Partitions and Their Afterlives

CRITICAL PERSPECTIVES ON THEORY, CULTURE AND POLITICS

Critical Perspectives on Theory, Culture and Politics is an interdisciplinary series, developed in partnership with the Centre for Critical and Cultural Theory, which is based in the School of English, Communication and Philosophy at Cardiff University, UK. The series focuses on innovative research produced at the interface between critical theory and cultural studies. In recent years much work in cultural studies has increasingly moved away from directly critical-theoretical concerns. One of the aims of this series is to foster a renewed dialogue between cultural studies and critical and cultural theory in its rich, multiple dimensions.

Series editors:

Glenn Jordan, Visiting Research Fellow, Cardiff School of Journalism, Media and Cultural Studies, Cardiff University. Former Director of Butetown History and Arts Centre.

Laurent Milesi, Reader in English, Communication and Philosophy and Chair of the Centre for Critical and Cultural Theory, Cardiff University.
Radhika Mohanram, Professor of English and Critical and Cultural Theory, Cardiff University.

Chris Müller, Department of Media, Music, Communication and Cultural Studies, Macquarie University.

Chris Weedon, Professor Emerita and Honorary Chair, Centre for Critical and Cultural Theory, Cardiff University.

Titles in the series:

Culture Control Critique: Allegories of Reading the Present, Frida Beckman

Prometheanism: Technology, Digital Culture and Human Obsolescence, Günther Anders and Christopher John Müller, translated by Christopher John Müller

Creole in the Archive: Imagery, Presence and the Location of the Caribbean Figure, Roshini Kempadoo

The Attention Economy: Labour, Time, and Power in Cognitive Capitalism, Claudio Celis

Performative Contradiction and the Romanian Revolution, Jolan Bogdan

Chinese Subjectivities and the Beijing Olympics, Gladys Pak Lei Chong

The Extreme in Contemporary Culture: States of Vulnerability, Pramod K. Nayar

Superpositions: Laruelle and the Humanities, edited by Rocco Gangle and Julius Greve

Credo Credit Crisis: Speculations on Faith and Money, edited by Laurent Milesi, Christopher John Müller and Aidan Tynan

Materialities of Sex in a Time of HIV: The Promise of Vaginal Microbicides, Annette-Carina van der Zaag

From Shared Life to Co-Resistance in Historic Palestine, Marcelo Svirsky and Ronnen Ben-Arie

Affective Connections: Towards a New Materialist Politics of Sympathy, Dorota Golańska

Homemaking: Radical Nostalgia and the Construction of a South Asian Diaspora, Anindya Raychaudhuri

Hypermodernity and Visuality, by Peter R. Sedgwick

Partitions and Their Afterlives: Violence, Memories, Living, edited by Radhika Mohanram and Anindya Raychaudhuri

Back Issues: Periodicals and the Formation of Critical and Cultural Theory in Canada, Gary Genosko, with Kristina Marcellus (forthcoming)

Contested Borders: Queer Politics and Cultural Translation in Contemporary Francophone Writing from the Maghreb, William J. Spurlin (forthcoming)

Partitions and Their Afterlives

Violence, Memories, Living

Edited by
Radhika Mohanram
and Anindya Raychaudhuri

ROWMAN &
LITTLEFIELD
INTERNATIONAL
London • New York

Published by Rowman & Littlefield International, Ltd.
6 Tinworth Street, London SE11 5AL, United Kingdom
www.rowmaninternational.com

Rowman & Littlefield International, Ltd., is an affiliate of Rowman & Littlefield
4501 Forbes Boulevard, Suite 200, Lanham, Maryland 20706, USA
With additional offices in Boulder, New York, Toronto (Canada), and Plymouth (UK)
www.rowman.com

British Library Cataloguing in Publication Data
A catalogue record for this book is available from the British Library

ISBN: HB 978-1-78348-838-4
PB 978-1-78348-839-1

Library of Congress Cataloging-in-Publication Data Available

ISBN: 978-1-78348-838-4 (cloth)
ISBN: 978-1-78348-839-1 (pbk.)
ISBN: 978-1-78348-840-7 (electronic)

Contents

Acknowledgments ix

Introduction xi
Radhika Mohanram and Anindya Raychaudhuri

1 The 1947 Partition Violence: Characteristics and Interpretations 1
Ian Talbot

2 The Sociohistorical Production of Partition in Palestine 23
Marcelo Svirsky and Ronnen Ben-Arie

3 Sexuality after Partition: The Great Indian Private Sphere 49
Radhika Mohanram

4 Lessons Not Learned from the Yugoslav Dismemberment and Their Implications for the European Union 83
Stefano Bianchini

5 Legacies of Partition: Remembering the German Democratic Republic 109
Chris Weedon

6 Memory Wars and Identity Construction: Return of the Suppressed as Afterlife of Partition under the Hindutva Rule in India 129
Samuel Sequeira

7 Postpartition Anxieties and the Matter of Authenticity in Ireland 157
Louise Harrington

8 Drawing Partition and Its Violence: Joe Sacco's *Palestine* and Vishwajyoti Ghosh's *This Side, That Side* 181
Vedita Cowaloosur

9 Advertising (Across) Borders: Fetishizing Humanism and the 'Magic' of Capitalism 201
Anindya Raychaudhuri

10 Following a Theory of Partition 223
Jennifer Yusin

Index 245

About the Contributors 251

Acknowledgments

The essays collected here were initially presented at a series of conferences organized under the auspices of the research network—*Partitions: What Are They Good For?* and funded by the Arts and Humanities Research Council. We are very grateful to the generous funding of the AHRC which allowed us to assemble a group of scholars who are working on partitions across a number of geographical and historical contexts, and from a number of different academic backgrounds.

We are also very grateful to our colleagues at the School of English, Communication and Philosophy, Cardiff University, and the School of English, University of St Andrews for all their support through the life of the network, and through the writing of this book.

Thanks are also due to all the contributors to this book, for their thoughtfulness and patience through the inevitably overlong editing and publication process.

We are grateful to Natalie Linh Bolderston and the entire team at Rowman & Littlefield International for their work to make this volume a reality. Thank you also to the anonymous reviewers who helped to improve the book through their generous and constructive comments.

Introduction

Radhika Mohanram and
Anindya Raychaudhuri

The years that marked the gestation and development of the work represented here, and *Partitions: What Are They Good For?*—the Arts and Humanities Research Council (AHRC)–funded research project that it was a part of were perhaps not coincidentally also marked by significant anniversaries of partitions past, and the foreshadowing of actual or potential partitions in the future. Since the launch of the project in 2013, there have been a number of actualized or attempted reorderings of national borders: 2014 saw the independence referendum in Scotland, and a referendum asking the people of Crimea if they wanted to remain in the Russian Federation or join Ukraine. In 2016, the United Kingdom voted in its own referendum to leave the European Union, while the following year Catalonia held its own independence referendum, albeit one that did not enjoy Spanish government recognition. These years have also seen significant anniversaries of the Palestinian Nakba, the India/Pakistan partition and the division of Cyprus. As the second decade of the twenty-first century comes to the close, there are plenty of reminders that even though the powers of the nation-state show no sign of abating, specific borders of actual nations remain as unstable and ambiguous as ever.

This book engages with political partitions and how their aftermath affects the contemporary life of nations and their citizens, in the process representing an important and innovative academic approach—comparative partitions studies. These essays seek to stretch our understanding of these conflicts and to show how elements of our day-to-day lives have been shaped by them. In juxtaposing scholarship about various partitions in a single volume, the book contributes to debates on citizenship, collective memory, nation-building and borders and boundaries. Such a focus also reveals how local communities as well as nations use their knowledge of the past and history. Some of the questions it engages with are: Can we theorize partitions differently? Can they produce new knowledges? How is the past constructed? How are new identities, moralities, polities and life constructed post-partition? How are children affected by partition violence? How are gender and sexuality recalibrated after partition? How can violence be theorized? What is the relationship between identity in the diaspora and identity after partition? What is the relationship between the movement of bodies, ideas, knowledges, technologies and capital and the newly created and newly configured national borders that are the mark of partition? How are all of these issues negotiated in the formal, official archives as well as the more informal world of cultural representation and oral history?

Depending on one's political position, one can read partition as either the effort of a disenfranchised and politically underrepresented people to gain greater self-determination, or violent territorial and political separation of groups, including the forced eviction and migration of populations—based on problematic notions of the desirability of ethnic, linguistic or cultural hegemony. Either way, partition has long-term repercussions on individual, familial, regional and national levels.

Partitions include the many variations of the disintegration of territories, the break-up of Empires, the whittling down of state boundaries, the secession of territories and decolonization. It generally involves three groups—two entities divided either by language, ethnicity, religion or political ideology competing against each other for territory and statehood and a third party that is supposedly neutral, whose role it is to resolve conflict by drawing boundary limitations, generally at the cost of local geographical and affective intricacies and practices. This neutral party, called the 'partitionist agent',[1] is further divided into two different types—the 'proceduralists' and the 'paternalists'.[2] Proceduralists consider themselves to be facilitators who offer legal and technical assistance to the process. Paternalists, on the other hand, do not perceive their roles to be dispassionate or neutral but rather as enforcing a peaceful resolution. In either case, the partitionist agent generally does not have a legal standing for their role, only an interest to arbitrate. Of foremost importance to the paternalists is the implementation of peace to which everything else such as consultation of all concerned parties and consent are subordinated. In the case of ethnic violence, partition is perceived to be 'the most humane form of intervention',[3] something for which the paternalists tend to stress partition as a realistic option. Partition as a form of maintaining ethnic homogeneity is problematic as such a goal is generally not achievable as this premise relies heavily on the notion of homogeneity but no matter the demographic reconstitution, the newly formed territory can never fully rid itself of minorities. As Rankin points out, '[s]eparation may help reduce inter-ethnic antagonism and moderate trenchant nationalist appeals, but as long as either side fears that it will be attacked by the other, past atrocities and old hatreds can easily be revived'.[4]

As a field of inquiry, the study of partitions and their political and historical significance has largely focussed to date on individual countries and within disciplinary boundaries. Such monolocal/monocultural approaches to partition studies are caused precisely by the incorporation of this topic within a nationalistic frame with a narrow focus that results in the ghettoization of each partition. As partition results in the formation of nations, the event itself is superseded by a focus on nationalism in the refractory light of heroic memory or the narration of its history. What is overlooked in such a narration is that '[i]n each of these "foundational fictions" the origins of national traditions turn out to be as much acts of affiliation and establishment as they are moments of disavowal, displacement, exclusion and cultural contestation'.[5]

Indeed, there is a small but significant body of scholarship that takes a comparative approach to the study of partitions. Mention in particular may be made of Joe Cleary's *Literature, Partition and the Nation-State: Culture and Conflict in Ireland, Israel and Palestine*, *The Partition Motif in Contemporary Conflicts* edited by Smita Tewari Jassal and Eyal Ben-Ari and *Partitions: Reshaping States and Minds* edited by Stefano Bianchini, Sanjay Chaturvedi, Rada Ivekovic and Ranabir Samaddar. This present volume continues to build on this existing work.

Partitions are a product of local histories yet they all have in common a long afterlife, and impact on the contours of societal and individual lives. Partitions generally lead to repeated eruptions of conflicts and, if they occur in countries which have a mixed population of different racial and ethnic groups, this results in political instability, ethnic cleansing or the presence of small enclaves of minority groups who feel that they lack proper representation in a democracy. Among other things, partitions affect group, familial and individual identities and generational dynamics, the formation of history and memories, political and social structures, and work and profession.

The intersection of memory and trauma frames that was developed in the study of the Holocaust underscored the urgency of keeping memory alive. This framework is also utilized in partition studies as the need to recuperate individual and personal memories in the face of a homogenising and forgetful national memory has gained ground in the last fifteen years. Juxtaposing memory work of various partitions allows us to focus on the art and strategies of forgetting rather than those of remembering. For instance, in a country like India the significance of the 1947 partition and losses has been displaced from public memory in order to focus attention on independence from imperial rule and the building of a new democratic nation. For Pakistan, this same moment became the foundational event of the achievement of a separate

Muslim nation in South Asia. In both contexts, memories of the partition and the ensuing violence have not been maintained or memorialized; yet they keep rematerializing in the form of enmity between the two nations and the unsettled issue of the state of Kashmir. This form of remembering and forgetting differs from the case of Israel/Palestine. Here, the collective memory of the Holocaust has been incorporated into the war of 1948 so that a seamless narrative emerges that transforms defeat, trauma and loss to heroism, survival and achievement—the partition of Palestine is renarrated as the War of Independence. For both Israel and Palestine, 1948 has been the defining moment of their identities and the partition resulted in a different experiential reality that constituted its citizens, but its memory has been excised in the narration of national Israeli history.

The comparative analysis of partitions also reveals them to be a *process* rather than an event, particularly because partitions impact on not only the past but second- and third-generation identities and lives. Partitions dictate foreign and defence policies of newly formed nations. For instance, Palestinians evicted from their homes, forced to become part of the diaspora, and rendered homeless nevertheless are now subjected to incarceration behind the barriers that Israel has built. Incarceration behind barriers or its opposite, migration, now constitutes Palestinian lives. In South Asia, the border between India and Pakistan which witnessed incredible violence is replayed in Kashmir in the present with both states claiming it as part of their territory. In reunified Germany, vestiges of its partition remain in the strong sense of 'Ostalgie' (from the German words *Ost* or East and *nostalgie* for nostalgia) that the former East Germans have for their past lives. Partition can thus be seen also as constitutive of social organization with people on both sides of the border defining themselves in terms of the other and both societies being organized in relation to the internal and external dynamics of each group.

Furthermore, comparing different partitions makes visible that which might be invisible in the study of only one. Such a comparative approach also sheds light on contemporary life—what constitutes the public sphere, social identities, citizenship, the nature of contemporary conflicts and the significance of borders and boundaries, memory and forgetting. Indeed, the juxtaposing of partitions allows us to see less their unique nature and concentrate more on the processes, organizations and new perceptions and theorizings of them. A comparatist perspective functions in several ways here. First, it allows for the specificity of history to emerge thus undermining the framework of nationalism that demands a shallow or mediated memory of its citizens. By focussing on history, we lose our fascination not only with the postmodern present but also escape its tendencies to homogenize the national past. The focus on history then allows us to explore how partitions affect the very constitution of memory and history as well as affect the development of emotional, national life. Secondly, by comparing political partitions in different parts of the world we can examine methodological challenges and the imperatives for scholars working on individual countries. For instance, how would we read the partitioning of Italy after the Second World War if we juxtapose it with that of Palestine/Israel? How would we read the silence around the exodus of Italians from Istria, the killing of the inhabitants of all the different ethnic groups and the shaping of cultural memory post war? Interdisciplinarity and comparative approaches will also allow the scholars to develop new models of analysis as well as see connections between different political and geographical areas and how research in one geographical context could allow for a development of new research questions in the other. A comparatist view also explores the myriad shapes and practices of nationalism, democracy and multiculturalism which are direct results of political partitions while also examining if they differ from those practised in unpartitioned nation states.

Finally, this multidisciplinary and multiregion volume will analyse the various convergences and departures between the different partitions and draw out lessons for the present. In so doing, this work will also examine methodological challenges and the imperatives for scholars working on individual countries. Interdisciplinarity and comparative approaches will allow the scholars to develop new models of analysis as well as to see connections between different political and geographical areas. This work also seeks to invigorate partition studies by seeing how research in one geographical context could allow for a development of new research questions in another. Furthermore, the essays in this collection emerge out of a number of different disciplines—history, literature, political science, cultural studies and critical theory—which, along with the different methodologies and different partitions, demand an interdisciplinarity from the partition studies scholar.

The first three chapters of the book all look at partition not just as a process, but as a *productive* process both in the sense that as an object partition is produced through a particular set of discursive and material processes, and because it then allows the production of certain types of identity-narratives, as well as certain phenomena that could be said to be peculiar to partition as a political process. Ian Talbot, in the first chapter, examines the violence that engulfed Punjab before, during and after the 1947 India/Pakistan partition, and explores how this violence is produced both on the ground, and later in and through formal and informal archival sources. Marcelo Svirsky and Ronnen Ben-Arie, in their chapter, explore the socio-historical processes that produced partition in Palestine. Svirsky and Ben-Arie share a notion of power as that which helps in the 'social production of the real', an argument which they use to critique partition in Palestine as a product of Zionist power. Radhika Mohanram shifts the lens to south Asia, but continues a similar analysis of power—in this case the power enacted on female bodies through sexual violence. Mohanram explores the ways in which these forms of power help to influence the practice of sexuality in south Asia after 1947. For all of these scholars, partition can and needs to be denaturalized, both in terms of its own origins as a political process, and in terms of the social reality of bodies and space that partition helps to produce.

The three subsequent chapters examine the legacies of partition in more detail. Stefano Bianchini examines the lessons that have not been learnt from the way the division of Yugoslavia was handled, and explores what this amnesia might mean for EU public policy in the face of crises such as the financial collapse of 2008, and (at the time of writing) the impending spectre of Brexit. Chris Weedon looks at the memorial legacy of the former German Democratic Republic, in contemporary unified Germany. She compares and contrasts the public narratives as constructed through museums and tourist attractions, with oral history testimonies to explore the fissures that exist between the two. Understanding the political dynamic of these gaps helps us better understand the ways in which the nation-state constructs narratives of partitions and reunifications. Samuel Sequeira finds echoes of the India/Pakistan partition in the rise of Hindu fundamentalism in contemporary Indian public and private life. These three chapters, taken together, demonstrate the necessity to read against the grain of notions of legacy, history and heritage, and critique the ways in which narratives of the past are put to political work in the present.

The next three chapters focus more closely on cultural representation. Louise Harrington examines the anxieties of authenticity that are apparent in contemporary Irish literature featuring immigrants and people of colour. Harrington's analysis reminds us of the dangers of connecting ethnicity with the national story at the moment of the nation's birth, and how subsequent generations have had to negotiate the various meanings of the nation that are constructed through partition. Vedita Cowaloosur compares the representation of the India/Pakistan partition with Israel and Palestine in graphic novels. In both cases, she argues that the graphic novels can be read as manifestos against the violence of partition, but that these representations are able to utilize the possibilities inherent within the comic form while 'reporting, recording, and safekeeping the violence of partition'. Anindya Raychaudhuri explores the way partitions are represented in advertising, making the case that advertising deploys a particular, uncritical narrative of humanism which functions by rendering the project of partition as unnatural, counterintuitive and dehumanising.

In the final chapter of the book, Jennifer Yusin moves away from conceptualising partition as a historically and geographically specific event, instead positing the possibility of partition theory. Such a theory, Yusin argues, leads to a conception of partition not just as a 'crisis of jurisdiction over space', but and perhaps more profoundly, as 'a crisis of space'. Some readers of this chapter may posit that, because it turns upon the ways partition presents a conceptual problem linked to the Western philosophical tradition, it produces a literal, or perhaps a forced, ahistorical reading of what the name 'Pakistan' signifies in relation to its political and historical evolutions. Such critiques, however, rely on the very disciplinary and cultural boundaries that this chapter moves away from in its exploration of the different ways a theory of partition functions in our practical approaches to understanding the realities of this type of historical event.

Taken together, the chapters of this book represent a variety of different ideological and methodological approaches to dealing with this central crisis. Whether imagined as historical, political, geographical, ontological or epistemological, partition represents a crisis and a challenge. The authors of this book believe that the best way to meet this challenge is precisely the kind of crossfertilization that is reflected in these pages.

NOTES

1. See K. J. Rankin, 'Theoretical Concepts of Partition and the Partitioning of Ireland', *Mapping Frontiers, Plotting Pathways Working Paper* no. 17 (2006): 6.
2. Rankin, 'Theoretical Concepts', 6.
3. Radha Kumar, 'The Troubled History of Partition', *Foreign Affairs* 76, no. 1 (1997): 23.
4. Rankin, 'Theoretical Concepts', 8.
5. See Homi K. Bhabha, 'Introduction: Narrating the Nation', in Homi K. Bhabha, ed., *Nation and Narration* (London and New York: Routledge, 1990), 5.

REFERENCES

Bhabha, Homi K. 1990. 'Introduction: Narrating the Nation'. In *Nation and Narration*, edited by Homi K. Bhabha, 1–7. London and New York: Routledge.

Bianchini, Stefano, Sanjay Chaturvedi, Rada Ivekovic and Ranabir Samaddar. 2006. *Partitions: Reshaping States and Minds.* Abingdon and New York: Frank Cass.

Cleary, Joe. 2002. *Literature, Partition and the Nation-State: Culture and Conflict in Ireland, Israel and Palestine.* Cambridge: Cambridge University Press.

Kumar, Radha. 1997. 'The Troubled History of Partition'. *Foreign Affairs* 76 (2): 22–34.

Rankin, K. J. 2006. 'Theoretical Concepts of Partition and the Partitioning of Ireland'. *Mapping Frontiers, Plotting Pathways Working Paper* no. 17. Centre for International Border Research. Belfast: Queen's University.

Tiwari Jassal, Smita, and Eyal Ben-Ari, eds. 2007. *The Partition Motif in Contemporary Conflicts*. New Delhi: Sage Publications.

Chapter 1

The 1947 Partition Violence

Characteristics and Interpretations

Ian Talbot

This chapter examines the characteristics of the end of empire violence in the Punjab area of northern India. The mass killings there were by no means unique and should not form the basis for a Punjab-centric understanding of India's partition turmoil.[1] Nonetheless, the drama and intensity of violence and uprooting in the region has come to represent the partition experience. It has provided the iconic images of the 1947 migration: men and women with their heavily laden bullock carts travelling across tracks of ground inundated with monsoon rains; trains with not only their carriages, but running boards and roofs, packed with refugees; and more disturbingly, trains arriving at their destinations stacked high with mutilated corpses. The Punjab massacres in August 1947 overshadowed violence elsewhere in India. They provide an important case for addressing the themes of partition-related ethnic conflict and forced migration.

The view, popularized by both nationalist and imperialist historiography, that the massacres were 'irrational' and 'spontaneous' occurrences has meant that the Punjab experience has been excluded from wider studies of religio-ethnic violence.[2] Recent works on ethnic conflict in South Asia together with local empirical studies have however questioned long-held assumptions. Far from being a spontaneous and temporary aberration, the violence was frequently marked by its cold-blooded planning and execution. Attacks on foot convoys and trains were carried out with military precision.[3] Such episodes suggest that concepts such as ethnic cleansing and genocide may be appropriate. It is also useful to consider the Punjab violence in the light of the Yale-based political scientist Stathis Kalyvas' theorization of mass collective violence.[4] He has conceptualised civil-war–type situations as having 'joint violence' that straddles the divide between the political and the private, the collective and the individual. The violence is engendered by a 'convergence of local motives and supra-local imperatives' which endow such situations with their 'particular character'. Before taking up these conceptual issues, it is necessary to consider the issues of casualty numbers, the characteristics of the most violent episodes and the timing of the Punjab killings.

CASUALTIES

Casualty numbers throughout India remain disputed, seven decades later.[5] Monsoon floods, mass disposal of bodies and administrative collapse meant that many corpses were never fully recovered or counted. In the absence of verifiable figures, writers have inflated them to promote community sacrifice and victimhood.[6] Contemporary propagandists exaggerated casualties to indict the Mountbatten administration and to demonise the aggressor 'other' community. Figures vary from two hundred thousand to two million. Whatever the number, there was immense human suffering. An unexpected and unprecedented mass migration was set in train in which around ten million Punjabis were caught up in a chaotic two-way flight over the new international boundary which divided the land of the five rivers.[7]

CHARACTERISTICS

Until the 1980s, the accepted view was that the 1947 partition violence was the result of a 'temporary madness' which had little to do with politics or modernity. It was, rather, a throwback to medieval barbarity. Recent scholarship has questioned these assumptions, by highlighting the organization that lay behind supposedly 'spontaneous' outbreaks.[8] The attacks by paramilitary groups, as in postindependence pogroms, were assisted by the quiescence, if not active involvement, of policemen, soldiers, civil servants and railway officials who divulged the running times of the refugee specials so that they could be waylaid.[9] Studies of ethnic violence from across the world reveal that where the police or the army quickly suppress violence its escalation is limited, with few casualties.[10] The high death rates in the partition violence reflect the failure of the police in particular to act impartially.

The partition violence was characterized by its brutality. In what has been termed a 'war on women', they endured terrible cruelties such as the lopping off of breasts and noses and impregnation by sticks and metal rods.[11] There were episodes of gang rape and parading women naked through the streets. Young children were also the target of brutal assaults. Earlier communal clashes had been deadly but had never been accompanied by such atrocities.

'Traditional' violence had taken place in public arenas, frequently around procession routes and disputed sacred space, with men from rival communities being the main victims. The recovery of the 'hidden history' of the partition violence has revealed that domestic space was increasingly invaded with women being targeted for murderous assaults and sexual humiliation. This new type of violence was rooted in notions of *izzat* (honour) and shame.[12] Disturbingly, fathers, brothers and husbands killed female family members to prevent their 'despoiling' by men from rival communities.[13]

Another new feature of the violence was the wholesale destruction of communities and the creation of refugees. Around ten thousand people shifted out of Calcutta following the August 1946 violence. There were forty thousand refugees in the Punjab following the March 1947 violence. Well before the British decision to divide and quit in parts of north India, the urban landscape had undergone a visible transformation as trust had completely broken down between communities, who retreated into barricaded enclaves. 'Traditional' communal violence in India had previously been about the 'renegotiation of local hierarchies of power', but not their destruction.[14]

THE LONG CYCLE OF PARTITION VIOLENCE

Standard accounts of the 1947 violence concentrate on the 'summer madness' of mid-August. This locates it in a 'special' time of flux and transition when conventional mores failed and anarchy prevailed.[15] The movement from 'traditional' communal violence to the more intensive and brutal violence we have examined above began however as early as the second half of 1946. Suranjan Das, in a detailed study, has revealed how the August 1946 killings in Calcutta differed from riots there twenty years earlier. He draws on colonial accounts that described the impact of the violence that claimed four thousand lives in just over seventy-two hours as a 'cross between the worst of London air raids and the Great Plague'.[16]

The episode is important not only because it marked a new violence, but initiated the spiral of killings that triggered India's partition. This action, designed to end violence, only intensified killings that continued another forty-two months with the violence in Calcutta and East Bengal of March 1950.

The cycle began and ended in eastern India, but was at its most deadly in the Punjab, commencing in March 1947 and peaking in August. The timing was different again in Sindh and Delhi with the outbreak only after the act of partition and the first influx of uprooted people. The extended timeframe means that the violence cannot be regarded as a temporary moment of madness. 'The new order in communal rioting' opens up theorization in terms of wider understandings of collective violence. Before turning to interpretations, it is necessary to look in more detail at the events in the Punjab, the epicentre of the violence in August–December 1947.

EVENTS IN THE PUNJAB

March 1947 saw the first signs of a new type of violence in Punjab. This was marked by horrific attacks on women and the complete destruction of minority communities, dwellings and businesses. The precipitating event was the resignation of the cross-community coalition government led by Khizr Hayat Tiwana on 2 March. The Punjab had been relatively peaceful at the time of the August 1946 Calcutta killings and its bloody aftermath in Bihar. There were however worrying signs of growing violence earlier in the year at the time of the March 1946 elections. Returning soldiers had also helped train the mushrooming numbers of paramilitary organizations in the province. The government's attempt to curb these created the civil liberties pretext for a six-week civil disobedience movement commencing on 24 January 1947 that was designed to unseat Khizr in what Jinnah termed the 'cornerstone of Pakistan'.[17] The pattern of the remaining period of British rule was set in Lahore following Khizr's resignation with stray stabbings; the erection of barricades and the first arson attacks on Hindu and Sikh localities. The eruption of this violence in Lahore is linked in the popular imagination with the Sikh leader Master Tara Singh unsheathing his sword on the steps of the Punjab Assembly building on hearing the news of the government's resignation.[18]

Clashes in Lahore and the neighbouring city of Amritsar rippled out to the Muslim majority areas of West Punjab. The attacks on largely defenceless minority populations have earned the violence the title of the Rawalpindi Massacres. Outlying villages in the Rawalpindi district witnessed shocking violence against Sikh inhabitants. Around seven thousand to eight thousand people were estimated to have died. The episode at Thoa Khalsa, a village surrounded by ten thousand to twelve thousand armed Muslims, where one hundred Sikh women committed suicide by jumping into a well to prevent their 'dishonouring' at the hands of Muslim attackers, has become a contested and iconic episode in partition historiography with its fictionalized version in Bhisham Sahni's award-winning partition novel *Tamas*.[19] The violence was seen as unprecedented and was the focus of an All India Congress Committee (AICC) investigation.[20] It found that the attacks of 6–13 March had been carefully planned. 'It is a mistake to call what happened in the Rawalpindi area, "Communal riots"', the AICC report records, 'These were not riots but deliberately organized military campaigns'.[21] It then goes on to record the holding of secret meetings in mosques, the declaration of a *jihad* and the roles of ex-military men, policemen and even Legislative Assembly members. The report maintains that the armed crowds which attacked such villages as Thoa Khalsa were 'led by ex-military men on horseback, armed with tommy guns, pistols, rifles, hand grenades, hatchets, petrol tins and some even carried field glasses'.[22]

Press reports of the violence throughout the West Punjab at this juncture noted that Muslim policemen were inordinately slow in responding to appeals for assistance. The Hindu residents of Traggar in the Multan district were attacked for eleven hours on 10 March but received no assistance from the police until troops arrived. A police contingent in the city of Multan stood by while a prominent Sikh leader and president of the Minorities Board, Sardar Nanak Singh, was done to death. They then abandoned the areas outside the walls where many Hindu-owned businesses were located, leaving them at the mercy of looters.[23] There are of course parallels here with major episodes of communal violence in postindependence India where Muslim minorities have been left defenceless.

Despite the naming and shaming by citizens' fact-finding committees, few of those involved in the March disturbances were brought to justice. The legal system was too polarized along communal lines and slow moving to bring many of the culprits to book. Concerning later violence in June in Amritsar, a British administrator recalled that 'thousands of mass murderers of the troubles could never be properly brought to book; and even when one could be caught red-handed it was not unknown for him to be released on bail at once by a co-religionist on the judiciary bench'.[24] British threats to relieve all those who were found guilty of their land grants and titles were empty, given their imminent departure.[25]

The legacy of the Rawalpindi Massacres was two-fold. First, they established a precedent that officials and the police could act in a biased manner with impunity. Secondly, they created a fierce desire for revenge amongst the Sikhs. Hindus may have suffered the greatest loss of property, but Sikhs suffered heart-rending brutalities in the scattered villages. The survivors, forty thousand of whom took refuge in temporary camps and some in the Golden Temple itself, retold the events to an enraged community. Personal desire for revenge fed into a politically motivated desire to carve out a Sikh state when the British departed. The leadership of the main Sikh party, the Akali Dal, shared this ambition with the rulers of the larger Sikh princely states.[26] The result was the widespread killing of Muslims in East Punjab in August 1947. Before turning to this, we will examine two notorious episodes of violence, the burning of the Shah Almi area of Lahore and the attack on refugees in Sheikhupura. They are important because of their scale, and because they span the actual event of partition. Finally, they are significant because of the insights they can lend to interpretations of the violence.

(i) Shah Almi

The commercial and residential area of Lahore around the Shah Almi gateway was the leading Hindu centre of population in the walled city.[27] Outside the gate there was a water tank, a *serai* and Shivala (known as Rattan Chand's temple.) Inside the gate, narrow alleyways linked the neighbouring Hindu-owned Gumti and Jaura Mori bazaars with the residential quarters (*Kuchas*). Hindu neighbourhoods stretched all the way from Shah Almi Gate to Rang Mahal's bustling market, where a well was situated sacred to the fifth Sikh Guru Arjun Dev. On the night of 21 June 1947, this whole area was destroyed in a great fire. Hundreds of Hindu residences and businesses were destroyed. In its aftermath, 'Shah Almi presented the look of a city that had just been subjected to a blitzkrieg', a memoir of the period recalls, 'heaps of bricks, twisted girders, roofless blackened walls and a deep mournful silence! Some of the lonely walls jutting out of the wreckage displayed typical Hindu decorations and mythological locales. Some were licked by fire, others washed away by the rain'.[28]

From the perspective of a Muslim League leader, this was an attack on 'an impregnable fortress (where) countless weapons and ammunition were stored'.[29] Conversely, it could be seen as an assault on the wealth of the Lahori Hindus, designed to ruin them and drive them from the city. Indeed, immediately after describing Shah Almi as a centre of Hindu terrorism, the writer cited above goes on to recount that 'As the locality burned down the Hindus lost heart and began to move towards Amritsar'.[30] This comment receives support from accounts by leading Hindu figures who saw the event as a significant turning point. The Lahore High Court Judge Gopal Das Khosla, who toured the area, recorded in his autobiography, 'the entire bazaar had been reduced to rubble and ashes and we could feel the heat radiated by the cinder . . . that day I realised that we would have to leave Lahore, our home town and seek safety elsewhere in India'.[31] Wealthy Hindus moved their businesses and bank accounts, although poor Hindus living elsewhere in the walled city did not have the luxury of anticipatory flight.

The destruction of Shah Almi was not only a significant turning point, but provides a number of valuable insights into the characteristics and motivations of the partition-related violence in the Punjab. First, it provides further evidence of the role of planning that lay behind it. Such a large area could not have been destroyed without preparation. This was not the work of just a handful of arsonists. Oral accounts gathered in the last decade prove this point. M. G. Chopra, who was a sixteen-year-old living some three kilometres away in Gowal Mandi, has recalled for example that 'The Muslims sprayed petrol in the area with a petrol tanker and set it on fire'.[32] Second, the episode illustrates the political purpose behind the violence. The destruction of Shah Almi occurred while the Punjab Boundary Commission was sitting in Lahore and hearing the contesting claims for the city's inclusion in India or Pakistan. While its deliberations were unaffected, the burning of the area signalled a Muslim victory by making it clear that Hindus and Sikhs would henceforth live in the city on Muslim terms.

(ii) Sheikhupura

The 25 August 1947 massacre at the Atma Singh Rice Mill in the Kucha Abdul Rahman neighbourhood of the West Punjab city of Sheikhupura was in all probability not only the worst attack on refugees, but the single worst massacre in the theatre of horrors which accompanied the partition. The Government of India report claimed over four thousand people were killed who had gathered in the factory and, 'more than 10,000 persons were either done to death by Muslim military and police or were burnt alive in the [neighbouring locality] . . . [in] well-planned and nicely executed' attacks.[33] These involved troops from the Third Baloch Regiment attached to the Punjab Boundary Force and local Muslim inhabitants. The Baloch Regiment's deployment on the eve of partition had raised tensions in the Sheikhupura district that was as contested between India and Pakistan as Lahore, because of the wealth of its irrigated colony areas and the presence of the Sikh shrines around the birthplace of Guru Nanak at Nankana Sahib.[34] The ferocity and the scale of the killings lend support to attempts to understand the partition-related violence as genocide. The vernacular term used for them was *burbadi* (destruction).

Desire for loot was seen in the robbing of the refugees trapped in the Atma Singh Rice Mill of about thirty or forty *lakhs* of rupees and 'seven or eight *maunds* of gold before they were mown down'.[35] The political context was that of the Muslim and Sikh communities preparing for violence by creating paramilitary organizations, while making counterterritorial claims for Sheikhupura to the Radcliffe Boundary Commission. Sikhs claimed what they termed 'the Shahidi Bar' for the Indian East Punjab, despite its Muslim majority. The Sheikhupura episode also points to the significance of 'target' populations and transport hubs in understanding the patterns of violence. There was little anticipatory migration in the district as Sikhs were confident that Nankana Sahib would be awarded to India. Sheikhupura city's strategic road and rail links led to a combustible influx of local and long-distance refugees at a time of administrative breakdown. Sheikhupura was flooded with Hindus and Sikhs from outlying villages and, because of its importance as a transport hub, also with Muslim refugees. Their arrival coincided with the pogrom.

AUGUST 1947 VIOLENCE IN THE EAST PUNJAB

The Muslim refugees in Sheikhupura had fled devastating violence in East Punjab orchestrated by Sikh paramilitary organizations and supported by Hindu militants and troops from the neighbouring Sikh princely states.[36] Community histories were later to emphasize the heroism and sacrifice of East Punjab Muslims in the achievement of Pakistan. Mashkur Hassan's harrowing account of what befell his family in Hissar forms the focus for his autobiography.[37] Khawaja Iftikhar's autobiographical work *Jab Amritsar jal raha tha* (When Amritsar Was Burning) is even more popular.[38] Iftikhar was vice president of the Amritsar Muslim League branch. He portrays the Muslims in the city as nonaggressors who valiantly defended their honour in face of overwhelming odds.

The East Punjab violence was so intense because of the role of ex-servicemen and of state forces from the Punjab's Sikh princely states. Indeed, the work of Saumitra Jha and Steven Wilkinson has revealed a high correlation between districts of wartime army combatants and partition-related violence.[39] The role of ex-servicemen reveals not only the organized element of the violence partition—but the fact that it was not simply the result of administrative breakdown in the region. This is also borne out by the role of the princely states. They provided havens for *jathas* (Sikh war bands) along with weapons. State forces joined in attacks on local Muslims. A curfew enforced only on the Muslims of Barnala preceded the massacre of three thousand members of the community.[40] State troops also attacked the refugee trains that passed through their territory. Trains coming from Ludhiana and Hissar, en route for Pakistan, were detained at Dhuri in the Patiala State where their passengers were systematically butchered and their possessions looted. The violence was so intense that it made it almost impossible for a Muslim to pass safely through the state.[41]

The princes denied that they had contacts with the Sikh *jathas*, and assured their minorities that they would be safe. However, high-ranking court state and military officers such as Bir Davinder Singh and Colonel Bhagwan Singh of Patiala, along with the Chief Minister of Jind, were widely believed to have connived with the *jathas*' activities.[42] Significantly, in the Muslim-ruled princely state of Malerkotla in East Punjab there was relative peace as Nawab Ahmad Ali Khan used his state forces to patrol the borders and discourage the incursion of Sikh war bands.[43]

The East Punjab Muslim community in all probability suffered a similar number of casualties to the minorities in the Pakistan areas. Hindus and Sikhs, because they were wealthier, abandoned more property than Muslims. They not only controlled the lion's share of industry and commerce in West Punjab, but possessed large landholdings in the fertile Canal Colony districts. Hindu and Sikh refugees vacated 9.9 million acres of land in Pakistan, while Muslims left behind 5.5 million acres in India.[44] The Muslims who fled or were massacred in East Punjab came mainly from small farming and artisan backgrounds.[45]

INTERPRETATIONS

(i) Genocide

Genocide is normally understood in terms of the Holocaust example of state-directed violence. It is also seen as directed against a single community. The apparent absence of state involvement in the 1947 violence has made such genocide scholars as Leo Kuper and Leonard B. Glick hesitant in describing it as an act of genocide.[46] Mark Levene similarly limits genocide to the involvement of the state apparatus.[47] Henry R. Huttenbach has adopted a wider interpretation. He has argued that not just states, but well-armed communal groups, 'with or without the collusion or cooperation of the instruments of the state', could embark on a genocide campaign.[48] The activities of war bands in the Punjab fall within Huttenbach's interpretation of genocide. During the last two weeks of British rule, there were reports of *jathas* attacking outlying Muslim villages in the Lahore district.[49] These were ruthlessly efficient killing machines which carefully targeted their victims. They were well armed with sten guns, rifles, pistols, swords and *kirpans* (steel daggers). The largest war bands had up to three thousand men. The violence intensified in the days after the formal declaration of the Boundary Award.[50] Jason Francisco, however, sticks with a state-sponsored view of genocide. He thus prefers to term the 1947 Punjab violence as fratricide. 'The partition stands as the archetype of what I call nationalist fratricide', he declares, 'the conflict between people of a common cultural heritage.[51]

Scholarship has also focused on how the preconditions for genocide emerged in the Punjab. Anders Bjorn Hansen for example draws on the work of such scholars as Robert Melson and Mark Levene to demonstrate how the preconditions for genocide were present in the late colonial Punjab.[52] He sees the March 1947 killings as a significant turning point. Thereafter, there was a new phase of 'reciprocal genocide'. It was characterized by organized killings that aimed at annihilating the 'Other' community. Paul Brass further conceptualized this approach, arguing for an extension of the understanding of genocide. He designated the Punjab massacres as 'retributive genocide'.[53] The retributive characteristic arose from the desire for revenge following reports and rumours of massacres elsewhere in Punjab. His reworking of the violence and adding it to the wider literature on genocide marked a major conceptual advance. However, there have been critics who maintain that while episodes of violence, whether attacks on refuge trains or the Sheikhupura episode, display genocidal intention and characteristics, the violence as a whole does not merit this description. This of course leads us back to the numbers game regarding the victims and to state and community attempts to displace the blame for the violence.

(ii) Ethnic Cleansing

Such episodes as the Rawalpindi Massacres, the burning of Shah Almi and the attacks on Muslims in the East Punjab possess a clear dimension of ethnic cleansing. Ishtiaq Ahmed has utilized firsthand accounts of the violence in Lahore to reveal the economic motives that lay behind the expulsion of the Hindu capitalist class.[54] There is controversy as to whether a 'Sikh Plan' existed, to clear out Muslims from the East Punjab in order to consolidate a Sikh state.[55] Actions on the ground by the Patiala authorities point to such an objective. Violence and the consolidation of the Sikh population went hand in hand. Such princes as Yadavindra Singh of Patiala were motivated by the ambition to carve out a Sikh state in the region.[56] The rulers of the states of Faridkot and Jind dramatically increased the size of their armed forces as the British departure grew closer.[57] The collusion between the Sikh princely rulers and militant groups in the East Punjab provide the clearest evidence of the role of 'ethnic cleansing' in the August outbreak. Some scholars have argued that 'ethnic' is an inappropriate term as Punjabis from similar tribes, castes and *biraderis* fought each other. If a label has to be applied it should be 'communal cleansing', as all other forms of political identity had been collapsed into that of religion.

Moreover, the notion of ethnic cleansing does not explain why there were widespread attacks on moving refugee columns or attacks on refugees in camps when the task of ethnic cleansing had been achieved. An attack on a Pakistan-bound Special just outside Khalsa College, Amritsar, for example, that was marked by military precision, resulted in the massacre of over one thousand Muslims.[58]

(iii) Personal Motives for Violence

Of course some of the violence in 1946–1947 was not politically motivated or organized. Individuals motivated by lust for loot and women spontaneously took advantage of the opportunity that came their way, operating in an environment in which such violence was socially sanctioned. We have seen this at work in the Sheikhupura mass killings. Such motivations for violence have received little serious attention aside from the reflection by Ayesha Jalal that the political struggle for territory in the Punjab was mirrored at the local level in 'strategies to appropriate the property of neighbours'.[59] Women as well as money and land could of course be regarded as property in this context. Early in 1948 the West Punjab Chief of Police reported that over one hundred thousand women were 'missing' as a result of abduction.[60] On 22 October 1947, the Lahore Civil Lines Police carried out a raid on the neighbouring village of Mian Mir. After two days of house-to-house searching, they recovered stolen goods worth Rs 150,000. According to reports, in August the villagers had ransacked houses on the Upper Mall and carried off cartloads of stolen goods.[61] A police drive the following month elsewhere in Lahore recovered property worth Rs 400,000. The recovery of stolen goods and weapons from policemen's houses revealed that they had also joined in the spree.[62] Indeed, a Meeting of the Joint Defence Council earlier on 16 May had made the serious charge that police in Lahore had 'joined mobs and carried out arson and murder'.[63]

Memoirs, and the vignettes provided by Saadat Hassan Manto in *Black Margins*, provide further evidence of the extent of looting in Lahore.[64] According to a pioneering study of local police records, in August alone there were reports of over fifty cases of looting in the jurisdiction of the Mozang police station in Lahore.[65] Its assistant subinspector provided an eyewitness account of the systematic looting of properties on Lahore's Bahawalpur Road, less than a week after independence.

> Today afternoon, some Muslims purposely burned the houses and shops of Hindus and Sikhs of Bahawalpur Road . . . they did this for the looting design. When a party of police reached there, some people (Muslims) were loading the looted things in their *tongas* (horse-carts).[66]

Police records reveal that looters were not only drawn from 'outsiders' and known criminals, but also from 'respectable' locals who knew their victims. Nathu Ram, who ran a wholesale shop in Lahore's Bibi Paak Daaman, reported to the Civil Lines Police Station on 13 August that:

> One part of my house is consisted of shop. Today between 10 and 12 Muslims attacked my shop. I ran away to the rooftop and thus narrowly escaped. They looted my shop. . . . The looted items included: Rs 550 net cash, 18 *pashmina* shawls and 10 leather bags . . . I have been living in this *mohalla* (locality) for the last 25 years. I know them and can identify their faces.[67]

The records of the same police station reveal that a couple of days later some 'notable traders', including Ayub Ghani, Dr Noor Mohamad, Khar Baksh, M. A. Shamin and Mohammad Sadiq, allegedly looted the shops of Hindu trading rivals in the Royal Park area.[68]

The looting in Lahore was not of course unique. Ilyas Chattha's work on Gujranwala and Sialkot has uncovered a similar story.[69] The two graphic eyewitness accounts provided below give insights into previously unreported episodes of violence in the Gujranwala district. The first from a local resident, Mohammad Ali, relates to an attack on a refugee train which is still remembered locally. The second which records attacks on outlying villages was provided by Sardara Dindar, who converted to Islam at the time of partition. Both testimonies point to the now well-established organized nature of the Punjab violence and emphasize the motivation for loot. Mohammad Ali, who was twenty at the time, recalled:

> Yes . . . I know they (Lohars and Kashmiris of Nizamabad) chopped that train and cut into pieces its Hindu and Sikh passengers. That train was on its way to Jammu railway track. . . . They attacked the train only because of loot. . . . Policemen were also in the train for the Hindus' safety. They also helped in killings and loot. The driver Rahmu connived with them and was the real culprit who stopped the train there. They blocked the track by placing trees on i. . . . He had even taken a (bribe) of Rs 10,000 from Hindus and had promised them that he would not stop the train . . . but he stopped it there.[70]

Sardara narrated his account as follows:

> Lohars of Nizamabad killed thousands of Hindus and Sikhs and looted their property. They used to attack with swords and guns which they made for themselves. . . . They raided in Jamkay, Manchar, Mansoorwali and Waziribad and so on. Sometimes local villagers of the area invited them to attack their villages to clear out the Hindus and Sikhs. . . . The local people also looted lots of properties of Hindus and Sikhs and eventually placed the blame on Lohars.[71]

District police record accounts of these incidents, in order to remove the need to prosecute locally powerful individuals and communities, merely report them under the British colonial heading as a 'communal riot'. One police report however acknowledges that violence was occasioned by competition for resources and the opportunity to pay off old scores rather than religious animosity. This concerns the case of the murder of Lambardar Bahader Singh Ghumman in the village of Kalra Singh. The case reporting reveals that this occurred to the backdrop of a fifteen-year-old land dispute between the Lambardar and a Jat Muslim landlord who paid village menials and a Christian to murder him.[72]

Nizamabad was a hotspot of violence not because its population was more bloodthirsty or avaricious than communities elsewhere, but because of its strategic location athwart the Waziribad-Gujranwala and Waziribad-Sialkot-Jammu railway lines. All trains on the way to Jammu and East Punjab passed through it. Research is yet to be done on this topic, but it is likely that any plotting of incidences of the 1947 violence in the Punjab would reveal key river crossings and road and railway junctions as frequent targets for attack. Refugee concentrations offered opportunities for loot and revenge, as we have seen with respect to Sheikhupura. 'From Phillaur to Jullundur', recalled a member of a Muslim convoy, 'mobs of armed Sikhs were seen collected along the railway track and road waiting to assault Muslim caravans by road or rail'.[73]

The fine-grained research on violence in Gujranwala and Lahore supports Stathis Kalyvas' comparative interpretation of mass collective violence in civil-war–type situations. He points to the 'selectivity' of targets and to the 'social approval' of individual acts of violence in a context of political breakdown and struggle. The latter, he argues, 'destroys social hierarchies that effectively act as social controls'.[74] It is the convergence of what might be termed political and private, or local and supra-local imperatives for violence that renders it so intensive in these circumstances.

Chattha's work in Gujranwala, including interviews with acknowledged perpetrators of violence, reveals that they felt that they had approval for what would otherwise be criminal activities. Indeed, it appears that some individuals were subsequently revered for their actions that occurred in a context of 'revenge' and *jihad*. One elderly respondent informed him that 'the people of our area still know of our house because of [his brother's] deed . . . in killing the Sikhs'.[75]

Lahore also provides numerous examples of the 'selective violence' that Kalyvas argues 'is a central form of civil war'.[76] Muslim properties were left untouched, while neighbouring Hindu and Sikh properties were destroyed. 'A [Hindu] shop in Bhaghban Pura Street, which displays an English-written signboard "H.Q. Chawala"', a police constable reported, 'has been set ablaze while neighbouring [Muslim] owned shops have been left unscathed'.[77] Where there were concentrations of non-Muslim residents and businesses as in Shah Almi, we have seen that whole localities were torched. My research has revealed that one Muslim participant in the burning of Shah Almi had recently settled in Lahore's nearby Chuna Mandi locality after losing his home in neighbouring Amritsar to violence.[78] Personal revenge drove his actions that assisted the wider political strategy of undermining the Hindu heart of the walled city.

Local imperatives for violence driven by a desire for loot and revenge were made possible by the territorial conflict at a provincial and all-India level.

At key moments in the final year of British rule, politicians saw violence carried out on the ground by a combination of criminal elements and members of organized paramilitary formations as a resource. The mounting violence in North India led the British to reluctantly agree to partition as a means of averting civil war. The March 1947 violence in the Punjab led to its minorities to demand the province's division. This made it impossible for the Muslim League to secure a homeland without paying its own price; the division of the Muslim majority provinces of Punjab and Bengal. Public acceptance of the 3 June Partition Plan did not however still the endemic violence in the Punjab. Administrative breakdown, Sikh desire for revenge and a growing realization that the Boundary Commission's consideration of 'other factors' would not outweigh the unfavourable Sikh demographic equation when drawing up its lines set the scene for future violence. This was highly dangerous in the context of a militarized province and of politicians thinking that they could control the use of violence as and when it suited their ends.

The circumstances were thus created for partition to intensify rather than abate the violence which had wracked North India during the final year of British rule. The shockwaves were felt across the subcontinent, but as we have shown here, its epicentre was in the Punjab.

CONCLUSION

Many of the factors in the Punjab killings were unique to the region and its colonial development. Undoubtedly, there would have been less turmoil if the region had not emerged as the main recruitment centre of the Indian Army[79] and if large numbers of Sikhs had not migrated to the farmlands of the Canal Colonies in the Muslim dominated areas.[80] The excellent road and railway connections that expedited the export of wheat provided mobility for armed gangs who were intent on looting refugees. Culturally derived notions of community honour encouraged the large numbers of assaults and abductions of women.

Nonetheless, the violence possessed many characteristics similar to other civil-war–type situations. Rape in such circumstances is a frequent occurrence, as is the breakdown of community life that sees violence perpetrated by 'insiders' as well as 'outsiders'. The use of force to move out minority populations is as much a feature of violence in the 1990s Balkans as the 1940s Punjab. There is much evidence in Kalyvas's terms of local turf wars feeding into the wider political conflict regarding the postcolonial power structure. Violence on the ground possessed both private and political purposes. It was this combination that made it so deadly. The violence was both spontaneous and politically purposeful. The organized attacks on villages, refugee trains and convoys belie accounts based on spontaneous religious passions, as does the extended chronology. Violence could take on 'genocidal' characteristics because of the involvement of heavily armed and organized war parties that were on occasion aided by policemen and soldiers.

Individuals killed and looted for personal gain and as part of a wider political process, confident that their actions had social approval and that they were unlikely to be held to account. The sense of impunity that began in the Punjab at the time of the March 1947 Rawalpindi Massacres was the product of the transition between empire and nation-state when the machinery of government was being dismantled.[81] However, recent studies of the violence in the Sikh princely states that bordered the Punjab and the relatively peaceful state of Malerkotla add a layer of complexity to simple notions of the killings being the result of state collapse. The lid was kept on violence where there were administrations, as in Malerkotla, that had nothing to gain from this. It could be intensified if functioning administrations had a political advantage in this.

NOTES

1. Gopal Das Khosla, *Memory's Gay Chariot: An Autobiographical Narrative* (New Delhi: Allied Publishers, 1985), 20.
2. For the view that the violence was spontaneous and unique to the temporary madness of August 1947 in Punjab, see Javeed Alam and Suresh Sharma, 'Remembering Partition', *Seminar* 461 (January 1998): 93–104.
3. In one such attack on a train outside Khalsa College, Amritsar, 1,200 Muslim refugees were massacred. *Civil and Military Gazette* (Lahore) 11 September 1947.
4. See Stathis Kalyvas, *The Logic of Violence in Civil War* (Cambridge: Cambridge University Press, 2006).
5. For the most authoritative discussion of the problem of the casualty figures, see Gyanendra Pandey, *Remembering Partition: Violence, Nationalism and History in India* (Cambridge: Cambridge University Press, 2001), 91.
6. In the 1990s, for example, the publications of the Mohajir Qaumi Mahaz maintained as many as two million *mohajirs* died in the achievement of Pakistan.
7. For an overview of the pattern of migration, see chapter 4 of Ian Talbot and Gurharpal Singh, *The Partition of India* (Cambridge: Cambridge University Press, 2009).
8. Ian Talbot, 'The 1947 Violence in the Punjab', in Ian Talbot, ed., *The Deadly Embrace: Religion, Politics and Violence in India and Pakistan, 1947–2002* (Karachi: Oxford University Press, 2007), 1–15.
9. For a discussion of the similarities with accounts of the 2002 Gujarat attacks on the Muslim minority, see Talbot and Singh, *The Partition of India*, 84–86.

10. Donald Horowitz, *The Deadly Ethnic Riot* (Berkeley: University of California Press, 2001), 490–91.

11. Pandey, *Remembering Partition*, 69.

12. Ritu Menon and Kamla Bhasin, *Borders and Boundaries: Women in India's Partition* (New Brunswick, NJ: Rutgers University Press, 1998).

13. Urvashi Butalia first uncovered this 'hidden history' of partition violence in her pioneering study, *The Other Side of Silence: Voices from the Partition of India* (New Delhi: Penguin, 1998).

14. Veena Das and Ashis Nandy, 'Violence, Victimhood and the Language of Silence', in Veena Das, ed., *The Word and the World: Fantasy, Symbol and Record* (New Delhi: Sage, 1986), 177–90.

15. For theories that link times of transition with increased potential for violence see, for example, Tamotsu Shibutani and Kian M. Kwan, *Ethnic Stratification: A Comparative Approach* (New York: Macmillan, 1965), 377.

16. Suranjan Das, *Communal Riots in Bengal, 1905–1947* (New Delhi: Oxford University Press, 1991), 171.

17. For the background both to the agitation and Punjab politics after the 1946 elections, see Ian Talbot, *Khizr Tiwana, The Punjab Unionist Party and the Partition of India* (Karachi: Oxford University Press, 2002), 145–56.

18. Syed Nur Ahmad, *From Martial Law to Martial Law: Politics in the Punjab 1919–1958* (Boulder, CO: Westview Press, 1985), 226.

19. For a discussion of the Thoa Khalsa episode from a feminist perspective, see Butalia, *The Other Side of Silence*.

20. Report on the Recent Disturbances in the Punjab (March–April 1947) AICC File No G-10/1947, Nehru Memorial Museum and Library, New Delhi.

21. Ibid.

22. Ibid.

23. Cited in Talbot, *The Deadly Embrace*, 6.

24. Cited in Catherine Coombs, 'Partition Narratives: Displaced Trauma and Culpability among British Civil Servants in 1940s Punjab', in Taylor C. Sherman, William Gould, Sarah Ansari, eds., *From Subjects to Citizens: Society and the Everyday State in India and Pakistan, 1947–1970* (New Delhi: Cambridge University Press, 2014), 234.

25. The British response is detailed in a report in *Civil and Military Gazette* (Lahore), 16 March 1947.

26. Ian Copland, 'The Master and the Maharajas: The Sikh Princes and the East Punjab Massacres of 1947', *Modern Asian Studies* 36, no. 3 (2002): 657–704.

27. Shah Almi was one of the walled city's famous thirteen gates. It was named after the Mughal Emperor Shah Allam, who died in Lahore in 1712.

28. Muhammad Saeed, *Lahore: A Memoir* (Lahore: Vanguard Books, 1989), 234–35.

29. Mian Amiruddin, 'Memories of Partition', in Ahmad Salim, ed., *Lahore 1947* (New Delhi: India Research Press, 2001), 290.

30. Ibid.

31. Khosla, *Memory's Gay Chariot*, 156.

32. Ian Talbot, *Divided Cities: Partition and Its Aftermath in Lahore and Amritsar 1947–1957* (Karachi: Oxford University Press, 2006), 45.

33. Rameshwari Nehru Papers, No. 25, Nehru Memorial Museum and Library, New Delhi.

34. Ian Talbot, 'The August 1947 Violence in Sheikhupura City', in Ian Talbot, ed., *The Independence of India and Pakistan: New Approaches and Reflections* (Karachi: Oxford University Press, 2013), 90–120. For the failure of the Punjab Boundary Force in containing the violence, see Robin Jeffrey, 'The Punjab Boundary Force and the Problem of Order, August 1947', *Modern Asian Studies* 8 (1974): 491–520; Daniel Marston, 'The Indian Army, Partition and the Punjab Boundary Force, 1945–1947', *War in History* 16, no. 4 (2009): 469–505.

35. The Punjab Police Abstract of Intelligence, week ending 13 September 1947, 375 (NIHCR).

36. Government of West Punjab, *The Sikhs in Action* (Lahore: Government Printing Press, West Punjab, 1948); Government of West Punjab, *RSS in Punjab* (Government Printing Press, West Punjab, 1948).

37. Mashkur Hassan, *Aazaadi ke charaagh*, third ed. (Lahore: no pub., 1986).

38. Khawaja Iftikhar, *Jab Amritsar jal raha tha.* The work ran to nine editions in the space of a decade. Its author has been awarded the gold medal of the Pakistan movement and the epithet, *Musavvir-e-Haqiqat* (The Painter of Realities).

39. Saumitra Jha and Steven Wilkinson, 'Does Combat Experience Foster Organizational Skill? Evidence from Ethnic Cleansing During the Partition of South Asia', *American Political Science Review* 106, no. 4 (November 2012): 883–907.

40. Copland, 'The Master and the Maharajas', 709

41. Ibid., 701.

42. Ibid., 693. Copland in fact cites evidence that the rulers of Kapurthala and Faridkot had direct contact with the *jathas*.

43. P. Virdee, 'Partition and the Absence of Communal Violence in Malerkotla', in Talbot, ed., *The Deadly Embrace*, 16–36.

44. Joseph Schechtman, 'Evacuee Property in India and Pakistan', *Pacific Affairs* 24 (1951): 411–12.

45. Recent scholarship has revealed that all communities had their victims and aggressors. There were also cases in which individuals risked their own lives to safeguard minority communities.

46. See the discussion in Anders Bjorn Hansen, *Partition and Genocide: Manifestation of Violence in Punjab 1937–1947* (New Delhi: India Research Press, 2002), 26–27.

47. Mark Levene, 'Is the Holocaust Simply Another Example of Genocide?' *Patterns of Prejudice* 28, no. 2 (1994): 4–5.

48. Henry Huttenbach, 'Locating the Holocaust on the Genocide Spectrum: Towards a Methodology of Definition and Categorization', *Holocaust and Genocide Studies* 3, no. 3 (1988): 296.

49. See the British Fortnightly Reports for the Punjab dated 30 July 1947 and 13 August 1947. L/P&J/5/250 India Office Records, British Library.

50. This demarcated the new international border in the Punjab region. Its judgements were controversially delayed until after the British transfer of power.

51. Jason Francisco, 'In the Heat of Fratricide: The Literature of India's Partition Burning Freshly', in Mushirul Hasan, ed., *Inventing Boundaries: Gender, Politics and the Partition of India* (New Delhi: Oxford University Press, 2000), 372.

52. Melson has maintained that genocides occur when state and society are in crisis. Mark Levene has developed the concept of 'zones of genocide'. They exist when competing national discourses clash in a context in which outside pressures impede traditional accomodationist mechanisms in multiethnic societies. Robert Melson, *Revolution and Genocide: The Origins of the Armenian Genocide and the Holocaust* (Chicago: University of Chicago Press, 1992), 15–17; Mark Levene, 'Creating a Modern "Zone of Genocide": The Impact of Nation and State Formation on Eastern Anatolia, 1878–1923', *Holocaust and Genocide Studies* 12, no. 3 (1998): 418 ff.

53. Paul Brass, 'The Partition of India and Retributive Genocide in the Punjab, 1946–47: Means, Methods and Purposes', *Journal of Genocide Research* 5, no. 1 (2003): 71–101.

54. See Ishtiaq Ahmed, 'Forced Migration and Ethnic Cleansing in Lahore in 1947: Some First Person Accounts', in Ian Talbot and Shinder Thandi, eds., *People on the Move: Punjabi Colonial and Post-Colonial Migration* (Karachi: Oxford University Press, 2004), 99.

55. Leading Sikh politicians maintained that Muslim CID officers had fabricated the Sikh Plan's existence to discredit the community. See, for example, Statement of Baldev Singh on Present Situation, n.d., T/3/1/174 IOR.

56. Copland, 'The Master and the Maharajas', 678.

57. Ibid., 681.

58. *Civil and Military Gazette* (Lahore), 19 September 1947.

59. Ayesha Jalal, 'Nation, Reason and Religion: The Punjab's Role in the Partition of India', *Economic & Political Weekly* 33/32 (8–14 August 1998): 2183–90.

60. *Inquilab* (Lahore), 12 January 1948.

61. *Pakistan Times* (Lahore), 24 October 1947.

62. *Pakistan Times* (Lahore), 17 September and 1 October 1947.

63. Joint Defence Council Meeting, 16 August 1947, Mountbatten Papers Mss Eur F200/130 IOR.

64. See Som Anand, *Lahore: Portrait of a Lost City* (Lahore: Vanguard Books, 1998), 74–75; Santosh Kumar, *Lahore Nama* (New Delhi: Vibha, 2002), 1, 19–20; Sa'adat Hassan Manto, *Siyah Hashiye* (Black Margins) was originally published as a collection in 1948. For a recent selection, see Muhammad Umar Memon, ed., *Black Margins: Stories Sa'adat Hasan Manto* (New Delhi: Katha, 2003).

65. Ilyas Chattha, 'The Patterns of Partition Violence in West Punjab', in Ian Talbot, ed., *The Independence of India and Pakistan: New Approaches and Reflections* (Karachi: Oxford University Press, 2013), 67.

66. FIR no. 340, Note Book no. 512, 23 August 1947, Thana Mozang, Lahore, cited in Chattha, 'Patterns of Violence', 71.

67. FIR no. 417, Note Book no. 249, 13 August 1947, Thana Civil Lines, Lahore, cited in ibid., 70.

68. FIR no. 418, Note Book no. 18/141, 15 August 1947, Thana Civil Lines, Lahore, cited in ibid.

69. Ilyas Chattha, *Partition and Locality: Violence, Migration and Development in Gujranwala and Sialkot 1947–1961* (Karachi: Oxford University Press, 2011).

70. Interview with Mohammad Ali Niamabad, 17 December 2008, cited in Chattha, *Partition*, 134.

71. Interview with Sardara Dindar, Tata Chanwa, Gujranwala, 21 February 2007, ibid., 135.

72. FIR no. 150, Note Book no. 66, 10 August 1947, District Police Record Office, Gujranwala, ibid., 130.

73. 'Statement of Sardar Abdul Aziz, Retired Superintendent of Police, Patiala State', in Saleem Ullah Khan, *The Journey to Pakistan: A Documentation on Refugees of 1947* (Islamabad: Government of Pakistan, Cabinet Division, National Documentation Centre, 1993), 201.

74. Kalyvas, *The Logic of Violence in Civil War*, 57.

75. Interview with Ghulam Nabi, Nizamabad, 27 February 2007, cited in Chattha, *Partition*, 134.

76. Kalyvas, *The Logic of Violence in Civil War*, 27.

77. FIR no. 377, Note Book no. 2/147, 12 August 1947, Thana Mughal Pura, Lahore, cited in Chattha, 'The Patterns of Partition Violence' in Talbot, *Independence*, 72.

78. Talbot, *Divided Cities*, 45.

79. On the Punjab's emergence as the 'sword-arm' of India, see Ian Talbot, *Punjab and the Raj 1849–1947* (New Delhi: Manohar, 1988), 41–46; Tan Tai Yong, *The Garrison State: The Military, Government and Society in Colonial Punjab 1841–1947* (Thousand Oaks, CA: Sage, 2005).

80. The British viewed the Canal Colony development from the 1880s as a crowning achievement of colonial rule. See Hugh Kennedy Trevaskis, *The Land of the Five Rivers: An Economic History of the Punjab From the Earliest Times to 1890* (London: Oxford University Press, 1928). On the reverse migration in 1947, see Ravinder Kaur, *Since 1947: Partition Narratives Among Punjabi Migrants of Delhi* (New Delhi: Oxford University Press, 2007).

81. For insights into how British officials understood and represented the deteriorating law and order situation, see Coombs, 'Partition Narratives', 216–41.

REFERENCES

Ahmad, Syed Nur. 1985. *From Martial Law to Martial Law: Politics in the Punjab 1919–1958*. Boulder, CO: Westview Press.

Ahmed, Ishtiaq. 2004. 'Forced Migration and Ethnic Cleansing in Lahore in 1947: Some First Hand Accounts'. In *People on the Move: Punjabi Colonial and Post-Colonial Migration*, edited by Ian Talbot and Shinder Thandi, 96–141. Karachi: Oxford University Press.

Alam, Javeed, and Suresh Sharma. 1998. 'Remembering Partition'. *Seminar* 461: 93–104.
Amiruddin, Mian. 2001. 'Memories of Partition'. In *Lahore 1947*, edited by Ahmad Salim, 251–90. New Delhi: India Research Press.
Anand, Som. 1998. *Lahore: Portrait of a Lost City*. Lahore: Vanguard Books.
Brass, Paul. 2003. 'The Partition of India and Retributive Genocide in the Punjab, 1946–47: Means, Methods and Purposes'. *Journal of Genocide Research* 5 (1): 71–101.
Butalia, Urvashi. 1998. *The Other Side of Silence: Voices from the Partition of India*. New Delhi: Penguin.
Chattha, Ilyas. 2011. *Partition and Locality: Violence, Migration and Development in Gujranwala and Sialkot 1947–1961*. Karachi: Oxford University Press.
———. 2013. 'The Patterns of Partition Violence in West Punjab'. In *The Independence of India and Pakistan: New Approaches and Reflections*, edited by Ian Talbot, 58–89. Karachi: Oxford University Press.
Coombs, Catherine. 2014. 'Partition Narratives: Displaced Trauma and Culpability among British Civil Servants in 1940s Punjab'. In *From Subjects to Citizens: Society and the Everyday State in India and Pakistan, 1947–1970*, edited by Taylor Sherman, William Gould and Sarah Ansari, 216–40. New Delhi: Cambridge University Press.
Copland, Ian. 2002. 'The Master and the Maharajas: The Sikh Princes and the East Punjab Massacres of 1947'. *Modern Asian Studies* 36 (3): 657–704.
Das, Suranjan. 1991. *Communal Riots in Bengal, 1905–1947*. New Delhi: Oxford University Press.
Das, Veena, and Ashis Nandy. 1986. 'Violence, Victimhood and the Language of Silence'. In *The Word and the World: Fantasy, Symbol and Record*, edited by Veena Das, 177–90. New Delhi: Sage.
Francisco, Jason. 2000. 'In the Heat of Fratricide: The Literature of India's Partition Burning Freshly'. In *Inventing Boundaries: Gender, Politics and the Partition of India*, edited by Mushirul Hasan, 371–93. New Delhi: Oxford University Press.
Hansen, Anders Bjorn. 2002. *Partition and Genocide: Manifestations of Violence in Punjab 1937–1947*. New Delhi: India Research Press.
Horowitz, Donald. 2001. *The Deadly Ethnic Riot*. Berkeley: University of California Press.
Huttenbach, Henry. 1988. 'Locating the Holocaust on the Genocide Spectrum: Towards a Methodology of Definition and Categorization'. *Holocaust and Genocide Studies* 3 (3): 289–303.
Jalal, Ayesha. 1998. 'Nation, Reason and Religion: The Punjab's Role in the Partition of India'. *Economic & Political Weekly* 33/32 (8–14 August): 2183–90.
Jeffrey, Robin. 1974. 'The Punjab Boundary Force and the Problem of Order, August 1947'. *Modern Asian Studies* 8:491–520.
Jha, Saumitra, and Steven Wilkinson. 2012. 'Does Combat Experience Foster Organizational Skill? Evidence from Ethnic Cleansing During the Partition of South Asia'. *American Political Science Review* 106 (4): 883–907.
Kalyvas, Stathis. 2006. *The Logic of Violence in Civil War*. Cambridge: Cambridge University Press.

Kaur, Ravinder. 2007. *Since 1947: Partition Narratives Among Punjabi Migrants of Delhi*. New Delhi: Oxford University Press.

Khan, Saleem Ullah. 1993. *The Journey to Pakistan: A Documentation on Refugees of 1947*. Islamabad: Government of Pakistan, Cabinet Division, National Documentation Centre.

Khosla, Gopal Das. 1985. *Memory's Gay Chariot: An Autobiographical Narrative*. New Delhi: Allied Publishers.

Kumar, Santosh. 2002. *Lahore Nama*. New Delhi: Vibha.

Levene, Mark. 1994. 'Is the Holocaust Simply Another Example of Genocide?' *Patterns of Prejudice* 28 (2): 3–26.

———. 1998. 'Creating a Modern "Zone of Genocide": The Impact of Nation and State Formation on Eastern Anatolia, 1878–1923'. *Holocaust and Genocide Studies* 12 (3): 393–433.

Marston, Daniel. 2009. 'The Indian Army, Partition and the Punjab Boundary Force, 1945–1947'. *War in History* 16 (4): 469–505.

Melson, Robert. 1992. *Revolution and Genocide: The Origins of the Armenian Genocide and the Holocaust*. Chicago: University of Chicago Press.

Memon, Muhammad Umar, ed. 2003. *Black Margins: Stories of Sa'adat Hasan Manto*. New Delhi: Katha.

Menon, Ritu, and Kamla Bhasin. 1998. *Borders and Boundaries: Women in India's Partition*. New Brunswick, NJ: Rutgers University Press.

Pandey, Gyanendra. 2001. *Remembering Partition: Violence, Nationalism and History in India*. Cambridge: Cambridge University Press.

Saeed, Muhammad. 1989. *Lahore: A Memoir*. Lahore: Vanguard Books.

Schechtman, Joseph. 1951. 'Evacuee Property in India and Pakistan'. *Pacific Affairs*, 24: 406–13.

Shibutani, Tamotsu, and Kian M. Kwan. 1965. *Ethnic Stratification: A Comparative Approach*. New York: Macmillan.

Talbot, Ian. 1988. *Punjab and the Raj 1849–1947*. New Delhi: Manohar.

———. 2002. *Khizr Tiwana, the Punjab Unionist Party and the Partition of India*. Karachi: Oxford University Press.

———. 2006. *Divided Cities: Partition and Its Aftermath in Lahore and Amritsar 1947–1957*. Karachi: Oxford University Press.

———. 2007. 'The 1947 Violence in the Punjab'. In *The Deadly Embrace: Religion, Politics and Violence in India and Pakistan, 1947–2002*, edited by Ian Talbot, 1–15. Karachi: Oxford University Press.

———. 2013. 'The August 1947 Violence in Sheikhupura City'. In *The Independence of India and Pakistan: New Approaches and Reflections*, edited by Ian Talbot, 90–120. Karachi: Oxford University Press.

Talbot, Ian, and Gurharpal Singh. 2009. *The Partition of India*. Cambridge: Cambridge University Press.

Trevaskis, Hugh Kennedy. 1928. *The Land of the Five Rivers: An Economic History of the Punjab From the Earliest Times to 1890*. London: Oxford University Press.

Virdee, Pippa, 'Partition and the Absence of Communal Violence in Malerkotla'. In *The Deadly Embrace: Religion, Politics and Violence in India and Pakistan, 1947–2002*, edited by Ian Talbot, 16–36. Karachi: Oxford University Press.

West Punjab, Government. 1948a. *RSS in Punjab*. Lahore: Government Printing Press.

———. 1948b. *The Sikhs in Action*. Lahore: Government Printing Press.

Yong, Tan Tai. 2005. *The Garrison State: The Military, Government and Society in Colonial Punjab 1841–1947*. Thousand Oaks, CA: Sage.

Chapter 2

The Sociohistorical Production of Partition in Palestine

Marcelo Svirsky and Ronnen Ben-Arie

> *We'll begin with the most important thing, with a matter of life-and-death for the State of Israel: If there will not be two states here, and fast, there will be one state here. If there will be one state here, it will be an Arab state, from the sea to the Jordan River. If there will be an Arab state here, I don't envy my children and my grandchildren.*
>
> —Amos Oz, 13 March 2015[1]

A string of international political events underwrites the legalistic-political focus of the scholarship on Palestine's partition. The bulk of this tradition studies the partition of Palestine as an instrument devised to solve a conflict construed in terms of just as worthy competing territorial claims between the Palestinian people and the Zionist movement. It all began towards the conclusion of the Great War with the 1917 Balfour Declaration that introduced the idea that modern Palestine does not belong to its native Arab population but should be rearranged for some form of Jewish sovereignty. The document was housed and validated as part of the British Mandate Charter for Palestine that earned legal ratification by the League of Nations (1922), and then in the Treaty of Lausanne (1923). In a world dominated by the old imperial powers, the Balfour text's potent impact resided in the discursive internationalization of Palestine as a new scene of national conflict, now to be steered by the British. Faced with a resolute Arab Revolt launched against Zionist settlerist encroachment and British imperial rule, in 1937 the Mandatory government introduced a proposal to partition Palestine (the Palestine Royal Commission headed by Lord Peel), a plan that was formally examined and de facto disallowed about a year later in the work of the Woodhead Commission (the Palestine Partition Commission). Immediately after the Second World War, the idea of partition was further recanted by the Anglo-American Commission of Inquiry, which recommended a unitary state in Palestine (report submitted in 1946), but it was resurrected in the Morrison-Grady Plan for Provincial Autonomy in the same year. As an upshot of the work of a special committee tasked to prepare a report on Palestine (the *United Nations Special Committee on Palestine*—UNSCOP), the partition of the country was internationally sanctioned by the United Nations General Assembly (UNGA) as Resolution 181, in November 1947. The dialectical relation inaugurated in the Balfour Declaration finally crystallized in the establishment of the state of Israel in 1948, a process that involved the ethnic cleansing of close to a million Palestinians. It took about three decades for the question of Palestine to be reintroduced in the UNGA agenda, via the 1974 Resolution 3236 (XXIX) that reaffirmed the inalienable rights of the Palestinian people to self-determination, national independence and sovereignty, and the right of the Palestinians to return to their homes and property. The Palestine Liberation Organization (PLO) began debating the acceptance of partition and the ensuing model of the 'two-states solution' by the mid-1970s, and in the 1988 Palestinian Declaration of Independence that proclaimed the State of Palestine, the UNGA Partition Resolution 181 is mentioned as the 'Resolution that still provides those conditions of international legitimacy that ensure the right of the Palestinian Arab people to sovereignty'.[2] A few years later, the old partition formula resurged in the context of the 1990s Oslo Accords in the form of the nowadays widely supported 'two-states solution'. In the reasoning that links Balfour to Oslo, the partition model became a paradigmatic framework back to which explanations of the Israeli–Palestinian conflict must refer.

What were the open and hidden positions of the Zionist and Palestinian political leaderships in regard to the different partition proposals from 1937 to 1947? Were there any cracks, that is, internal disagreements, within these leaderships in relation to the question of partition? Did these positions change over time, and if so, how and why? What were the internal governmental dynamics in the camp of the partition proponents? What were the political alliances with the international actors that accelerated or slowed the furthering of partition-oriented Palestinian and Zionists interests? These are the sort of questions that have mostly preoccupied the research agenda in relation to the question of the partition of Palestine. Basically, these questions survey—in a morally neutral realpolitik form of analysis—political interests, political circumstances, the creation and maintenance of advantages, and at times also their relation to the realm of ideas.[3] This view of power has brought the study of the Palestine partition to be stapled to a political science infatuated with the political behaviours and the explicit and covert political positions of the various actors involved—the Arab–Palestinian leadership, the Jewish settlement leadership, the British government, the World Zionist Organization (WZO), the Arab nations and, post-World War II, the Arab League, the United Nations and the American government. The ultimate upshot of these analyses is answering the question of who supported the partition proposal, why and when.[4] Others have conducted analyses of the arguments around partition, justifications and its critiques.[5] Yet, these topicalities, important as they might be, cannot explain a profounder social reality: how could a political model that did not even emerge formally from within the people in conflict, evolve to the point that it devoured these people's passions, and pedals today their political imaginations? Why it is that the sentiment behind partition frames the rational and affective methods with which Palestinians and Israelis remember their interrelated modern history, interpret their present and envisage political solutions for historic Palestine—regardless of their differing, typically oppositional understandings? Partition is in fact entrenched in their collective soul; it is the lifeblood of these societies. Its defiance by those reflecting upon an alternative shared future is no less than a rebuked profanation. See, for instance, Amos Oz's quotation in the epigraph: the idea of a shared homeland, which Oz defines as necessarily an 'Arab state' sort of fortune, horrifies the acclaimed liberal writer. It can hardly be argued that partition expresses itself as the most instinctual paradigm to think about the whole spectrum of modern Palestine experience. One reasonable explanation for this condition is that the factuality of partition that resulted from the 1948 war and the ethnic cleansing of the Palestinian people set the initial material and cultural conditions that eventually, over the years, led Israelis and Palestinians to embrace the segregated character of that fabricated common reality as an inescapable destiny that was projected in mind and soul backwards in time as much as forward. Public memory and education immortalized that framing. From this point of view, then, it might make sense to study partition mainly as a political model that augured a new reality, and a new collective consciousness common to all.

Plausible as this answer might be, it is ahistorical, and therefore, naturally apolitical. It neglects the formative events that took place in Palestine, before partition plans of sorts began filling the political discourse about this Middle Eastern corner. Partition as a political model and an internationally recognized instrument perhaps did not arise from within the region, politically or ideologically, but at the time the idea of partition was suggested by the British, *partition was in fact the dominant social reality of Palestine.* In contrast to the pre-Zionist period, by the mid-1930s Palestinians and Jews lived mostly apart or were in the process of deepening their physical, cultural and economic separation. The political model first presented by the British officially in 1937 echoed that existing reality, regardless of the support or rebuff voiced regarding this model by the political leaderships in the two camps, natives and settlers. Though some authors have acknowledged this segregative reality in Palestine,[6] not many have explained the historicity of this reality: partition was the most unambiguous indication of the settler colonial process that Palestine was going through, not just an aspect of this project. In other words, and to get to the point, in Palestine, partition was artificially engineered—in all aspects of life—as an unfolding rationality of the settler-colonization of the country by the Zionist movement: the social production of partition fashioned the conflict. That begs the question of why in academic as much as journalistic work, and also in popular culture, partition is analysed as a cure to the conflict.

Partition might be studied as a legal-political instrument that was or can be hypothetically moulded to solve the conflict, but historically, partition in all its social forms emerged as the expression of the causative forces at work that incrementally brought about and formed the conflict between settlers and natives. To make use of Michel Foucault's terminology, partition became the landscape that defined the fields of visibility and sayability not only for Arab-Palestinians and Jews on the ground, but also for the British administration in Palestine and in the Colonial Office in London, and eventually it shaped the worldwide political language that enveloped Palestine more generally; and that partition models of sorts between the two world wars were a fold of the modern geist of nationalist ideology is to state the obvious.[7] The partition state of mind in academic scholarship and other forms of writing that flagrantly ignore the explanative role of the causative forces of the social reality that in the early twentieth century created partition on the ground long before it was suggested as a political model is a fact we should regret, as it has contributed—and continues to do so—to a perverse historical representation which has greatly benefited Zionism with regard to its intentions and materializations. This is very typical of writers not critical of Zionism. If settler colonial Zionism is absolved from any historical responsibility for partitioning Palestine's life and land de facto, we are left with a twisted understanding of history, society and politics that not only obscures the causes and evolvement of the conflict but reaffirms the validity of a racially segregated existence and future. Alternatively, other writers have offered nuanced accounts of the UNGA Partition Resolution. For instance, renowned Palestinian scholar Walid Khalidi discussed the Resolution in the context of a variety of international events from a viewpoint of international justice, in conjunction with an analysis of the demographic and land ownership realities of the time.[8]

Essentially, the problem with the legalistic-realpolitik analysis of partition lies in its poor understanding of power. Power is not to be understood only at the level of political interests, but rather it needs to be grasped also at the level of the social production of the real. Central to power is the micro-sociological ways by which communities create their own social reality. We ascribe to an understanding of power that focuses on how differential social forces produce new forms of actualizing the real, permanently struggling to consolidate and maintain social hierarchies.[9] But by positioning the question of partition on the plane of circumstantial political interests responding to legal and political documents—which represents a reduction of power to the administration of domination—whatever relation may exist between the event of partition and the historical construction of society can be surfaced only partially, and incongruently. Our basic claim is that it is at the level of social production that we are able to explain how partition became the spirit of this conflict, its guiding axiom and a form of political-cultural receptacle within which the partition political proposal made sense and came to be considered obvious. It is therefore our task in this chapter to rewrite the place and role of partition in the history and politics of the settler colonial conflict in modern Palestine.

BEFORE PARTITION, OR BEFORE ZIONISM

Ottoman Palestine, echoing the rest of the empire, had its major social groups defined along the axes of religion (defined mainly in terms of Muslims vs. non-Muslims), ethnos (Turks and others) and class (defined mainly by profession and the urban/rural divide)—altogether making a very diverse, multilingual society.[10] These divisions were not so rigid as to prevent the existence of everyday practices shared by members of the Muslim, Christian and Jewish communities. That is, these divisions did not resonate in ways that made wide-ranging social intersections impossible. As far as it concerned intercommunal relations, homogeneity was not the imperial Ottoman logic but was in fact to the contrary, at least until the consolidation of the driving force of Turkism just before the Great War. In Ottoman Palestine, Arabs and Oriental Jews[11] (or Arab-Jews) shared a wide range of social practices from the sheer neighbourhood and the cohesions that common housing creates—'The residential compound was the basis of the local identity, and neighbours shared celebrations and tragedies'[12]—to elite cooperation, commercial partnerships, sharing pastime activities, even political activism and to some extent, also shared education. According to Michelle Campos, 'many memoirs argued that "native" Sephardi and Maghrebi Jews shared cultural, spatial, and everyday practices with their Muslim neighbours that sharply differentiated them from "newcomer" Ashkenazi Jewish co-religionists'.[13] Members of the three religions not only lived in the same neighbourhoods and at times in the same apartment building or courtyard, but they also:

> belonged to the same craft guilds, worked and shopped in the same markets, went into business together, and frequented the same cafés and law courts. The popular tradition of visiting the tombs of holy men and saints further bridged the religious gap and brought Muslims, Christians, and Jews to pray together for divine intercession.[14]

Odd as it may sound to the contemporary observer, mental boundaries did not exist between Muslim and Christian Arabs and Jews, and since most Palestinian Jews spoke Arabic, the walls of language and culture were low ones.[15] Arab-Jewish identity was a fact of life and that identity 'meant more than coexistence and residing one beside the other; lifestyles, languages and culture created a common identity that centred on a sense of belonging to a place and to the people who live there'.[16] Though education was mostly segregated, there was some mixed attendance at schools in the urban centres, in public and private schools. As Salim Tamari explains, 'One should not forget . . . the impact of . . .public schools established by the Ottoman authorities in the last third of the nineteenth century in bringing together in one classroom children who had previously gone to their own Qur'anic *kuttab* or Talmud schools (*heder*)'.[17] Wasif Jawhariyyeh, the famed Arab musician and storyteller from Jerusalem, did not spare words to describe the religious celebrations during the Easter week in the early twentieth century: 'It is amazing to see how the huge festivals and wide national celebrations of each religion and every confession followed one another in this small region, in peace and security'.[18] 'These solidarities'—explains Tamari—'undermined the fixity of a confessional system derived from a premodern—perhaps even primordial—network of affinities'.[19] The works of Menachem Klein, Michelle Campos, Salim Tamari, Issam Nassar, Moshe Behar, Ami Dockser Marcus, Mahmoud Yazbak, Yair Wallach, Julia Philips Cohen, Yuval Ben-Bassat, Hillel Cohen and Abigail Jacobson are replete with similar chronicles by Arab and Jewish writers drawn from memoirs, newspapers and other sources that documented their close relations in Jerusalem, Tiberias, Safed, Hebron, Jaffa and Haifa before Zionism. The genealogy of this interfaith familiarity characteristic of Ottoman imperial society is to be sought in the ways Islamic Caliphates created that possibility for long periods of time, in sharp contrast with the fate European Jews had to endure during medieval times.[20]

Oriental Jews were seen by the Arabs of Palestine as natives, indigenous people of the land or 'abna al balad' (sons of the country), 'compatriots', and 'yahud awlad Arab' or sons-of-Arabs Jews.[21] The source of this indigeneity derived from a shared sense of Arabness: this means to think of this form of sociability within the age-old everyday framework given by Arab culture and traditions, the common use of the Arabic language by Arabs and Jews, the free movement and use of the geographical space, their physical proximity in urban centres and the Islamic character of their shared space that facilitated the sort of interfaith relationship and intercultural proximity.

Driven by centuries of antisemitism and by an emergent collective will to forge a secular modern nation capable of self-determination, Zionist Jewish immigrants coming into Palestine from the early 1880s were equipped with xenophobic assumptions vested in them during their long presence in the European continent. So, when they came to 'The Orient', white European Zionists racialized all things Arab as inferior. In other words, as a European project, Zionism was pregnant with racial assumptions and rationalities. European Zionists conceived the Palestinian native content as racially and culturally incompatible with their own. Not only did they not see the reality of shared life in Palestine as one they desired to become part of, but their cultural preaccumulation[22] left no room in their national project for their Oriental brethren. As Hillel Cohen explains, 'The Eastern-European immigrants, particularly those who came from socialist frameworks, did not wish or need to integrate as part of the existent Sephardic community in Palestine, nor did they desire to integrate this community in the new Zionist system they were forming'.[23] In the eyes of the natives, this isolationism construed the Jewish Zionists in Palestine as strangers. The cultural coordinates of the Oriental Jews, their commitment to the Arabic language, their loyalty to the Ottoman Empire and their preference to continue cultivating productive Arab-Jewish relations—all these patterns indicated, in the eyes of the Jewish European settlers, an unbridgeable lack of obligation to 'Zionist emancipation' while these components meant nativeness for the Arab Palestinians. As Hayyim Ben-Kiki diagnosed in 1921, 'When the new [European-Zionist] settler comes to the Land, he does not come to accommodate and adjust. The precise opposite is the case: he comes to make others adapt to him'.[24] More as a general pattern, this is what distinguishes white settlers in colonial processes, according to Raef Zreik:

> The settler colonialist refuses to come under local laws. He is the law. He brings with himself his own law, his totality, and his terms of reference. He accepts no partners in making the law. The native can benefit from the colonialist's arrangements as a contingent beneficiary, but he cannot be the co-author of the nomos of the land.[25]

The next section examines how the oppositional relation between the Palestinian natives—Arabs and Jews—on the one hand, and the European Jewish immigrant-settlers on the other hand, had destructive effects on the former. As has already been noted, we carry out this political reading of history by using the lens that settler colonial theory provides. In its most structural aspect, the settler strives *to dispossess life from its native forms*. In the process, native routines, sociabilities and institutions—wither away. This means decreasing the potentiality of a life by fatally debilitating the supports that nurture and animate native spaces. Processes that entail the assault on, and at times the extinction of, the sociabilities and ecologies of life that sustained and spatialized native existence were defined by late Australian historian Patrick Wolfe as processes hinged on native elimination.[26] Making the inherited coordinates of these spaces unavailable to the native is the most treasured of the settler's aspirations. In terms of process, dispossessing life from its native forms means the creation of a replacement structure emerging during the course of the struggle to eliminate the native. The inquiry into how the structure of invasion is formed begins by charting the forces of native elimination, and in our case, by answering the question of what exactly settler forces sought to displace in Palestine.

PARTITION, OR ZIONISM

Given that the social, cultural and economic partition of Palestine 'predated geopolitical partition by many years and was well underway by the end of the 1920s' as Barbara Smith argued,[27] research questions should not shy away from elucidating the processes that produced that reality. That is, between the opposite poles of social integration and social scission, it should be asked what were the various social phenomena that gradually brought about the segmentation of Palestine's social texture, and eventually, made the notion of partition a common sense, a logical assumption and a driving force. In a recent work we have offered a comprehensive answer to this question, one that lies in the social constructions between power and resistance in the course of the settler colonization of Palestine during the first three to four decades of the Zionist invasion, starting from the early 1880s.[28]

The notion of *Aliyah* is used to denote Jewish immigration to Israel, but it literally means 'ascension', since for Zionism immigration to *Eretz Israel* (The Land of Israel) is an act of ideological and moral elevation quite distinct from immigration to any other country. The historiography of Zionism distinguishes between several waves of immigration into Palestine or *Aliyot* (plural), which were no innocent immigrations but evolved on the ground as forms of settler invasion of a particular kind. Though already the first *Aliyah* (1882–1903) implanted itself in Palestine, avoiding merging with the existing local community, it was the second *Aliyah* (1904–1914) that was the most significant in terms of its impact in the long run as formative of the Zionist settler colonial project. Their dealings with land, their separatist practices and their cultural mannerisms awakened more than just preoccupation among

Palestinian Arabs and Jews. It did not take long—based on the recurrence of certain emergent practices—for settlerism in Palestine to shape a tendency and a form that not only opposed but sought to destroy the conditions of existence of the traditional forms of life in the region. However, this was not by any means a linear and uninterrupted development. Resistance to the Zionist project began with the first steps of Zionist settler colonization; the first violent incident took place on 28 March 1886 at Petah Tiqva (the first Jewish settlement in the Zionist era) because of disputes over grazing rights and rights of access to land.[29] Before Arab resistance reached a sound level of local and national political organization, it was incubated via different actions. At first, Arab peasant opposition to Zionist land purchases and evictions comprised acts of violence and petitioning the Sultan.[30] Political intervention by means of parliamentary activity (during the second constitutional Ottoman era, 1908–1922) was another sphere of protest, and lastly the press was invoked.[31] Later on, during British rule, armed resistance was organized for the first time in the early 1930s, and it reached its peak during the Arab Revolt of 1936–1939.

Jewish immigration to Palestine was seen by those Sephardim and other Oriental Jews supportive of Zionism as a just remedy for those persecuted Jews in Eastern Europe, and they believed that Zionism could contribute to the wellbeing of all Palestinian Ottomans by way of its economic activities. More generally, they saw in Zionism an opportunity to revive Jewish culture, but significantly, they consciously divorced these principles from the territorial-political aspirations of the European Zionist movement.[32] Not only the emphasis on cultural Hebraism rather than political territorialism stood at the centre of this Zionist belief, but no less importantly was the determination to maintain close Arab-Jewish relations and the call to Jewish immigrants to learn Arabic and immerse themselves in the local culture. For the Sephardim, these ideas were inseparable from the general project of Jewish revitalization in Palestine. Though the Zionist leadership in Palestine was content with whatever form of instrumental mediation the Sephardim could offer that would help bypass the legal restrictions on Jewish European immigration and land purchasing set by the Ottoman government, they categorized non-European Jews as backward and primitive, and left them no role or place in the leadership of the emergent Jewish-Zionist settlement in Palestine.[33] As much as the Oriental Jews asked to extend a bridge between the Arab natives and the Jewish newcomers and somehow prolong Arab-Jewish shared life into the future, it proved hard to extend a bridge between two emerging nationalisms on the background of a native–settler confrontation. The balance was tilted finally in 1929. According to Hillel Cohen, the 1929 riots were the break point in the effort of the Arab-Jews to navigate between identities.[34]

For Cohen, the Arab attacks on their old Jewish neighbours in Sefad, Hebron, Jerusalem, Haifa and Jaffa—killing 133 of them—needs to be explained in terms of the end of an era: 'when the Arabs attacked, they made no distinction between Jews of different political views, or between those who came from long-established families and those who were relative newcomers'.[35] At that point, for the Arabs they were all Jews somehow involved in the project of dispossessing them from their ancestral land;[36] internal Jewish differences did not matter anymore. For the Oriental Jews, this was the end of dual loyalty and the inauguration of the attempts to become an integral part of the Zionist institutions, an attempt that—given the racial topography of Zionism—was doomed to fail. As Tim Sontheimer showed, the British administration in Palestine contributed to deepening the gap between the Ashkenazi Zionists and the Sephardi communities.[37] For the realization of the 'Jewish national home' promise given in the Balfour Declaration, the 'British partners envisioned for this endeavour were neither the Sephardi nor the Ashkenazi anti-Zionist Orthodox communities of Palestine . . . British key statesmen had been closely connected to European Ashkenazi Zionists, with the brilliant lobbyist Chaim Weizmann leading the way'.[38] For this purpose, the British created the 'Zionist Commission', a semigovernmental organization comprised of European Zionist Jews only. Their policies of exclusion of local Jews were endorsed by the British Mandate, and the positions of the Oriental Jews and the Orthodox Jewish community, who called for the fostering of peaceful Arab-Jewish relations, ignored. For the British administration, there was only one Jewish form of representation for the Jews in Palestine, and this was embodied in the Zionist organizations.

The differentiation with the Oriental Jewish community was but an aspect of the variety of Zionist settler practices that lacerated the integrity of the native Palestinian society. More generally in relation to the wholeness of this society, the bifurcation of the economy and the society, and the emergence of a Jewish enclave extricated from the Palestinian space, became finally visible by the end of the 1920s.[39] This process was the result of several Zionist separatist policies in the areas of land, labour, everyday economic relations, education and culture. One such important strategy was the exclusivist relation to land established by the Zionist movement. The general pattern that arose was that following purchasing of land from Arab absentee landowners, land that was aimed for settling Jewish immigrants, 'villagers [peasant-tenants] were forcibly removed from lands sold to Zionists'.[40] In 1901 at the Fifth Zionist Congress held in Basel, the Jewish National Fund (JNF) was founded. Its task was to organize buying and developing land for settlement in Palestine. At that Congress, the most fundamental racial principles of Jewish colonization were established: land purchased by the JNF could not be resold, and could be leased only to Jewish settlers. Land was made into national capital. This method of national Jewish permanent ownership, Shafir explains, accomplished three complementary tasks:

> It not only did exclude non-Jews from control of land once acquired by the JNF, but at one fell swoop abolished private ownership of land and replaced it by hereditary land leasing. Land purchased by the JNF could not be resold, as it was held in trusteeship for the whole nation. Nor it could be sublet in order to ensure that the usufruct would belong to the actual cultivator.[41]

Yet, it would be only after 1907 that the JNF's involvement in the purchasing of land for Jewish settlement would begin to have significant impacts. Until then, and since the First Zionist Congress of 1897, the WZO and the Jewish immigrants in Palestine were preoccupied with creating stable conditions of employment, without which no further immigration could be called for.

Another important strategy of colonization was that of the 'conquest of labour' or the Jewish-only labour strategy adopted in 1905, coined in Hebrew as *Avoda Ivrit* (Hebrew labour). Basically, this strategy was meant to take work from the hands of Arab workers; this logic began being applied in agriculture and rapidly spread to encompass urban workplaces.[42] At first, its success was quite limited, but in one sphere the doctrine had rapid success. On 29 September 1907, the paramilitary Bar-Giora group was established with the aim of replacing Arab guards in the agricultural colonies of the first *Aliya*. The group evolved in 1909 into the *Hashomer* (The Guard), in 1920 eventually becoming the nucleus of the *Haganah* (The Defence), itself the forerunner of the contemporary IDF, the Israeli Defence Forces.[43] As Shafir explains, 'Bar-Giora was not born solely as a guard organization, but rather as a self-selected elite group in which "Hebrew Labour", settlement, and guarding all occupied pride of place'.[44] By 1910, *Hashomer* had secured a number of contracts with small and large plantations in the *Yishuv*.[45] Soon *Hashomer* extended their activities to the 'conquest of land', the purchasing of land and expulsion of Arab peasants.

Avoda Ivrit was not met with approval on the side of the native Jewish community. As Ella Shohat explains, '*Avoda Ivrit* had tragic consequences engendering political tensions not only between Arabs and Jews, but also between Sephardim and Ashkenazim as well as between Sephardim and Palestinians'.[46] As Behar noted from a reading of the Sephardi newspaper *Haherut*, its writers 'warned against the exclusion of Palestinian *fellahin* (Arab tillers, peasants) from newly established Zionist farms, arguing that this ran the risk of harming the long-term interests of Jewish revival in Palestine'.[47] Dockser Marcus also reported on the issue that the Sephardi public activist Antébi 'disliked the way the Zionists loudly proclaimed that they would hire only

Jews to work on their settlements, angering Muslim peasants who had toiled on the land for years'.[48] The doctrine aroused even more anger among the Oriental Jews as a result of the Yemeni experiment (the infamous 'Yavnieli mission')—to recruit 'Jews in the form of Arabs'[49]—another failed strategy to homogenize the labour force. As Shafir states, the reconfiguration of the labour market 'left its imprint on all social relations in the *Yishuv*, and excited the passions more than any other single question',[50] but in practical terms, as said above, it took long to consolidate the racial preferences of the Jews in Palestine. To achieve correspondence between the conquest of land and the conquest of labour, Jewish settlers found themselves experimenting with what would become the *kibbutz*.

This was an organizational metamorphosis that conjoined land, labour and housing in the creation of the cooperative settlement. The story of the emergence of the *kibbutz* has its roots in colonization methods borrowed from central Europe that were adapted for and articulated with the Zionism movement by the German sociologist Franz Oppenheimer. His model was based on public ownership of land and cooperative settlement. By 1903, at the Sixth Zionist Congress, Oppenheimer's ideas were already discussed:[51] the model was meant to reverse the antisettler colonial tendency created by the first *Aliyah* plantation style of colony, according to which a few Jewish families attracted hundreds of Arab peasants to whom work was offered. To make Jewish colonization work, Oppenheimer's model aspired to address several issues at once: demography, agricultural labour and settlement. Basically, this meant strategies 'to transform the agricultural workers into settlers'.[52] The new model of colonization would renew Zionist expansion by simultaneously securing land, labour and housing in the form of the co-operative settlement. From 1907, the JNF would effectively procure land, placing it in Jewish national ownership, on which cooperative settlements would be established. At the heart of this settler colonial type, demography and agricultural work were interwoven to assure control of the land and provide permanent work for the settler: an enclosed piece of Judaised land to be collectively worked by a highly motivated group of Jewish settlers. Without conquering land, labour could not be conquered and vice versa. By settling the workers and providing them with permanent work, their predicament was resolved, independently of the labour market.[53] Importantly, at the level of the whole, the logical tendency of this process of expanding frontiers would be to accumulate and cluster together land-labour 'redeemed' spaces as part of the growing skeleton of the Jewish society. After World War I, the 'pure ethnic colony' in the form of the cooperative settlement had replaced the 'plantation type colony' as the method of colonization of Palestine. By circumventing it via the creation of separated, isolationist, racialized, new existential territories of the Zionist pioneers, Arab competition—within these realms of life—was finally eliminated. Protected from the labour market and built on the exclusion of Arabs and populated almost entirely by Eastern European Jews, the *kibbutz* became the most homogenous body of the future Israeli society. The importance of the *kibbutzim* (plural) as a nucleus and model for the future Jewish state lay not only in its ultra-segregative nature but also in the fact that agriculture was its initial means of reproduction, thus adding farming production to the plantation type colony of the first *Aliyah* owners. As Wolfe has stated, 'Agriculture not only supports other sectors. It is inherently sedentary and, therefore, permanent. . . . [It] is geared to vouchsafing its own reproduction, generating capital that projects into a future where it repeats itself'.[54] The late 1880s are the starting point of Zionist agriculture in Palestine (First *Aliyah*), and figures show that during the Mandate period (1922–1948) this sector grew at an average rate of 12.6 per cent annually, providing employment during the 1930s for about a quarter of the Jewish labour force.[55] 'In settler colonial terms', Wolfe explains, 'this means that an agricultural population can be expanded by continuing immigration at the expense of Native lands and livelihood',[56] and Jewish immigrants into Palestine, though not huge in numbers, were not lacking.

The separatist ideas and racial logic explored in land and labour had spread to encompass all occupations: under the banner of *Avoda Ivrit*, Jewish-owned industries and businesses were called on to employ only Jews, thus increasingly fracturing the economy in Palestine into two separate entities. The policy was supported and campaigned for by the *Histadrut* (the General Organisation of Hebrew Workers in the Land of Israel), a key multifaceted institution established in 1920 which became vital in the formation of core social and economic functions in the Jewish prestate society.[57] Its own organizational capacities, heavy subsidies by the World Zionist movement and the facilitation of its activities provided by the colonial British administration—these factors enabled the *Histadrut* to embark on and succeed in the creation of a Jewish economic sector and eventually to become the largest Jewish employer at the time it provided a range of social and cultural services. The *Histadrut*-controlled urban employment for Jews was complemented by Jewish-only work (and membership) in the agricultural settlements, the *kibbutzim* and *moshavim* (cooperative smallholders farms), each having their own role in the continuing colonization of Palestine.[58]

Another exclusivist racial campaign was launched on 20 January 1924 in Tel Aviv by the *Tozeret Haaretz* First National Convention. Literally, *Tozeret Haaretz* means 'made in the country', and today is translated as 'made in Israel'. In the political atmosphere of early-twentieth-century Palestine, *Tozeret Haaretz* meant 'Jews should buy only Hebrew-labour made products, sold by Jewish businesses even at a higher price for an inferior product. The boycott on Arab labour expanded now to Arab produce, so as a matter of fact 'Jewish production was designed primarily for Jewish consumption and export and not for the majority of the Palestinian population'.[59] From early 1930s, the *Histadrut* had a central role in promoting the *Tozeret Haaretz* campaign, and soon companies, small as well as large, had the *Tozeret Haaretz* motto stamped in their advertising; the campaign was introduced in schools, and Jewish unions were called to hold informational meetings to promote it. Everyday consumption was now an active realm of Zionist action.

The separatist sentiment was present in an interrelated number of practices. The racialization of labour and everyday consumption, the Jewish-only social institutions that the *Yishuv* created, Hebraist education, the composition of a highly distinctive settler culture, the establishment of Jewish paramilitary forces and the consolidation of Jewish autonomous and vibrant political institutions—these became the social territories on which a new social aggregation was being cultivated. Eventually, three societies emerged in Palestine. Two societies, torn apart along an emerging national axis (Arabs and Jews) under the Mandatory umbrella, and two communities torn apart along an emerging ethnic axis (Ashkenazim and Oriental Jews) relocating their standings in the *Yishuv*.

The imprint of British rule on the native–settler struggle and the economic and social bifurcation of Palestine cannot be underestimated. The Mandate administration's tragic intervention that began with the Balfour Declaration became felt in minor and major ways—in the mundane details of everyday life and in institutional political dimensions. Fatally, the British Mandate operated as an echo chamber for the segregationist operations that the Zionist leadership had been advancing before the war. As Tamari and Nassar explain,

> In British discourse, the backwardness of the indigenous population was always assessed by comparison with the images of modernity and progress associated with the new Jewish pioneers, and the argument in favor of development, the ultimate moral justification for domination, made the Zionist enterprise coincide with the British one, as if the 'sacred mission of civilization' were in this case taken charge of by both the British and the Zionists.[60]

A major gift to the Zionist movement given by the British was the conceptual structuration of Palestine as inhabited by two communities with equally legitimate needs and demands. The discourse of 'parity' was initially introduced by means of an alleged 'dual obligation' to both communities as promised in the 1917 Balfour Declaration, and then replicated in the Mandate Charter sanctioned by the League of Nations (1922). The overwhelming

Arab majority in Palestine was no obstacle for the British to redact these documents in such a way. In these documents, there were no Arabs and Jews, neither colonists nor natives. Rather, the still small Zionist *Yishuv* featured as 'the Jewish people aspiring to establish a National Home', while the Arabs were minimized under the label of the 'non-Jewish communities' in Palestine, as if they were some minority group. Thus, the political discourse introduced by the British not only disregarded the facts on the ground, but it did so as part of an exercise in imperial political benevolence.[61] On the ground, 'the Civil Administration clearly placed its commitment to promote the Jewish National Home above its obligation to protect the rights of the non-Jewish population'.[62] In practice, a range of specific policies and laws that promoted the Jewish National Home programme were materialized. These included the arbitrary implementation of the criterion of economic absorptive capacity that facilitated Jewish immigration (by means of which the Arab side had no say in the immigration quotas given to Jews but rather, these are determined by the economic capacity of the *Yishuv*); protective tariffs favouring new Jewish industries; granting monopolistic concessions to profit from Palestine's resources that also amplified Jewish employment; budgetary proportional spending that increased the economic autonomy of the *Yishuv*; allowing discriminatory employment policies and enabling the establishment of exclusivist social frameworks such as the *Histadrut*, Hebrew education and health services; and also the lack of positive protection for Arab peasants who were exposed to eviction from the land by Zionist purchases.[63] As in other settler geographies, the British pursued 'discriminatory policies, suppressing natives, and promoting the interests of the European settlers', in so doing, 'the colonial administrators obviously reinforced the developmental cleavage and the exceedingly unequal income distribution between the two population segments [Arabs and Jews]'.[64] To facilitate the overall privileging of the Jewish-Zionist community in Palestine, 'a corollary of British policy had been', as Walid Khalidi claims, 'the suspension of democracy and representative government'. As Khalidi explains, this measure was 'integral to the very formation and growth of the Jewish national home in Palestine' simply because it permitted the dismissal of the majority of the population's preferences.[65] Some of these pro-Zionist policies were scrutinized and criticized by British commissions of enquiry (such as the 1929 'Shaw Commission' and the 1930 'Hope Simpson Commission') but all in all, the colonial administration provided the necessary governmental framework for the *Yishuv* to advance its settlerist aims and for world Zionism to coordinate its importation into Palestine of international finance and East European immigrants, an arrangement that enabled them to marshal capital, culture and labour with unparalleled effectiveness.[66]

PARTITION, ETHNOCIDE AND SETTLER COLONIALISM

The 1937 Peel proposal for partition was not an omen, a notice of what is about to happen. Rather, it was an event telling that 'something significant had already happened; some turning points had already occurred in the material constitution of the political'.[67] From this viewpoint, one way to characterize the qualitative difference in the systems of life between Ottoman Palestine and Mandatory Palestine is to look at the buildup of the segmentation of social life along the axis of race. The change was deeply transformative. Yet, this social transformation is of a very special sort. In the production of the Zionist society in Palestine, practices that were marked as referents, that had social attraction—such as the racialization of land, labour and consumption, the exaltation of the Hebrew language as a negation of Arabic, separate housing and education—functioned as focal points around which life was organized and given sense. New zones of thought, hope and expectations followed. These focal points of power shared common denominators—specific settlerist logics—that make them resonate, thus producing an increasing centralized and homogeneous space.[68] This is a description of the internal Jewish-Zionist landscape. From a wider perspective, these new Zionist arrangements brought about a dualist organization of social existence, where everything is either Jew or Arab, settler or native. A new social universe emerged. The flexible divisions that characterized Palestine before Zionism have now been eradicated.

This new geopolitical geometry of social life in Palestine reveals yet a third point of view, given by 'the power of the scalpel',[69] eviscerating native geographic and social continuity. That is, native discontinuity is the first name of the emerging settler societal silhouette. This explains how settler colonial projects are premised on the incremental attrition of native life. In the sequence of accumulation-aggregation of acquired settler spaces—the process of formation of the settler colony—native life as a collective form of life is interrupted. In Palestine, shared life was interrupted never to be resumed. The settler's scalpel cuts by partitioning native life: it first secures a small territoriality—land or a sphere of social life, in the process displacing the forms of native life that animated it previously; it then fences it and incorporates exclusion as its functioning axiom; aggregation is the last stage in this initial process, and yet, obsessive securitization of the robbed space haunts the settler for eternity. At the level of the whole, the logical tendency of this process of expanding frontiers would be to accumulate and cluster together land-labour-housing 'redeemed' spaces as part of the growing skeleton of the Jewish society.

Remarkably, in the Zionist settler colonial project, the notion of 'frontier' materialized not just via the expansion of physical boundaries of the territorial Jewish enclaves moving in an accelerated rhythm from 1907 onwards—a result of the synthesis of the Jewish National Fund's land purchases and its racial codex, Jewish immigration and the cooperative settlement movement. Rather, as explained, in Zionist settler colonial expansion, land was but one realm of action. Zionist conquest during the first decades of the project was based on the race-motivated invention of frontiers, and frontiers were created literally everywhere. In racializing workers, their tools and skills, Jewish settlers created frontiers in the labour market, making the conquest of labour a horizon of expansion. As we explained, domestic consumption was another such new frontier, where from whom one purchases bread, cigarettes, flour, meat and other products had national significance. By following the axiom that Jews buy only from Jews who have produced their goods on the basis of Hebrew labour only, one was contributing to a double movement: to strengthen the Jewish economy meant to weaken the Arab one. One existential territory arises on the dwindling of another; a life for another. An either-or alternative was created; rejecting the Eastern brethren; splitting the economic sphere into production and consumption—in all these actions and more, *Zionists were devising sociocultural frontiers that never existed before in Palestine*. In the manufacturing of segregated enclaves, Zionism invented frontiers, hence it could expand, it could conquer. In the case of Palestine, territorial conquest was dependent on settler colonial *social* expansion. It is worth remembering that by 1947 the *Yishuv* held only about 7 per cent of the total land area of Palestine (national and private holdings), while by early 1949, with the signing of the Armistice Agreements with Egypt, Lebanon, Jordan and Syria, Israel found itself dominating 77 per cent of Palestine. This dramatic change ensued in the course of the 1947–1949 war. The competence, strength and hunger to conquer territories beyond the lines of the 1947 UN Partition resolution—these attributes were the product of a long process of frontier expansion in the social realm. That is, the number 7 per cent might be misleading. Within that 7 per cent a full functioning society was developed, equipped as a state. Its territorial expansion was predicated on its institutional aptitudes, its internal cohesiveness, its ability to recruit, its international network of support provided by the Jewish diaspora and the Western powers, not less than on the determination of this society and its sense of entitlement.

In setting apart new existential zones that were to incubate the new forms of life, the integrity of native life has been fragmented, partitioned. Thus, it seems essential to claim that in the context of settler colonial processes, partition is the form the process takes while it encroaches on native spaces, a form that eventually—forced by the repetition of this dynamic—becomes indistinguishable from content. It can be claimed that until 1948, the whole project of Arab-Palestinian resistance was one against the dissection of the native polity. 'Rather than replacing one owner with another', Wolfe claimed, 'settlers seek to replace an entire system of ownership with another. The settler/Native confrontation, in other words, is not between claims to ownership but between frameworks for allocating ownerships'.[70] It is not just natives who are replaced in settler colonial formations, but fundamentally, their systems of life are replaced.

Settler colonial constructions produce what Robert Jaulin defined as ethnocide. What characterizes a process of ethnocide is that the ways social reproduction takes place in a society begins to escape the members of the group.[71] Laden with the new Zionist rationalities and practices, everyday life practices of common housing, joint business initiatives and informal social gathering of sorts shared by Arabs and Oriental Jews in Palestine became transvalued using national standards nonexistent before. The role and significance of interfaith relations being coextensive with a number of spheres in the social field declined. This impact on Arab-Jewish shared life was only an aspect, though a central one, of a more comprehensive process through which Arab native life was threatened, its legitimacy challenged, and its material sources of income emaciated. All in all, in ethnocide, the universe of the colonized is reduced:

> The condition of the colonized can lead to a reduction in the humanization of the universe, so that any solution that is sought will be a solution on the scale of the individual and the restricted family, with, by way of consequence, an extreme anarchy or disorder at the level of the collective: an anarchy whose victim will always be the individual–with the exception of those who occupy the key positions in such a system, namely the colonizers, who, during this same period when the colonized reduce the universe, will tend to extend it.[72]

Wolfe captured this inverse relation of growth between colonizers and colonized in the following way: 'Settler colonialism has both negative and positive dimensions. Negatively, it strives for the dissolution of Native societies. Positively, the ongoing requirement to eliminate the Native alternative continues to shape the colonial society that settlers construct on their expropriated land base';[73] the second dimension is unthinkable without the first. Both dimensions constitute one reality; that is, the practices of elimination of the native and the products of settler formation are reciprocally constitutive, and in fact, from an ontological point of view, they cannot and should not be differentiated. These are not two sides of a machine, nor two dimensions, but inseparable operations forming one reality. For instance, the rejection of the exile paradigm in European Zionism favoured instead the constitution of a new Jewish subjectivity, a new Jew, incarnated in a muscular settler

Jew to be shaped by physical training and hard labour. But that rejection remains an unchallenged myth without supplementing it with a reading that takes into account the realities of the 'conquest of land' and the 'conquest of labour'. These doctrines created the theoretical tools for a future colonial sovereignty that would develop as necessarily separated from native life, and hence, they preempted immersion in the native society against the wishes of the Oriental Jewish community; but in the long run, and because of British support, among Arab workers the doctrines effected unemployment and economic hardship. Jewish productivity in Palestine—articulated by means of favouring race over class solidarity ultimately adopted by the workers of the second *Aliyah*—could not have been accomplished without the contraction of the labour market that affected the life opportunities of Arab workers. In the same vein, if land supplied the vehicle with which to grow the Jewish pioneer's muscle, the expulsion of the *fellahin* from that land provided the biopolitics of that process. Historically, the continuous efforts to eliminate Palestinian life and to suppress the Arab-Jewish horizon on the one hand and settler formation and social reproduction on the other hand are immanently entangled and form one body. That is, there is no Israeli society without Palestinian impossibilities.

AFTER PARTITION, OR AFTER ZIONISM

Acknowledging the role of the Zionist settler-colonial machines in the dissection of Palestine bears not only on our understanding of the past, but also on the present and future. Irrespective of the preferred political model—two-states, one-state, a binational state and so forth—the devastating part that the partition impetus played, and plays, in the shaping of social life between the Mediterranean Sea and the Jordan River needs to be reversed. No form of reconciliation can take place on the background of political cultures driven by segregation. Overturning the legacy of partition seems to us the only way forward.

NOTES

1. Amos Oz, "Amos Oz Has a Recipe for Saving Israel," *Haaretz*, 13 March 2015.
2. "Declaration of Palestinian Independence," 18 November 1988, http://www.declarationproject.org/?p=397.
3. For an interesting discussion on the last theme, see Yair Wallach, 'The Genealogy and Logic of Palestine's Partition', *Qadaya Israiliyya* 67 (2017): 9–18.
4. For such a discussion see, for instance, Avi Shlaim, *The Politics of Partition: King Abdullah, the Zionists, and Palestine 1921–1951* (New York: Columbia University

Press, 1990); Benny Morris, *Righteous Victims: A History of the Zionist-Arab Conflict, 1881–2001* (New York: Vintage Books, 2001), 135–258.

5. See, for instance, Brendan O'Leary, 'Debating Partition: Justifications and Critiques', *Working Papers in the British-Irish Studies* 78 (2006).

6. See, for instance, Aaron Klieman, 'The Resolution of Conflicts through Territorial Partition: The Palestine Experience', *Comparative Studies in Society and History* 22, no. 2 (1980): 281–300.

7. Laura Robson, *States of Separation: Transfer, Partition, and the Making of the Modern Middle East* (Berkeley: University of California Press, 2017).

8. Walid Khalidi, 'Revisiting the UNGA Partition Resolution', *Journal of Palestine Studies* 27, no.1 (1997): 5–21.

9. Gilles Deleuze and Félix Guattari, *Anti-Oedipus: Capitalism and Schizophrenia* (Minneapolis: University of Minnesota Press, 1983); Gilles Deleuze and Félix Guattari, *A Thousand Plateaus: Capitalism and Schizophrenia* (Minneapolis: University of Minnesota Press, 1987); Michel Foucault, *The History of Sexuality. Volume 1: The Will to Knowledge* (New York: Pantheon, 1978).

10. Yuval Ben-Bassat and Eyal Ginio, eds., *Later Ottoman Palestine—The Period of Young Turk Rule* (London and New York: I. B. Tauris, 2011); Gad Gilbar, ed., *Ottoman Palestine 1800–1914: Studies in Economic and Social History* (Leiden: Brill, 1990); Albert Hourani, *A History of the Arab Peoples* (London: Faber and Faber, 1991), 209–64; David Kushner, ed., *Palestine in the Late Ottoman Period* (Jerusalem: Yad Izhak Ben-Zvi, 1986); Donald Quataert, *The Ottoman Empire, 1700–1922* (Cambridge: Cambridge University Press, 2000).

11. By 'Oriental Jews' we mean the Sephardic (Iberian descent), Maghrebi (North African descent) and Mizrahi (Eastern descent—Iraq, Iran, Yemen and Afghanistan mainly) communities. However, today the most used designation is 'Mizrahi' for all these Jewish groups. A small community of Ashkenazi Jews, mainly religious orthodox, was also part of the Jewish minority in Palestine prior to Zionist immigration.

12. Menachem Klein, *Lives in Common—Arabs and Jews in Jerusalem, Jaffa and Hebron* (London: Hurst & Company, 2014), 37.

13. Michelle Campos, *Ottoman Brothers* (Stanford: Stanford University Press, 2011), 18.

14. Ibid., 11.

15. Klein, *Lives in Common*, 45.

16. Ibid., 19–21.

17. Salim Tamari, *Mountain against the Sea: Essays on Palestinian Society and Culture* (Berkeley: University of California Press, 2008), 153.

18. Salim Tamari and Issam Nassar, eds., *The Storyteller of Jerusalem—The Life and Times of Wasif Jawhariyyeh, 1904–1948* (Northampton, MA: Olive Branch Press, 2013), 46–47.

19. Ibid., xviii.

20. Marcelo Svirsky and Ronnen Ben-Arie, *From Shared Life to Co-Resistance in Historic Palestine* (London: Rowman & Littlefield International, 2017), 67–70.

21. Salim Tamari, *Mountain against the Sea*, 164. See also Hillel Cohen, *Year Zero of the Arab-Israeli Conflict: 1929* (Waltham, MA: Brandeis University Press,

2015), 8; Abigail Jacobson and Moshe Naor, *Oriental Neighbors—Middle Eastern Jews and Arabs in Mandatory Palestine* (Waltham, MA: Brandeis University Press, 2016); Klein, *Lives in Common*, 21; Mahmoud Yazbak, *Haifa in the Late Ottoman Period 1864–1914: A Muslim Town in Transition* (Leiden: Brill, 1998), 219.

22. Patrick Wolfe, *Traces of History: Elementary Structures of Race* (London: Verso, 2016).

23. Hillel Cohen, "The Life and Death of the Arab-Jew in Palestine and Beyond," *Yiunim beTkumat Israel* 9 (2015): 185.

24. Moshe Behar and Zvi Ben-Dor Benite, eds., *Modern Middle Eastern Jewish Thought—Writings on Identity, Politics, and Culture, 1893–1958* (Waltham, MA: Brandeis University Press, 2013), 105.

25. Raef Zreik, 'When Does a Settler Become a Native? (With Apologies to Mamdani)', *Constellations* 23, no. 3 (2016): 357.

26. Patrick Wolfe, *Settler Colonialism and the Transformation of Anthropology* (London: Cassell, 1999); Patrick Wolfe, 'Settler Colonialism and the Elimination of the Native', *Journal of Genocide Research* 8, no. 4 (2006): 387–409.

27. Barbara Smith, *The Roots of Separatism in Palestine: British Economic Policy, 1920–1929* (Syracuse, NY: Syracuse University Press, 1993), 3.

28. Svirsky and Ben-Arie, *From Shared Life to Co-Resistance.*

29. Neville J. Mandel, *The Arabs and Zionism before World War I* (Berkeley: University of California Press, 1976), 36–37.

30. Yuval Ben-Bassat, "Rural Reactions to Zionist Activity in Palestine Before and After the Young Turk Revolution of 1908 as Reflected in Petitions to Istanbul', *Middle Eastern Studies* 49, no. 3 (2013): 349–63; Yuval Ben-Bassat, *Petitioning the Sultan—Protests and Justice in Late Ottoman Palestine 1865–1908* (London: I. B. Tauris, 2013).

31. Rashid Khalidi, *Palestinian Identity—The Construction of Modern National Consciousness* (New York: Columbia University Press, 1997), 63–144; Mandel, *The Arabs and Zionism*, 71–116.

32. Abigail Jacobson, *From Empire to Empire: Jerusalem between Ottoman and British Rule* (Syracuse, NY: Syracuse University, 2011), 165–82.

33. Svirsky and Ben-Arie, *From Shared Life*, 70–88.

34. Hillel Cohen, *Year Zero*, 192–97; Hillel Cohen, 'The Life and Death'.

35. Cohen, 'The Life and Death', 256.

36. Cohen, *Year Zero*, 194–96.

37. Tim Sontheimer, 'Bringing the British Back in: Sephardim, Ashkenazi Anti-Zionist Orthodox and the Policy of Jewish Unity', *Middle Eastern Studies* 52, no. 2 (2016): 165–81.

38. Ibid., 167.

39. Ilan Pappé, *A History of Modern Palestine* (Cambridge: Cambridge University Press, 2004), 93–94.

40. Gershon Shafir, *Land, Labor and the Origins of the Israeli–Palestinian Conflict 1882–1914* (Berkeley: University of California Press, 1989), 41–44.

41. Ibid., 155.

42. Svirsky and Ben-Arie, *From Shared Life*, 97–108.

43. Walid Khalidi, *All That Remains: The Palestinian Villages Occupied and Depopulated by Israel in 1948* (Washington, DC: Institute of Palestinian Studies, 1992), 105–07; Shafir, *Land, Labor*, 135–45.
44. Shafir, *Land, Labor*, 138.
45. The term is used to describe the nascent Zionist Jewish collective entity in Palestine. In Hebrew, literally 'settlement'; it means 'the community' or 'the inhabited place'.
46. Ella Shohat, 'Sephardim in Israel: Zionism from the Standpoint of Its Jewish Victims', *Social Text* 19/20 (1988): 13.
47. Moshe Behar, 'The Foundational Antinativism of Mizrahi Literature', *Journal of Levantine Studies* 5 (2015): 123.
48. Amy Dockser Marcus, *Jerusalem 1913: The Origins of the Arab-Israeli Conflict* (London: Penguin Books, 2007), 53.
49. Shohat, 'Sephardim in Israel'; Svirsky and Ben-Arie, *From Shared Life*, 74–76.
50. Shafir, *Land, Labor*, 215.
51. Ibid., 148–51.
52. Ibid., *Land, Labor*, 155.
53. Ibid., *Land, Labor*, 160–63.
54. Wolfe, *Traces of History*, 79.
55. Jacob Metzer, *The Divided Economy of Mandatory Palestine* (Cambridge: Cambridge University Press, 2002), 142–54.
56. Wolfe, *Traces of History*, 179.
57. Tamar Gozansky, *Between Expropriation and Exploitation: Status and Struggles of Arab Workers in Palestine and Israel* (Tel Aviv: Pardes Publishing House, 2015); Zachary Lockman, *Comrades and Enemies—Arab and Jewish Workers in Palestine 1906–1948* (Berkeley: University of California Press, 1996); Shafir, *Land, Labor*.
58. Svirsky and Ben-Arie, *From Shared Life*, 103–05.
59. Smith, *Roots of Separatism*, 179.
60. Tamari and Nassar, *Storyteller of Jerusalem*, xxvii.
61. See Ilan Pappé, 'Revisiting 1967: The False Paradigm of Peace, Partition, and Parity', *Settler Colonial Studies* 3, nos. 3–4 (2013): 341–51.
62. Smith, *Roots of Separatism*, 159.
63. Smith, *Roots of Separatism*.
64. Metzer, *Divided Economy*, 201.
65. Walid Khalidi, 'The Hebrew Reconquista of Palestine: From the 1947 United Nations Partition Resolution to the First Zionist Congress of 1897', *Journal of Palestine Studies* 39, no.1 (2009): 32.
66. Wolfe, *Traces of History*, 223.
67. Iain MacKenzie, 'What Is a Political Event?' *Theory and Event* 11, no. 3 (2008): 17.
68. Deleuze and Guattari, *A Thousand Plateaus*, 224–26.
69. Ibid., 212.
70. Wolfe, *Traces of History*, 34.

71. Robert Jaulin, *La paix blanche: introduction à l'ethnocide* (Paris: Editions du Seuil, 1970); see also Deleuze and Guattari, *Anti-Oedipus*, 189.
72. Jaulin, *La paix blanche*, 309.
73. Wolfe, *Traces of History*, 33.

REFERENCES

Behar, Moshe. 2015. 'The Foundational Antinativism of Mizrahi Literature'. *Journal of Levantine Studies* 5: 107–36.
Behar, Moshe, and Zvi Ben-Dor Benite, eds. 2013. *Modern Middle Eastern Jewish Thought—Writings on Identity, Politics, and Culture, 1893–1958*. Waltham, MA: Brandeis University Press.
Ben-Bassat, Yuval. 2013a. *Petitioning the Sultan—Protests and Justice in Late Ottoman Palestine 1865–1908.* London: I. B. Tauris.
———. 2013b. 'Rural Reactions to Zionist Activity in Palestine Before and After the Young Turk Revolution of 1908 as Reflected in Petitions to Istanbul'. *Middle Eastern Studies* 49 (3): 349–63.
Ben-Bassat, Yuval, and Eyal Ginio, eds. 2011. *Later Ottoman Palestine—The Period of Young Turk Rule*. London and New York: I. B. Tauris.
Campos, Michelle. 2011. *Ottoman Brothers*. Stanford, CA: Stanford University Press.
Cohen, Hillel. 2015. *Year Zero of the Arab-Israeli Conflict: 1929*. Waltham, MA: Brandeis University Press.
Cohen, Hillel. 2015. 'The Life and Death of the Arab-Jew in Palestine and Beyond'. *Yiunim beTkumat Israel* 9: 171–200 (Hebrew).
Declaration of Palestinian Independence. 1988. 18 November. http://www.declarationproject.org/?p=397 (accessed 18 February 2018).
Deleuze, Gilles, and Félix Guattari. 1983. *Anti-Oedipus: Capitalism and Schizophrenia*. Translated by R. Hurley, M. Seem and H. R. Lane. Minneapolis: University of Minnesota Press.
———. 1987. *A Thousand Plateaus: Capitalism and Schizophrenia*. Translated by Brian Massumi. Minneapolis: University of Minnesota Press.
Dockser Marcus, Amy. 2007. *Jerusalem 1913: The Origins of the Arab–Israeli Conflict*. London: Penguin Books.
Foucault, Michel. 1978. *The History of Sexuality. Volume 1: The Will to Knowledge*. New York: Pantheon.
Gilbar, Gad, ed. 1990. *Ottoman Palestine 1800–1914: Studies in Economic and Social History*. Leiden: Brill.
Gozansky, Tamar. 2015. *Bein nishul lenitzul: Skhirim Aravim—matzavam uma'avakeihem (Between Expropriation and Exploitation: Status and Struggles of Arab Workers in Palestine and Israel)*. Tel Aviv: Pardes Publishing House (Hebrew).
Hourani, Albert. 1991. *A History of the Arab Peoples*. London: Faber and Faber.
Jacobson, Abigail. 2011. *From Empire to Empire: Jerusalem between Ottoman and British Rule*. New York: Syracuse University.

Jacobson, Abigail, and Moshe Naor. 2016. *Oriental Neighbors—Middle Eastern Jews and Arabs in Mandatory Palestine*. Waltham, MA: Brandeis University Press.
Jaulin, Robert. 1970. *La paix blanche: introduction à l'ethnocide*. Paris: Editions du Seuil.
Khalidi, Rashid. 1997. *Palestinian Identity—The Construction of Modern National Consciousness*. New York: Columbia University Press.
Khalidi, Walid. 1992. *All That Remains: The Palestinian Villages Occupied and Depopulated by Israel in 1948*. Washington, DC: Institute of Palestinian Studies.
———. 1997. 'Revisiting the UNGA Partition Resolution'. *Journal of Palestine Studies* 27 (1): 5–21.
———. 2009. 'The Hebrew Reconquista of Palestine: From the 1947 United Nations Partition Resolution to the First Zionist Congress of 1897'. *Journal of Palestine Studies* 39 (1): 24–42.
Klein, Menachem. 2014. *Lives in Common—Arabs and Jews in Jerusalem, Jaffa and Hebron*. London: Hurst & Company.
Klieman, Aaron. 1980. 'The Resolution of Conflicts Through Territorial Partition: The Palestine Experience'. *Comparative Studies in Society and History* 22 (2): 281–300.
Kushner, David, ed. 1986. *Palestine in the Late Ottoman Period*. Jerusalem: Yad Izhak Ben-Zvi.
MacKenzie, Iain. 2007. 'What Is a Political Event?' *Theory and Event* 11 (3): 1–28.
Mandel, Neville J. 1976. *The Arabs and Zionism before World War I*. Berkeley: University of California Press.
Metzer, Jacob. 2002. *The Divided Economy of Mandatory Palestine*. Cambridge: Cambridge University Press.
Morris, Benny. 2001. *Righteous Victims: A History of the Zionist–Arab Conflict, 1881–2001*. New York: Vintage Books.
O'Leary, Brendan. 2006. 'Debating Partition: Justifications and Critiques'. *Working Papers in the British-Irish Studies* 78.
Oz, Amos. 2015. 'Amos Oz Has a Recipe for Saving Israel'. *Haaretz*. 13 March. https://www.haaretz.com/.premium-amos-oz-has-a-recipe-for-saving-israel-1.5335960.
Palestine Royal Commission Report. 1937. Cmd 5479. House of Commons Parliamentary Papers Online.
Pappé, Ilan. 2004. *A History of Modern Palestine*. Cambridge: Cambridge University Press.
———. 2013. 'Revisiting 1967: The False Paradigm of Peace, Partition, and Parity'. *Settler Colonial Studies* 3 (3–4): 341–51.
Quataert, Donald. 2000. *The Ottoman Empire, 1700–1922*. Cambridge: Cambridge University Press.
Robson, Laura. 2017. *States of Separation: Transfer, Partition, and the Making of the Modern Middle East*. Berkeley: University of California Press.
Shafir, Gershon. 1989. *Land, Labor and the Origins of the Israeli-Palestinian Conflict 1882–1914*. Berkeley: University of California Press.
Shlaim, Avi. 1990. *The Politics of Partition: King Abdullah, the Zionists, and Palestine 1921–1951*. New York: Columbia University Press.

Shohat, Ella. 1988. 'Sephardim in Israel: Zionism from the Standpoint of Its Jewish Victims'. *Social Text* 19/20.

Smith, Barbara. 1993. *The Roots of Separatism in Palestine: British Economic Policy, 1920–1929*. Syracuse, NY: Syracuse University Press.

Sontheimer, Tim. 2016. 'Bringing the British Back in: Sephardim, Ashkenazi Anti-Zionist Orthodox and the Policy of Jewish Unity'. *Middle Eastern Studies* 52 (2): 165–81.

Svirsky, Marcelo, and Ronnen Ben-Arie. 2017. *From Shared Life to Co-Resistance in Historic Palestine*. London: Rowman & Littlefield International.

Tamari, Salim. 2008. *Mountain against the Sea: Essays on Palestinian Society and Culture*. Berkeley: University of California Press.

Tamari, Salim, and Issam Nassar, eds. 2013. *The Storyteller of Jerusalem—The Life and Times of Wasif Jawhariyyeh, 1904–1948*. Translated by Nada Elzeer. Northampton, MA: Olive Branch Press.

Wallach, Yair. 2017. 'The Genealogy and Logic of Palestine's Partition'. *Qadaya Israiliyya* (Israeli Affairs) 67: 9–18 (Arabic).

Wolfe, Patrick. 1999. *Settler Colonialism and the Transformation of Anthropology*. London: Cassell.

———. 2006. 'Settler Colonialism and the Elimination of the Native'. *Journal of Genocide Research* 8 (4): 387–409.

———. 2016. *Traces of History: Elementary Structures of Race*. London: Verso.

Yazbak, Mahmoud. 1998. *Haifa in the Late Ottoman Period 1864–1914: A Muslim Town in Transition*. Leiden: Brill.

Zreik, Raef. 2016. 'When Does a Settler Become a Native? (With Apologies to Mamdani)'. *Constellations* 23 (3): 351–64.

Chapter 3

Sexuality after Partition

The Great Indian Private Sphere

Radhika Mohanram

August 1947 defined the national border between the new states of India and Pakistan, yet as I argue in detail below, its significance went far beyond geographical boundaries, as it redefined the boundaries between public and private, morality and sexuality, citizen and the other, and notions of the norm and the abnormal, especially of the body. From August 1947 through the months that followed, the movement of refugees between the newly formed nations numbered between twelve to fifteen million, and in by far the largest transaction of population in history, the death toll reached two million with the abduction of about 75,000 to 120,000 women, and 50,000 children lost or abandoned.[1] This moment saw the formation of three zones and two nations in South Asia—India and West and East Pakistan. August 1947, in short, conflated citizenship with violence so that bodily, spatial and violent signifiers and practices came together in the production of a language of nation, religion and political subjecthood in both countries. Indeed, extremely violent acts conducted during partition—murder, arson, rape, maiming and so forth—underpinned the other event of 1947, the 'nonviolent' protest that brought about Indian independence. Notwithstanding lengthy imperial rule, the origin of both countries was this separation event, a demarcation from a historical continuum of being one people and from a single landmass to one where both nations, now in postmodernity, perceive this 1947 origin myth as being the only truth, as if Hindus and Muslims had only a relationship of enmity from prehistoric times and as being natural and real to millennial generations in both nations.

Yet it is this event of partition and its influence on the Indian future that remains generally unexamined in much political analysis of nation formation in India. Focussing on the partition is generally considered to be unproductively fixated on the past; in contemporary India this topic is supposed to belong to a particular historic moment, relegated to descriptions of affect, emotions, subjective feelings, people's mourning of the losses and memories of the pre-partitioned Indian past. As such, it is defined as being outside of the fields of present-day politics which is focussed on neoliberal economics, globalization and the future, generally considered to be the proper sites of formal, political rationalities.[2] This separation of partition violence and postindependence nation building suggests that the latter term is unrelated to the violence of the former. In postmodern India, partition studies is not pursued with any degree of urgency and is often dismissed as being nostalgic or as looking to an imagined past of happy communities that never as such existed. Yet contemporary events in India, the attacks on Mumbai and the Indian parliament, the three wars with Pakistan and the waxing and waning of border tensions between the two countries all endow this backward glance, this history, this spatial metaphor with coherence of meaning.

In this chapter, I explore the tight imbrication of violence, spaces, citizenship, bodies and sexuality in South Asia that was instigated in 1947 and that continues to reverberate today. Partition violence and the violation of the body, in particular, suggests that the body is usefully theorized as a political institution, a political instrument through which social transformation is effected; the body is also closely tied to spatial demarcations in that the 1947 partition was the time of ethnic cleansing in South Asia. In the first section of this chapter, I examine the relationship of violence to space and how these two terms are central to the formation of the citizen-subject. I argue that the production of all three terms is mutually generative. The first section of the chapter focusses on how, in the pursuit of utopia, violence transforms places and constructs citizenship. The second section focusses on issues of gender and explores the significance of bodies and gendered violence in the construction of sexuality and their implications for citizenship. In this section I examine the postcolonial public sphere to analyse how partition sexual violence reverberates in contemporary India. In the final section I investigate the symptomatic return of sexual violence as a phenomenon that gestures at a seamless continuum between 1947 and 2012 in India, especially within the context of gender and the public sphere.

I

Space and Bodies

> *If I should die, think only this of me/That there is some corner of a foreign field/That is forever England.*[3]

It is a critical commonplace to posit the tight imbrication between bodies and space/place in that our identities are always already spatially located.[4] Bodies are specifically linked with nations. For instance, in Germany of the Third Reich concepts such as 'fatherland' and 'blood and soil' are linked to the imagining of the perfect German body.[5] Rupert Brooke's famous poem 'The Soldier', quoted above, conflates the two terms, suggesting that the nationality of the person who leaves behind the body transforms the piece of land in which it is buried. The connection between bodily identity and home country is also conveyed in nondiscursive forms as when exiled people traditionally carry soil or plants to a new country to indicate symbolic transplantation. Women's bodies signify as the initial home for unborn children. In Freud's work, the woman's body and particularly her sexuality is a dark continent;[6] in Plato, the woman is place itself: 'chora', 'unnameable, improbable, hybrid, anterior to naming, to the One, to the father, and consequently connoted'.[7]

The formation of the body is closely linked to the formation of the public subject. For Hegel, the slave's labour and the master's consumption together form paradigmatic spaces;[8] for Foucault, the prison, the clinic and the asylum were all spaces that formed the modern body.[9] In India, the political citizen-subject came into being in 1947 with an inbuilt sense of loss, of India having lost its Eastern and Western arms now renamed Pakistan even as it became a free country, as what Faisal Fathehali Devji refers to as 'a nation unachieved'.[10] The inception of the two nations was sustained and reinforced by ideology, religious differences and violence.

The command of space in 1947 demanded the reorganization of the senses as well as those of internalized maps, topographies and the various performances of national belonging. Indeed, in the sites of the Punjab and Bengal in 1947 identification between citizen and 'enemy' was predicated on the physical mark of circumcision, previously an insignificant difference to the community of Hindu, Sikh and Muslim that had lived together for millennia. Was there much (social and cultural) difference between a peasant who was Muslim and peasants who were Sikh or Hindu? Like the Ephraimites in the Old Testament and in Derrida, this trace upon the body that is circumcision identified religious affiliations, nationalist ideologies, and life and death.[11] While women could change their religious identities with a change of clothes because they were not bodily marked or could be bodily marked by rape, the mark of circumcision on the men implicated them of belonging or not belonging, Sikh, Hindu or Muslim.

1947 also reinterpellated the citizens of South Asia from being British subjects to becoming Indian and Pakistani citizens, showing the complex relationship between bodily marks, citizenship and community. In fact, repeated debates about whether citizenship should be granted along lines of *jus solis*, according to territorial definitions or *jus sanguinus*—by right of blood—were conducted by both the Indian National Congress and the Muslim League leaders around 1947.[12] Traditional forms of community based on residence and kinship competed with an emergent imagined community based on ideology and religion. Traditional forms of community prior to 1947 inhabited space not only according to the social order, including religious and ethnic categories, but also through relationships, everyday life, work and death. In contrast the new form of imagined community restructured, reordered and remade new political representations through violence in Punjab and Bengal. As Yasmin Khan points out, at the time of partition many people on both sides of the border performed selfless acts in sheltering large numbers of people from different religious communities, smuggling food and providing transportation and armed protection. Yet this valorization of community spirit was often outweighed by the ethnic cleansing which caused the deaths of tens of thousands and forced millions to become refugees.[13] For perpetrators, the historical narrative that violence transcended the individual helped facilitate its repression as unconnected to them. It could be considered detachable, transcending cultural and personal limits. These perpetrators, suffused with a sense of emergent nationalism, often identified members of the other religious communities for lynching mobs and participated in the meting out of violence as a form of national/religious justice to their former neighbours and friends whom they had known for decades.

This transformation of identity was also linked to a transformation of a sensory landscape in that the body became an ideological text and the eyes were given the added sensory duty of identifying the ethnic/religious other.[14] In the case of men the question was: Is he circumcised or is he not? Is he same or other? Identifying or detecting the female ethnic other did not work as simply, as the religious markers on her body were detachable, discardable, based upon clothing rather than physical appearance. Therefore, women were identified by their menfolk's facial appearance, clothing, corporal comportment, linguistic specificity and the residential areas occupied by the men that immediately indicated their religion. One could state that partition violence towards women was also a partial displacement of violence towards men who were ethnic others: in short, their bodies became a metaphor for the men in whose name they were being attacked and violated. If women were the property of their men, then the sexual violence inflicted on women by men of the other community was aimed at violating the men of the other community. To miscontextualize Marx, these women could not even represent themselves; in patriarchal South Asia, they were represented by the men.[15] Furthermore, in partition violence, identifying, organized around ethnic purity, allowed the perpetrator not so much to avoid polluting contact but *to reorganize interactions* with the women—they moved from being community members to victims to be violated. The ethnic texture of the body that previously was just one of many multicultural signifiers in a united India attained a particular intensity—a confessional signification of the self—through the text of the body.

The practice of identifying produced a new sign system in 1947 India: it suggested that bodies encountered in the Punjab especially were a synecdoche of a particular sociohistorical space. Identifying suggested that Hindu, Muslim and Sikh bodies naturally belonged to specific topographies and this apparently organic, naturalized relationship between the two produced and reproduced a particular form of nationalist ideology and became a new moral order and a new semantic system of community. This new order, which intertwined spatial and somatic ideology, shifted the focus away from the immediacy of lived experience. Thus, the partition was not just a drawing on the map but also a violent transcription of ethno-historical codes onto material surfaces of the body, which transformed social life and popular memory. The command of spaces achieved through ideology and violence, particularly gendered violence, entailed a reorganization of the senses, mental maps, topographic origin myths and spatial performance. A clear example of this is visible in the daily flag ceremony at the Wagah border.[16] The demarcation of borders at partition thus demanded a profound discontinuity of social spaces that had been established through long custom.

In contemporary South Asia, the competing discourses of old forms of community and new utopian and imagined forms is played out most strongly in the state of Jammu and Kashmir. This state, which has a highly diverse population of Muslims and Hindus, has been recodified into confrontational zones divided by the line of control (LOC) that separates Pakistan-administered Kashmir (or POK as it is known in India—Pakistan-*occupied*-Kashmir; in Pakistan, it is known as Azad Kashmir or Free Kashmir) from Indian-administered Kashmir. The cross-border infiltration that India accuses Pakistan of pursuing is a mix of historical symbolism, command of space and boundary transgression. Cross-border infiltration by Pakistan transforms the authorities on the Indian side of the border into objects of ridicule and defilement in that it suggests that the border is easily penetrable. This leads to retaliatory violence by the Indian army against the Muslim population in Kashmir. In the highly militarized zone of the Kashmir Valley, no Muslim civilian is to be trusted as all are suspected of being sympathetic to Pakistan. Kashmir is replete with checkpoints, insurgents intent on ethnic cleansing, forced disappearances and extra-judicial killings. Notwithstanding the Shimla agreement of 1972,[17] which upheld peaceful solutions to border disputes between the two countries, both sides perform rituals and postures that exacerbate the violence, temporarily shifting the symbolic centres of Jammu and Kashmir from its civilian population, its cultural capital, and commerce, to insurgents, the borders and the military. This is not unlike the situation during the partition. Thus, the line of control, far from being in the margins, becomes political theatre that is central to the construction of the civilian population as political subjects in an extremely rigid replay of the partition.

Partition violence also scrambled long-established meanings of the difference between the home and the world in that domestic space was often the site of politically and religiously motivated assaults and murder. Thus, the private spaces of affective links increasingly became the space of politics and sectarian violence. Personal, familiar spaces once violated became, instead, the spaces of the repressed, uncanny, unfamiliar and estranged, affecting subsequent generations. The walls of the house, the zigzagging of the lanes and streets and the borders of the nation turned into a repository of the history of violence, effecting a physical connection between the violator and the violated. Raping a woman of the other community became a political act of terrorism and ethnic cleansing as well as an individualized act representing the breakdown of law and order. The former home, the community with its designated roles for individuals, was turned inside out and the woman's body unfolded and exposed in order to violate and contaminate the domestic spaces previously associated with purity. This space of imagined domestic purity was thus made other, the distinction between the outside (the space of the other) and inside collapsing through the rape of women. Once women and the home were polluted by the other, a new home had to be sourced across the border in the newly constituted country to which the refugee belonged by default.

Whilst partition stories of women's abduction by men of the other community have the status of archetypal material, stories of women killed by their own menfolk to enable them to avoid the fate of abduction are deemed less important—but nevertheless significant. Even before independence and partition, the story of ninety Sikh women in Thoha Khalsa village who jumped into a well and drowned themselves to avoid abduction by Muslim men had iconic status amongst oral narratives. These women had 'sacrificed' themselves not only to preserve their own 'honour' but also, particularly, those of their men. The well filled up with dead bodies and women who jumped on top of these bodies somehow tried to submerge their heads under water so that they too could drown. Other stories of men who shot their wife and daughters, only to find more women from their community demanding to be shot as well, abound in these narratives.[18] These women attained the status of martyrs in such narratives. Their men invariably remarried to begin a new cycle of reproduction once they had fled to the 'right' country.

The threat of rape combined with the victim's fear converted rape into an insignia of a politically legitimized ethnic cleansing. Thus, the central issue in analysing partition rapes is *not* how ethnic cleansing leaks into the rationalized objectives of the newly formed political entities of India and Pakistan but rather *how the fear of the other provides the foundation for the very rationalization of power and subsequent actions of the state and South Asian patriarchy*. Thus, intrinsic to the continuation of patriarchal authority is a kind of rationalization and legitimation of rape. On the political level in this context, rape or the violation of the body is only the mimetic act by individuals of what the state considers to be the rightful fate of the other. On the cultural level, South Asian patriarchy sacrificed these women to preserve itself. Two metaphysical intangibles collide and mingle in the body of the rape victim—first, the force of anarchy and disorder that had her abducted and second, the will/desire of the newly formed states to establish their space and regain control of their domain after colonialism. If the body can be theorized as a political institution, then the woman's body is a political orifice, a passageway into the state and its others. The woman multiply violated and mutilated loses what little individuated identity she had in the first place completely; rape reduces her to silence. If the state did manage to rescue her eventually,[19] her family members, inevitably, often refused to take her back, now that she had been contaminated, having cohabitated and even reproduced with men of the other community. She was just effaced flesh, a body that had been subtracted from any individuated identity by violence. She became a corpse, silent, disembodied, her body being no more her own, effectuating a separation of self from body, of body from language. In this condition/status of lack, the woman is outside of time, this removal being tantamount to a simulation of death. Exiled and in limbo, at home and not at home, her body experiences social death: a position outside of time, outside of politics, outside of her value as a woman, and outside of her status in the family. These transactions on the body conferred political power on the names 'India' and 'Pakistan'. Or, to put it in another way, the names 'India' and 'Pakistan' bore down upon the women's bodies with violence and invested them with political lack. The silencing of the woman, however, is necessary. It must silence discourse that suggests that these are states legitimated by violence that also empower patriarchy. This silencing would have profound implications for the present.

Bodies and Gendered Violence 1947 and 2012

Thus far, I have discussed how violence reembodies as much as it reconstructs space and difference. I have suggested that partition violence caused Indian citizens' senses to shift and re-identify friends as foe and neighbours as strangers. I have also implied that, notwithstanding their accession to equal citizenship in

August 1947, Indian women (along with the poor and the minorities) were seen as marked citizens (or rather, carried the meaning of the bodily marks of their men). Partition violence transformed each of them from being an individual to a metaphor. In this next section I want to disentangle from this process the legacy of partition violence for the postcolonial construction of sexuality in India. I want to examine the question, 'Did partition violence influence the practice of sexuality after 1947?' Did sexuality get reconfigured by the intensified nationalist ideologies (generated by the independence movement) in postcolonial South Asia? Did new forms of power and their deployment also influence sexuality and sexual practices in South Asia after 1947? Did the masses of women abducted and raped during partition reconfigure attitudes and knowledges about sexuality? In *The History of Sexuality* (*Volume 1*), Foucault suggests that sexuality is neither a naturalized act nor one which is strictly about sex. Sexuality is shaped by the twists and turns of history and also takes a plethora of different forms. For Foucault, both reticence about sexuality as well as the proliferation of discourses around population, architecture, criminal justice and medicine (to just name a few) were all sites for the construction of sexuality in the West.[20] In India, too, sexuality has been shaped by the vagaries of power relations, and the road from the ancient text *Kamasutra*, which celebrated human sexual behaviour, to the recent restoration (2013) of the colonial era Indian Penal Code Section 377, which has recriminalized gay sex, has had remarkable twists and turns. And in 2018, the Supreme Court of India finally decriminalized homosexuality.

If the history of British colonialism continues to influence the practice of sexuality in India, how can we read partition violence's influence? I want to suggest that independence and partition, which combined to redefine citizenship, concepts of democracy and an awareness of the body have also been influential in the reshaping of sexuality and gender. Such an argument is in line with George Mosse's thesis that nationalism aligned itself to the notion of respectability and changed the nature of nineteenth-century European sexuality. Furthermore, in his examination of German sexuality in the interwar period, Mosse points out that 'the line drawn between normalcy and abnormalcy had to be tightly drawn in order to protect the nation against its enemies'.[21] In this discourse, 'perverted' sexuality is perceived to be practised by racial others who were seen as degenerate. For Mosse, the rise of the Nationalist Socialist Party in Germany and the othering of the Jewish people that led to the Holocaust are directly connected to shifting comprehensions of nationalism. Thus, we can see that gender and sexuality are not categories in themselves but, as Foucault argued, they are imbricated in and shaped by multiple factors including the economy, nationalism, war and peace and, in India's case, also colonialism and the partition.

Since the 1990s, much scholarly attention has been given to tracing the status of women refugees in the partition.[22] The horrific statistics for women refugees—between 75,000 to 120,000 Hindu, Muslim and Sikh women abducted by men of the other communities (or sometimes even their own) and subjected to multiple rapes, mutilations and, for some, forced marriages and conversions—raise the question of what is the relationship between citizenship in emergent democracies in South Asia and the sexual violation of women. This question is important to me as Western media coverage of Indian culture now predominantly consists of rape stories in which Indian men are being represented as predominantly sexually violent towards women.[23] Are the over half billion Indian men only sexual predators? Is there no love or decency or sense of ethical behaviour? Of course, the media are highly selective in what they choose to report. Yet this leads me to ask: Is there any hermeneutic link between 1947 and the present in the acts of sexual violence inflicted on women? In 1947, women refugees with newly conferred equal citizenship rights to male refugees faced the dismal prospect of experiencing their bodies and identities as vulnerable and having to fear for their safety from men. Is it the same for women in India now? Can we juxtapose the statistics of sexual violence in 1947 to the frequent and well-publicized cases of sexual assault of women in India today?[24] I want to make the comparison between two disconnected dates, 1947 and 2012, when in New Delhi, a young woman and her male friend caught a private bus one evening after having been to the cinema. The bus had only six other people in it all of whom, in a conspiracy, then severely beat up the young man and proceeded to rape the young woman for several hours. Finally, they tossed her and her friend out of the bus. The young woman, eventually identified as Jyoti Singh Pandey, died several days later of the severe wounds she had received. Because Indian laws prevent the publication of a rape victim's name, she was initially identified as *Nirbhaya*, or 'fearless'. With the use of ubiquitous social media, there has been a visible shift in attitudes about sexuality, especially sexual violence in India. Nowhere was this shift more visible than in this case and its aftermath. The incident led to civil unrest for over a month in Delhi and all the other major cities, with the public protesting against the lack of safety for women in public spaces and the lax enforcement of the laws on rape and demanding that the government address this situation immediately. This shocking event in 2012 received world-wide coverage and, since then, has led to the publicising of rape cases in India on the front pages of Western newspapers.[25] I wish to argue that it is this event that makes visible the spoor, the scent, the track of partition rapes in attitudes to sexual violence in India today and how 1947 led to the diminished status of the Indian woman citizen and the indifference of the state to her victimization.

My attempt to see the connection between 1947 and 2012 is problematized by India's long history of misogyny. During the colonial period, the justification for colonial rule was often based upon India's 'lack of civilization', which was seen to include the mistreatment of women by patriarchal authorities. Colonial bills such as those against widow burning (1829), the Widow Remarriage Act (1856), the Age of Consent Bill (1891) and the Sarda Bill (1929) had positioned the colonial rulers as the saviours of Indian women,[26] resulting in women's bodies being perceived to be 'not simply sites for discourse , but . . . also sites of patriarchal constraint and violence'.[27]

To facilitate a more nuanced way of exploring the link between 1947 and 2012, I draw on the Derridean notion of the trace.[28] The trace carries the meanings of otherness and alterity embedded within it, an imprint or a mark, and refers to the vestiges of something that was left behind and that does not exist anymore. It is the irreducible mark of otherness in every sign. Tracing as a potential pathway leads to an elsewhere (in meaning), a useful metaphor for the ongoing reverberations of historical events in the present, that calls into question history's linearity. The notion of the trace allows history to be perceived as 'a continuous movement across geographical, cultural and temporal borders, becoming through its non-linear passages a condition or cultural system that attempts to rethink the relationship between the past and the present'.[29] In this view of history, the link between the partition and the present becomes visible. Indeed, the visibility of trace—in this case, the past intruding upon the present—is not unlike the structure of trauma in which the past intrudes upon and shapes the present. The contours and traces of partition become visible in India through different signifiers—the periodic communal violence between Hindus and Muslims in particular, and through sexual violence towards women. I will speculate further on this equivalence between communal violence and sexual violence later in this chapter, but for now I will concentrate on the signification of sexual violence.

Works by Urvashi Butalia and Ritu Menon and Kamla Bhasin, published in 1998, suggest that women who underwent the partition were inserted differently in the national narrative of independence struggle that culminated in violence. Butalia engages with oral testimonies from men and women who experienced the partition and points out that neither Pakistan nor India has commemorated the losses and dispossession of the refugees in any way.[30] Both nation states have tended to foreground the story of independence or nation formation instead of the partition. In tracking the lives of abducted women, both works, by Butalia and by Menon and Bhasin, have underscored the lack of agency of these women, abducted first by men and then by the state, especially in the case of recovered women. In one instance, Butalia points out how she had come across a ledger in a secondhand book store which consisted of 1,414 pages with a list of 21,809 names of abducted women and children compiled by the Commissioner of Ambala and Jalandhar districts. The compilation itself was a list of non-Muslim abducted women and children in Pakistan and in the Pakistan side of the state of Jammu and Kashmir.[31] The descriptions of women are brief but mournful: 'Prakash Kaur, 22 years, w/o Pritam Singh, Vill. Dinga, Teh. Kharian, Distt. Gujrat'. In the column for the particulars of abductors we find that Prakash Kaur 'is likely to be found in or about Dinga' or, in other words, Prakash Kaur was abducted by men from her own village and was likely to have been made a prostitute in her own village. In the case of 'Pooro, 25 years, d/o Sardar Singh, Vill. And P.O Bhagowal, Teh and Distt, Gujrat', the names of the abductors are specifically Muslim: 'Rahmat Khan and Ghulam Qadir, Bhagowal, Distt., Gujrat'.[32] There are many more examples of women and children abducted by men from the same village and the table of names is also a commentary on desire, crime, violent sexuality and, likely, score settling by the abductors. These names, Butalia discovered, had never been published 'out of deference for the feelings of those whose relatives were listed' in the ledger.[33] The discarding of this ledger, a refusal to archive it, an excision of the abducted women's feelings, an excision of state responsibility to make it public in any way reveals the hierarchy of the stakeholders: the government and the officials valuing the feelings of family members of abductees over the urgency of rescuing the women who were abducted. This refusal carries the trace of the violation of the abducted woman's rights not only by the abductors but also by the state; the erasure of her equal right as a citizen of the newly democratic country is in its semiosis, etched in the very process of the signification of India. In the Constituent Assembly in 1949, it was recorded that of the fifty thousand Muslim women abducted in India, eight thousand of them were recovered and of the thirty-three thousand Hindu and Sikh women abducted, twelve thousand were recovered.[34] In short, of all the women abducted only one in four was ever recovered. The Ministry of Relief and Rehabilitation in the newly formed states demanded that these women be returned to their respective countries, even the ones who had come to terms with their abductors and started a family with them. In most of the instances of the recovered women, their voices, their preferences and their wishes were not heard and they were deprived of agency, subject to the whims of the men and patriarchy and the policies of the state, which were structurally in a relation of equivalence with each other.

A key issue here is the nature of the archive. In *The Archaeology of Knowledge*, Foucault defines the archive as being not only 'the whole mass of texts that belong to a single discursive formation' but also as underscoring 'the law of what can be said'; the archive 'defines at the outset the system of its enunciability . . . it is that which defines the mode of occurrence of the statement-thing; *it is the system of its functioning*'.[35] Foucault suggests that the archive determines the shape of the articulation of the discourse, arguing that the politics that permit the collection of the archive are present in the archive itself. The archives relating to the abduction of women in the partition well illustrate this point. This focus on thinking about the law that brings about an archive is also present in Jacques Derrida's *Archive Fever*.[36] For Derrida, the archive is a juridical concept, part of a theory of how the law becomes institutionalized as law through the figure of the *archon*, a word that refers both to the keeper of the archive and to the place where the law is conceived. For Derrida, social order is instituted not discursively as Foucault would have it, but hermeneutically by *archons* through the interpretation of texts.

My question here is whether Derrida and Foucault's notions of the archive can shed new light on the abducted women of the partition. Can one even call it an 'archive' if the names of these women were never made public by the district commissioner nor the volume kept safe among the mountains of bureaucratic papers that any colonial office would have produced? If the *archon* does not think of particular material as relevant enough to be archived, can the discourse it embodies ever become audible or a part of history? There is a silence around these women's names and fates and a careless disposal of any evidence of them ever having existed. Butalia's recovery of the ledger resurrects these names *as a trace*, not only of the women themselves but the indifference of the patriarchal state. To echo Gayatri Spivak, there is no discursive space from which the abducted women can speak and the archival work consists of 'measuring silences'.[37] In this instance the silence is not only that of the state and the government officials, but also that maintained by the recovered women themselves. Butalia adds that ashrams (residential houses) were set up for abducted women who were recovered but cast out by their families as they were considered to be 'polluted', and that these ashrams continued to house these women (unclaimed and with nowhere to go) in 1997, fifty years after independence and partition.[38] Veena Das points to the zone of silence that surrounded recovered women when she questioned them about their experiences. She states:

> This silence was achieved either by the use of language that was general and metaphoric but that evaded specific description of any events so as to capture the particularity of their experience, or by describing the surrounding events but leaving the actual experience of abduction and rape unstated. . . . [O]ne woman warned me, it was dangerous to remember.[39]

In short, all parties concerned—the state, the bureaucracy, the men and the recovered women themselves—have no desire to remember or fear remembering this event. In another work, *Life and Words*, Das suggests that 'the circulation of the figure of the abducted woman, with its associated imagery of social disorder as sexual disorder, created the conditions of possibility in which the state could be instituted as essentially a social contract between *men* charged with keeping male violence against women in abeyance'.[40] Das refers to the privileging of male citizens and to women being denied the justice, equality and liberty promised by the constitution, arguing that this points to the limits within which women were placed in the formation of the nation-state.

II

Public/Private

What I have suggested thus far is that 1947 not only brought about a political shift in India—independence, democracy and the division of the subcontinent into two states—but also the reembodiment of the Indian citizen. Whereas during the independence movement Indian-ness was defined by racial difference, in 1947 at independence, it was constituted by visible religious difference. This shift in the comprehension of the body, along with the independence struggle for democracy and universal suffrage, inevitably reshaped gender and gender relations as well. I have also indicated that the relationship between 1947 and the events of 2012 in terms of violence towards women is metonymically linked to the redrawing of the public sphere. In this section I want to examine what space women occupy and why the occupation of this space results in sexual violence towards women or, in other words, how notwithstanding independence and democratic rights, the present seems to be repeating the misogynistic past. To do this, I want to slow down my argument in this chapter about sexuality after partition and approach it from another angle—the division between the public and private spheres—as this will illuminate the complex meanings around sexual violence that adhere to 1947 and 2012 in India.

The public and private are widely perceived as two distinct zones that are often positioned in opposition, a distinction that is central to the liberal tradition but challenged by most feminists, including many liberal feminists.[41] The liberal resituating of individuals as having (individual) rights that went beyond their public legal status allowed them to flourish as private citizens. Locke suggests that private citizens, motivated by self-interest, yielded good public benefits. In his categorization, he distinctly divides the public (or political) from the private (or natural) realms of the individual, thus presenting liberalism with an egalitarian landscape as long as it is limited to the public sphere. Feminists like Carole Pateman, however, argue that the division of the public and private actually refers to the unequal spatial opposition between men and women in that whilst men have access to both the public and private spheres, women could generally occupy only the private or domestic sphere. Furthermore, these two spheres are in a hierarchical relationship, with the public sphere occupying the position of domination and the private an inferior sphere, the space where women generally resided, thereby becoming invisible. For Pateman and other second-wave feminists, women's exclusion from equal rights was connected to the entitlement to democratic participation accorded to men.[42] Additionally, second-wave feminists point to a conflation of the state, the official economy of paid employment and arenas of public discourse in their interpretation of the public.[43] Indeed, feminist reinterpretations of the public emerge from a critique of the concept of *res publica* in Roman law which, among other things, referred to property held in common by many people. The spatial dimension of this term emerged during the medieval period to mean anything in the open or outside domestic space.[44]

A different concept of the spatial implications of public and private emerges from the works of Kant and Habermas.[45] Kant's work suggests that there are multiple publics, which need not all be aligned with any polity but which form a public by the use of critical discourse. In other words, the public is not necessarily aligned with an office, a state or a nation.[46] It is this *circulation of discourse* between writers and readers that is also pertinent to Habermas for whom the public is a reading public that was formed in the Enlightenment through the circulation of print.[47] It is this collective use of reason by a 'critically debating reading public'[48] that established the public sphere for Habermas. Here we can see that the physical dimension of the public sphere inherent to both liberal and feminist conceptualizations is missing in Kant and Habermas's definitions. While the circulation of independence discourse galvanized India prior to 1947, Habermas's notion of a critically debating reading public that represented the public sphere is perhaps more appropriate to Western Europe than to India in 1947. The 1951 census indicated that 92 per cent of women and 75 per cent of men were illiterate at that time.[49] Furthermore, with twenty-four different languages with equal status in the Indian Constitution, the 'reading public' was extremely fragmented and regionalised and consisted, for the most part, of the educated and urban elite. A public sphere divorced from its spatial element as Kant and Habermas have it, also throws little light on Indian women because sexually assaulted women, both during partition and in the present, were and are generally perceived to be outside of their 'assigned' domestic space. Thus, any notion of the public in India has to include a sense of their spatial dimension, a sense of an inside and an outside.

So how are the public and private constituted in India? Partha Chatterjee's essay, 'The Nationalist Resolution of the Women's Question', gives a different genealogy of nationalism in India from the one espoused by European Enlightenment thinkers for whom the Enlightenment in Europe was the outcome of the development of the bourgeoisie, nationalism and democracy. For Chatterjee, nationalism and democracy in India emerged from an anticolonial movement and consequently had a different trajectory. Chatterjee points out that in anticolonial India, the world was perceived to be divided into the material and spiritual realms, with Western thought and civilization with its science, technology and economic advancement being located in the material realm and Indian tradition and national culture located in the spiritual realm.[50] This division of material and spiritual, the West and India, cohered into a paradigm of mutually exclusive terms that were also gendered. Indian men were located in the paradigmatic cluster of the spiritual and the inner, but contaminated themselves every day with the other realm due to their occupations, the need to earn their livelihood by entering Western, material culture. Therefore, it was the Indian woman who had to maintain the spiritual nature of this paradigmatic cluster. The woman located inside the home, embodying the spiritual nature of India, had to maintain its pure and unsullied traditions. It was this role assigned to Indian woman in the nationalist cause that gave strength to the whole movement. She embodied the space from which India's strength emerged in independence struggle discourse. To a large extent, this role bestowed upon the women by the nationalist cause—to represent the uncontaminated inner world, to maintain timeless traditional values and to be located within the home and not the harsh world outside—was not that different from bourgeois Western Victorian values of separate spheres, which positioned women in the home and as the angel in the house. However, in addition to this wider paradigm, women in India were entrusted this role in the nationalist cause, in a way naturalizing the political. Furthermore, Indian patriarchy rewrote itself as a new patriarchy that placed women inside the home, while also demanding that women have a formal education, which was meant to inculcate in women the virtues—the typically 'bourgeois' virtues characteristic of the new social forms of 'disciplining'—of orderliness, thrift, cleanliness and a personal sense of responsibility, and the practical skills of literacy, accounting and hygiene, and the ability to run the household according to the new physical and economic conditions set by the outside world.[51] The implications of Chatterjee's thesis are that the Indian woman in the home was not meant to be confined or a prisoner but, in fact, her virtuous presence *actually recharged and shifted the meaning not only of the home but also that of the indigenous world that had been contaminated by the presence of the British.* The woman embodied both tradition and an Indian modernity that did not follow the same historical trajectory as Western Enlightenment. Her presence was thus not transformative but re-creative, and this shifted the paradigmatic cluster so that the terms 'public' and 'private' did not quite work oppositionally anymore within nationalist discourse. She embodied the Indian home and values but also the new India in the world outside that represented spirituality and modernity. In sum, the reworking of the state, citizenship and the polity in 1947 was a seismic event which changed the lives of South Asian citizens in tremendous ways, shifting notions of private and public alongside those of stranger and neighbour, coloniser and colonised, citizen and enemy, friend and foe, masculinity and femininity, sexuality and violence, and private and public. The division between the public and private is also an affective one in that, if the public is supposedly governed through objectivity, logic and common sense, the private is perceived to be the space of emotions. In this, any form of emotional trauma is precluded from entering public discourse except in very specific ways which allows it to be governed through logic and the law. In *The Archive of Feelings*, Ann Cvetkovich examines the affective practices of queer communities in the aftermath of sexual abuse and the HIV/AIDS crisis in the United States. This crisis was perceived to be marginal by the public and of relevance only to queer communities. Nor was there any recognition of trauma or genocide and the perception of queer community trauma as being worthy of entering public discourse. Cvetkovich suggests that marginalized forms of trauma require 'new genres of expression, such as testimony, and new forms of monuments, rituals, and performances, that can call into being collective witnesses and publics'.[52] For Cvetkovich, the ephemeral quality of trauma demands an unusual archive and approach to perceive the trauma under erasure. Most importantly, echoing Cvetkovich, Rosann Kennedy has also pointed out the significance of the witness of trauma in the creation of the new public (or counterpublic).[53] The witnessing and acknowledgement of trauma permits the articulation and visibility of unacknowledged or invisible trauma, making it a part of public discourse.

Both Cvetkovich and Kennedy's comprehension of the witness of trauma is influenced by the notion of the 'counterpublic' popularized in Nancy Fraser's work.[54] This term is suggestive in that it goes beyond Habermas' notion of the bourgeois public in which political participation is enacted through talk leading to the formation of public opinion and a common good. Unlike Habermas though, for Fraser, the interlocutors in the public sphere are not social equals, leading to the silencing of minority groups. Counterpublics are formed by those excluded from deliberation in the public sphere and is a significant concept, among others, within queer, feminist and racial discourses as they challenge the dominant public sphere. The witnessing of trauma, then, creates an archive of feeling, a sentiment which, as Lauren Berlant indicates, transforms the public sphere to include the concerns of counterpublics. The 'pain of intimate others burns into the consciousness of classically privileged national subjects, in such a fashion that they feel the pain of flawed or denied citizenship as their [own] pain. . . . Identification with pain, a true universal feeling, then leads to structural social change'.[55]

But how is sexuality imbricated with the spatial element of the public and private? In the division between the public and the private spheres, sexuality and sexual behaviour are considered to belong to the private realm. Indeed, anything that deals with the body and bodily sensations—pleasure, pain, shame, display, appetite and purgation—are presumed to belong to privacy because this realm is also the space of selfhood and the development of an individuated identity. If raped and recovered women during the partition had no archive, then we can posit that the women's rapes in India are neither remembered nor given public attention. In rural and urban spaces, Indian women of both lower and upper castes are located within an 'amnesia archive' as defined by Lauren Berlant and Michael Warner[56]—amnesia within the judicial system, the courts, the police, the government and the patriarchy. The public/private split which structurally differentiates between work and the domestic, and politics and intimacy furthers the notion of the private as a pre-political space. However, partition rapes and abductions showed that sexual violence towards women, far from being in the realm of the private, was politically motivated in the name of nation and community. Furthermore, in hegemonic Indian culture, making sexuality private reintensifies sex within marriage as the only legitimate form of female sexuality, and thus replaces laws against sexual violence with a privatized ethics of responsibility ('what was she doing being without a male family member accompanying her at that time of the night') and rape myths ('dressed that way she was asking for it'). *In short, the privatization of sex leads to the privatization of sexual violence*. The sexual violence towards the raped Indian woman who has no legal recourse because the law is unenforced within the context of a hegemonic patriarchy gets transformed into a private misery for the woman. At best, it can only be articulated as a violence towards the individual or the family. The privatization of sexual violence and the consequent shame forces the raped woman to retreat from the public completely. Thus, public places are reinforced as spaces of patriarchy.

Is there any continuum, then, in the signification of sexual violence towards women between 1947 and 2012? In partition rapes, the politicization of sexual violence was moved to the zone of the private by the government, the law, the families and the archive itself. In 2012, women's sexuality and sexual violence are again relegated to the private, untouched by the law or any form of justice. Such a signification of sexual violence emerges from a patriarchal public that acts only to protect the zone of patriarchal privacy with the institutions of economic and sexual privilege, informing its practices and organizing its ideal world and demonizing any woman who confesses to being sexually violated.

III

Gender and Sexuality: Past and Present

In this chapter, I have suggested thus far that the connection between partition abductions and the rapes in present-day India lies within the resituation of the public and private spheres. In 1947, the citizenship rights bestowed upon both men and women in India caused a major shift in the meanings and understandings of the two spheres. Yet this has not been the only force for change in play. Since 1991, the economic liberalization and globalization in India that led to the deregulation of the market and greater foreign investment have not only effected a further shift in the meaning of the public sphere but have altogether reshaped interpersonal relations and relocated gender roles in postmodern India. In general, gender relations have been strongly affected by neoliberalism in that there have been changes in the traditional androcentric division of productive labour (for men) and reproductive labour for women. With the inclusion of large numbers of women into the waged economy due to the rising cost of living caused by increasing privatization of services in neoliberal economies, there has been a power shift in gender relations. As Naila Kabeer points out, women have become 'the flexible labour force par excellence for the highly competitive labour intensive sectors of the global economy'.[57] This increase in working women has its counterpart in declining numbers of employed men, as the male labour force is associated with fixed costs that do not apply to women, working in large proportions in part-time work.[58] In addition, in an ostensibly 'postfeminist' age, the proportion of men with poor educational attainment and low usage of health services has meant that the number of women who attain economic autonomy has increased, leading to changing power relations within the family. Deborah Tudor adds an important caveat to this scenario of increasing autonomy for women by pointing out that, while they have increasingly occupied the public sphere through participating in the work force, this has not resulted in any changes in the nature and structure of the workplace for women.[59] For Tudor, neoliberal economies have strengthened dominant patriarchies which now coexist with certain pragmatic feminist ideas.[60] One can say that the narrative of women's advancement under the neoliberal cause conceals the reality of the increasing difficulty in women's lives caused in part by savage cuts made to social spending and welfare. Yet the changing nature of masculinity and femininity in the present era go beyond its effects in the workplace. In metropolitan areas of India there is a conflation of 'sexual liberation [and] economic liberalization'[61] in the sense that sexual freedom and sexual agency both symbolize freedom.[62] As Ashwini and Shruti Tambe point out, the increasing participation of women in the public sphere in India and their new aspirations have resulted in greater threats of violence by a traditional patriarchy. In her assessment of gender violence's connection to neoliberalism, Tithi Bhattacharya also suggests that the last four decades of neoliberalism have seen a marked escalation of violence towards women in most countries.[63] Bhattacharya argues that gender violence is in part an outcome of socioeconomic processes and states that, after the global financial crisis of 2008, there was a rise in gendered violence; for instance, domestic violence rose by 35 per cent in 2010 in the United Kingdom, in Ireland by 21 per cent and, in the United States, over 80 per cent of domestic violence shelters reported an increase in domestic violence year on year.[64] Bhattacharya observes that multiple and interlocking factors such as increased participation of women in subsistence work, or women working longer hours for lower pay, produce 'the conditions of possibility'[65] for gendered violence. Under neoliberalism, more women are employed in low-paying jobs. As Cynthia Enloe remarks, 'The risk-taking globalised banker needs the conscientious seamstress to hold his world together'.[66] Globalization has also meant that work life is no longer restricted to 9 a.m. to 5 p.m. but continues through the night. This has resulted in a complete shift in the meaning of public spaces and the public sphere with women being out and working late at night. One can also speculate that the sexual and gendered anxiety of men now having to compete with women for low-paying jobs often manifests itself in rape as a form of protest against women's increased visibility in the public sphere and in public spaces brought about by globalization and neoliberalism.

If economic shifts brought about by neoliberalism in the present have created changes in the definitions and gendering of the public sphere that have consequently percolated downwards to change the shape of masculinity and femininity, can we look back at 1947 to see whether there were any parallel changes in masculinity and femininity in India at that time? How did Indian independence coupled with partition reconfigure the public sphere and the concepts of masculinity and femininity? Earlier I suggested via Chatterjee that the independence struggle and Indian nationalism had created a neo-patriarchy that located women in the private sphere that was, nevertheless, politically charged and informed by late nineteenth-century conceptualizations of gender. Yet there was no neat gender division amongst Indians that was solely determined by (Western) conceptualizations of the public and private spheres. As Mrinalini Sinha has pointed out, the understanding of gender in

India during the long nineteenth century was also shaped by the discourses of colonialism.[67] In colonial discourse, masculinity was a condition that was bestowed only upon the colonizer, and the colonized were relegated to effeminacy. Sinha notes that this gendering of the Indian versus the British also needs to be contextualized by events taking place in late nineteenth-century Britain. She states that 'the emergence of the 'New Woman;' the 'remaking of the working class'; the legacy of 'internal colonialism'; and the 'anti-feminist backlash of the 1880s and 1890s' were all factors that contributed to the politics of colonial masculinity[68] where only the white British male was represented as properly masculine. In this formula, the supine, colonized nation, along with its people, by default, occupied the passive feminine position. Elsewhere, I have argued that the nineteenth century in Britain saw an increasingly strident demand for inculcating proper masculine virtues, particularly amongst young British schoolboys in the aftermath of the Sepoy rebellion of 1857 in India and the Morant Bay rebellion in Jamaica in 1865, both of which together shook the perception of white supremacy that underwrote the imperial project.[69] Only hypermasculine youth was perceived to be valuable in governing Britain's large colonial holdings. The perception of India as feminine was not only based on her colonized condition but also on the lack of understanding of the significance of the Indian to European thought and modes of being. Sinha points out that educated Indians were, therefore, perceived as an aberration and effeminate because they 'represented an "unnatural" or "perverted" form of masculinity'.[70] Furthermore, the British divided populations according to their fighting abilities, with Sikh and Muslim populations often being categorized as martial and male whereas vegetarian Hindus in particular were perceived to be feminine, notwithstanding the vast numbers of Hindu soldiers that composed the Indian army. It is within this imperial context of feminization that nationalists felt an urgency to rewrite gender relations in India. The revisions to gender relations, inevitably, reinscribed women within the private sphere. As for the Indian men, especially those who experienced the partition, to echo Veena Das, if they moved from being colonial subjects to autonomous citizens, they also turned from being men to becoming monsters.[71]

Yet another aspect of Indian independence/partition highlights how gender roles were affected during the independence movement. Gandhi's shaping of passive resistance, which was a key strategy to winning independence and a national identity that cohered the heterogeneous population in India, hinged around two mutually related platforms—spinning and *khadi* (homespun cloth). Among other things, both spinning and *khadi* had great symbolic value as they represented India's rejection of Western modes of being and refusal to be a captive market for Britain's industrial products. Gandhi's focus on spinning and *khadi* derived from his observations of passive resistance in his wife and mother. Kumari Jayawardena notes that Gandhi felt that since women were 'used to passive forms of resistance in their daily lives', they could 'more effectively participate in socially organised passive resistance and non-cooperation'.[72] Spinning and the production of *khadi* were, however, not exclusively for women participants of the independence movement but also demanded the participation of the men. Ketu Katrak observes that Gandhi's enjoining of 'Indian men and women to engage in acts of passive resistance . . . feminised the usually masculinist struggle against the coloniser'.[73] Indeed, underpinning traits of passive resistance such as purity, suffering and self-sacrifice were deemed to be 'feminine' and as such the participants of the independence movement had not only to act according to these traits, but were also encouraged to abnegate themselves sexually in order to dedicate themselves exclusively to the nationalist cause. Gandhi's encouragement of traditionally feminine characteristics in the public sphere as his main strategy for achieving Indian independence rendered this entire space feminine. If femininity was a trait that was necessary to achieve independence, a 'masculine' aggression was needed to retain it at partition. The asexuality, self-sacrifice and passivity that was demanded from the Indian by the independence movement is at odds with the violence, murders and rapes that marked the partition. It is this binding of opposites—nonviolence with violence, passivity with aggression, strong sense of a coherent national identity with an unravelling national identity because of partition, and a sense of belonging with a deep sense of loss of one's autochthonous identity—that led to this emergent form of identity in South Asia in 1947. If read only within the frame of gender predicated on the public/private split, we could interpret partition violence, especially that directed at women, to be a reclaiming of the newly formed public sphere as a male, neo-patriarchal space and as a violent reaction to aspects of the passive resistance that was demanded to free a country.

The hermeneutic link between 1947 and 2012, I posit, lies in the shift in the definition of the public sphere resulting in violence against women in India. Both dates witnessed massive changes in the lives of women, neoliberalism's seeming bestowal of equal opportunity for women and partition the democratic future's bestowal of equal rights. However, while the threat of rape might restrict women to the private sphere, women's lives changed radically after partition, especially for the refugees. Partition was a 'critical event' in modern Indian history, to borrow Veena Das's term, an event that transformed definitions of space and people's lives in completely new and unexpected ways; it instituted 'a new modality of historical action' and new forms of categorization of race, of markets and of imperial advances which were not 'inscribed in the inventory of that situation'.[74] While this event was meant to be a solution to speed up and not postpone independence any further, it also changed the social landscape of India. It changed everyday lives in the form of domestic arrangements and familial lives as well as transforming the lives of women. Refugees from the same villages or districts were often housed together in clusters in camps with two or three families having to share the same room.[75] As a result of this event, more women were single—due to the death of either their spouse or other menfolk in the family at partition—requiring them to become the head of the household, earning money and supporting their remaining family. Middle-class and upper-class women who became refugees also had to provide a second income to support a suddenly impoverished family. Indeed, an entire generation of young partition refugee women could not participate in normal life practices such as marriage. It was not just the nation that needed to be reconstructed but also refugee families and every family member had to be in paid work. Volunteers who worked in camps and women's service centres as doctors, teachers and counsellors, who were often refugees themselves, acquired immense organizational skills through the experience. Addressing how the partition spelt an opportunity for women, Menon and Bhasin point out that 'the tragedy of partition created a cadre of women workers many of whom subsequently became employees of the government and retired only after thirty or forty years of service'.[76] The importance of education for girls was underscored especially among partition refugees because of the increase in working mothers amongst them. Karuna Chanana points out that the '[p]artition narrowed the physical spaces and enlarged the social spaces available to women thereby affecting the practice of *parda* or seclusion, modified the impact of caste and regional culture on marriage arrangements and widened the channels of educational mobility and employment for girls and women'.[77] A final qualifier to be made about women and the partition is that, while the partition predominantly affected only those women who were from the states of the Punjab and Bengal, all Indian women were offered new models of femininity after 1947. Bipan Chandra, Mridula Mukherjee and Aditya Mukherjee suggest that the legal, political, educational and political status of all Indian women changed because 'the improvement of the position of women had been at the heart of the social reform movement from the first quarter of the nineteenth century'.[78] They suggest that from the early twentieth century onwards, women had participated in the various nationalist movements for independence, including the Gandhian, socialist, communist and revolutionary terrorist causes. Since the 1930s, women had demanded a rise in the age of consent and marriage, the end of polygamy, a right to divorce, to maintenance and to inherit, and for dowry to be treated as women's property.[79] These rights were achieved in the 1950s. However, these changes could not have been effected so easily without the lives of partition women offering new possibilities of social structures. Read from within a

Foucauldian framework, one can suggest that the partition was not a discrete but an emancipatory event that redefined the relationship between agency and change, resistance and power. It recreated agency for the new citizens of India through economic necessity, living in a diaspora and being subjects of a modern, emergent but impoverished nation after centuries of colonial rule that transformed social structures and women's lives.

CONCLUSION

In this chapter I have attempted to show the effects of the Indian partition on the status of women, their occlusion from the archive and how the events of the partition have continued to influence gender and sexuality in India since 1947. I have suggested that 1947 left a legacy for Indian women that has shaped attitudes about violence against women that became internationally visible in 2012 with the case of Nirbhaya. I have argued that the link between the two events, insofar as women are concerned, lies within the political/discursive shift that the public sphere underwent in India. An outcome of both these events has been that women have attained a few more rights as citizens. In locating these two moments within a cultural history, I have attempted to denaturalize the lives of Indian women who are generally located outside of the history of the public sphere and official history and outside of temporality, represented as a natural essence of being unchanged by the past and history. Indeed, the Indian woman has always been an underdeveloped figure for Indian history, always subordinate, always perceived to lack will, reason or any form of agency.[80] My intervention was not simply to recover her at two specific moments but also to rethink the pattern of independence history and what has been lost to view. The woman of the partition has not only been obscured from Indian history, but this obscuring has been premised to a large extent on women's irrelevance to political thought. The logic that excludes socially and hierarchically inferior beings or subalterns from rigorous analysis is connected to the logic that ignores the legacy of partition, while foregrounding the glorious struggle for independence. If the history of the partition has been a history of ethnic cleansing, murders, extreme violence, rapes, abductions and abandonment then, given its close imbrication with independence, one should concede that this latter event was not just a product of nonviolence but also of ethnic cleansing, murders, violence and so on. This foreclosure of partition history permits India to see contemporary communal violence and sexual violence against women as one-off events, and thus to avoid looking at the wider context and at trauma's compulsion to repeat itself. A more progressive sexual politics in India requires a willingness to look at how the past, in this case colonialism and partition, has shaped gender relations and to examine that which national history has occluded. I also wanted to see if any other meaning of partition women could be extrapolated beyond woman's victim status as she is located in Butalia and Menon and Bhasin's works. Indeed, I found the Subaltern Studies group's work very inspiring as well. For them, the subalterns were a people without history and Butalia's shocking tale of the lost ledger of names of partition abductees—names dislocated from history—made me see the connection between the two. I focussed on the opening of the public sphere to women to give a political aspect to the figure of the woman and to underscore the politics of her agency. In *Routine Violence*, Pandey posits the notion of a 'fragment', which resembles the Derridean supplement and which, he states, is not the dictionary's 'piece broken off' from a preconstituted whole. Rather, it is

> a disturbing element, a disturbance, a rupture, shall we say, in the self-presentation of particular totalities and those who uncritically uphold them. The mark of the fragment is that it resists the whole (the narrative). It cannot be assimilated into the narrative and its claim to wholeness. It speaks to us of what cannot be written of the whole (and indeed of the fragment), and in that sense becomes symptomatic of a particular claim to wholeness or completeness.[81]

One can say that the history of partition rapes functions as a fragment and forces the South Asianist scholar to read against the grain of the hegemonic history of independence. Another way of saying this is that *the occlusion of partition abductees becomes the condition by which the triumphant narrative of independence can be rendered.* But the fragment *does* interrupt this narrative and becomes 'an answer without a question'.[82] In this chapter, I have tried to formulate and answer the missing question, namely: Can we ascribe more meaning and significance to partition abductees than that of being 'victims' of spontaneous violence? The answer is clearly 'yes'.

NOTES

1. For more details, see the chapters on 'Facts' and 'Women' in Urvashi Butalia, *The Other Side of Silence: Voices from the Partition of India* (Durham, NC: Duke University Press, 2000). The chapter 'Facts' is on pp. 53–84 and 'Women' is on pp. 85–136.
2. Only since 1997, fifty years after partition, have South Asian scholars started engaging with affect in the reading of this event. Previously the focus had been solely from traditional engagements in politics and history about the facts that surrounded this event. See, for instance, Gyanendra Pandey, *Remembering Partition: Violence, Nationalism and History in India* (Cambridge: Cambridge University Press, 2004);

also see his work, *Routine Violence: Nations, Fragments, Histories* (Palo Alto: Stanford University Press, 2006) and Kavita Daiya, *Violent Belongings: Partition, Gender, and National Culture in Postcolonial India* (Philadelphia: Temple University Press, 2008).

3. Rupert Brooke, *1914 and Other Poems* (London: Sidgwick and Jackson, 1917).

4. See Doreen Massey, *Space, Place and Gender* (Minneapolis: Minnesota University Press, 1994); Radhika Mohanram, *Black Body: Women, Colonialism and Space* (Minneapolis: Minnesota University Press, 1999); David Harvey, *Spaces of Capital: Towards a Critical Geography* (London: Routledge, 2001); Steve Pile and Nigel Thrift, eds., *Mapping the Subject: Geographies of Cultural Transformation* (New York and London: Routledge, 1995).

5. See George Mosse, *Nationalism and Sexuality: Middle Class Morality and Sexual Norms* (Madison: University of Wisconsin Press, 1985).

6. See Sigmund Freud, 'The Question of Lay Analysis', in James Strachey, ed., *Standard Edition of the Complete Psychological Works of Sigmund Freud, Vol XX*, trans. A. P. Markaer-Branden (London: Vintage, 1999), 211.

7. As quoted in Kaja Silverman, *The Acoustic Mirror: The Female Voice in Psychoanalysis and Cinema* (Bloomington and Indianapolis: Indiana University Press, 1988), 102. Also see Julia Kristeva's chapter on 'The Semiotic and Symbolic' in *Revolution in Poetic Language* (New York: Columbia University Press, 1984), 19–132.

8. Georg Hegel, *Phenomenology of Spirit*, trans. A. V. Miller (Oxford: Clarendon Press, 1977).

9. See the vast corpus of Michel Foucault's works, especially *Madness and Civilization* (New York: Vintage, 2006); *Discipline and Punish*, trans. Alan Sheridan (New York: Vintage 1979); *The Birth of the Clinic*, trans. Sheridan-Smith (New York: Vintage 1977).

10. See Faisal Fatehali Devji, 'Hindu/Muslim/Indian', *Public Culture* 5, no. 1 (Fall 1992): 1.

11. Circumcision as an identifying mark in the discursive field of sameness and otherness is the focus of Derrida's 'Shibboleth' on Paul Celan's use of language, a work which opens up alternative readings of circumcision beyond their religious and cultural significance. In the Old Testament in *Judges*, the Hebrew word 'shibboleth' was used as a test to distinguish the Gileadites from the Ephraimites—the latter being unable to pronounce the 'sh' sound of the word. They could only pronounce it as 'si', as a result of which they were not given a safe passage across the Jordan and that resulted in the slaughter of forty-two thousand Ephraimites. Thus, the word was the diacritical difference that could spell the difference between life and death and, for Derrida, 'marks the multiplicity within language, insignificant difference as the condition of meaning'. Here Derrida points out that the insignificant difference between 'Si' and 'Shi' (in the pronunciation of the term 'Shibboleth'), which is the condition of the granting of safe passage or the denial of life, is like the circumcision or the mark of the Jew which is the visible difference between belonging and not belonging. This mark of difference, additionally, becomes comprehensible *only in relation to a particular site or place*. The mark thus allowed both to participate as well as to set apart. In this reading of circumcision, Derrida suggests that it could also be seen for

its potential to discover, to invent, to come upon something new and the coming of the other. See Derrida, 'Shibboleth for Paul Celan', in Aris Fioretos, ed., *Word Traces: Readings of Paul Celan*, trans. Joshua Wilner (Baltimore: Johns Hopkins University Press, 1994), 31. Also see John Caputo, *The Prayers and Tears of Jacques Derrida* (Bloomington: Indiana University Press, 1997), 251–52.

12. See Joya Chatterji, 'South Asian Histories of Citizenship, 1946-1970', *The Historical Journal* 55, no. 4 (Dec. 2012): 1052–53.

13. See chapter 'Blood on the Tracks' in Yasmin Khan, *The Great Partition: The Making of India and Pakistan* (New Haven, CT and London: Yale University Press, 2007).

14. See Allen Feldman, *Formations of Violence: The Narrative of Body and Political Terror in Northern Ireland* (Chicago and London: University of Chicago Press, 1991). See especially the chapter 'Spatial Formations of Violence'.

15. These lines are a reference to Marx's 'The Eighteenth Brumaire of Louis Bonaparte' written in 1853. These lines were made famous by Edward Said, who used it as an epigraph to his ground-breaking *Orientalism.* But Said himself misuses the sense in which Marx had originally written it. Marx had referred to the poverty-stricken French peasants who were small holders who could not unite and enforce their interests in their own name. Marx said of these peasants, 'They cannot represent themselves. They must be represented. Their representative at the same time must appear as their master'. See Karl Marx and Frederick Engels, *Selected Works*, vol. 1 (Moscow: Progress Publishers, 1969–1970), 303. But in *Orientalism*, Said uses the term 'represent' not in a political sense as Marx intended it, but rather as meaning 'depiction'. See Edward Said, *Orientalism* (New York: Vintage Press, 1978). In my context, the Partition women could not mean anything on their own but came into meaning only as the property of men. Violating women, then, was meant to be a violation of men; only the men's bodies were not the ones being violated.

16. Wagah is a Pakistani village near the Radcliffe Line that marks the border between India and Pakistan. (In India, the bordering village is called Atari.) The Wagah border ceremony takes place at the gate two hours before sunset and consists of a coordinated flag-lowering ceremony and high drama and theatrical aggression from soldiers on both sides. This ceremony is very popular with tourists but some of the audience find it a bit appalling.

17. The Shimla agreement was signed in 1972 by Indira Gandhi and Zulfikar Ali Bhutto after the 1971 war between India and Pakistan. It was a comprehensive agreement to promote good, neighbourly relations between the two countries.

18. See, for instance, the chapter 'Honourably Dead' in Ritu Menon and Kamala Bhasin, *Borders and Boundaries: Women in India's Partition* (New Brunswick: Rutgers University Press, 1998), 31–64.

19. The two governments of India and Pakistan quickly recognized that female citizens had a symbolic value as well and signed an Inter-Dominian Agreement in December 1947 for the recovery of women. However, cultural taboos coupled with issues considered more important meant that two years later, in December 1949, only around 18,800 women out of an estimated 100,000 or more who had been abducted

were recovered and returned on both sides of the border. See 'Borders and Bodies' in Menon and Bhasin, *Borders and Boundaries*, 69–70.

20. Michel Foucault, *The History of Sexuality, Volume 1: An Introduction*, trans. Robert Hurley (New York: Vintage, 1978).

21. George Mosse, 'Nationalism and Respectability: Normal and Abnormal Sexuality in the Nineteenth Century', *Journal of Contemporary History* 17, no. 2 (April 1982): 229.

22. See Menon and Bhasin's *Borders and Boundaries* and Butalia, *The Other Side of Silence* for some of the earliest analyses of women's lives in the partition. That they only have been published fifty years after the partition suggests the muting of women's voices in the recording of history of this event.

23. See, for instance, Soutik Biswas, 'Why India's Rape Crisis Shows No Sign of Abating', BBC.co.uk, 17 April 2018, http://www.bbc.co.uk/news/world-asia-india-43782471 (accessed 19 April 2018); also Manveena Suri, 'Indian Women's Commissioner on Hunger Strike over Rape Laws', CNN.com, 18 April 2018, https://edition.cnn.com/2018/04/18/asia/india-bjp-rape-law-hunger-strike-intl/index.html (accessed 19 April 2018); see Ellen Barry and Mansi Choksi, 'Gang Rape in India, Routine and Invisible', *New York Times*, 27 October 2013, https://www.nytimes.com/2013/10/27/world/asia/gang-rape-in-india-routine-and-invisible.html (accessed 19 April 2018).

24. The newspaper *Indian Express* reported that over 34,600 rapes were reported in India. See 'Over 34,600 Rape Cases in India, Delhi Tops among Union Territories', *Indian Express*, 30 August 2016, http://indianexpress.com/article/india/india-news-india/over-34600-rape-cases-in-india-delhi-tops-among-union-territories-3004487/ (accessed 19 June 2017). This figure doesn't include the unreported rape figures which is calculated as only one rape in thirty being reported. See 'Majority of Rape Cases Go Unreported', *The Hindu*, 27 August 2013, http://www.thehindu.com/todays-paper/tp-national/tp-newdelhi/majority-of-rape-cases-go-unreported-mps/article5063089.ece (accessed 19 June 2017).

25. See the sources of note 24.

26. See, for instance, Gayatri Spivak, 'Can the Subaltern Speak?' in Cary Nelson and Larry Grossberg, eds., *Marxism and the Interpretation of Culture* (Urbana: University of Illinois Press, 1988), 271–316.

27. See Debali Mookerjea Leonard, 'Quarantined: Women and the Partition', *Comparative Studies of South Asia, Africa and the Middle East* 24, no. 1 (2004): 37.

28. The term 'trace' in French, translated as 'trace' in English, is rich, dense and saturated with meaning that is linked to a variety of significant Derridean terminologies: différance, supplément, writing and even hauntology. This notion of trace is central to Derrida's *Of Grammatology*, which is generally perceived as a supplement to Saussure's theory of the sign. See Jacques Derrida, *Of Grammatology*, trans. Gayatri Chakravorty Spivak (Baltimore and London: Johns Hopkins University Press, 1976). In *Course on General Linguistics*, Saussure points out that the function of the signifier is to give access to the signified, showing its investment in logocentrism. Moreover, in Saussure, writing is simply a means of representing speech. Derrida posits the primacy of writing over speech (speech as a form of writing rather than the other

way around), and deconstructing the relationship between speech and writing. In this, *Of Grammatology* functions like a supplement (an inessential extra to something complete which simultaneously undercuts that which is complete as it supplements its lack) to Saussure's work.

29. Jenny Yusin, 'The Silence of Partition: Borders, Trauma and Partition History', *Social Semiotics* 19, no. 4 (2009): 454.

30. In 2017, seventy years after the partition, India has finally acknowledged the profound losses of the refugees of 1947, not in terms of territory or property but in terms of emotions that cohere around it, by opening a museum to this historical event in Amritsar. It is the only museum dedicated to partition in all of South Asia.

31. Butalia, *The Other Side of Silence*, 107.

32. Ibid., 108–09.

33. Ibid., 107.

34. See Veena Das, *Life and Words: Violence and the Descent into the Ordinary* (Berkeley: University of California Press, 2007).

35. Michel Foucault, *The Archaeology of Knowledge*, trans. A. M. Sheridan Smith (New York: Pantheon Books, 1972), 127, 129. Emphasis in original.

36. Jacques Derrida, *Archive Fever: A Freudian Impression* (Chicago: University of Chicago Press, 1998).

37. Spivak, 'Can the Subaltern Speak', 286.

38. Butalia, *The Other Side of Silence*, 129–30.

39. Veena Das, 'Language and Body: Transactions in the Construction of Pain', in Arthur Kleinman, Veena Das and Margaret Lock, eds., *Social Suffering* (Berkeley: University of California Press, 1997), 84.

40. Das, *Life and Words*, 21. Emphasis in the original.

41. The origins of the liberal tradition lie in its critique of patriarchy. In his *Second Treatise* (1689), John Locke suggests that political power is different from patriarchal power exerted by the monarch or father figure in that it requires *consent* from free and equal adult individuals. In contradistinction to monarchy, in a Republic, in liberal thought private persons were not defined as powerless but as having 'publicly relevant rights'. Michael Warner, *Publics and Counterpublics* (New York: Zone Books, 2005), 39.

42. See, for instance, Carole Pateman, *The Sexual Contract* (Cambridge: Polity, 1988), and *The Disorder of Women* (Cambridge: Polity, 1989). Also Michelle Zimbalist Rosaldo, 'Women, Culture and Society: A Theoretical Overview', in Michelle Zimbalist Rosaldo and Louise Lamphere, eds., *Women, Culture and Society* (Palo Alto, CA: Stanford University Press, 1989) and Jean Bethke Elshtain, *Public Man, Private Woman: Woman in Social and Political Thought* (Princeton, NJ: Princeton University Press, 1981).

43. See, for instance, Nancy Fraser's critique of both Habermas and second-wave feminism in 'Rethinking the Public Sphere', in Craig Calhoun, ed., *Habermas and the Public Sphere* (Cambridge, MA and London: MIT Press, 1997), 109–42. Fraser's objection to such a conflation is because 'it has practical political consequences when, for example, agitational campaigns against misogynist cultural representations are confounded with programs for state censorship or when struggles to deprivatize house-

work and child care are equated with their commodification. In both of these cases the result is to occlude the question of whether to subject gender issues to the logic of the market or of the administrative state is to promote the liberation of women' (p. 110).

44. Michael Warner points out the various meanings that adhere to these two associated terms that are often defined against each other. For instance, the hierarchically superior term 'public' included meanings of what is open to everyone, accessible for money, the public sector, official, impersonal, national, outside the home and circulated in print. The term 'private' carried overtones of what is restricted, nonstate, nonpolitical, nonofficial, personal, concealed, domestic and only circulated orally. Warner, *Publics and Counterpublics*, 29.

45. For Kant, 'public' and 'private' are terms which are closely linked to freedom and enlightenment, both terms being constituted by reason and common sense. (Kant distinguishes between the use of public and private reason and states, 'By "public use of one's reason" I mean that use which a man, as *scholar*, makes of it before the reading public. I call "private use" that use which a man makes of his reason in a civic post that has been entrusted to him'. Immanuel Kant, 'Answering the Question: What is Enlightenment', in James Schmidt (ed.) *What is Enlightenment?: Eighteenth-Century Answers and Twentieth-Century Questions* (Berkley: University of California Press, 1996), 58–64.

46. In contrast, for Locke, a critical public had to be aligned with a state or a national people.

47. Habermas, *The Structural Transformation of the Public Sphere*, 27.

48. Ibid., 106. He states, 'The bourgeois public sphere may be conceived above all as the sphere of private people come together as a public; they soon claimed the public sphere regulated from above against the public authorities themselves, to engage them in a debate over the general rules governing relations in a debate in the basically privatized but publically relevant sphere of commodity exchange and social labour'.

49. See Bipan Chandra, Mridula Mukherjee and Aditya Mukherjee, *India Since Independence, 1947–2000* (Gurgaon, India: Penguin, 2000), 3, 19.

50. See Partha Chatterjee, 'Nationalist Resolution of the Women's Question', in Kumkum Sangari and Sudesh Vaid, eds., *Recasting Women: Essays in Colonial History* (New Delhi: Kali for Women Press, 1989), 233–53.

51. Ibid., 247–48.

52. See Ann Cevtkovich, *The Archive of Feelings: Trauma, Sexuality and Lesbian Public Cultures* (Durham, NC: Duke University Press, 2003), 7.

53. Rosann Kennedy, 'An Australian Archive of Feelings', *Australian Feminist Studies* 26, no. 69 (2011): 257–79.

54. See Nancy Fraser, 'Rethinking the Public Sphere: A Contribution to the Critique of Actually Existing Democracy', *Social Text*, 25/25 (1990): 56–80. She states:

> On the contrary, virtually contemporaneous with the bourgeois public there arose a host of competing counterpublics, including nationalist publics, popular peasant publics, elite women's publics, and working class publics. . . . [T]he relations between bourgeois publics and other publics were always conflictual. Virtually from the beginning, counterpublics contested the exclusionary norms of the bourgeois public, elaborating alternative styles of political behavior and

alternative norms of public speech. Bourgeois publics, in turn, excoriated these alternatives and deliberately sought to block broader participation. (61)

55. Lauren Berlant, 'The Subject of True Feeling: Pain, Privacy and Politics', in Austin Sarat and Thomas R. Kearns, eds., *Cultural Pluralism, Identity Politics and the Law* (Ann Arbor: University of Michigan Press, 1999), 53.

56. Lauren Berlant and Michael Warner, 'Sex in Public', in Warner, *Publics and Counterpublics*, 549.

57. Naila Kabeer, 'Marriage, Motherhood and Masculinity in the Global Economy: Reconfigurations of Personal and Economic Life', *Institute of Development Studies Working Papers* 290 (2007), 12.

58. Ibid., 12.

59. Deborah Tudor, 'Twenty-First Century Neoliberal Man', in Jyotsna Kapur and Keith Wagner, eds., *Neoliberalism and Global Cinema: Capital, Culture and Marxist Critique* (New York and London: Routledge, 2011), 59–75.

60. Ibid., 60.

61. Ashwini Tambe and Shruti Tambe, 'Sexual Incitement, Spectatorship and Economic Liberalization in Contemporary India', *Interventions* 15, no. 4 (2013): 495.

62. Gargi Bhattacharya as cited in ibid., 496.

63. See Tithi Bhattacharya, 'Explaining Gender Violence in the Neoliberal Era', *International Socialist Review*, 91 (Winter 2013–2014). https://isreview.org/issue/91 (accessed 17 June 2017).

64. Ibid., n.p.

65. Ibid.

66. See Cynthia Enloe, *Bananas, Beaches and Bases: Making Feminist Sense of International Politics*, second edition (Berkeley: University of California Press, 2014), 279.

67. See Mrinalini Sinha, *Colonial Masculinity: The 'Manly Englishman' and the 'Effeminate Bengali' in the Late Nineteenth Century* (Manchester: Manchester University Press, 1995).

68. Ibid., 2.

69. See Radhika Mohanram, *Imperial White: Race, Diaspora, and the British Empire* (Minneapolis: University of Minnesota Press, 2007).

70. Sinha, *Colonial Masculinity*, 2.

71. Das, 'Language and Body', 86.

72. Kumari Jayawardena, *Feminism and Nationalism in the Third World* (London: Zed Press, 1986), 97.

73. Ketu Katrak, 'Indian Nationalism, Gandhian "Satyagraha" and Representations of Female Sexuality', in Andrew Parker, Mary Russo, Doris Sommer and Patricia Yaeger, eds., *Nationalisms and Sexuality* (New York: Routledge, 1992), 395.

74. See Veena Das, *Critical Events: An Anthropological Perspective on Contemporary India* (New Delhi: Oxford University Press, 1996), 5. Das uses Francois Furet's work on the French revolution 'as an event *par excellence* because it instituted *a new modality of historical action* which was not inscribed in the inventory of the situation'.

75. Menon and Bhasin, *Borders and Boundaries*, 133.

76. Ibid., 169.

77. Karuna Chanana, 'Partition and Family Strategies: Gender Education Linkages among Punjabi Women in Delhi', *Economic & Political Weekly* 28, no. 17 (April 24, 1993): 25.

78. Chandra, Mukherjee and Aditya Mukherjee, *India Since Independence, 1947–2000*, 641.

79. Ibid., 642.

80. See the final section of Spivak's 'Can the Subaltern Speak', 90–104 for an elaboration of this understanding.

81. Gyanendra Pandey, *Routine Violence: Nations, Fragments, Histories* (Stanford, CA: Stanford University Press, 2006), 66–67.

82. Althusser as quoted in Gyanendra Pandey, 'Subaltern Citizens and their Histories', *Interventions: International Journal of Postcolonial Studies* 10, no. 3 (2008): 278.

REFERENCES

Barry, Ellen, and Mansi Choksi. 2013. 'Gang Rape in India, Routine and Invisible'. *New York Times*. 27 October. https://www.nytimes.com/2013/10/27/world/asia/gang-rape-in-india-routine-and-invisible.html (accessed 19 April 2018).

Berlant, Lauren. 1999. 'The Subject of True Feeling: Pain, Privacy and Politics'. In *Cultural Pluralism, Identity Politics and the Law*, edited by Austin Sarat and Thomas R. Kearns, 43–84. Ann Arbor: University of Michigan Press.

Bhattacharya, Tithi. 2013. 'Explaining Gender Violence in the Neoliberal Era'. *International Socialist Review* 91 (Winter 2013–2014). https://isreview.org/issue/91 (accessed 17 June 2017).

Biswas, Soutik. 2018. 'Why India's Rape Crisis Shows No Sign of Abating'. BBC.co.uk. 17 April. http://www.bbc.co.uk/news/world-asia-india-43782471 (accessed 19 April 2018).

Brooke, Rupert. 1917. *1914 and Other Poems*. London: Sidgwick and Jackson.

Butalia, Urvashi. 2000. *The Other Side of Silence: Voices from the Partition of India.* Durham, NC: Duke University Press.

Caputo, John. 1997. *The Prayers and Tears of Jacques Derrida.* Bloomington: Indiana University Press.

Chanana, Karuna. 1993. 'Partition and Family Strategies: Gender Education Linkages among Punjabi Women in Delhi'. *Economic & Political Weekly* 28 (17): 25–34.

Chandra, Bipan, Mridula Mukherjee and Aditya Mukherjee. 2000. *India Since Independence, 1947–2000*. Gurgaon, India: Penguin Books.

Chatterjee, Partha. 1989. 'Nationalist Resolution of the Women's Question'. In *Recasting Women: Essays in Colonial History*, edited by Kumkum Sangari and Sudesh Vaid, 233–53. New Delhi: Kali for Women Press.

Chatterji, Joya. 2012. 'South Asian Histories of Citizenship, 1946–1970'. *The Historical Journal* 55 (4): 1049–71.

Cvetkovich, Ann. 2003. *The Archive of Feelings: Trauma, Sexuality and Lesbian Public Cultures.* Durham, NC: Duke University Press.
Daiya, Kavita. 2008. *Violent Belongings: Partition, Gender, and National Culture in Postcolonial India.* Philadelphia: Temple University Press.
Das, Veena. 1996. *Critical Events: An Anthropological Perspective on Contemporary India.* New Delhi: Oxford University Press.
———. 1997. 'Language and Body: Transactions in the Construction of Pain'. In *Social Suffering*, edited by Arthur Kleinman, Veena Das and Margaret Lock. Berkeley: University of California Press.
———. 2007. *Life and Words: Violence and the Descent into the Ordinary.* Berkeley: University of California Press.
Derrida, Jacques. 1976. *Of Grammatology.* Translated by Gayatri Chakravorty Spivak. Baltimore and London: Johns Hopkins University Press.
———. 1994. 'Shibboleth for Paul Celan'. Translated by Joshua Wilner. In *Word Traces: Readings of Paul Celan*, edited by Aris Fioretos, 3–74. Baltimore: Johns Hopkins University Press.
———. 1998. *Archive Fever: A Freudian Impression.* Chicago: University of Chicago Press.
Devji, Faisal Fatehali. 1992. 'Hindu/Muslim/Indian'. *Public Culture* 5 (1): 1–18.
Elshtain, Jean Bethke. 1981. *Public Man, Private Woman: Woman in Social and Political Thought.* Princeton, NJ: Princeton University Press.
Enloe, Cynthia. 2014. *Bananas, Beaches and Bases: Making Feminist Sense of International Politics*, second edition. Berkeley: University of California Press.
Feldman, Allen. 1991. *Formations of Violence: The Narrative of Body and Political Terror in Northern Ireland.* Chicago and London: University of Chicago Press.
Foucault, Michel. 1972. *The Archaeology of Knowledge.* Translated by A. M. Sheridan Smith. New York: Pantheon Books.
———. 1977. *The Birth of the Clinic.* Translated by Alan Sheridan Smith. New York: Vintage.
———. 1978. *The History of Sexuality, Volume 1: An Introduction.* Translated by Robert Hurley. New York: Vintage.
———. 1979. *Discipline and Punish.* Translated by Alan Sheridan. New York: Vintage.
———. 2006. *Madness and Civilization.* New York: Vintage.
Fraser, Nancy. 1990. 'Rethinking the Public Sphere: A Contribution to the Critique of Actually Existing Democracy'. *Social Text* 25/25: 56–80.
———. 1997. 'Rethinking the Public Sphere'. In *Habermas and the Public Sphere*, edited by Craig Calhoun. Cambridge, MA, and London: MIT Press.
Freud, Sigmund. 1999. 'The Question of Lay Analysis'. Translated by A. P. Markaer-Branden. In *Standard Edition of the Complete Psychological Works of Sigmund Freud, Vol XX*, edited by James Strachey, 177–258. London: Vintage.
Habermas, Jürgen. 1989. *The Structural Transformation of the Public Sphere: An Inquiry into the Category of Bourgeois Society.* Trans. Thomas Burger. Cambridge, MA: MIT Press.
Harvey, David. 2001. *Spaces of Capital: Towards a Critical Geography.* London: Routledge.

Hegel, Georg. 1977. *Phenomenology of Spirit*. Translated by A. V. Miller. Oxford: Clarendon Press.
Jayawardena, Kumari. 1986. *Feminism and Nationalism in the Third World*. London: Zed Press.
Kabeer, Naila. 2007. 'Marriage, Motherhood and Masculinity in the Global Economy: Reconfigurations of Personal and Economic Life'. *Institute of Development Studies Working Papers* 290.
Katrak, Ketu. 1992. 'Indian Nationalism, Gandhian 'Satyagraha' and Representations of Female Sexuality'. In *Nationalisms and Sexuality*, edited by Andrew Parker, Mary Russo, Doris Sommer and Patricia Yaeger, 395–406. New York: Routledge.
Kennedy, Rosann. 2011. 'An Australian Archive of Feelings'. *Australian Feminist Studies* 26 (69): 257–79.
Khan, Yasmin. 2007. *The Great Partition: The Making of India and Pakistan*. New Haven, CT and London: Yale University Press.
Kristeva, Julia. 1984. *Revolution in Poetic Language*. New York: Columbia University Press.
'Majority of Rape Cases Go Unreported'. 2013. *The Hindu*. 27 August. http://www.thehindu.com/todays-paper/tp-national/tp-newdelhi/majority-of-rape-cases-go-unreported-mps/article5063089.ece (accessed 19 June 2017).
Marx, Karl, and Frederick Engels. 1969. *Selected Works*, vol 1. Moscow: Progress Publishers.
Massey, Doreen. 1994. *Space, Place and Gender*. Minneapolis: Minnesota University Press.
Menon, Ritu, and Kamala Bhasin. 1998. *Borders and Boundaries: Women in India's Partition*. New Brunswick, NJ: Rutgers University Press.
Mohanram, Radhika. 1999. *Black Body: Women, Colonialism and Space*. Minneapolis: University of Minnesota Press.
———. 2007. *Imperial White: Race, Diaspora, and the British Empire*. Minneapolis: University of Minnesota Press.
Mookerjea Leonard, Debali. 2004. 'Quarantined: Women and the Partition'. *Comparative Studies of South Asia, Africa and the Middle East* 24 (1): 35–50. https://doi.org/10.1215/1089201X-24-1-35.
Mosse, George. 1982. 'Nationalism and Respectability: Normal and Abnormal Sexuality in the Nineteenth Century'. *Journal of Contemporary History* 17 (2): 221–46.
———. 1985. *Nationalism and Sexuality: Middle Class Morality and Sexual Norms*. Madison: University of Wisconsin Press.
'Over 34,600 Rape Cases in India, Delhi Tops among Union Territories'. 2016. *Indian Express*. August 30. http://indianexpress.com/article/india/india-news-india/over-34600-rape-cases-in-india-delhi-tops-among-union-territories-3004487/ (accessed 19 June 2017).
Pandey, Gyanendra. 2004. *Remembering Partition: Violence, Nationalism and History in India*. Cambridge: Cambridge University Press.
———. 2006. *Routine Violence: Nations, Fragments, Histories*. Palo Alto, CA: Stanford University Press.

———. 2008. 'Subaltern Citizens and Their Histories'. *Interventions: International Journal of Postcolonial Studies* 10 (3): 271–84.

Pateman, Carole. 1988. *The Sexual Contract.* Cambridge: Polity.

———.1989. *The Disorder of Women.* Cambridge: Polity.

Pile, Steve, and Nigel Thrift, eds. 1995. *Mapping the Subject: Geographies of Cultural Transformation.* New York and London: Routledge.

Rosaldo, Michelle Zimbalist. 1989. 'Women, Culture and Society: A Theoretical Overview'. In *Women, Culture and Society*, edited by Michelle Zimbalist Rosaldo and Louise Lamphere. Palo Alto, CA: Stanford University Press.

Said, Edward. 1978. *Orientalism*. New York: Vintage.

Silverman, Kaja. 1988. *The Acoustic Mirror: The Female Voice in Psychoanalysis and Cinema.* Bloomington and Indianapolis: Indiana University Press.

Sinha, Mrinalini. 1995. *Colonial Masculinity: The 'Manly Englishman' and the 'Effeminate Bengali' in the Late Nineteenth Century.* Manchester: Manchester University Press.

Spivak, Gayatri. 1988. 'Can the Subaltern Speak?' In *Marxism and the Interpretation of Culture*, edited by Cary Nelson and Larry Grossberg, 271–316. Urbana: University of Illinois Press.

Suri, Manveena. 2018. 'Indian Women's Commissioner on Hunger Strike over Rape Laws'. CNN.com. 18 April. https://edition.cnn.com/2018/04/18/asia/india-bjp-rape-law-hunger-strike-intl/index.html (accessed 19 April 2018).

Tambe, Ashwini, and Shruti Tambe. 2013. 'Sexual Incitement, Spectatorship and Economic Liberalization in Contemporary India'. *Interventions* 15 (4): 494–510.

Tudor, Deborah. 2011. 'Twenty-First Century Neoliberal Man'. In *Neoliberalism and Global Cinema: Capital, Culture and Marxist Critique*, edited by Jyotsna Kapur and Keith Wagner, 59–75. New York and London: Routledge.

Warner, Michael. 2005. *Publics and Counterpublics*. New York: Zone Books.

Yusin, Jenny. 2009. 'The Silence of Partition: Borders, Trauma and Partition History'. *Social Semiotics* 19 (4): 453–68.

Chapter 4

Lessons Not Learned from the Yugoslav Dismemberment and Their Implications for the European Union[1]

Stefano Bianchini

In an interview published by *Le Monde* in 2014, Jacques Rupnik remarked that 'the greatest obstacle to the Europeanization of the Balkans is the Balkanization of Europe'.

The sentence may be perceived to be too alarming, particularly in the circles that neglect the relevance of the Yugoslav war, or it may simply nurture the illusion that some sort of pacification in the region is under way. Actually, there are lessons not learned from the Yugoslav dismemberment whose cultural, mental and political implications are still producing effects. Moreover, the rationale of these lessons impact on a number of dynamics that affect the development of the European project. Therefore, they deserve to be analyzed and critically elaborated, rather than exorcized using stereotypes such as the 'Balkan violence' or its 'irremediable backwardness' or its 'long-century unsettled instability' and so on. On the contrary, in-depth considerations of the lessons not learned from Yugoslavia might be helpful in the identification of alternative patterns to be carried out in the European Union, particularly in the current historical phase, which is affected by a deep institutional, economic and cultural crisis while facing accelerated social changes. These social changes are marked by people's mobility, interculturality and syncretism, which are also rejected either socially or politically by important social sectors of the member states in terms of neonational (sometimes racist or xenophobic) resistances, which include a special emphasis on local traditions, ethnonational homogenization, one religion and homophobia.

1. UNDERESTIMATED LESSONS FROM THE YUGOSLAV DISMEMBERMENT

Basically, the general underestimation of the dynamics that led to the Yugoslav dismemberment is due to a variety of reasons: (a) the role of anticommunist feelings which were addressed not only towards the Soviet Union and its Camp, but also towards the nonaligned Yugoslavia, as Brzezinski explicitly stated in Uppsala in 1978 during the World Congress of Sociologists.[2] In particular, these feelings reinforced the Western predisposition to support secessionist nationalisms when they appeared to be functional to the weakening and, then, the eradication of communism; (b) a widespread Western belief that the violence that erupted in Yugoslavia was an evident manifestation of an uninterrupted, medieval 'Balkan' brutality, unrelated to the 'European democratic traditions'; (c) alternatively, that the violence was generated by nationalisms in opposition with each other, whose mutual hatred had been nurtured for centuries; and (d) the Western conviction that an international nonaligned position in Europe (Yugoslavia, in effect, promoted and led the Non-Aligned Movement) was unsustainable as soon as the socialist statehood experience started vanishing in the late 1980s.

By contrast, regardless of the ideology of the dictatorship of the proletariat and the predominant role of the League of Communists, the Yugoslav federalism deserves a special consideration since the way its institutions worked offers critical insights about the experimented mechanisms of representation and decision making in multinational societies.[3]

To explain briefly, Yugoslavia after the 1974 Constitution was closer to a confederation rather than a federation because of the remarkable empowerment of its units, the republics and the regions. A deep decentralization shifted *de facto* the key powers to the republics and the regions which were expected to negotiate and harmonize their interests within the federal bodies. With a yearly rotating presidency among these units, the representatives of the federal components had the right of veto, each of them having one vote regardless of the number of their members in the two parliamentary chambers. The federal government was set up on the basis of a rigid and well-balanced distribution of the responsibilities of the ministries among republics and regions. Moreover, the representative groups of republics and regions mirrored an ethnic ratio, according to the census outcomes, although both republics and regions were supposed to represent, within the highest federal bodies, all the six 'constituent peoples' of the federation (Serbs, Croats, Slovenes, Muslims, Montenegrins and Macedonians) and the two main minorities (Albanians and Hungarians).[4]

Given this institutional structure, a better understanding of what happened in the Yugoslav federation during the 1980s will widely improve our interdisciplinary and comparative knowledge of the nexus of partitions processes, geopolitical balances and the development of democracy. This analysis is underpinned by the *international interdependence* that European socialist countries increasingly developed as soon as destalinization and economic reforms were implemented from the second half of the 1950s onwards. Indeed, this is an aspect that has been essentially ignored by the literature in argument with rare exceptions. In effect, the communist parties gradually abandoned the Stalinist protectionist policy thanks to two main factors: the intensification of the relations with the newly established postcolonial states (the so-called 'Third World') and the access to international loans from the West.

Despite the existing differences between socialist states, their leaders pursued this policy of international openness even during the Brežnev stagnation (with the exception of Albania, which preferred a sharp isolation). However, Gorbačëv was the first high-ranked policy maker who explicitly elaborated both a domestic and foreign policy strategy based on the interdependence of 'three worlds' (the capitalist, the socialist and the nonaligned ones). In short, the implementation and public recognition of global interdependence had far-reaching consequences for the whole Socialist Camp in Europe. This was particularly true for Yugoslavia, which had not belonged to the Camp since 1948, but was a socialist country. Belgrade applied the most radical reforms in this regard, strengthening its own ties worldwide and implementing distinctive forms of pluralism, in spite of domestic social inequalities and political differentiations among republics.

In this way, however, interdependence, as an early form of globalization, deeply penetrated all of the socialist societies, especially the Yugoslav federation, playing a pivotal role in generating long-term, unpredictable, social and cultural consequences. The previous isolation policy, emphasized by the theories of the 'besieged fortress' and the 'socialism in one country',[5] later applied to an expanded Socialist Camp, proved to be unsustainable in the long term, while the will of competing internationally in a comprehensive way, including the promotion of social patterns worldwide, increased dependency. In other words, since the end of the 1950s, socialism began to compete with capitalism, promoting itself as the most effective model for postcolonial countries.[6] Under these circumstances, socialist societies gradually diversified, even if all of them originated, and remained ideologically inspired, by the Bolshevik revolution. The USSR, Yugoslavia and China, in particular, began to compete with the United States (and the West in general). The 'race' intensified globally but occurred under conditions that exposed socialist countries to fluctuating international contingencies, progressively contributing to encompassing them mentally within a wider European context. In the end, the variety within the European socialist experiences vanished.

These aspects rarely have been analyzed by scholars,[7] but are important because interdependence and globalization not only created the conditions for exhausting the communist 'otherness', but also produced the broader cultural framework which led—once the socialist system collapsed—to the widening and the deepening of the European Union, the brutal dismemberment of the Yugoslav federation and the partitioning of the Soviet Union and Czechoslovakia. Consequently, an analysis of the lessons not learned from the Yugoslav dismemberment requires us to keep in mind both the globalizing background and the dichotomy of comprehensive integration trends and national sovereign isolation demands. These were further compounded by three other issues: the impact of a prolonged economic crisis, ineffective governance and the quality of the appeals to mass mobilization.

a. The Implications of a Prolonged Economic Crisis

The first lesson concerns the impact that a prolonged economic crisis may generate in inter/multicultural societies. From the beginning of the 1980s, the Yugoslav economic crisis was characterized by a high foreign debt (20 billion dollars) with unproductive domestic investments. The amount of the debt was, to a large extent, contracted by republics and regions: therefore, in order to avoid nationalist recriminations on responsibilities and repayments, the federal government in Belgrade published only the total amount, classifying the debts by republics and regions. Then, restrictive austerity measures were adopted, with a drastic import reduction, in order to restore a budget balance. As a result, public investments rapidly declined, family consumerism (encouraged since 1965) was affected and the rate of unemployment increased which, then, coincided with the country being suddenly excluded from new technology developments, particularly in the field of IT. The existing gaps in development of the six republics (Slovenia, Croatia, Bosnia-Herzegovina, Serbia, Montenegro and Macedonia) and the two regions (Kosovo and Vojvodina) escalated severely. The perception that sacrifices were unequally distributed among republics and regions increased as well, thus fuelling frustrations and resentments. The sense of social and financial solidarity sharply declined, while mutual complaints about the quality of investments and the use of the money for the most underdeveloped regions escalated, weakening the credibility of the leaderships and raising their antagonisms. Meanwhile, the repayment of the foreign debt proved to be extremely costly. At the end of the decade Yugoslavia had paid the interest only for an amount equal to the debt, but not the debt itself.[8] Furthermore, because the crisis was deepening and Yugoslavia was a federation with a high level of devolution, the prevailing reaction of the authorities of the eight constituent units was to protect their local economies as much as they could. They also interfered in the business relations between republics and regions, thus hindering the definition and/or the application of contracts between enterprises. In so doing, they generated an economic nationalism, which had a detrimental impact on the unity of the Yugoslav market.[9]

***

Broadly speaking, the Yugoslav experience tells us a lot about the consequences generated when a long period of economic crisis is tackled with austerity measures without investments for growth, as the European Union has experimented since 2007 when the crisis of the sovereign debts exploded and monetary measures rather than social support investments have been taken. In a context of the rapid decline of the standard of life, increased unemployment and social impoverishment, restrictive measures produce divergent interests between the autonomous components of an integrated society and generate trends in support of economic nationalism.[10] These trends become particularly acute when the economic and social differences between regions (or states) are escalating and may encourage the adoption of a policy of 'everyone for him/herself' in blatant contrast with either the needs and the advantages of free trade, free circulation of capital, labor, people and services or the morality of solidarity and equality. The consequences are, on the one hand, a growing limitation of the exchanges within narrower geopolitical spaces, which trigger further economic effects of recession and on the other, a worsening of the relations between regions (or states), based on the perception that sacrifices are unequally distributed and financial resources are diverted to some territories to the detriment of others. Furthermore, the political economy polarization between budget policy priorities or expansive investments widens the gap not only in terms of strategies to be applied, but also in terms of social implications.[11] This situation can encourage local authorities, bankers or entrepreneurs to clamor for alternative solutions, derogations, differentiations, which can ultimately result, for example, in conflicting economic visions between the North and the South, in divisive currency policy proposals (for example the creation of two or three Eurozones) or in more radical decisions by suggesting to hold a referendum for quitting a currency, the European Union or an existing nation-state. The months-long controversial debate among EU member states over the strategies to be adopted on the Greek crisis, whether to offer a bailout (under stricter or softer conditions of reforms) or a hopefully agreed pathway to a

'Grexit' from the Euro is emblematic of the political atmosphere that has affected EU internal relations.[12] In substance, the arguments used to express discomfort within the European Union, member states or third parties in the Continent after the explosion of the economic and financial crisis in 2007 are to a large extent reminiscent of the arguments that opposed Slovenia, Serbia and Croatia between 1981 and 1988.

b. Problematic Governance

A second lesson concerns the effectiveness of governance and decision making. As mentioned above, Yugoslavia was a deeply decentralized federation, with both ethnic ratio and regular one-year rotations in all representative bodies at the federal level, in the eight constituent units exercising a *de facto* veto power and in the municipalities. These mechanisms concerned the state institutions at any level, the League of communists and other social organizations; even the supreme command of the army represented the ethnic plurality. Nevertheless, under a depressing economic context, the decision-making system crucially showed a lack of effectiveness. In a time of crisis, people need to understand who is responsible for what and how their civic and economic rights are protected.[13] Furthermore, they expect from leadership a vision, a strategy for a way out with decisional capacity in solving the problems and passing consistent institutional reforms, when needed and in time. Nevertheless, the Yugoslav federal system was unable to make rapid decisions, since the tortuous negotiations among the eight units of the federation with the need to achieve their consensus imposed a timetable increasingly incompatible with the quick economic requirements. Particularly problematic was the adoption of budgetary measures able to reduce significantly the welfare expenses without changing the political system (under the dictatorship of the proletariat), because the latter appeared to be ideologically intolerable.[14] As a result, the decision-making system was increasingly powerless in reforming welfare and when it was finally able to do so, it was too late for producing beneficial effects. Meanwhile, *ad hoc* commissions for reforms were established and worked for years without achieving any effective synthesis (this was in particular the case of the economic commission led by Sergej Krajger and the political commission led by Josip Vrhovec). The governmental attempts to introduce stimulating measures in economics and politics failed miserably because they were inadequate to the rapid worsening of the situation. Accordingly, Republics and Regions, as well as the population at large, increasingly did not see the advantages of sharing (ineffective) institutions; as a result, they started to search for alternatives (separation) outside Yugoslavia.[15]

***

Differently from socialist Yugoslavia, the EU member states are democratic states, but the decision-making system of the European Union has proved so far to be too slow and inadequate to face the crisis that started in 2008 with the sovereign debt, followed by a sharp decline of production and consumption. Divergent interests are multiplying as an effect of the economic crisis: different divides crosscut EU membership, from Eurozone policies to national Constitutional Courts invited to scrutinize the legitimacy of the decisions (as in the cases of Portugal, when austerity measures negotiated for the bailout were rejected in 2013, or Germany, when it was repeatedly requested to verify the compatibility of EU decisions with the national Constitution). Furthermore, the budgetary measures—required by the more economically successful countries—have imposed austerity measures and higher taxations, generating dramatic social costs. As a result, angry social protests are intensifying, particularly in Southern Europe. With the deepening of the North/South polarization, Eurosceptic and nationalist parties are trying to maximize their electoral benefits. In a search for consensus, they appeal for a 'return' to an imaginary sovereign nation-state, criticizing the hyperbureaucracy of 'Brussels' and/or their own central government. Since people have been educated for almost two centuries to nation-state values, the idea of returning to this political concept holds great appeal. Nevertheless, neonationalist arguments are increasingly conflicting with the everyday reality, marked by globalization and societal diversifications, which are two of the driving forces of a post-nation-state configuration. In such antithetical circumstances, the existing institutions (of both the European Union and its member states), being weakened by the financial crisis and inadequate to face it, are severely affected by multilevel challenges, while the dissatisfaction toward shared institutions is intensifying all over Europe. The Yugoslav federation experienced similar dynamics. Over the years, these dynamics threatened its society, where both multiculturalism and interculturalism operated. The former pertained to the institutional representation, based on an ethnic ratio without democracy, which restricted dialogue and mediation to ethnic group dynamics. The latter concerned a century-long social reality based on people's mobility, mixed marriages, education and cross-national university course enrollments, military service and the access to services. The simultaneous double crisis of (a) the economic (self-managed) system and (b) the institutional governance paved the way to a radical collapse of the federation, under the assumption that a democratic transition would have been possible only in its constituent units, rather than in a federal framework.[16] The latter assumption was encouraged (whether consciously, it may be debated) by the United States and the European Community. Neither ever insisted on pluralistic elections at the

Yugoslav federal level for Yugoslavia in 1990–1991, nor offered any alternative pattern in terms of democratic (or liberal) federalism to be followed in the post-Socialist transition. Despite the differences between Yugoslavia and the European Union (that is the former was a state under dictatorship, the latter is not a state, but an original conglomeration of democracies), similarities can be recognized, particularly in the tensions between (neo)nationalist and integrative arguments when supranational frameworks operate.

Therefore, under a prolonged economic crisis and with an inadequate governance, whether democracy is able to offer effective room for diversity management in intercultural contexts and stimulate people's support for shared, reformed institutions remains an open question.[17] Another question that cannot be excluded is whether the prospect of integration runs the risk of being overwhelmed by neonationalist discourses.

c. People's Mobilization in Time of Crisis

The third lesson refers to the quality of the appeals to people's mobilization in time of crisis. In general terms, historical experience shows that economic and institutional crisis encourages leadership to redefine their sources of legitimacy. In the Yugoslav case, this process was gradually influenced by the decline of the self-management system in the political and economic spheres. The decline affected the convincing role of ideology, which was the lever of power legitimacy in socialist societies. Consistently, political elites began to worry about their future role and look for electoral consensus. The *economic nationalism* and the institutional role of republics and regions offered to them the opportunity to rely increasingly on territory (soil) and people, rather than ideology. With the aim of defending local interests and its own power positions, the communist leadership began to criticize the 'hyper-bureaucracy of the federal government' in Belgrade. Slobodan Milošević particularly encouraged an 'anti-bureaucratic revolution'[18] that actually facilitated the shifting of the administrative personnel in republics and regions from the communist ideology to a visible support of nationalist discourses, meeting the arguments of those intellectuals, mainly from the humanities, who were endorsing a primordialist vision of the nation. This approach, in fact, appeared to be helpful in many respects as the mental and cultural borders of the nation are supposed to be clearly marked and the sense of belonging to the group could be reinforced in times of crises through a call to ethnic recognition and solidarity.

Ethno-identification between rulers and ruled sounded simpler and more effective. Appealing to emotions rather than to reason facilitated mass mobilization, fuelling resentments against the 'other', regarded as 'responsible' for the crisis. Additionally, this approach made possible convergence with that part of the anti-Communist émigré community that promoted a mental return to the past. Rather than an inspiring vector for the future, crimes soared as did a sense of injustices allegedly or effectively suffered. Historical revisionism became a crucial aspect of this process. This would not only distance the new political systems from the communist legacy and its ideology, but also offered the opportunity to rehabilitate local anticommunism as a 'patriotic' movement by obfuscating its Nazi and/or Fascist collaboration.

Within this context, the conflicting nationalist players with the increasing participation of religious leaders, especially of the Croatian Catholic Church, as if the Second World War was not yet over, acted and voiced fully in continuity with the animosities of fifty years earlier. In the end, a nexus was firmly established between soil and blood (or group homogenization) in full contrast to the existing in-depth intercultural individual relations within Yugoslavia. Predictably, this step paved the way to a new war and ethnic cleansing.

***

On the other hand, ethno-nationalist claims are only apparently less influential in the European Union and within member states. In reality, the political culture based on the 'us/them' polarization which adamantly rejects the 'other' (whatever category the 'other' falls into, in terms of gender, migrants, refugees or asylum seekers, EU citizens from another member state, people with different religious prescription, sexual orientation, transnational or cosmopolitan cultures, etc.), is vivid and shared by a growing number of political protagonists, activists and ordinary people. The reactions to the movement of refugees since 2015, mostly from the Southern Mediterranean and the Middle East to EU member states, has adamantly highlighted the antipathy toward the other. Racism, xenophobia and anti-Semitism are, in fact, well-rooted feelings in European populations, easily spread worldwide by social networks, despite the sharp rejection of these emotions by the democratic political cultures, civil societies projects of inclusion and EU institutional behaviors/recommendations. Migration flows, both between EU member states and from third countries, have been manipulated mainly by far right and anti-EU parties (but also by media, particularly when they have to report news on criminality), which aim to inflame a mass hysteria against 'otherness'. The economic crisis and the search for a job are additional contexts that contribute to inflaming contentious situations when the opportunities for employment are offered to migrants: the United Kingdom's Prime Minister Cameron's suggestion in October 2014 to reduce even the mobility of EU citizens coming to the United Kingdom was not only a violation of a key value of the EU integration, but it was also a dramatic concession to policies of exclusiveness promoted by the far right as well as a cultural failure of the Conservative Party. In fact, public opinions are often and increasingly influenced by these attitudes; sometimes even democratic movements have been culturally contaminated by these phenomena and democratic parties have compromised because of the prevalence of these narratives. As a result, the third lesson that stems from the Yugoslav tragedy concerns the mechanisms that determine how mutual trust evaporates and the sense of threat that spreads within and among ethnic groups or nations when discriminatory and exclusive policies are justified and claimed. In the end, instead of strengthening democracy, the homogenization of the groups on the basis of the 'us/them' dichotomy demolishes the bridges of communication and threatens peace.

2. THE POLITICAL MORALITY OF THE LESSONS NOT LEARNED AND THE LIMITS OF EU SOFT-POWER

In addition to the above-discussed main lessons, a fourth one can be also considered: Actually, its character is mainly encoded into the local (Balkan) context. Nevertheless, as the reader will see, this lesson includes a crucial political morality, whose implications concern liberal ideology, the political culture of the nation-state and Western political behavior, with evident implications for the Soft-Power policy of the European Union.[19] In a sense, the considerations that follow are a direct consequence of the three aforementioned lessons, but their content easily reminds us of Rupnik's sentence quoted at the beginning of this chapter. In fact, his alarming statement mirrors a broader concern about the mutual flow of 'negative' interdependences, which stem from either the lack of will to pass key reforms in the Western Balkans or the EU's reluctance to further enlargements (summarized by 'enlargement fatigue' and 'lack of absorption capacity'). To a large extent, this behavior did not motivate post-Yugoslav élites to support reconciliation, cooperation, integration and consistent reforms.

Undeniably, the European Union has undertaken a long-term commitment to supporting peace and stabilization in the Balkans since the beginning of the 1990s, but its concrete improvements in the region largely depend on, and are deeply affected by, the way peace has been established between the Yugoslav successor states, as argued here below. Furthermore, the EU project faces difficulties since the Constitutional treaty had been rejected in 2005, thus leading to the question of whether local authorities would reform local institutions by making them institutionally compatible with membership, bringing about EU integration.

In 1995, in fact, a fragile peace treaty, the Dayton agreement, was imposed by US and EU diplomats to the warlords (that is, the warring leaders of the

Yugoslav successor states). The agreement successfully put an end to the war in Bosnia-Herzegovina, but the ethno-national compromise that dominated the agreement made postwar decision making impossible, affecting the prospective peace consolidation.[20]

This failure, however, depended to a large extent on the political culture of the nation-states that the diplomacies of the United States and European Union perversely continued to comply with during the consultations with the warring parties. Consistently acting on the basis of this cultural background, they negotiated the peace with leaders who have a crucial war goal: the establishment of ethnic-homogeneous nation-states. Despite the Western diplomats' rejection of violence, there was a close cultural predisposition from both sides to find a solution that respected *de facto* a 'shared rationale', based on the supremacy of ethno-national homogenization. Admittedly, they were speaking the same 'national language' (even if with different interpretations). Therefore, the morality of the ethnic separation deeply shaped the Dayton agreement.

When Western diplomats realized the mistake, they negotiated a different accord for Macedonia in 2001 in Ohrid, rejecting partition in entities, confirming the unity of the state, and assuming the municipal devolution to be the unique acceptable compromise able to guarantee an equal representation of ethnic groups. In other words, while the Dayton agreement strengthened *de facto* the ethnic partition of people with its configuration of cantons and entities (although preserving a loose common framework), the Ohrid agreement limited the ethno-territorial devolution to municipalities, ascribing greater competencies to state institutions.

Consequently, a contradictory message was launched, since these agreements (and the others that were signed between 1995 and 2003) could be interpreted either as a temporary achievement *before* the final state partition, or as the *first step toward* the preservation of the territorial unity and leading to national reintegration.[21] Consistent with this equivocal rationale, even when social unrests emerged unconnected to ethnicity, as occurred for a short while in Bosnia-Herzegovina in February 2014,[22] the political parties not only in Bosnia-Herzegovina, but also in Croatia and Serbia, reinterpreted the events in ethnic terms, trying to silence any other discourse.

Ultimately, the Dayton agreement represents a cultural defeat of the Western liberal vision based on a pretended supremacy of the 'civic nation', but whose main characteristics have been deeply tarnished by the predominant and broader ethnic solutions incorporated into the agreement. This paradoxical outcome was generated not only by the influential role of the warlords during the negotiations, but also—and more disturbingly—by the substantial cultural convergence of the Western diplomacy, whose ethno-national inclinations actually remained on track, even when it was publicly rejected.

This effect is not surprising, if considered in the light of the historical experiences of the twentieth century. The civic/ethno ambivalence in liberal praxis has emerged repeatedly since the House Inquiry, the *ad hoc* US presidential commission established in 1917, presented their conclusions on desirable peace arrangements after World War I to President Wilson, when he was elaborating his famous fourteen points.[23] Similarly, the way in which Great Britain withdrew from its various colonies is also indicative of ethno-national inclinations. London rarely transferred civic values together with independence, as the ethno-national instabilities generated by the British *divide et impera* policy have confirmed in India, South Africa, Cyprus and the Middle East.

Furthermore, the lack of recognition of any minorities in France stems from a rooted liberal belief, according to which primacy is assigned to the rights of *citoyens* as individuals, therefore undermining the impact of assimilation policies, which are—or have been—actually practised (and sometimes even violently pursued in the past). This approach has been absorbed by other countries in different contexts, where the obsession for security and territorial integrity has coincided with the belief that citizenship rights should be granted to an ethno-national homogeneous population without minorities. Greece and Turkey are two, among other significant examples in this regard, that have been inspired by the French political culture. The monarchic interpretation of Yugoslavism and the Czechoslovakism of Tomáš Masaryk between the two World Wars are additional examples in this sense.

Truly, most of these beliefs have been softened after the Second World War, particularly under the process of European integration. For instance, Italy has recognized minority languages in its Constitution and the law passed in 1999 mentions, among others, Albanian, Catalan, Friulan, Sardinian, Occitan, Greek, Slovenian, Croatian, German and so on. In its turn, France recognized some devolution rights to Corsica after the launching of the Balladur Initiative for Stability pact in Eastern Europe (with the aim of isolating the 'nationalist virus' ready to expand outside the Yugoslav borders). Then, in 1993, the European Union approved the Copenhagen criteria, which require the respect of minority rights prior to submitting the application for membership.[24]

This is however a key point. The European Union conditionality, as a crucial expression of its soft power, has been successful in the 1990s thanks to two main factors.[25] On the one hand, a crucial role has been played by the strong will of the political élite of the candidate countries to join the Union regardless of their political orientations (to such an extent that alternate governmental coalitions never questioned the desirability of EU membership, but worked toward achieving the goal anyhow). On the other, the influential capacity of the European Union in convincing candidates to pass reforms was consistently reinforced by its serious commitment to increase its inner harmonization and develop its integration further by reforming and adapting its institutions to the new challenges. In other words, the European Union has a convincing inclusive perspective because widening and deepening the Union were political goals that were simultaneously pursued.[26]

As a result, the years between 1995 and 2004 were the most successful and dynamic period for carrying out the integration of the Union and affirming its soft power to the external world. These transformations were positively perceived by many scholars and journalists overseas who began to follow and analyze carefully the new inputs issued by former warring states. In 2004, Jeremy Rifkin published *The European Dream* where he captured the momentum of the European Union by comparatively analyzing the declining 'American dream' against the insurgent 'European dream'.[27] He was particularly impressed by the fact that after a long history of violent clashes and genocide, the Europeans were developing an integrative pattern based on cooperation, soft power, democratic values and peaceful coexistence, which was able to attract the former socialist countries of East Central Europe, jointly passing the Charter of Fundamental Rights and paving the way to a Constitutional treaty. His seminal book was not the only one which recorded this fervent phase of openness and reforms. Previously, in 2000, Elisabeth Pond addressed to still incredulous Americans her passionate interpretation of the fresh and vibrant reshaping of Europe in *The Rebirth of Europe*.[28] Similarly, the *New York Time*s bestseller list in 2004 included T. R. Reid's *The United States of Europe* with the subtitle *The New Superpower and the End of American Supremacy*. Focusing on the ability of the European Union to 'invent peace', the author extensively described the European social model and networking policy as being able to bind together a Europe undergoing deep transformation and concluded by warning American readers that a revolution was taking place with a 'profound effect on the world'.[29] Other studies suggested that the European Union and the United States might gradually diverge and grow apart.[30]

In short, there was a time when the European integration project was shaking consciousness, attracting international admiration and interest, and representing an evident novelty in a globalizing and uncertain world. Nevertheless, this proactive phase vanished in 2005, when the Constitutional treaty was rejected in the French and Dutch referenda. A Gallup poll revealed after the vote that the main contentious argument that led to the failure of the treaty proposal was related to demands for a more Social Europe,[31] that is, a European Union committed to struggle against social exclusion and in support of solidarity. Moreover, the constitutional document was expected to include, in a clear and readable way, the main legal principles on which the Union should have been based.[32] Instead, the document was a huge list of decisions approved by the European Councils without an inspiring project for the future. This aspect played a key role in strengthening the negative vote, far beyond the criticism against the Bolkestein directive on services in the internal EU market, which however offered the opportunity for new divisive behaviors within the European Union, summarized by critiques against the 'Polish plumber'.[33]

Significantly enough, the campaign against the 'Polish plumber' was able to stimulate a critical attitude from the public against the free mobility of people within the European Union just a few months after the first great enlargement of 2004 and the years of excited rhetoric about the 'reunification of Europe' once communism had collapsed. Such a campaign was a divisive sign that revealed a growing reluctance of old member states' populations towards the policies of inclusiveness that the EU had been pursuing. Indeed, this was an indication that a 'return' to national and sovereign values in terms of homogenization was coming again to the surface. The governments of member states were able to seize the opportunity and take advantage of it. Consistently with this new 'renationalization' trend, the new Lisbon treaty, which was designed to replace the failed Constitutional Treaty, excluded the reference to any state symbols like the flag, the anthem, the coat of arms, which were included in the Constitutional treaty, maintaining only the Charter of Fundamental Rights. However, the institutional provisions of the second part of the Constitutional treaty were encompassed in the new one. As a result, the Union gradually abandoned the communitarian approach for a more assertive intergovernmental one, imposed the approval of the treaty to a reluctant Ireland, and *de facto* reinvigorated the negative assessment of public opinion about the democratic deficit in the European Union.[34]

This reconstruction is crucially important to understand what has been the political impact of the economic and global crisis that started in 2007. Since then, in fact, enlargement has been increasingly perceived within the Union as a weight, rather than an opportunity; moreover, the institutional effectiveness of the European Union was measured in relation to its managerial capacity for facing the implications of the crisis. Nevertheless, the outcomes so far achieved have recorded a failure in promoting a general recovery first, followed by a new phase of growth and social security, particularly in the Eurozone.

With the intensification of social and political uncertainties, the prospect of implementation of the integrative project has been affected, generating visible negative effects in some candidate or potential candidate countries in the Balkans, especially in Bosnia-Herzegovina and Macedonia, whose commitment for the reforms has evaporated.[35] Even if Serbia and Kosovo, under pressure from the European Union, made some efforts for normalizing their relations (Belgrade and Tirana organized the first visit of the Prime Minister of Albania to Serbia in sixty-eight years; Serbia and Croatia announced for the first time their participation in joint military exercises of NATO in Serbia along with a stronger cooperation in the healthcare system), the level of understanding, tolerance and reconciliation within social realities remains poor in the Balkans as a whole.

Several polls in different periods have recorded the persistence of animosities in the Balkans. Scholars and anthropologists with their methodological observations and contextual interpretations have easily confirmed this situation and lobbied authorities to take actions for bridging this gap, which was persisting despite the generous commitments of part of the civil society to facilitate dialogue, cooperation and trust. More recently, in 2014, the Belgrade magazine *Nin* published an opinion poll conducted in Serbia, Albania and Kosovo which offers insightful data. First of all, 62 per cent of Serbs who were questioned admitted they never visited Kosovo, or Albania (97 per cent). Furthermore, if 47 per cent of the Albanians supported the project of Greater Albania,[36] 43 per cent believed themselves to have more in common with than differences from the Serbs. Nevertheless, 39 per cent of the Serbs (against 37 per cent) thought that long-term peace with Albanians was impossible. The lack of trust is mutually evident when the question concerns the dialogue between Belgrade and Priština: the majority of Kosovar Serbs (43 per cent against 2 per cent) believed that the dialogue was beneficial for Kosovo rather than for Serbia, while the general perception in Kosovo (34 per cent against 19 per cent) was diametrically opposed.[37]

The outcome of this poll is just one example, among others, that explains why a mere sports match can inflame team supporters in nationalistic terms, as occurred in Belgrade in October 2014 when a drone with a flag representing the map of Great Albania landed in the playground, resulting in violent reactions. On the other side, however, the European Union is no longer an affirmative project; on the contrary, to the outside world it reflects its own sharp divisions on the future of its integration, of its economic policy and institutional reforms, its understanding of its inner solidarity and its deep uncertainties while facing migration flows or the Ukrainian crisis. In doing so, however, the risk for the European Union to suffer what has been so far called a 'Balkanization' becomes an option that cannot be excluded.[38]

As a matter of fact, the renationalization of domestic and foreign policies of the member states, which is evident in many respects—as for instance in the energy sector, or in the reluctance of old member states to comply with the directive of the European commission in some national policy aimed to preserve its own bank autonomy—has dramatic implications for making joint decisions in economic policy. The controversy over the most effective measures aimed to consolidate the common currency is increasingly strengthening the decisional uncertainty of the Union. On the one hand, in fact, the Bundesbank in a more radical way and the German chancellor, Angela Merkel, more softly are insisting ideologically on neoliberal principles, based on the priority of monetarist and budgetary policies (although agreed by twenty-five out of twenty-seven member states when the Stability Treaty was signed in 2012). On the other, a wide number of economists (from Joseph Stiglitz to Jean Paul Fitoussi and Paul Krugman) are fervently discouraging this option in newspapers and magazines by supporting a neo-Keynesian approach, which is also influencing the most recent behaviors of the governments of France and Italy, which would prefer to focus on public investments for growth and welfare protection.[39]

In addition to the internal implications of such a dichotomy, the divergent strategies in the political economy of the European Union generates several external effects, among these the weakening of the effectiveness of conditionality. In fact, by propelling an image of uncertainty and inability in making decisions, the convincing capacity of the EU project remains deeply affected both among its own citizens, and towards the Balkan countries interested in gaining membership, but still struggling with unimplemented reforms.

In this context, the European Union is going to face multiple challenges concerning its own future. These challenges affect not only, as is said, the economic policy and the common currency, after a long-term financial and economic crisis whose recovery still appears uneven, fragile and volatile. They also affect, in a broader way, the project of integration as a whole (including its values and morality based on the respect of diversities and 'otherness'), because the lines of fractures are multiplying within the EU level as well as within member states. In this sense the European Union is suffering from the implications of multiple divergences that may lead to multiple partitions between the following: Euro and non-Eurozone countries; Schengen and non-Schengen member states; countries whose security priorities are related to Russian aggressive policies and countries whose security priorities are related to the Southern Mediterranean/Middle East wars and fragmentations; countries who are on the frontline in facing a wave of migration flows and countries who are interested in protecting their borders on the basis of the Dublin regulation.

In addition to Brexit, the European Union also faces other potential risks in member states: the fragmentation of the United Kingdom with Scotland (and prospectively Northern Ireland and possibly Wales); in Spain with Catalonia and possibly Galicia and Basque regions, without mentioning the risks of dissolution for Belgium.[40] To a large extent these challenges have been generated or aggravated by both the economic crisis and the inadequacy of the EU institutional system after the great enlargements of 2004–2013. Racism and xenophobia (like ethno-nationalism) emphasize blood homogeneity and spread fears of any cultural syncretism, which is unavoidably produced by the implementation of the four liberties of the European Union, that is the free movements of capitals, goods, services and people.

Right-leaning parties have even managed to create a group in the EU Parliament where they are urging a return to the (small) nation-state sovereignties, which are actually under liquefaction and unable to restore the previous links of communication and power exercise, because the world has meanwhile radically changed. Nevertheless, these claims are poisoning relations within the European Union and contribute to deepening mistrust among leaderships by appealing to populist and irrational mobilizing factors, whose main seeds are represented by social and economic dissatisfactions.

As a result, under the current multifaceted crisis and the respective uncertainties it is producing, both the EU institutions and the members-states appear to be mentally and politically unprepared to face the comprehensive challenges that are affecting their societies, and particularly the dynamics of fusion and amalgamation that the EU integration processes and globalization have generated in the last decades.

NOTES

1. This research was realized in the framework of the TÁMOP 4.2.4.A/2-11-1-2012-0001 'National Excellence Programme—Elaborating and operating an inland student and researcher personal support system convergence programme'. The project was subsidized by the European Union and cofinanced by the European Social Fund. The contents of this chapter are elaborated excerpts from my book *Liquid Nationalism and State Partitions in Europe* (Cheltenham: Edward Elgar, 2017).

2. See Raif Dizdarević, *From the Death of Tito to the Death of Yugoslavia* (Sarajevo: Šahinpašić, 2009), 491.

3. Compare Jovan Đorđević 'Federalism', in Jovan Đorđević, Savin Jogan, Mitja Ribičič and Anton Vratuša, eds., *Self-Management, the Yugoslav Road to Socialism* (Beograd: Jugosloveski Pregled, 1982); Jovan Mirić, *Sistem i kriza* (Zagreb: Cekade, 1984); Stefano Bianchini, *Sarajevo: le radici dell'odio* (Roma: Edizioni Associate, 2003) and Julie Mostov, *Borders: Rethinking Sovereignty and Democracy* (New York: Palgrave Macmillan, 2008).

4. More extensively in Stefano Bianchini, *La diversità socialista in Jugoslavia. Modernizzazione, autogestione e sviluppo democratico dal 1965 ad oggi* (Trieste: Editoriale Stampa Triestina/Založba Tržaška Tiska, 1984), 189–211.

5. The 'besieged fortress' was a popular Stalinist expression aimed to emphasize how the USSR was surrounded by enemies and had to protect itself like a Bastille. The 'socialism in one country' was, again, a sentence originally used by Stalin, but later theoretically elaborated by Bukharin. The notion suggested that the USSR had the task to build socialism despite the failure of the world revolution that Bolsheviks had expected in the 1917–1923 years.

6. Stefano Bianchini, *Eastern Europe and the Challenges of Modernity 1800–2000* (London and New York: Routledge, 2015), 132–42.

7. Among the rare contributions, see Marie Lavigne, *The Economics of Transition: From Socialist Market to Market Economy* (New York: St. Martin's Press, 1998); Iván Berend, *Central and Eastern Europe 1944–1993: Detour from the Periphery to the Periphery* (Cambridge: Cambridge University Press, 1998) and Bianchini, *Eastern Europe and the Challenges of Modernity 1800–2000*, 194–202.

8. Compare Will Bartlett, 'The Problem of Indebtedness in Yugoslavia: Causes and Consequences', *Rivista internazionale di Scienze economiche e commerciali* 34, no. 11–12 (1987): 1179–95; Paolo Brera, 'L'économie yougoslave face au programme de stabilisation', *Revue d'études comparatives Est-Ouest* 16, no. 1 (1985): 121–52 and Dizdarević, *From the Death of Tito to the Death of Yugoslavia.*

9. Among the authors that extensively wrote about the Yugoslav crisis before the collapse, see Marijan Korošić, *Jugoslavenska kriza* (Zagreb: Naprijed, 1989); Branko Horvat, *Jugoslavensko društvo u krizi* (Zagreb: Globus, 1985) and *Jugoslovenski Centar za Teoriju i Praksu Samoupravljanja* (JCTPS), *Društveno-ekonomski aspekti međunacionalnih odnosa u Jugoslaviji* (Ljubljana: Delavska Enotnost, 1982).

10. On this issue, compare Grigory Yavlinsky, *Realeconomik: The Hidden Cause of the Great Recession (and How to Avert the Next One)* (New Haven, CT: Yale University Press, 2011); Gérard Duménil and Dominique Lévy, *The Crisis of Neoliberalism: From Subprime Crash to the Great Contraction* (Cambridge, MA: Harvard University Press, 2011) and Jože Mencinger, 'The Global Financial Crisis and the European Union', paper presented at the international conference *The EU, Russia and the Global Crisis*, Forlì, 17–18 April 2009.

11. Zoltán Pogátsa, *Heterodox International Political Economy* (Sopron: University of West Hungary Press, 2011), 91–117.

12. Stuart Holland, *Europe in Question and What to Do About It* (Nottingham: Spokesman, 2015).

13. Valerie Bunce, *Subversive Institutions: The Design and the Destruction of Socialism and the State* (Cambridge: Cambridge University Press, 1999), 83–88.

14. Yugoslav leaders considered the possibility to restrict the access to the welfare system for free, by offering to the people an alternative: political reforms which would affect the dictatorship of the proletariat and expand democracy. However, this option was ideologically rejected by communist hardliners and orthodox. As a result, in search of an agreement, decisions were postponed indefinitely.

15. The literature on this topic includes a wide variety of contributions. In particular, stimulating interpretative approaches are those of John B. Allcock, *Explaining Yugoslavia* (New York: Columbia University Press, 2000); John R. Lampe, *Yugoslavia as History. Twice There Was a Country* (Cambridge: Cambridge University Press,

1996); Susan Woodward, *The Balkan Tragedy* (Washington, DC: The Brookings Institute, 1995) and Lenard J. Cohen, *Broken Bonds: Yugoslavia's Disintegration and Balkan Politics in Transition* (Boulder, CO: Westview Press, 1995).

16. See Stefano Bianchini, ed., *L'enigma jugoslavo. Le ragioni della crisi* (Milano: Angeli, 1989) and Vladimir Goati, *Politička anatomija jugoslovenskog društva* (Zagreb: Naprijed, 1989).

17. Neil E. Reichenberg, *Best Practices in Diversity Management* (New York: UN Export Group Meeting on Managing Diversities in the Civil Service, 3–4 May 2001); David Turton and Julia González, eds., *Ethnic Diversity in Europe: Challenges to the Nation State* (Bilbao: University of Deusto, 2000); and Mitja Žagar, 'Diversity Management and Integration: from Ideas to Concepts', *European Yearbook of Minority Issues* 6 (2007): 307–27.

18. See more details in Dejan Jović, *Jugoslavija država koja je odumrla* (Zagreb: Prometej, 2003); Eric D. Gordy, *The Culture of Power in Serbia* (University Park: The Pennsylvania State University Press, 1999) and Zoran Obrenović, *Srbija i novi poredak* (Niš: IFDT, 1992).

19. The EU soft power was successfully implemented through a set of conditionality measures that were applied to candidate or potential candidate countries in the perspective of membership. By means of persuasion the European Union was able to stabilize postsocialist countries of the former Soviet bloc, whose leaderships were willing to join the Union. By contrast, when the crisis began to affect the European Union, such conditions lost both effectiveness and attractiveness.

20. The Dayton agreement was signed in Ohio, under US and EU pressure. It established two different entities, the Federation of Bosnia-Herzegovina, subdivided into ten ethnic cantons, and the centralized Republika Srpska. The two entities were loosely bounded by some shared institutions.

21. Stefano Bianchini, Joseph Marko, Craig Nation and Milica Uvalić, eds., *Regional Cooperation, Peace Enforcement and the Role of the Treaties in the Balkans* (Ravenna: Longo, 2007).

22. Compare 'Bosnia-Herzegovina Hit by Wave of Violent Protests', *Guardian*, 7 February 2014, https://www.theguardian.com/world/2014/feb/07/bosnia-herzegovina-wave-violent-protests and 'Bosnia-Hercegovina Protests Break Out in Violence', BBC.com, 7 February 2014, http://www.bbc.com/news/world-europe-26086857.

23. More details in Derek Heater, *National Self-Determination: Woodrow Wilson and His Legacy* (New York: St. Martin's Press, 1994) and Victor. S. Mamatey, *The United States and East Central Europe 1914–1918* (Princeton, NJ: Princeton University Press, 1957).

24. See Pál Dunay and Wolfgang Zellner, *The Pact on Stability in Europe—A Diplomatic Episode or a Lasting Success?* 1997, last accessed 10 May 2018, https://ifsh.de/file-CORE/documents/yearbook/english/95_96/Dunay.pdf and Stefano Bianchini, ed., *Self-Determination and Sovereignty in Europe: From historical legacies to the EU external role* (Ravenna: Longo 2013).

25. Othon Anastasakis, 'The EU's Political Conditionality in the Western Balkans: Towards a More Pragmatic Approach', *Southeast Europe and Black Sea Studies* 8, no. 4 (2008): 365–77, https://doi.org/10.1080/14683850802556384 (accessed 10

October 2009) and Heather Grabbe, *The EU's Transformative Power. Europeanization through Conditionality in Central and Eastern Europe* (New York: Palgrave Macmillan, 2006).

26. See Frank Schimmelfenning and Ulrich Sedelmeier, *The Europeanization of Central and Eastern Europe* (Ithaca, NY: Cornell University Press, 2005) and Milada Anna Vachudova, *Europe Undivided* (Oxford: Oxford University Press, 2005).

27. Jeremy Rifkin, *The European Dream* (New York: Tarcher/Penguin, 2004).

28. Elizabeth Pond, *The Rebirth of Europe* (Washington, DC: Brooking Institutions Press, 2000), 14–18.

29. T. R. Reid, *The Unites States of Europe: The New Superpower and the End of American Supremacy* (New York: Penguin, 2004), 26–62.

30. Jeffrey Kopstein and Sven Steinmo, eds., *Growing Apart? America and Europe in the Twenty-first Century* (Cambridge: Cambridge University Press, 2008), 4–21.

31. Róbert Manchin, *After the Referenda* (Brussels: Gallup Europe, June 29, 2005).

32. Stuart Holland, 'The Life and Death of Democracies', in Jody Jensen and Ferenc Miszlivetz, eds., *Reframing Europe's Future: Challenges and Failures of the European Construction* (Abingdon/New York: Routledge, 2015), 189–206.

33. The Bolkestein directive is a EU law whose aim was to establish a European market of services. The law was strongly criticized in 2005 as prospectively responsible for the decline of the quality of services. In particular, the directive was considered an encouragement to 'exploit' the cheap labor of the East European new member states. During the referendum campaign, therefore, the posters against the 'Polish plumber' epitomized such concerns.

34. See details in Jacques Ziller, *Il nuovo trattato europeo* (Bologna: Il Mulino, 2007), 167–99 and Krzysztof Michalski, ed., *What Holds Europe Together?* (Budapest: CEU Press, 2006), 93–102.

35. Useful details in Michael Emerson, Senem Aydin, Julia De Clerck-Sachsse and Gergana Noutcheva, *Just What Is This 'Absorption Capacity' of the European Union?* (Brussels: CEPS Policy Brief, September 2006).

36. The project of Greater Albania, advocated by Albanian ethno-nationalist movements, intends to redraw the map of the Balkans by uniting Albania with Kosovo, Western Macedonia, the Preševo valley in Serbia, Southern Epirus (in Greece) and some territories of Montenegro. About the Albanian-Kosovar relations, see, for example, Shaban Murati, *The Albanian Question after the Independence of Kosovo* (Tirana: Globus R., 2012) and Stephanie Schwandner-Sievers and Bernd J. Fischer, eds., *Albanian Identities. Myth and History* (London: Hurst & Co., 2002).

37. Vera Didanović, 'Hlađanje glava ili odnosa' (Freezing heads or relations), *Nin*, 23 October 2014, 11–13.

38. See, for instance, the broad and in-depth analysis of Jim Yardley, 'Has Europe Reached the Breaking Point?' *New York Times*, 15 December, http://www.nytimes.com/2015/12/20/magazine/has-europe-reached-the-breaking-point.html?ref=world (accessed 16 December 2015).

39. Compare Joseph E. Stiglitz, *The Price of Inequality: How Today's Divided Society Endangers Our Future* (New York: Norton, 2013); Paul Krugman, *End this Depression Now!* (New York: Norton, 2013); Jean-Paul Fitoussi and Jacques Le Cacheux, *Report on the State of the European Union: Crisis in the EU Economic Governance* (New York: Palgrave Macmillan, 2009); Joseph E. Stiglitz, *Interpreting the Causes of the Great Recession of 2008*, lecture to have been delivered at BIS Conference, Basel (June 2009), https://fcic-static.law.stanford.edu/cdn_media/fcic-testimony/2009-1020-Stiglitz-article-2.pdf (accessed 3 September 2009) and Joseph E. Stiglitz, 'The Current Economic Crisis and Lessons for Economic Theory', *Eastern Economic Journal*, 35 (2009): 281–96, doi:10.1057/eej.2009.24.

40. See, for example, Montserrat Guibernau, 'Catalan Secessionism: Young People's Expectations and Political Change', *The International Spectator* 49, no. 3 (September 2014): 106–17; Euan McKirdy, Bryony Jones and Susannah Cullinane, 'Five Secessionist Movements That Could Learn from Scotland', CNN.com, 19 September 2014, http://edition.cnn.com/2014/09/17/world/scotland-five-other-separatist-movements (accessed 12 October 2014); David McKittrick, 'Scottish Referendum Results: Outcome Divides Opinion in Northern Ireland', *Independent*, 19 September 2014, http://www.independent.co.uk/news/uk/scottish-independence/scottish-referendum-results-outcome-divides-opinion-in-northern-ireland-9745192.html (accessed 20 September 2014) and Tom Van Grieken, 'Flemish Independence: Better to Become Good Friends Than Stay Together in a Bad Marriage', RT.com, 18 September 2014, http://rt.com/op-edge/188684-flanders-independence-referendum-belgium (accessed 5 October 2014).

REFERENCES

Allcock, John B. 2000. *Explaining Yugoslavia*. New York: Columbia University Press.

Anastasakis, Othon. 2008. 'The EU's Political Conditionality in the Western Balkans: Towards a More Pragmatic Approach'. *Southeast Europe and Black Sea Studies* 8 (4): 365–77. https://doi.org/10.1080/14683850802556384 (accessed 10 October 2009).

Bartlett, Will. 1987. 'The Problem of Indebtedness in Yugoslavia: Causes and Consequences'. *Rivista internazionale di Scienze economiche e commerciali* 34 (11–12): 1179–95.

Benhabib, Seyla. 2002. *The Claims of Culture: Equality and Diversity in the Global Era*. Princeton, NJ: Princeton University Press.

Berend, Ivan. 1998. *Central and Eastern Europe 1944–1993. Detour from the Periphery to the Periphery*. Cambridge: Cambridge University Press.

Bianchini, Stefano. 1984. *La diversità socialista in Jugoslavia. Modernizzazione, autogestione e sviluppo democratico dal 1965 ad oggi*. Trieste: Editoriale Stampa Triestina/Založba Tržaška Tiska.

———. ed. 1989. *L'enigma jugoslavo. Le ragioni della crisi*. Milano: Angeli.

———. 2003. *Sarajevo: le radici dell'odio*. Roma: Edizioni Associate.

———, ed. 2013. *Self-Determination and Sovereignty in Europe: From Historical Legacies to the EU External Role*. Ravenna: Longo.

———. 2015. *Eastern Europe and the Challenges of Modernity 1800–2000*, London and New York: Routledge.

Bianchini, Stefano, Joseph Marko, Craig Nation and Milica Uvalić, eds. 2007. *Regional Cooperation, Peace Enforcement and the Role of the Treaties in the Balkans*. Ravenna: Longo.

Bianchini, Stefano, Sanjay Chaturvedi, Rada Ivekovic and Ranadir Samaddar. 2005. *Partitions: Reshaping States and Minds*. London: Frank Cass (Indian Reprint in 2007).

Brera, Paolo A. 1985. 'L'économie yougoslave face au programme de stabilisation'. *Revue d'études comparatives Est-Ouest* 16 (1): 121–52.

Buchanan, Allen. 1991. *Secession: The Morality of Political Divorce from Fort Sumter to Lithuania and Quebec*. Boulder, CO: Westview Press.

Bunce, Valerie. 1999. *Subversive Institutions: The Design and the Destruction of Socialism and the State*. Cambridge: Cambridge University Press.

Cohen, Lenard J. 1995. *Broken Bonds. Yugoslavia's Disintegration and Balkan Politics in Transition*. Boulder, CO: Westview Press.

Cohen, Stephen F. 2004. 'Was the Soviet System Reformable?' *Slavic Review* 63 (3): 459–88.

Dejan, Jović. 2003. *Jugoslavija država koja je odumrla*. Zagreb: Prometej.

Didanović, Vera. 2014. Hlađanje glava ili odnosa (Freezing heads or relations). *Nin*. 23 October, 11–13.

Dizdarević, Raif. 2009. *From the Death of Tito to the Death of Yugoslavia*. Sarajevo: Šahinpašić.

Donskis, Leonidas, and Ineta Dabašinskienė, eds. 2010. *European Memory: A Blessing or a Curse?* Ravenna: Longo.

Đorđević, Jovan. 1982. 'Federalism'. In *Self-Management, the Yugoslav Road to Socialism*, edited by Jovan Đorđević, Jogan Savin, Mitja Ribičič and Anton Vratuša. Beograd: Jugosloveski Pregled.

Duménil, Gérard, and Dominique Lévy. 2011. *The Crisis of Neoliberalism: From Subprime Crash to the Great Contraction*. Cambridge MA: Harvard University Press.

Dunay, Pál, and Wolfgang Zellner. 1997. *The Pact on Stability in Europe—A Diplomatic Episode or a Lasting Success?* https://ifsh.de/file-CORE/documents/yearbook/english/95_96/Dunay.pdf (accessed 10 May 2018).

Emerson, Michael, Senem Aydin, Julia De Clerck-Sachsse and Gergana Noutcheva. 2006. *Just What Is This 'Absorption Capacity' of the European Union?* Brussels: CEPS Policy Brief.

Fitoussi, Jean-Paul, and Jacques Le Cacheux. 2009. *Report on the State of the European Union. Crisis in the EU Economic Governance*. 2009. New York: Palgrave Macmillan.

Gingrich, Andre, and Marcus Banks, eds. 2006. *Neo-nationalism in Europe and Beyond: Perspectives from Social Anthropology*. New York: Berghahn Books.

Goati, Vladimir. 1989. *Politička anatomija jugoslovenskog društva*. Zagreb: Naprijed.

Gordy, Eric D. 1999. *The Culture of Power in Serbia*. University Park: The Pennsylvania State University Press.

Grabbe, Heather. 2006. *The EU's Transformative Power: Europeanization through Conditionality in Central and Eastern Europe*. New York: Palgrave Macmillan.

Guibernau, Montserrat. 2014. 'Catalan Secessionism: Young People's Expectations and Political Change'. *The International Spectator* 49 (3): 106–17.

Heather, Derek. 1994. *National Self-Determination: Woodrow Wilson and His Legacy*. New York: St. Martin's Press.

Holland, Stuart. 2015a. 'The Life and Death of Democracies'. In Jody Jensen and Ferenc Miszlivetz, eds., *Reframing Europe's Future: Challenges and Failures of the European Construction*. New York: Routledge.

———. 2015b. *Europe in Question and What to Do About It*. Nottingham: Spokesman.

Horvat, Branko. 1985. *Jugoslavensko društvo u krizi*. Zagreb: Globus.

Huttenbach, Henry, and Francesco Privitera, eds. 1999. *Self-Determination from Versailles to Dayton*. Ravenna: Longo.

Iveković, Rada. 2003. *Dame Nation. Nation et Différence des Sexes*. Ravenna: Longo.

Iveković, Rada, and Julie Mostov, eds. 2002. *From Gender to Nation*. Ravenna: Longo, 2002.

Jensen, Jody, and Ferenc Miszlivetz, eds. 2015. *Reframing Europe's Future: Challenges and Failures of the European Construction*. New York: Routledge.

Jugoslovenski Centar za Teoriju i Praksu Samoupravljanja (JCTPS). 1982. *Društveno-ekonomski aspekti međunacionalnih odnosa u Jugoslaviji*. Ljubljana: Delavska Enotnost.

Kopstein, Jeffrey, and Sven Steinmo, eds. 2008. *Growing Apart? America and Europe in the Twenty-first Century*. Cambridge: Cambridge University Press.

Korošić, Marijan. 1989. *Jugoslavenska kriza*. Zagreb: Naprijed.

Krugman, Paul. 2013. *End This Depression Now!* New York: Norton.

———. 2014. 'Scots, What the Heck?' *New York Times*, 7 September. http://www.nytimes.com/2014/09/08/opinion/paul-krugman-scots-what-the-heck.html?_r=0 (accessed 10 October 2014).

Kymlicka, Will. 1995. *Multicultural Citizenship*. Oxford: Clarendon Press.

Lampe, John R. 1996. *Yugoslavia as History: Twice There Was a Country*. Cambridge: Cambridge University Press.

Lavigne, Marie. 1998. *The Economics of Transition: From Socialist Market to Market Economy*. New York: St. Martin's Press.

Mamatey, Victor. S. 1957. *The United States and East Central Europe 1914–1918*. Princeton, NJ: Princeton University Press.

Manchin, Róbert. 2005. *After the Referenda*. Brussels: Gallup Europe.

McKirdy, Euan, Bryony Jones and Susannah Cullinane. 2014. 'Five Secessionist Movements That Could Learn from Scotland'. CNN.com. 19 September. http://edition.cnn.com/2014/09/17/world/scotland-five-other-separatist-movements (accessed 12 October 2014).

McKittrick, David. 2014. 'Scottish Referendum Results: Outcome Divides Opinion in Northern Ireland'. *Independent*. 19 September. http://www.independent.co.uk/news/uk/scottish-independence/scottish-referendum-results-outcome-divides-opinion-in-northern-ireland-9745192.html (accessed 20 September 2014).

Mencinger, Jože. 2009. 'The Global Financial Crisis and the European Union'. Paper presented at the international conference *The EU, Russia and the Global Crisis*. Forlì, 17–18 April.

Michalski, Krzysztof, ed. 2006. *What Holds Europe Together?* Budapest: CEU Press.

Mirić, Jovan. 1984. *Sistem i kriza*. Zagreb: Cekade.

Mostov, Julie. 2008. *Soft Borders: Rethinking Sovereignty and Democracy*. New York: Palgrave Macmillan.

Murati, Shaban. 2012. *The Albanian Question after the Independence of Kosovo*. Tirana: Globus R.

Noiriel, Gérard. 2001. *État, nation et immigration. Vers une histoire du pouvoir*. Paris: Belin.

Obrenović, Zoran. 1992. *Srbija i novi poredak*. Niš: IFDT.

Pogátsa, Zoltán. 2011. *Heterodox International Political Economy*. Sopron: University of West Hungary Press.

Pond, Elizabeth. 2000. *The Rebirth of Europe*. Washington, DC: The Brooking Institute.

Puri, Jyoti. 2004. *Encountering Nationalism*. Malden-Oxford: Blackwell.

Reichenberg, Neil E. 2001. *Best Practices in Diversity Management*. New York: UN Export Group Meeting on Managing Diversities in the Civil Service, 3–4 May.

Reid, T. R. 2004. *The Unites States of Europe: The New Superpower and the End of American Supremacy*. New York: Penguin.

Rifkin, Jeremy. 2004. *The European Dream*. New York: Tarcher/Penguin.

Schimmelfenning, Frank, and Ulrich Sedelmeier. 2005. *The Europeanization of Central and Eastern Europe*. Ithaca, NY: Cornell University Press.

Schwandner-Sievers, Stephanie, and Bernd J. Fischer, eds., 2002. *Albanian Identities: Myth and History*. London: Hurst & Co.

Stiglitz, Joseph E. 2009a. *Interpreting the Causes of the Great Recession of 2008*. Lecture to have been delivered at BIS Conference, Basel (June 2009). https://fcic-static.law.stanford.edu/cdn_media/fcic-testimony/2009-1020-Stiglitz-article-2.pdf (accessed 3 September 2009).

———. 2009b. 'The Current Economic Crisis and Lessons for Economic Theory'. *Eastern Economic Journal* 35:281–96. doi:10.1057/eej.2009.24.

———. 2013. *The Price of Inequality: How Today's Divided Society Endangers Our Future*. New York: Norton.

Turton, David, and Julia González, eds. 2000. *Ethnic Diversity in Europe: Challenges to the Nation State*. Bilbao: University of Deusto.

Vachudova Milada, Anna. 2005. *Europe Undivided*. Oxford: Oxford University Press.

Van Grieken, Tom. 2014. 'Flemish Independence: Better to Become Good Friends Than Stay Together in a Bad Marriage'. RT.com. 18 September. http://rt.com/

op-edge/188684-flanders-independence-referendum-belgium (accessed October 5, 2014).

Woodward, Susan. 1995. *The Balkan Tragedy*. Washington, DC: The Brookings Institute.

Yavlinsky, Grigory. 2011. *Realeconomik: The Hidden Cause of the Great Recession (and How to Avert the Next One)*. New Haven, CT: Yale University Press.

Žagar, Mitja. 2007. 'Diversity Management and Integration: From Ideas to Concepts'. *European Yearbook of Minority Issues* 6: 307–27.

Ziller, Jacques. 2007. *Il nuovo trattato europeo*. Bologna: Il Mulino.

Chapter 5

Legacies of Partition

Remembering the German Democratic Republic

Chris Weedon

In Germany, a country where the borders marking two separate states have been consigned to history, life under partition is remembered by those directly affected by it through family stories and more widely in the museums, tourist venues, media and publications that continue to depict it for subsequent generations. The German Democratic Republic (GDR) past is a recurrent subject of public history and media, regularly profiled on the annual anniversaries of the fall of the Berlin Wall and of reunification. It is also a focus for tourism—particularly in Berlin—and of a nostalgia industry. This chapter looks at the afterlives of political partition and reunification as they shape how the GDR is represented in public history and in individual and collective memory. It draws on examples from museums, documentary media, oral history and written life stories with particular reference to how they are narrated and mobilized, ideologically and affectively. The chapter looks at what is emphasized and what is excluded as part of a broader concern with the politics of individual and collective memory and considers the wider ideological implications of hegemonic modes of representation. It further seeks to identify issues of relevance to broader understandings of the social and affective legacies of partitions.[1]

POSTPARTITION REPRESENTATIONS OF THE GDR

The fall of the Berlin Wall is widely regarded as marking the end of the Cold War. Well-known images of this event, widely available in museums, books and tourist publications, in the media and online, show huge crowds of jubilant people from East and West celebrating on and around the wall and seemingly endless lines of East Germans on foot and in their Trabants, Wartburgs and Skodas, queuing to cross from East to West. The dominant motifs here are escape from oppression to freedom and access to that 'better life' long enjoyed by West Germans. These images, widely reproduced in various media, set the tone for the wider treatment of the GDR in public history.

In most current representations of the GDR in museums, tourism and popular culture, the emphasis is on life in the GDR in the years from 1949 onwards, with particular emphasis on the period between the building of the Berlin Wall in 1961 and its fall in 1989. As I will argue in more detail below, these representations tend to recycle well-established motifs and stereotypical, clichéd representations of GDR life. The majority of exhibitions, TV programmes, books, films and DVDs about the GDR produced in Germany since 1990 make little attempt to understand the prehistory of the state and how it came into being other than at the geopolitical level of occupation and the Cold War. Digitally remastered newsreels from the immediate postwar years give some sense of the destruction caused by war and key events leading up to the founding of two separate German states in 1949. Detailed empirical histories such as volume one of Stefan Wolle's three-volume *Die heile Welt der Diktatur: Alltag und Herrschaft in der DDR 1949–1989* (The Safe World of Dictatorship: Everyday Life and Domination in the GDR) mirror the newsreel narratives surprisingly closely, focusing on events that includes the physical destruction wrought by the final phases of the war, the displacement of populations, Soviet occupation, the merging of the Social Democrat and Communist Parties to form the SED (Socialist Unity Party) and the Soviet-style centralization of state power in all areas of life. Key motifs in coverage of the 1950s are the uprising of 1953, land reforms, state takeovers of the small and medium business sector, ideological reeducation and state repression. While considerable oral history work has been done since 1989, these sources tend only to surface in the representation of specific themes, such as the building of the Berlin Wall, restrictions on travel and divided families.[2] There is little detailed material available in public history from the perspectives of those who lived through the period from 1945 until the building of the Berlin Wall in 1961. It is here that oral history narratives have the potential to bring day-to-day experience alive and capture the ideological, material and affective dimensions of everyday life, including the idealism and commitment that motivated many during the immediate postwar years of reconstruction (*Aufbaujahre*). An important question in the politics of representation in relation to the GDR today is why more differentiated narratives are still largely invisible or absent.

Factors common to many political partitions shaped subjectivities in East Germany in the early postwar years: the immediately preceding history of fascism, war and forced migration and the forms and everyday practices of the state apparatuses.[3] Those who survived mass flight brought with them experiences and stories of violence, pillage and rape, which were traumatic and as such hard to retell because they were both painful and often sources of shame.[4] Refugees also brought with them a deep and lasting sense of loss and dispossession that was given material form with the redrawing of national boundaries and the partition of both Germany and Berlin. Experiences of war and its aftermath and revelations of the full horrors of the Nazi regime fed a felt need among many for a new form of society in which fascism, genocide and war would become impossible. Political experiences from the Weimar years and under the Nazis were also important in shaping the subjectivities of those committed to building a new state. Many members of this *Aufbau* generation, which included socialist, communist and Jewish returnees from exile, made positive choices to help build what they hoped would be a new and better society. Without an understanding of the trauma and idealism of the early years, many aspects of later life in the German Democratic Republic cannot be well understood.

The partition of Germany was imposed for political reasons and did not reflect ethnic or religious differences or internal conflict within the former territory of the German Reich. Germany had a strong regional character and had only been unified as a nation-state since 1871. As in other divided societies, those who lived near the border, those who had relatives on the other side and those who were anxious to move across it, for whatever reasons, felt the effects of partition most strongly. While the border remained permeable until the building of the Berlin Wall in August 1961, divergent ideologies, currency reforms, restrictions on access to media and print culture and to travel in the East, as well as increasing differences in wealth between the two Germanies, soon made moving between the two sides problematic. Moreover, the drain of highly educated professionals from East to West Germany and the depletion of a skilled and unskilled workforce moving west across the open border quickly became a real economic and social threat to the survival of the East German state.

In postpartition public history and media programs about the period 1945–1989, partition tends to be represented as an East German problem. The fact that there were two sides to the border and that partition affected relations on both sides tends only to figure in relation to the movement of people from East to West. The constant barrage of negative Cold War propaganda in the years before the building of the Berlin Wall, which was produced on both sides of the border, is hard to imagine in the twenty-first century. In postpartition accounts of this history, West Germany is consistently taken to be the norm and the GDR an aberration from that norm.

Since the end of German partition, a number of hegemonic discourses have emerged about life in the GDR in which lack, restriction and oppression play dominant roles, be they geographical, sociocultural, ideological or material. Physical and ideological restrictions that are violently imposed and policed, accompanied by shortages and a standard of living that was for most people way below that of West Germans in equivalent jobs play a central role, yet it is dictatorship and surveillance that feature most strongly. In the documentaries about the GDR, shown regularly on German television, the term 'Deutsche Demokratische Republik' has largely been replaced by 'SED Diktatur' (Socialist Unity Party dictatorship). This designation, together with the term 'Stasi Staat', (Stasi state) dominates representational practices with particular emphasis on the themes of ideological indoctrination and physical containment. GDR citizens are represented as locked into the Soviet Bloc, often indoctrinated, sometimes imprisoned and always with little or no freedom of thought or movement. They tend to be represented as either *Mitlaüfer* (fellow travellers) or dissidents, rather than as complex subjects shaped by a range of competing interests, influences and internal and external constraints. In most representations, agency tends to be equated only with resistance and is subject to the constant threat of punishment by the Stasi, if criticisms threaten to enter the public sphere.[5]

Like many other partitioned or previously partitioned societies, Germany has no museum of partition that shows it from multiple perspectives as a force that shaped the history of *both* sides of the divide. The Berlin Museum of German History includes sections on both states, but many important aspects are absent from its narrative. Its exhibits, like those on display in the Tränenpalast (the former border crossing between East and West Berlin at Friedrichstrasse) are notable not so much for what they say but for what they fail to mention. While there is no national museum of partition, there are a number of GDR-related museums, buildings and archives mostly in the larger East German cities. Of these, the DDR Museum in the centre of Berlin is perhaps the best known. It was opened with private capital as a tourist venue in 2006 and is marketed as the eleventh-most visited museum in Berlin.

The provision of a museum about the GDR in Berlin had originally been left to West German private enterprise. The DDR Museum's founder, Robert Rückel from Freiburg in the Black Forest, began advertising for GDR objects and collected ten thousand in the first two years. He commissioned the Stuttgart architect Frank Wittmer and the GDR historian Stefan Wolle to design and curate the museum. Today, huge advertisements for the museum are among the prominent things that catch your eye as you enter the arrivals hall at Schönefeld Airport. The collection of original GDR products that forms the core of this museum are displayed within a confined and oppressive space, designed to produce specific affective responses in the visitor as they engage with the depiction of everyday life in the GDR. In the words of curator Stefan Wolle on the occasion of the museum's opening:

> You enter a crypt like space with pillars and enter it through a wall like structure. Then you go down a few steps and find yourself right in the middle of GDR everyday life. The first thing you encounter is a model of the *Palast der Republik* [the GDR parliament building] and you can look inside through little windows to where Erich Honecker is giving a speech at the 9th Party Congress. On the other side you see an ice cream shop and bowling alley and in this way the *Palast der Republik* is also experienced symbolically as signifying both these sides of the GDR: dictatorship and idyll. In no way is what you find here a 'museumised' Ostalgie show. We have classified and firmly tied everyday life in the GDR to the political system.[6]

This linking of everyday life to the political system inevitably creates highly reductive narratives. The DDR Museum's text panels and its guidebook make very questionable links between GDR social structures and practices and generalized and clichéd claims about former GDR citizens displaying authoritarian personalities, lack of initiative and fascist leanings in the postunification period. The selection of exhibits plays into a widespread repertoire of stereotypes of the GDR citizen summarized in the East German *Sächsische Zeitung* in 2009 in an article entitled 'The Ossi, the Banana and German-German clichés'. The stereotypes are identified as 'lazy, incompetent, irresponsible whiners, incapable of democracy . . . who were put on the chamber pot too soon and as a result were so psychically deformed that change is probably impossible'.[7] In the DDR Museum, ideals of the society and its achievements are ignored, satirized or downplayed. This produces an othering effect that makes it impossible to take up a positive position toward any aspect of life in the former GDR. Moreover, the displays lack any sense of history as contested or as process. The GDR is presented as in some ways 'quaint', but always repressive, static and unchanging.

A more balanced treatment of everyday life in the GDR opened in 2012 in a free museum located in the *Kulturbrauerei*, a cultural centre in the old Schultheiss brewery in Prenzlauer Berg in East Berlin. It was developed by the foundation, Stiftung Haus der Geschichte der Bundesrepublik Deutschland using a comprehensive collection about design and everyday culture in the GDR, which the foundation acquired in 2005. If the DDR Museum works in the words of its curator with the binary opposition between 'dictatorship and idyll', the Museum of Everyday Life looks at 'ideology and reality' (*Ideologie und Wirklichkeit*) in the GDR, attempting to depict how life was experienced at the level of both individual and group. The museum has both permanent and changing exhibitions and its publicity materials give a good sense of what the visitor might expect from the permanent display:

> You begin by learning about the ideology of the SED state by looking at large-scale propaganda posters and short texts. The ways in which the Soviet Union

> was a model can be seen clearly. The SED promoted the idea of the collective both at work and in leisure time. Listen to recordings of songs valued by the collectives. Have a look at the brigade books kept by groups of workers: a lively mixture of political slogans and impressions from workplace events, such as football matches. The museum also thematises shortages of everything. There weren't large enough living spaces, electrical appliances, fruit and vegetables. One contemporary witness complains about the long waiting time for her wall unit and tape recorder, and another about Christmas without oranges. Look inside a typically furnished, high-rise apartment. Fashion produced by the textile industry is also part of the exhibition. Many East Germans found happiness in private life. Be amazed by the inventiveness of people: tents on the roof of the 'Trabi' [Trabant] for a holiday on Rügen or Usedom and the imaginative extensions to weekend cottages (*Datschen*) in the countryside.[8]

While the selection of themes is in many ways similar to those found in the DDR Museum, the treatment of them is much more sympathetic and does not dismiss the ways of life on display as indicative of indoctrination and naiveté.

THE *OSTALGIE* INDUSTRY

As I have discussed in more detail elsewhere, the built environment of post-unification Berlin includes a number of key sites of memory—Checkpoint Charlie, a preserved section of the Berlin Wall, the Stasi Museum and the 'Stalin style' architecture build in the 1950s—that are now marketed as visitor attractions.[9] Others include museums related to the wall, the Friedrichstrasse border crossing and a Stasi prison. Running alongside this form of public history, which stresses repression, is a profitable market in memorabilia and GDR products and their reproductions. This belongs to the controversially termed '*Ostalgie*' industry. In dropping the 'n' from nostalgia, this neologism cleverly signals the German word for east, 'Ost,' creating a term that has acquired the negative connotations of being uncritical about the past. This distortion of the term 'nostalgia' is characteristic of more general moves, commonplace among West Germans, to dismiss positive accounts of everyday life in the GDR as mere blinkered denials of the oppressive nature of the state. The *Ostalgie* tendency was critiqued by scholars in the later 1990s but has subsequently become normalized. As Daphne Berdhal suggested in her 1999 article, '"(N)Ostalgie" for the present: Memory, Longing, and East German Things':

> The last several years have witnessed the birth and boom of a nostalgia industry in the former East Germany that has entailed the recuperation, (re)production,

> marketing, and merchandising of GDR products as well as the 'museumification' of GDR everyday life.[10]

Despite critiques of the term, *Ostalgie* is now a firm part of consumer culture directed at Germans and non-Germans alike and there are many businesses and websites that market themselves using this term. For example, the website *Top 10 Berlin* includes an *Ostalgie* page which lists a restaurant, shops, design and food outlets which seek to evoke a lost era:[11]

> In OSTEL you quickly feel that you are back in the past. Everything is furnished in the old Ost-Chic with yellow patterned wallpaper, standard lamps with beige lampshades and functional furniture.[12]

This is the marketing of affect for profit. Its various nostalgic or voyeuristic effects will necessarily vary according to the age, knowledge and experience of the visitor but like many representations of the GDR past, it is likely to be experienced as at best quaint or retro and as a pointer to how much better things are nowadays.

In an interesting appropriation and partial reversal of dominant discourses about life in the GDR, a shop in Strausberg on the outskirts of East Berlin is now marketing the '*Ostpaket*'. This references the '*Westpaket*', the term given to parcels of West German products that East Germans with relatives or friends in the West sometimes received and which have become a familiar motif in museum representations of life in the GDR. Like the *Westpaket* in the GDR, the *Ostpaket* contains goods not easily accessed on the other side of the former border (or even in mainstream stores in contemporary East Germany). Many of the varied contents are specially manufactured for the *Ostpaket* and their contents are described online as: 'pure nostalgia'. In the words of the *Top10 Berlin* website: 'Under the motto "Products Made in East Germany" Ostpaket in Stausberg near Berlin offers a broad palette of products from the former GDR and produced in East Germany'. The products on offer include food, beers, wines and soft drinks, East German films and cosmetics.[13] In addition to Ostpaket, there are also a number of Internet-based companies supplying East German products, for example, Ostprodukte-Versand, 'as seen on TV and in the press'. This business offers forty-one different boxes of products, most ranging in price between twenty and fifty Euros. In addition to food and drink, they include selections aimed at specific audiences and tailored to specific interest groups. Examples include a 'Trabi [Trabant] box', '24 GDR products for real Ossie [east German] men' and an 'NVA' (National People's Army) box. The contents of these boxes satirize the original GDR practice or institution. For example, the 'Held der Arbeit' (literally 'hero of work') box takes up the GDR honorary title, initiated in 1950, which was awarded annually by the state to up to fifty people for innovative contributions to the development of the socialist economy, particularly in industry, agriculture, transport and trade. Such contributions included scientific discoveries and technical inventions. Recipients received a medal and a bonus of up to ten thousand Marks. In the 'Held der Arbeit' box, the title is awarded for exceptional contributions to 'family, people [Volk] and fatherland'. The contents of the box include shower gel, a lapel badge, a bottle opener, a mug, a ruler and a certificate.[14]

This example shows how meaningful GDR state practices have become material for satire in ways that undermine their legitimacy and that of those who worked hard and achieved the award. It points to the reasons why there is a widespread feeling among ordinary people who lived and worked in the GDR, expressed in oral history interviews and frequently in conversation, that the things that made their lives meaningful are now treated negatively in ways that deny the legitimacy of their voices and experience. Interestingly the enterprises that market the *Ostpaket* do not use the term 'Ostalgie' but 'nostalgia' in their publicity, a term which does not necessarily have the negative connotations of *Ostalgie*.

LIVING WITH STEREOTYPES

The delegitimization of positive experience in the GDR is not the only negative aspect of how the past is remembered former GDR citizens and their families that regularly confront in public history. Stereotypes are another powerful form of silencing alternative ways of seeing the past. Various scholarly analyses of postunification mediatized culture have identified and discussed the stereotypes of the GDR in circulation. For example, writing in 1997, Kathrin Hörschelmann analysed filmic and TV representations of life in the GDR, concluding that:

> East Germans are often said to be more authoritarian and nationalistic, old fashioned in social attitudes, less confident, less used to taking care of themselves, and generally unable to adapt to the new, western, pluralist state. . . . Differences such as these between East and West Germans have come to be seen as self-evident and unquestionable, a 'fact' that simply needs to be accounted for. Their ongoing social construction in present-day political, academic and media discourses is seldom addressed.[15]

Recent forms of public history documenting the GDR in media programmes have largely been produced from perspectives in which the collapse of the State, at the end of forty years, determines the discursive strategies employed, including choice of archival film sequences, pictures and commentaries. This perspective tends to stress failings and downplay the positive features of life in the GDR and does not allow for the possibility that some aspects of this life might have been preferable to West Germany. TV programmes and DVDs produced since 1990 often focus on the 'SED Diktatur', the politicization of everyday life and on political interference in private life, themes that are omnipresent in documentaries.[16] Major among these themes is the Stasi, that is, the state security.

Yet recent years have also seen a number of documentary series shown on television that aim to show the younger generation what the GDR was 'really' like. A good example of this is the series 'Not everything was bad' (*Nicht alles war schlecht*). Sequences start in a positive way, mentioning achievements GDR citizens were proud of and invariably end in abstract negative statements. They depict GDR citizens as funny, often childishly naive and creative in the face of shortages, loving wild parties, music and alcohol. Many familiar stereotypes recur; for example, we are shown families enjoying the aroma of parcels sent by relatives or friends in the West. On close reading these television films might more accurately be titled: 'nearly everything was bad'.

It is possible to argue convincingly that these representations of life in the GDR tend to present a repertoire of socialist signs and signifiers, now voided of their contextual meanings. These undergo secondary semanticization, as for example in the case of state rituals, organizations and GDR products including furniture, food, clothing, music and TV. Effectively both history and the type of experience that oral history interviews describe are lost in the process. Dr Isolde Neubert-Köpsel has suggested that from the perspective of the East German viewer: 'The images presented become pure material to play with according to one's affectivity, mental state etc. One's lived history becomes a burlesque performance, especially in the "not everything was bad", ("Nicht alles war schlecht") approach to everyday life'.[17]

This mode of presentation sells well since it addresses people's needs to identify: an individual can pick out the signs which she or he might feel to be splinters of his or her personal history. This affective process can be experienced as comforting, convenient and/or individually empowering. Neubert-Köpsel comments:

> It is an important and legitimate strategy for most filmmakers, because individualism was largely neglected in the GDR. Viewers find themselves more at home in the (soothing) little signs of everyday life than in depictions of the social structure. This is represented as negative and doomed from the very beginning, and one might feel inclined to repress/ignore the impression that nearly all episodes are from the historical perspective of the winner looking down on the loser.[18]

East German viewers' emotional reaction to these films include feelings of loss and of being ridiculed and misunderstood. They often find their individual history denied and their individual life achievements devalued. As Neubert-Köpsel argues, this may well in part account for the nostalgic wish to revive aspects of a GDR that did not exist in quite the ways they are often remembered. Memories that may today be reconfigured as the negative sides of life in the GDR are edited out, and even negative experience is sometimes evaluated more positively from a position of historical distance. The danger here is that an individual's own knowledge/experience/memory becomes his/her referential framework, and this knowledge is unreliable.

CONTESTING BINARIES: THE STASI STAAT

No one wants to be a conformist. And yet we all did it. Are still doing it. Back then and today.[19]

The term 'Stasi state' plays a major role in hegemonic discourses of the GDR past and together with the trope of dictatorship, often appears to sum up life in the GDR. Many of those who lived and worked in the GDR and supported socialism, as well as those who opposed the State, remain critical of how the Stasi is represented in postpartition public history. It can be argued that while the role of the Stasi was clearly very extensive and often extremely brutal and repressive, the dominant role that it assumes in public history and tourism often serves to silence other factors that made the GDR what it was. Moreover, it often appears as unique to the GDR in more than its methods and extensiveness, and as if Western societies did not also have secret services.[20] The partial nature—in both senses of the term—of representations that privilege dictatorship and the Stasi implicitly suggest that people need look no further into the lives of people in the GDR than the role of these institutions in order to understand how and why the State survived for forty years. Yet such an approach cannot explain the real engagement and positive feelings and memories that persist both among older generations and their children in East Germany. The last two decades have seen a wide range of texts published on the Stasi ranging from histories, personal accounts of arrest and imprisonment to discussions of the ways in which the issue has been handled since 1989. They have also seen the publication of popular fiction and films thematizing the repressive aspects of the East German state.

For those who suffered detention, imprisonment and expatriation, the trauma of their encounters with the Stasi was often life changing. Many hours of oral history have been dedicated to collecting the stories of victims of the Stasi. Individuals have written about their experience of clandestine political protest, arrest, imprisonment and interrogation.[21] Central here has been a coming to terms with the role of the Stasi and people's complicity with it in everyday life. For those arrested for political dissidence, imprisoned and/or deported by the organs of state security and the legal apparatus, for those imprisoned for trying to leave the GDR for the West and for the families of those shot while trying to cross the border, there is a strongly felt need to make public individual, personal memories in the face of a homogenizing and often forgetful national memory.[22]

Much of this writing attempts to understand how the repressive apparatuses of the GDR remained largely unchallenged by the majority of those living there. For example, in his book *Wir Angepassten: Überleben in der DDR* (We Conformists: Survival in the GDR, 2014), Roland Jahn (born in 1953) draws on his own memories of his life in the GDR up to 1983 to explore and undermine a dominant binary—conformism or resistance—in post-1990 discourses on life in the GDR. Jahn was a student critic of the expatriation of singer-poet Wolf Biermann in 1976, a critique that cost him his university place.[23] He was finally arrested and found guilty of activities hostile to the state (*staatsfeindliche Aktivitäten*) in 1982. In 1983 he was released early, only to be deported to the West against his will. In the preface to his book Jahn writes: 'I believe that talking about the GDR offers an opportunity. Much remains to be said about this past. To speak openly of it can be liberating'.[24] Liberation in this context signifies a move beyond the binary lens through which most GDR citizens are seen as either conformists or rebels. Through description of concrete experiences, Jahn explores what makes people get used to things, remain silent and go along with the status quo, but also what motivates them to overcome fear and express overt resistance. He comments: 'All these memory share one thing. They show that life under conditions of dictatorship often confronts people with impossible decisions. One's own humanity is tested every now and then in an absurd way'.[25]

Jahn explains that one important objective of his text is to create a form of consciousness in which people could maintain the freedom to express themselves 'as they are', that is in ways that allow for exploration of questions of conformity and responsibility, unconstricted by binary ways of seeing.[26] Reflecting on public discourse, he writes of how the binary—perpetrator versus victim—dominates public discussion about the GDR. The victims are those who, aware of their human rights, fought and suffered for their right to self-determination. Some were imprisoned, some even paid with their lives. He comments:

> They have earned our regard, respect and sympathy. They experienced injustice, they were damaged in body and spirit, their lives often went off the rails as a result of the suppression of human rights in the GDR. And for this reason,

> coming to terms with this injustice requires that perpetrators and responsibility be named. The SED regime functioned because of the actions of many people responsible for the injustice. This pole of GDR society embodies the extreme and this makes it particularly interesting and insightful. But it does not reflect the whole picture: the majority of people who lived in the GDR cannot identify either with the definition of a perpetrator or a victim. The big debates about Stasi entanglement and the analysis of dictatorship sweep straight over their memory. The word 'dictatorship' does not immediately occur to many people when they think about their life in the GDR. The sun also shines in a dictatorship.[27]

The inability of much current discourse to include the memories and self-perception of most people who lived in the GDR is perhaps nowhere more pronounced than among the *Aufbau* generation, who dedicated their lives to building a state that they believed would ensure peace, put pay to fascism and rule out the exploitation and crises that governed the Weimar years. Yet arguably, it is the formative experience of this generation, to which many major political figures in the GDR belong, that throws most light on the reasons why people conformed to or supported the state and why dictatorship is not foremost in the minds of so many former GDR citizens. Moreover, it can be argued that it is the neglect of this history that leads to a situation in which stereotypes and clichés can flourish. Jahn suggests that the process of coming to terms with the past is necessarily slow:

> It has to be admitted that the path to honest memory is long. Not least, because we have talked about the GDR in clichés already for far too long. About guilt and shared guilt. About the perpetrators and repression. Not a few people react to this defensively having experienced the GDR themselves.[28]

As Jahn argues, recognition that life in the GDR was part of a 'functioning dictatorship' is uncomfortable. Yet the issue here is in part a recognition that the term 'dictatorship' is never one thing and that in the Marxist tradition the dictatorship of the proletariat was not regarded as a negative but as a necessary stage in the path to socialism. This points to a wider problem in current representations of life in the GDR, according to which all life and agency tends to be related directly back to an unspecified category of dictatorship that does not allow for the different, contested and changing understandings in the GDR of what Marxist theory termed the 'dictatorship of the proletariat'. However flawed the Leninist/Stalinist GDR state was, it was nonetheless rooted for many in the belief in the possibility of a better socialist society. The impossibility of achieving this, given the Cold War context and the lure of the Federal Republic, is an important and often missing aspect of this past.

PARTITION AND ITS LEGACIES

The constitutions drawn up in 1949 in the two Germanies and subsequent changes to them illustrate the nature of this partition and the form taken by its partial resolution in 1990. The preamble to the GDR constitution of 7 October 1949, speaking as if for all German people, framed its aims in the language of universal values, asserting that:

> The German People, imbued with the desire to safeguard human liberty and rights, to reshape collective and economic life in accordance with the principles of social justice, to serve social progress, and to promote a secure peace and amity with all peoples, have adopted this Constitution.[29]

In contrast, the Grunggesetz (Basic Law) of the Federal Republic, passed in May 1949, stressed its incomplete and transitory status:

> The German people in the regions of Baden, Bayern, Bremen, Hamburg, Hessen, Niedersachsen, Nordrhein-Westfalen, Rheinland-Pfalz, Schleswig-Holstein, Württemberg-Baden und Württemberg-Hohenzollern, conscious of their responsibility to God and mankind, driven by the will to preserve their national and state unity and to serve peace as an equal member of a unified Europe, have passed this basic law of the Federal Republic in order to give the life of the state a new form for a transitory period. It has also acted on behalf of those Germans prevented from participating. It remains the task of the whole German people in free self-determination to complete the unity and freedom of Germany.

After reunification in 1990, this preamble was modified to include the statement that the German people 'have achieved the unity and freedom of Germany in free self-determination. This Basic Law thus applies to the entire German people'.

After 1990, the territory of the GDR became once again a collection of regions within a larger Germany rather than a country in its own right, and the Basic Law offers useful pointers to dominant motives in postreunification discourse. This tends overwhelmingly to characterize the GDR as unfree and repressive and partition as an issue that only concerns those who lived in the former GDR. It is seldom acknowledged that the GDR had alternative ideas of 'freedom' and a value system and set of educational and social welfare provisions that were in many ways positive. The two postwar German states held very different ideas of 'freedom' and 'democracy'. In the GDR, the emphasis was on freedom from social ills such as war, unemployment, ignorance, poverty and ill-health, whereas in West Germany emphasis was very much on freedom to do things. However much truth there is in the postpartition characterization of the GDR regime as repressive and as a (self-proclaimed) dictatorship (ostensibly of the proletariat), differentiation is seldom made in postpartition discourse between the good and the bad aspects of the system.

The focus in public history on the internal political and economic culture of the GDR tends to leave the question of the other side of the partition and the role played by West Germany out of the frame. In critiquing the GDR, questions are rarely asked about West German society, politics and culture between 1949 and 1989 or the effects of its policies and propaganda on the GDR and its citizens' perceptions of the West. Yet, it is undoubtedly the case that however morally superior many East Germans believed their ideals and values to be, for those in power, these were perceived as legitimizing a centralized state under Socialist Unity Party rule and a planned economy that was impervious to critique and relentless in its pursuit of dissidents.[30] State practice was marked by a consistent overestimation of the power of ideology that led to restricted travel and attempts to control access to Western media, censorship of social and political writing and of literature and the arts. It also underpinned the rapid expansion of the Stasi after the suppressed uprising of 1953. Education of the population in socialist ideas and values was seen as crucial, more especially in the years before the border was completely sealed with the building of the Berlin Wall in August 1961. In reality, no amount of socialist rhetoric or felt moral superiority could outweigh the limitations of the planned economy in providing consumer goods and a standard of living comparable to that experienced in West Germany, even though after the sealing of the border in 1961, the GDR became a much richer society than its socialist neighbours in the Eastern bloc. Yet while East Germans were well aware of the different standards of living in East and West, many continued to endorse the idea of a more moral socialist society and looked eagerly for a third way in 1989.

Positive memories of life in the GDR preserved in oral history interviews are necessarily tempered (like the actual lived experience at the time) by the very real material constraints under which people lived, including shortages of many nonbasic commodities, restrictions on travel and the role of the Stasi. Both the oral history interviews that I conducted in 1993 and more recent ones from 2014 to 2017, as well as those by other researchers,[31] suggest that these constraints were experienced very differently by different people and need to be weighed against positive aspects of everyday life in the GDR, many of which radically contradicted the privileging of neoliberal Western subjects of 'freedom', choice and consumption.

For East Germans, East and West Berliners and their families, partition remained a lived reality until 1989. Subsequently, as many scholars have argued, partition lives on in the different ways of thinking and socioeconomic opportunities in East and West Germany. Aspects of the different cultures produced in East and West under partition have remained a site for the articulation of discontent with reunified Germany. Where memory is concerned, I would argue that despite the decades that have passed since the founding and the collapse of the East German state, the battle over the meanings of its history remains important, and unless the 'united' Germany promotes a more complex and 'just' memory of the past,[32] serious divisions will remain, living on in family memory and serving as a site for ongoing forms of resistance.

The tendency in West Germany to dismiss any positive recollections of life in the GDR as *Ostalgie* not only testifies to a discursive strategy that seeks to delegitimize GDR voices, but also one that refuses to recognize aspects of GDR society and social provision that were arguably better than in the West. It also denies the positive aspects of nostalgia. Viewed as an 'affective space', nostalgia can function in various ways: for example, as a site of pleasure in past memories, or as a technique for coping with the present by granting access to places that have become inaccessible. A good example of this is the success of GDR rock music since the fall of the Berlin Wall. It can serve as an empowering counter-narrative and source of positive identity as well as a form of pleasurable escapism.[33]

Among the effects of dominant modes of representations of the GDR is the exclusion of the majority, who in the words of Isolde Neubert-Köpsel:

> Settled down in the GDR and made a living. Identified with their state and became neither advocates of 'evil' nor uncritically conformist.
> Accepted the 'dictatorship of the proletariat' and the restrictions on travel as a possibly/hopefully transitory period to a better society.
> Raised a family and benefited from the social provisions and health care, and were thankful not to be threatened by unemployment and financial problems.
> Liked their jobs and the working environment and socialized with friends and members of the collective at work and even at the weekends and in their spare time.
> Enjoyed the admittedly restricted domestic holiday resorts or went abroad to get to know the other socialist countries.
> Developed a lot of spare time activities according to their interests not prescribed by the state.[34]

The idea that the GDR was morally superior to West Germany and that socialism was at least potentially a better and more just system than capitalism survived among many East Germans until the 1990s and lives on among many members of the older generation who at the time of the *Wende* hoped for a third way. In thinking about what we can learn from depictions of German partition and its aftermath it becomes clear just how important public sites of memory and media representations are in shaping how the past is remembered. At issue here are whose voices and whose perspectives are heard. Perhaps the most important aspect of how the past is remembered concerns our understanding of how the past came to be and how it might have been different. This is important for imagining different futures.

NOTES

1. The chapter is part of a larger project on the politics of memory that looks at what I would term 'located memory'. Its focus is on social forgetting and remembering; resistance to hegemonic narratives; counter memory; and memory and identity in relation to the GDR.

2. As discussed below, less-negative narratives about life in the GDR, where they occur at all, most often surface in relation to the clichés of everyday life in the GDR after 1961.

3. For more on this see, for example, Eric D. Weitz, *Creating German Socialism, 1890–1990* (Princeton, NJ: Princeton University Press, 1997), 311–87 and Stefan Wolle's three-volume history *Die heile Welt der Diktatur: Alltag und Herrschaft in der DDR 1949–1989* (Berlin: Ch. Links Verlag, 2013).

4. See R. M. Douglas, *Orderly and Humane: The Expulsion of the Germans after the Second World War* (New Haven, CT: Yale University Press, 2012).

5. Between 1950 and 1989, the Stasi employed a total of 274,000 people in the GDR. Statistics for 1989 include 173,081 unofficial informants.

6. http://www.deutschlandfunk.de/ostalgie-und-alltagskultur. 691.de.html?dram:article_id=49825 (accessed 23 May 2015).

7. 'faule, unfähige, verantwortungslose und demokratieunfähige Jammerlappen . . . , die man zu früh kollektiv auf den Nachttopf gesetzt hat, so dass aufgrund der psychischen Verformung Änderung wohl nicht in Sicht sein kann'. Heinz Eggert, 'Der Ossi, die Banane und deutsch-deutsche Klischees', 2 October, http://www.sz-online.de/nachrichten/der-ossi-die-banane-und-deutsch-deutsche-klischees-1869193.html (accessed 1 June 2015).

8. Available at https://www.visitberlin.de/de/museum-der-kulturbrauerei (accessed 11 November 2017).

9. See Chris Weedon, 'Place and Space and the Politics of Memory', in David Walton and Juan A. Suárez, eds., *Culture, Space and Power: Blurred Lines* (Lanham, MD: Lexington Books, 2016), 1–18.

10. Berdhal, Daphne. 1999. '"(N)Ostalgie" for the Present: Memory, Longing and East German Things'. *Ethnos* 64 (2): 192.

11. See the Visit Berlin website: http://www.visitberlin.de/en/see/berlins-locations-of-world-history/the-gdr (accessed 13 June 2016).

12. Available at http://www.top10berlin.de/de/cat/freizeit-268/ostalgie-1967 (accessed 11 October 2017).

13. See http://www.top10berlin.de/de/cat/freizeit-268/ostalgie-1967/ostpaket-2095#1 (accessed 31 October 2017).

14. https://www.ostprodukte-versand.de/ostpaket.html (accessed 11 October 2017).

15. Kathrin Hörschelmann, 'Watching the East: Constructions of "Otherness" in TV Representations of East Germany', *Applied Geography* 17, no. 4 (1997): 387–88.

16. See, for example, 'Goodbye, GDR. Das Ende der DDR', 'Das war die DDR', especially episodes 6 and 7; 'So war die DDR', Kinder des Ostens, especially part 2/school and 3/leisure. Available at https://www.zdf.de/dokumentation/zdfinfo-doku/ddr-geschichte-von-der-staatsgruendung-1949-bis-zum-100.html (accessed 29 January 18).

17. Isolde Neubert-Köpsel, who sadly died in 2016, was a long-term friend and colleague in Berlin with whom I regularly discussed my research and who commented on aspects of it.

18. Email correspondence with Isolde Neubert-Köpsel.

19. 'Niemand will ein Anpasser sein. Und doch haben wir es alle getan. Und tun es noch. Damals und heute'. Roland Jahn, *Wir Angepassten:* Überleben *in der DDR* (Munich/Berlin: Piper, 2014), 13. Ostprodukte-Versand, https://www.ostprodukte-versand.de/ostpaket.html (accessed 10 November 2017).

20. Interestingly, the 2013 film *West*, in which a mother and child escape from East to West Berlin, shows how she is interviewed by the US secret service in much the same way as by the Stasi.

21. See, for example, the account of Stasi interrogation by Jürgen Fuchs, *Vernehmungsprotokolle: November 76 bis September 77* (Berlin: Jaron Verlag, 2009).

22. Various anthologies and single-authored texts about attempts to leave the GDR illegally have been published since 1990, as well as novels about the lives of children left behind.

23. Born in Hamburg in 1936, Wolf Biermann moved to the GDR at the age of seventeen and became a critical singer-songwriter committed to a better form of socialism. From 1965 he was no longer allow to publish or perform in public and he was refused reentry to the GDR and deprived of his citizenship in 1976 while on an authorized tour of West Germany. A number of writers and artists protested openly about his expatriation.

24. Jahn, *Wir Angepassten*, 11.

25. Ibid., 12.

26. Ibid., 79.

27. Ibid., 16.

28. Ibid., 167.

29. A translation is available at https://www.cvce.eu/content/publication/1999/1/1/33cc8de2-3cff-4102-b524-c1648172a838/publishable_en.pdf (accessed 12 November 2017).

30. As historians, social scientists and oral history interviews suggest, it had become clear by 1961—the year that the Berlin Wall was built—that the state was unviable. Rather than beginning from the 1.448 billion-dollar input of financial re-

sources that were invested in the Federal Republic via the Marshall plan (1948–1952), the GDR was stripped of much of its industrial and infrastructural assets which were dismantled and transported to the Soviet Union as reparations. (While the Allied plans for dismantling German industry were implemented in all zones, this strategy largely came to an end in 1949 and ceased completely in 1951.) The Marshall Plan had strings attached that related, for example, to dismantling trade barriers and would have given the United States a say in the economic development of the Soviet bloc. For this reason, American money was refused by the Soviet Union both for itself and the countries of the Eastern bloc.

31. The interviews that I collected will be published in English in due course. There is a range of anthologies by other scholars of published interviews in German as well as archives of audio-visual interviews and short films on YouTube. See http://www.defa-stiftung.de/zeitzeugen-archiv and http://www.ddr-zeitzeuge.de (accessed 29 January 2018).

32. Paul Ricoeur, *Memory, History, Forgetting*, trans. K. Blamey and D. Pellauer (Chicago: University of Chicago Press, 2004), xv.

33. See for example, Peter Wicke, '"Born in the GDR": Ostrock between Ostalgia and Cultural Self-assertion', *Journal of Contemporary Central and Eastern Europe* 6, no. 2 (1998): 148–55.

34. Email correspondence with Isolde Neubert-Köpsel.

REFERENCES

Berdhal, Daphne. 1999. "(N)Ostalgie" for the Present: Memory, Longing and East German Things'. *Ethnos* 64 (2): 192–211.

Douglas, R. M. 2012. *Orderly and Humane: The Expulsion of the Germans after the Second World War.* New Haven, CT: Yale University Press.

Eggert, Heinz. 2009. 'Der Ossi, die Banane und deutsch-deutsche Klischees'. http://www.sz-online.de/nachrichten/der-ossi-die-banane-und-deutsch-deutsche-klischees-1869193.html (accessed 1 June 2015).

Fuchs, Jürgen. 2009. *Vernehmungsprotokolle: November 76 bis September 77.* Berlin: Jaron Verlag.

'Goodbye, GDR. Das Ende der DDR'. n.d. https://www.zdf.de/dokumentation/zdfinfo-doku/ddr-geschichte-von-der-staatsgruendung-1949-bis-zum-100.html (accessed 29 January 2018).

Hörschelmann, Kathrin. 1997. 'Watching the East: Constructions of "Otherness" in TV Representations of East Germany'. *Applied Geography* 17 (4): 385–97.

Jahn, Roland. 2014. *Wir Angepassten:* Überleben *in der DDR*. Munich/Berlin: Piper. *Ostprodukte-Versand.* https://www.ostprodukte-versand.de/ostpaket.html (accessed 10 November 2017).

Museum of Everyday Life. *Visit Berlin.* https://www.visitberlin.de/de/museum-der-kulturbrauerei (accessed 11 November 2017).

Ricoeur, Paul. 2004. *Memory, History, Forgetting*. Translated by K. Blamey and D. Pellauer. Chicago: University of Chicago Press.

Top 10 Berlin. http://www.top10berlin.de/de/cat/freizeit-268/ostalgie-1967 (accessed 11 October 2017).

Visit Berlin. n.d. http://www.visitberlin.de/en/see/berlins-locations-of-world-history/the-gdr (accessed 13 June 2016).

Weedon, Chris. 2016. 'Place and Space and the Politics of Memory'. In *Culture, Space and Power: Blurred Lines*, edited by David Walton and Juan A. Suárez, 1–18. Lanham, MD: Lexington Books.

Weitz, Eric D. 1997. *Creating German Socialism, 1890–1990.* Princeton, NJ: Princeton University Press.

Wicke, Peter. 1998. '"Born in the GDR": Ostrock between Ostalgia and Cultural Self-assertion'. *Journal of Contemporary Central and Eastern Europe* 6 (2): 148–55.

Wolle, Stefan. 2013. *Die heile Welt der Diktatur: Alltag und Herrschaft in der DDR 1949–1989*. Berlin: Ch. Links Verlag.

———. n.d. 'DDR Museum'. http://www.deutschlandfunk.de/ostalgie-und-alltagskultur (accessed 23 May 2015).

Chapter 6

Memory Wars and Identity Construction

Return of the Suppressed as Afterlife of Partition under the Hindutva Rule in India

Samuel Sequeira

On 18 February 2018 a small province, Tripura, in the North East of India went to the polls. This was a province that had been ruled by the Left Front (a coalition of Communist parties) for the previous twenty-five years. But with this election the Bharatiya Janata Party (BJP), the Hindu nationalist party, also known for its adherence and promotion of Hindutva[1] ideology, won a majority and formed the government. In Indian democracy, the norm consists of holding elections with political parties winning or losing the elections and the subsequent smooth transfer of power. But what was not so normal in this instance was what followed the Tripura Assembly poll results. Soon after the results were announced on 3 March 2018, a BJP-supporting mob used bulldozers to raze to the ground two statues of Lenin in the towns named Belonia and Sabroom. The justifications offered by Hindutva ideologues for this vandalism was that Lenin is a terrorist and the communist ideology is not indigenous but foreign to India. In a tit for tat that followed in the subsequent days, statues of several other icons revered by different identity groups were vandalized. In West Bengal, a mob vandalized the statue of Hindu nationalist leader Shyamaparasad Mukherjee. In Kerala, the glass cover protection of Mahatma Gandhi's statue was broken. In Tamil Nadu, following comments from a BJP leader, the statue of Periyar Ramaswamy, a non-Brahmin Dravida icon of the Tamils, was defaced. In Uttar Pradesh, several statues of Dr Ambedkar, the Dalit icon, were vandalized.[2] To top it all, on 3 May 2018 a group of Hindutva supporters barged into Aligharh Muslim University (AMU) demanding the removal of Muhammad Ali Jinnah's portrait from the Student Union building. Jinnah was once the leader of the Indian National Congress and a strong proponent of Hindu–Muslim unity and then, due to the evolving nature of prepartition Indian politics, was forced to be the leader of the Muslim League which claimed to represent the interests of Muslims in prepartition India. But Jinnah's portrait adorned the wall of the Student Union building of AMU for a different reason—his portrait was alongside other illustrious alumni of the institution and those who represented and furthered Muslim interests and identity in India.[3] However, for the 'nationalist' Hindutva party in India, he is a traitor because of his alleged role in partitioning the nation, the oft-repeated myth and assumption perpetuated by the historiography of the Indian partition which is effectively challenged by historians such as Ayesha Jalal.[4] But for the Muslims, as well as for secular Indians, Jinnah was a great leader who fought for the freedom of India. He is also remembered for his achievements as a highly educated and illustrious legal luminary in British India who represented Indian causes and defended the freedom fighters of India in the law courts of London.[5] This memory of the role of Jinnah and the Muslims in India's freedom struggle is under interrogation by the Hindutva ideologues and the BJP government of India today.

The aforementioned incidents are a glimpse of how India is reenacting today a version of the discourses and conflicts that led to the partition of the country in 1947. In the early years after independence and the partition, India, under its first Prime Minister Jawaharlal Nehru, embarked on a secular, socialist model of nation building despite the party and its leaders' chequered history in their role in the partition of the country, their open espousal of Hindu majoritarian interests and even perpetration of communal politics.[6] However, after partition for a relatively long period, identity conflicts were not dominant or as sharp as today. In fact, in the first few decades following independence, all identity conflicts were subsumed under the goal of nation building. The other reason for the domination of Nehru's secularist vision was the dormancy of today's dominant ideology, Hindutva, which as the brain child of the Rashtriya Swayamsevak Sangh (RSS) was banned due to its alleged involvement in the assassination of Mahatma Gandhi, the father of the nation. However, since the 1980s, India's gradual adoption of globalization and neoliberal economic policies has resulted in the resurfacing of the identity conflicts.[7] The phoenix-like rise of the Hindu Right, subscribing to the Hindutva ideology, which has consciously initiated memory wars throughout the country, is a significant change witnessed in recent years. These conflicts over memory are enacted in multiple spheres and through multiple strategies, often attracting backlash but vehemently furthered through violence against and between various groups that stand in their way.

In this article I would like to focus on how, in India, multiple memories have been vying for hegemony during the independence movement and how, even after seventy years since independence and the partition, the struggle over memory between ideologies, religious groups, castes, genders, languages and regions continues to grip the nation. The current vexed phenomenon of nationwide unrest among various groups such as students, farmers, job seekers, intellectuals, political parties, women (protesting against the normalizing of rapes and violence against them), Muslims and Dalits (protesting against lynching and discrimination) warrants a longer discussion about how the suppressed or rejected ideology of Hindutva has managed to emerge as hegemonic in recent times and has been trying to claw back the social, economic and democratic progress achieved over previous decades. The discussion will focus on how the BJP or the Hindutva Party in power has been trying to erase the secular, inclusive memory that dominated until now and, in its place, reinstall the once discredited casteist, communal, hierarchic and upper caste/class hegemonic memory by revising historical writings and by trying to erase the symbols of secular, inclusive national memory. This section is elaborately dealt with because the very dynamics of communal politics that resulted in the partition have been brought to centre stage by Hindutva ideology in India today along with the discourses of communal violence, caste and linguistic divisiveness and Hindu majoritarianism. The chapter will also discuss how the Dalits,[8] minorities and the secular forces are fighting back to reestablish the secular, democratic and inclusive memories that held the nation together since independence. This entire conflict of memory politics is playing out through media debates, political discourses and physical violence by means of which certain memories are legitimized while others are being forced into erasure. This dynamic is also a vindication of the relationship between power, memory and history.

HISTORY, MEMORY, POWER

History is an ever-contested area of discourse because it has to stand the test and claims of memory. In any country, multiple competing identities force themselves to be recognized and represented within discourses on national identity. At the same time, dominant historical discourse is underpinned by multiple powers that try to establish their hegemony over national memory, which then generally gets accepted as official history.[9] While the governments with competing ideologies and agendas try to 'own' and mould history, individuals and groups also vie for a place within the national narrative.[10] Very often this process involves the use and abuse of power and violence. This violent and forceful character of inscribing memory in historical writings stems from the role played by social actors who wield social, political and economic power and by those that are involved in archiving, narrating and legitimizing these memories through the process of cultural representations and social practices.[11] As an outcome of this struggle some memories and identities find adequate recognition and representation while others are subjugated, ignored, lost, suppressed and often forcefully erased in order that a particular narrative gets its dominant place.[12] Hence, when one particular historical narrative that is propagated by the powerful groups becomes official history of a nation, then, in a democracy, multiple actors and movements that are aggrieved by their lack of representation fight for their legitimate memory-space. In order to do so, they have recourse to the collective memory of their group or community. This entire effort and struggle is undertaken to forge an identity for the group or community.[13] In other words, this identity construction is a strategy for group survival. In a democracy where numbers can counter the power of money, groups strive to organize themselves around an identity that offers them numerical strength with the clear objective of gaining political recognition.[14]

The dominant historical narratives pertaining to independence struggle, the partition and the new nation states that emerged after partition try to show how three opposing sets of memories and ideologies adhered to predominantly by three groups (the Indian National Congress,[15] the Hindu Mahasabha[16] and the Muslim League[17]) vied for recognition and/or dominance.[18] According to this generally accepted myth, the entire movement was a clash of predominantly two types of nationalistic narratives: secularism, multiculturalism and inclusivism on the one side as against majoritarianism, communalism and exclusionary discourse on the other, though during the preindependent days this distinction was not so clear cut. It is because even many within the Congress Party who advocated inclusiveness were neither the strongest votaries of inclusiveness nor secularism, as some leaders wanted the Congress Party to strongly advocate for Hindu interests. Moreover, most Congress leaders, including Gandhi, were very religious and used religion as part of the political movement.[19] In contrast, not all from among the Muslim League could be branded totally communal. This is borne out by the fact that Muhammad Ali Jinnah, the leader of the Muslim League, had been a staunch secularist and was once the president of the Indian National Congress. However, during this period of political evolution and the increasing communalization of society, the general perception was that Congress predominantly represented the majority Hindu interests and the Muslim League the majority of the Muslims.[20] Despite these volatile realities, the secular and inclusive discourses were perceived to be represented by the Indian National Congress and the communal, majoritarian and exclusionary discourses were perceived to be represented by the votaries of Hindutva, with the Hindu Mahasabha claiming to represent all Hindus and the Muslim League claiming to represent all Muslims. These groups vied for a certain kind of memory to dominate in the kind of nations that they visualized. Accordingly, historical discourse in the newly constituted countries (India and Pakistan) veered towards legitimizing the successful narratives in view of building them into national narratives. In the case of India, between the 1950s, to the 1980s it was the purported secular narrative of the Indian National Congress, with the motto 'unity in diversity', that found legitimacy while the exclusionary, divisive, majoritarian Hindutva discourses got suppressed. Also, the weight of the grand narrative of 'unity in diversity' suppressed subaltern discourses of women, Dalits, tribals and even farmers.[21] Hindutva ideology, represented by its political wing Hindu Mahasabha, suffered a backlash because of its involvement in the assassination of Mahatma Gandhi while Dalit memory remained unrepresented due to the domination of the independence movement by the elite class and due to the poor socioeconomic condition of the Dalits within society. In turn, Pakistan had initially adopted a secular constitution in 1956 but had amended it in 1973 to reflect an Islamic bias so that the national memory was recast to reflect a Sunni majoritarianism and an exclusionary nationalism. The fruits of this change are visible to the present day in the mushrooming of the majoritarian vigilante groups of Sunni Muslims, who continually attack minorities and their cultural symbols. A similar change is taking place in India today. With the emergence of Hindutva politics, the secular discourses and memories that dominated India for the last seventy years since independence have been challenged by the once 'vanquished' or subservient discourses of the time, both the Hindutva groups as well as the subalterns, especially the Dalits and the Adivasis (tribals). The ascendency of these new discourses, especially the majoritarian Hindutva discourses, started emerging with full force from the 1980s. By mobilizing majority Hindus along communal lines and gaining state power in 1998 and again in 2014, and by controlling power in many provincial assemblies, Hindutva groups have already succeeded in bringing into the political mainstream the once suppressed and discarded majoritarian, communal and divisive discourses. Due to the lack of social, economic and political power, the same has not happened with the subaltern groups such as the Dalits, Adivasis and minorities, who still fight for their legitimate place and memories to be inscribed in postindependent India.

Current Hindutva hegemony is accompanied by an attempt to erase or reinterpret national memories through violence, the use of state machinery as well as the use of media that the government has co-opted to fall in line with its official revisionist project. In so doing, there is a systematic delegitimization of the secular and minority groups such as Dalits whose marginalized memories and voices had found some space in Nehruvian secularism. This is the key difference between the current Hindutva rule and the previous regime of other supposedly secular parties, especially the Indian National Congress[22] where multiple memories, including the Hindutva, found a level of place and space in the public domain. Previously I alluded to how the struggle over memory resulted in the destruction of symbols and icons representing different groups and ideologies. Other strategies for the manipulation of memory include: the renaming of streets, buildings, railway stations; the alteration of school syllabi, the revisions and rewritings of history books; the renaming of monuments and even the violent razing to the ground of monuments and places of worship.

In tracing the 'afterlife of the Indian partition' here I would like to focus on the contesting discourses and violent conflicts around two historic symbols and memory narratives that are in question today: Tipu Sultan, the Muslim ruler of Mysore, the commemoration of whose birthday represents the secular, inclusive (minority) narrative of nationalist history; and the Bhima Koregaon event and its annual commemoration in Maharashtra which represents the memory of Dalit valour in the battle against upper-caste atrocities against them. By attacking these and many other symbols which once represented secular, minority or Dalit memories, the Hindutva narrative is trying to delegitimize the identities represented by these symbols and reinscribe them with the chauvinistic, upper-caste, hierarchic version of memory. The typical means used to achieve this objective are violence, use of state machinery, communal riots, falsification of history and the use of 'nationalism/antinationalism' discourses. These discourses are deployed to delegitimize certain groups of citizens that question upper-caste hegemony and prejudices that are being imposed on the nation and resist this violent appropriation of memory and history. The most recent use of the state machinery to silence critics and those associated with fighting for the rights of the Dalits and tribals was evident in the attempt to accuse five human rights activists of inciting violence at Bhima Koregaon on 2 January 2018.[23] These examples are just instances of the Hindutva agenda for expanding the space of their influence by provoking flashpoints along multiple sites. However, through discursive reclamation of the very same symbols that the Hindutva is trying to appropriate or delegitimize, the secular, democratic and inclusive nationalist as well as Dalit assertion movements are fighting back.

At the root of these conflicts lie two opposing ideological perspectives that define nationalism. Before discussing further the pitfalls of the violent nature of the exclusionary Hindutva war on inclusive national memory, it is pertinent to focus briefly on the different ways nationalism is articulated by the Hindutva groups represented by the Hindu Mahasabha and the secular democratic groups represented by Indian National Congress (despite its chequered history of appeasing the majority Hindus and not acting firmly in times of majoritarian communal violence). This discussion is because the concept of nationalism and the articulation of national identity as well as the inclusionary and exclusionary discourses that form part of these wars are at the root of the past and present memory wars.

INDIAN NATIONALISM: CLASH OF IDEOLOGIES AND WAR OF MEMORY

Indian national consciousness or the idea of nationalism was not something that was always there when India was ruled by monarchies, princely states or even the Europeans. Its origin is attributed to the 1857 uprising and it took a definite shape during the struggle for independence and with the establishment of the Indian National Congress in 1885.[24] Also, Indian nationalism considerably differs from how nationalism had evolved in the West in that European nationalism stressed the importance of a single religion and language as the constitutive elements of nationalism.[25] Furthermore, in order to hold the nation together, European nationalism also considered minorities to be second-class citizens and identified an enemy within who also needed to be fought against, though most of these nations have evolved into multicultural societies today. In short, in its original defining features, it is an exclusionary nationalism. In contradistinction to the European model, Indian nationalism was an outcome of the national independence movement. It was essentially a democratic and egalitarian nationalism as opposed to the aggrandizing European form.[26] It was a nationalism that is inclusive of religious, caste and class differences in its character. That's the reason India is at home with multiple languages, cultures, religions and ethnicities. This was the idea of secular, democratic, pluralist nationalism that was associated with the independence movement and personalities such as Mahatma Gandhi, Jawaharlal Nehru, Maulana Azad, Vallabhbhai Patel and others who were part of the Indian National Congress. However, it must also be noted that great personalities associated with the congress including Gandhi, Patel and Azad were deeply religious people, but unlike the proponents of Hindutva they were neither fanatics nor supremacists.

In opposition to the above conception of nationalism, the two other ideologies, Hindutva[27] and Islam were strictly in line with the European[28] kind of nationalism where majoritarianism is the key feature of the nation, and where one single language and religion were forced upon the nation (of course with little success) while those who differ from this definition were to be treated as second-class citizens. Accordingly, after the partition, and though in 1956 Pakistan adopted a secular constitution, since 1973 it has evolved into an Islamic state where Sunni Islam has become the official state religion, Urdu the national language and minorities treated as unequal citizens. Similarly, Hindutva groups in India desire that Hinduism be the religion of India and Hindi imposed throughout the country as the national language. In this perspective too, minorities are to be treated as unequal citizens.[29] But due to the victory of secular nationalism for reasons mentioned already India shunned officially the majoritarian, exclusionary and unitary vision of the nation.

In today's context of Hindutva domination in India, however, the once discarded version of majoritarian Hindu nationalism is being reimposed upon the nation. Anyone who opposes this view is treated as an antinational and often punished by mobs, defamed by the media and intimidated through social media by Hindutva trolls. In this category are included dissenting scribes, intellectuals, NGOs, university students, journalists, Dalits, minorities, women and even the secular opposition parties.[30] Very often even the state itself officially tries to punish the individuals and institutions through the use of archaic laws, withholding funding or instituting legal action. With this approach, a large section of society finds itself on the wrong side of the dominant ideology and becomes the target of intolerance. This ideological war waged by Hindutva resembles the doctrines of European fascism and Nazi ideology of ethnic and religious supremacism.[31] Before discussing Hindutva and its strategies of memory wars further, it is necessary to have a brief discussion about how a once vanquished ideology (Hindutva) has been able to occupy the national mainstream.

NEOLIBERALISM, FAILURE OF THE STATE AND IDENTITY POLITICS

During the first few decades after independence, successive governments in India had followed a socialist economic model where state participation, either as a monopoly player or in competition with the private sector, was the norm in most sectors of the economy. During this period the government, while being a major economic player, was also an important employment generator. This was also the period when the job reservations policy in the public sector for economically and socially disadvantaged groups was enacted. Being a new democracy, this was the time when people had placed their faith in the state to effect changes in their lives through various socio-economic programmes. Hence, as part of its planned development model the government was intervening positively in the agricultural sector through land reforms and enabling modern ways of farming that had ushered in the famous 'Green Revolution'. However, in view of aligning the Indian economy with world capitalism, successive governments since the 1990s opened the Indian economy to the private sector and international capital along with the privatization of state assets. With this, India was opened to the forces of 'globalization' or neoliberal economic practices.[32] Also, with this development, Radhika Desai argues, India entered into the realm of communitarian and nationalistic politics.[33]

The two key characteristics of a capitalist state in the era of neoliberalism described by Prabhat Patnaik are:

> One relates to the change in the nature of the State, from being an entity apparently standing above society and intervening in its economic functioning in the interests of society as a whole, even at the expense of the unbridled interests of finance capital (such as for instance the State in the era of Keynesian demand management), to being an entity acting exclusively to promote the interests of finance capital. This change in the nature of the capitalist State, which is sometimes mistakenly called the 'retreat of the State', is manifest in the shift that occurs from its being a spender, an investor and a producer, to its new role in carrying out 'privatization' and 'disinvestment' (all of which benefit finance capital) and undertaking State expenditure deflation (which accedes to a perennial demand of finance capital).[34]

Having transformed from being a state working to improve the wellbeing of its citizens to working to further the interests of finance capital, or from being a spender, investor and producer to one reducing state expenditure by carrying out privatization, the state has become virtually incapable of taking care of its citizens' needs effectively. Instead, due to the free flow of capital and the opening of the market for big business, the small producers, artisans and farmers are pushed out of their businesses, trades and farms. This phenomenon generates a huge number of jobless people migrating to the cities, living on sustenance-level wages earned through jobs without security and tenure. Lacking both state support and social security, they add to the already swelling numbers of the urban poor. With this surplus labour at their beck and call, the corporate world succeeds in entrenching its power against the workers' collective bargaining power. To make things worse for democracy, by financing state functionaries in exchange for their policy support to help corporate interests, the corporate world strengthens its stranglehold over the governments. To put it in Patnaik's words again: 'the increase in the political power of the corporate financial elite, integrated to the world of globalised finance, has as its counterpart a decline in the political power of the working class, as well as of the peasantry and petty producers, who are pushed increasingly into penury and distress. The era of globalisation thus brings about a decisive shift in the balance of class forces'.[35]

This new situation where the state becomes incapable of taking care of its people while at thc same time being beholden to finance capital and multinational businesses results in people losing faith in the political system. The economic degeneration suffered by people engenders social anxiety which forces them to take shelter under the security of their *archaic* or *traditional* identities based on caste, religion, language, territory, race, gender and so on, and, in most cases, people choose religion and nationalism as their preferred response. These two primordial identities offer them security and hope.[36] One of the main features of this 'identity politics' is called the 'identity fascist' politics.[37] In this category are included Hindutva in India, Zionism in Israel, and White Supremacism in the United States and Europe, all of which campaign virulently against another target group such as Muslims, Palestinians, immigrants, minorities and so forth.

NEOLIBERALISM AND THE RISE OF HINDUTVA

In the case of India, the ushering in of globalization set in motion a political flux. According to Radhika Desai, this political flux towards communitarian and nationalistic politics began at the 'decisive point at which the crucial component of independent India's early development strategy—the social transformation of its agriculture as the basis of a sustained, broad-based and domestic capitalist industrialization in India—was pronounced [to be] a failure'.[38] The social transformation saw the agricultural bourgeois finding their economic interests in the urban and industrial sectors bringing them in alignment with provincial propertied classes that resulted in the formation of regional parties as well as the Hindutva party, the BJP. Thus began the decline of the once ubiquitous Indian National Congress Party which espoused pan-Indian secular, inclusive political values, alongside the rapid rise of the Hindutva Party that espoused Hindu identity and nationalism as the dividing parameter among citizens.[39] Eventually, as the effects of globalization began to percolate downwards to all groups—even the middle classes and castes began to feel the anxiety of downward mobility. While the upper castes and upper middle classes were, through their social connections and cultural capital, able to garner lucrative jobs and business opportunities, large sections of the lower educated classes and castes ended up being losers. Even some among the lower castes enjoyed economic advantage due to affirmative action. This further infuriated the middle classes, who lacked that advantage. However, in this game of fierce competition for government and private-sector jobs, it is the lower castes that have largely lost out, resulting in deep existential anxiety. This, in turn, pushed them into the fold of identity groups that offered them solace.[40] In most cases the solace offered was by religious figures such as the babas, gurus and, of course, the right-wing 'identity fascist' political groups who, very often, work in the interests of Hindutva groups in India. Hence, in conclusion, one could argue that it was the neoliberal economic policies ushered in by the successive Congress governments that prepared the ground for the rise of identity politics of the regional parties first, followed by the rise of identity politics of the Hindutva. The following section discusses this phenomenon in detail.

HINDUTVA AND MAJORITARIAN DISCOURSE

In postindependent India for over five decades the inclusive and the so-called secular ideology espoused by the Congress Party held sway and it defined the national space in economic terms. In this conception of the nation, whoever contributed to the nation in any productive capacity was included as a citizen. The nation thus comprised patriotic producers and the 'other', that is, the 'nonnational', a shirker who does not want to work and produce for the nation. This was the Nehruvian vision of India.[41] This was in principle at least an inclusive vision as it was ideologically impartial towards various communities, though in practice it discriminated against minorities, Dalits, women, tribals and so forth. It all changed with the arrival of the Hindutva movement beginning in the 1980s.

The rise of Hindutva is marked by what is known as the Ram Temple movement and the subsequent violent destruction of the Babri Masjid[42] in 1992. This marked the ideological inscription of intolerant majoritarianism in Indian polity which is diametrically opposed to the secular democratic character of Indian national belonging as visualized by the constitution. This intolerance is evident in the majoritarian, antiminority, anti-Dalit, antiwomen, antisecular, anticommunist and antiliberal politics in the country. The gradual rise of this Hindutva ideology also marks the intense and often violent contestation of memory over the symbols and sites of syncretic culture and inclusive nationalism.[43] Their exclusionary ideology purports to establish a Hindu majoritarian nation which they call 'Hindu Rashtra' where all others except Hindus will be treated as second-class citizens. This national belonging is determined by one's triple affinities[44] with the motherland by birth, caste-based social positioning and cultural belonging by treating India as the holy land. By corollary, one can say that the Buddhists, the Sikhs and the Jains belong to the Hindu family, while the Muslims and Christians do not because their holy lands are outside India. Hence, one could say that this ideology was built on ethnic supremacy of Aryan Hindus and resembles the race ideology of the Nazis, built on the mystical conceptions of sacred geography, ethnic affinity and cultural choice.[45] According to this definition, Muslims and Christians, whose 'holy land' is not India, are suspected to be stooges of Pakistan or of the West, respectively. Dalits and other lower castes have no place in this envisioning of Hinduism because they do not form part of the religion in the strictest sense. That, precisely, is why they are excluded from the very social fabric of upper-caste life. Given the kind of alienation and mistreatment felt by the Dalits within the Hindu society, many have embraced Buddhism, Islam or Christianity. As there is a growing self-consciousness about their political and economic rights among the Dalits today, they have started organizing themselves politically and socially. This is evident amongst many Dalit intellectuals who prefer not to follow Hinduism.[46] This self-assertion by the Dalits and minorities in postindependent India has been used by Hindutva forces to manufacture anxiety among the majority Hindus. In today's globalized world where more and more people suffer economic anxiety, they become a fertile ground for politics of identity. Hindutva groups have succeeded in harvesting this anxiety and capturing power through democratic means but have already embarked upon their exclusionary agenda by attacking secular, minority and Dalit symbols of identity.

While the once suppressed Hindutva ideology aims to build a *Hindu Rashtra* (Hindu Nation)[47] that would not only make all minorities into second class citizens but also establish the BJP as the only legitimate party to represent the Hindus, it also considers only those who support this party to be true Hindus. Hence, along with other minorities, even political parties and ideologies that oppose Hindutva are treated as antinational. As most of the Dalit, secular and leftist parties are opponents of Hindutva they are also targeted in various ways by state machinery and direct physical violence is deployed against them through Hindutva mobs. The display of such blatant use of state power and draconian laws against political opponents and social activists was evident in New Delhi in the arrests of five eminent Dalit and leftist social activists under the pretext of hatching a plot to assassinate the prime minister.[48]

To emphasize their objective of inscribing Hindutva ideological memories on the nation, Hindutva forces have adopted certain spatial strategies which have succeeded in disarming the various minority groups discursively as well as physically. As a discursive strategy, history and mythology are invoked to establish the claim of Hindutva history while physically destroying or occupying spaces that belonged to these 'enemy' groups for centuries. In this way, a memory of minority or syncretic culture is overwritten or erased from existence. Ever since the destruction of Babri Masjid[49] in 1992, there have been numerous attacks on minority groups, by way of killing, destroying houses and property by burning, and systematically attacking and destroying their communal symbols, especially mosques, churches, prayer halls and so on.

Other strategies of memory wars include violent protests against interreligious and intercaste marriages, as well as exclusion of non-Hindus in cultural events like Holi or Garba dancing, which were once cultural meeting points for people of all religions and castes. To these must be added the 'politics of beef' as well as nonvegetarianism where beef eating is associated with Muslims and lower, unclean castes.[50] With the lame-duck politics of the supposedly 'secular' Congress Party governments, and due to the stupendous success of the Hindutva discourses, a large portion of Indian society and the administrative apparatus has adopted the fundamentalist ideology of Hindutva as 'communalised common sense'.[51] This soft communal violence is fitted into the day-to-day Indian social fabric which is overwhelmingly unequal and racist towards various communities within Hindu tradition itself. With the election of Narendra Modi, who tacitly played a part in the 2002 massacres of Muslims in Gujarat, what message the minorities should get is well explained by the renowned journalist Harish Khare in an opinion piece written on the NDTV website:

> Soft communal violence is practiced with considerable finesse. It is intended to generate a sense of disquiet and vulnerability among the minorities, without overt violence against them. The idea is to tell them never to cross the lines drawn by the local power structure. Be content with your reduced status; don't raise your voice or hopes.[52]

The result of this long-term strategy was able to bear political dividends in abundance in the national election of 2014, giving absolute majority to the BJP, the party that subscribes to Hindutva. With this, India is rendered to be a locus of memory wars reminiscent of partition-time conflicts. The sites of such memory wars are myriad but I have chosen a few typical ones to discuss.

ATTACK ON SECULAR SYMBOLS AND ATTEMPTS AT ERASURE OF MEMORY

As previously mentioned, since 2014 when the BJP formed the government, attempts have been made to erase the symbols and practices associated with the secular state. By 'secular' here I refer to the inclusive nationalism that evolved during the anticolonialist movement and was eventually enshrined in the constitution of India and upheld during the last six or so decades by various governments in power. However, Hindutva rule of the present has initiated revisions of history books prescribed in schools, and renamed streets and national symbols such as railway stations, universities, streets and even government programmes. Hence, any non-Hindu name carrying Muslim, Christian or colonial references is treated as alien and antinational. Two events and discourses surrounding those events are a testimony to the violent as well as discursive erasure by the Hindutva forces of those memories of secular, inclusive India. One is the effort to erase the memory of Tipu Sultan and the other is the case of the Bhima Koregaon obelisk.

The Case of Tipu Sultan

Karnataka is one of the largest provinces in southern India. From the middle of the fourteenth to the end of the eighteenth centuries, this province was ruled by Muslim rulers. Northern regions of what is now Karnataka had been under the rule of the Adil Shahi dynasty since the fourteenth century and, later, in the eighteenth century with the rise of Hyder Ali followed by Tipu Sultan, the southern regions of modern Karnataka also came under Muslim rule. The contribution of Muslim rulers to Karnataka's polity, culture, economics and military technology is well documented. Accordingly Varija Bolar[53] argues:

> Islam played an important role in Karnataka in the introduction of arts and crafts based on Persian models. A large number of Persian words belonging to the field of public administration entered Karnataka. In the same way, in business and legal proceedings, especially those of courts of justice, words of Persian origin abound in Kannada language. Many words of apparel, words denoting kinds of food entered Kannada through Persian Language. Islamic influence can be seen in the fields of economy, education, religion, language, art and architecture, paintings and music.

The rule of Tipu Sultan not only belonged to the history and memory that cohered with an identity for Muslims in Karnataka but, as observed by Bolar,[54] due to his contribution to the history of Karnataka, it was treated as the social, cultural and political heritage of Karnataka. Hence, the government of the province recently began to celebrate his birthday (Tipu Jayanthi) every year. This celebration is also considered to be the recognition of the secular, multicultural identity and the cultural, linguistic and religious mix of the province of Karnataka. But in the unidimensional view of Hindutva, anything Muslim needs be purged from its narrow interpretation of Indian culture, polity and society. Hence, every time Tipu's birthday is celebrated, Hindutva supporters would organize protests and brand the government of the day, often the Congress government, as anti-Hindu and pro-Muslim. In political parlance they accuse the government of appeasing the minorities. The protests can be seen as a ploy to discredit and erase Muslim history from Karnataka and, in so doing, construct a discourse to delegitimize Muslims as equal citizens. This begs the question: who was Tipu and was he a bigot as the Hindutva claims him to be?

Tipu, the Most Maligned Ruler

When Tipu was born on 20 November 1750, his father, Haider Ali, was the ruler of Mysore, the role he had assumed after the Raja of Mysore, a Hindu ruler, who had decided to retire. At the time the kingdom of Mysore was surrounded by British, French and Portuguese territories as well as the Maratha Kingdom. In order to maintain his rule, Tipu, who assumed power at the death of Haider Ali, in 1782, had to fight the British. Also, in the process of consolidating his rule he had to ruthlessly put down any signs of betrayal or alliance with colonial powers such as the British, French and the Portuguese by some of the diverse communities within his kingdom. Hence, some communities that came under suspicion and ruthless suppression such as the Catholics of Dakshina Kannada, Kodavas of Coorg and Nayars of Kerala consider him a bigot who persecuted their ancestors. Among the others, some Kannada chauvinists consider him anti-Kannadiga because he changed names of places and introduced Persian vocabulary into his administration. Hindutva groups claim that he was a 'tyrant' who forcefully converted many Hindus to Islam. However, to some Marxist historians, Tipu was also 'one of the foremost commanders of [the Indian] independence struggle' and a 'harbinger of new productive forces'.[55] According to Muzaffar Assadi,[56] history has been very unkind to Tipu primarily because the early history of India was written by colonial historians and missionaries who depicted him as a 'tyrant' to which Hindutva groups also subscribe. However, Assadi maintains that:

> Tipu cannot be reduced to a singular narrative or tradition of intolerance or bigotry as he represented multiple traditions. He combined tolerant inter-religious traditions, liberal and secular traditions, anti-colonialism and internationalism. He could do this as he had strong roots in Sufism, which is not explored much by historians. He belonged to the Chisti/Bande Nawaz tradition of Sufism.[57]

The fact of his professional approach to administration was displayed when the Hindu Marathas attacked and ransacked the Hindu temple of Shringeri, one of the foremost Hindu religious places in Karnataka. Tipu gave grants to rebuild the temple to its former glory and considered the seer of the temple as his guru (teacher). There are several such examples where he treated his citizens with respect but also ruthlessly put down those whom he suspected of colluding with his enemies.

So, Karnataka's commemoration of his birth anniversary is as much about its celebration of a multicultural heritage and an acknowledgement of its history as it is an acknowledgment of the role of Islam in Karnataka's social, religious and cultural sphere. In so doing, Karnataka's minority populations, and Muslims in particular, find a validation of their memories, histories, heritage and place in secular India. Given their anti-Muslim ideology, Hindutva groups see this as pandering to the minorities. With this approach the Hindutva groups play divisive politics along religion lines strongly reminiscent of the communal politics of 1947. Partition discourse and partition violence were the outcome of this exclusionary communal politics of both Hindus and Muslims who had subscribed to the majoritarian and religion-based politics of the Hindu Mahasabha and the Muslim League.

If the erasure of Tipu Sultan's legacy reveals a desire to erase the memory of India's Muslim past, the Bhima Koregaon violence of 2 January 2018 was an attempt to obliterate Dalit history from that of the nation. This incident relates to an obelisk erected by the British that commemorates the Mahar caste of Dalits who aligned with the colonial rulers to defeat a large and powerful army of the Hindu Brahmin rulers, the Peshwas. Dalits, in this case, are targeted by Hindutva supporters for being supporters of the British; but more importantly they are seen to be developing an assertive political identity and challenging upper-caste hegemony. For the upper-caste dominated Hindutva groups, Dalits' effort to reclaim their rightful place in the memory of the nation runs contrary to the Hindutva view of history.

The Case of Bhima Koregaon

The Dalits of Maharashtra celebrate *Shaurya Diwas* (bravery day) every New Year's day). This is celebrated in memory of the twenty-two martyred soldiers belonging to a Dalit caste called Mahar who fought alongside the British and defeated the Peshwas, the Brahmin rulers of the area 200 years ago. The main reason that the Mahars (leather workers) joined the British was to avenge the mistreatment they were undergoing under the upper-caste Hindu rulers. Shraddha Kumbhojkar describes the inhumane manner in which lower-caste people were treated by the Brahmin Peshwas during their rule:

> The Peshwas were infamous for their high-caste orthodoxy and their persecution of the untouchables. Numerous sources document in detail that under the Peshwa rulers the untouchable people who were born in certain low castes received harsher punishment for the same crimes committed by those from high

> castes. They were forbidden to move about public spaces in the mornings and evenings lest their long shadows defile high-caste people on the street. Besides physical mobility, occupational and social mobility was denied to these people who formed a major part of the population.[58]

This illustrates why the Mahars did not hesitate to join the British East India Company army to fight the oppressive rule of the upper-caste Brahmin rulers, the Peshwas. Given the kind of inhumane treatment they received and the lack of means for survival, they were quick to choose an opportunity in the British Indian army that allowed them socioeconomic mobility. At this stage, political freedom or nationalism meant hardly anything because India had not developed a national consciousness. For this reason, the Bhima Koregaon battle of 1818 where the Mahars along with the British managed to defeat the formidable army of Peshwas becomes a very significant event for the Mahars and other Dalits because the battle had no connotation of antinationalism whatsoever. This victory and the martyrdom of a total of forty-nine soldiers, twenty-two of which were Mahars, was officially recognized by the British government of the time, resulting in an obelisk being erected at the site of Koregaon, which eventually became the site of memory and identity for Mahars. In 1927, Dr B. R. Ambedkar, the architect of the Indian constitution, who also belonged to the Mahar caste and whom Dalits look up to as their icon, visited the Bhima Koregaon memorial. Over the years, more and more Dalits began to visit the site and on the first of January of every year commemoration events started taking place. However, there has been a consistent effort by right-wing historians to negate the role of Mahars as Dalits by claiming that at this time in history there was no Dalit consciousness among lower castes and hence the Bhima Koregaon battle cannot be perceived as a conscious battle by Dalits against Brahmanic oppression. Not merely that, the Hindu Right has also resorted to fabricating pseudo-histories as well as pseudo-memories of the event through literature and historical writings where they even claim that it was the Peshwas who had won the battle and not the British.[59] This is a typical example of how right-wing historians systematically resort to the fabrication of history by erasing memories that are inconvenient to its linear narrative of Hindu supremacy. Despite these efforts, history has enough evidence to prove the participation of Mahars in British wars and the defeat of the Peshwas in the Bhima Koregaon battle. Kumbhojkar mentions this fact thus: 'The valour of the Mahar regiment, however, continued to be manifested in the battles of Kathiawad (1826), Multan (1846) and the second Afghan War (1880)'.[60]

However, rising Dalit consciousness paralleled by a rising number of atrocities against the Dalit groups since 2014 has led to the added significance of the Bhima Koregaon memorial for their identity. This is clear from the huge participation that the bicentenary celebrations attracted on 1 January 2018 when over three hundred thousand Dalits gathered to commemorate this event. This congregation was brutally attacked by two right-wing organizations named Shiv Pratishthan and Hindu Ekta Manch, led by Sambhaji Bhide (alias Manohar Bhide) and Milind Ekbote, respectively. In the violence that followed, one Dalit youth was killed while several others were injured along with a number of vehicles damaged. At the same event the upper-caste Hindutva groups made it a point to destroy the shops belonging to the Muslims.[61] This violence against the Dalits and the simultaneous damaging of Muslim property seemed premeditated and conducted in line with their discursive construction of minorities as being antinational.

Dalits as Antinational

As the Hindutva ideology is predominantly an upper-caste discourse that subscribes to the maintenance of caste hierarchy, the votaries of Hindutva do not waste time finding antinationals everywhere. Along with other religious minorities, the Dalits are easy targets because they are not instinctive subscribers to the hierarchic ideology of Hindutva. In reality, lacking caste and class privilege, they are also positioned as opponents to Hindutva's alignment with neoliberal capitalism. In fact, the Indian state, which is required to follow affirmative action, by privatizing state-owned institutions, reduces Dalits' chances of employment in the public sector where there are jobs reserved for the lower castes. The Bhima Koregaon obelisk and the commemoration by Dalits of a battle against native rulers which shows them as having allied with colonial rulers automatically positions them among the 'newly constituted' group of antinationals. This branding of Dalits as antinational legitimizes the violence against Dalits by Hindutva groups, just as violence against Muslims is legitimized by branding them as the progeny of Muslim invaders and as Pakistani sympathizers. Hence, Bhima Koregaon is a site of contesting memories and a site that offers special identity to the Dalits in India notwithstanding Hindutva forces trying to erase and overwrite that memory by means of falsifying history and creating pseudo-memories. This assault on memory to suppress the growing identity consciousness amongst Dalits and trying to deny them any political gains is not unlike the Hindutva approach to delegitimize Indian Muslims and Christians. This is caste politics in its naked form.

Notwithstanding nationalistic feelings, for the Dalits, British colonial rule proved to be more benevolent and helpful for social mobility than upper-caste Indian rule. This also explains why Dalits did not show much enthusiasm for the independence struggle as well as partition-time violence. This antinomy towards an upper-caste-dominated independence struggle was trenchantly expressed by the Dalit leader, Dr B. R. Ambedkar. Though the Gandhi-led independence movement was perceived to have represented all Indians, Ambedkar viewed it differently. Kumbhojkar puts it thus:

> There were major ideological differences between Ambedkar and Gandhi. For the India represented by Gandhi and the Indian National Congress, the primary contradiction was between colonial supremacy and Indian aspirations for political freedom; for Ambedkar and the untouchable masses he represented, the oppression was not located in the political system but in the socio-economic sphere. There was a clash of interests. The Congress under Gandhi sought to represent all Indians in a unified front against colonial rule; Ambedkar and the untouchables, for their part, were certain that replacing colonial rulers with high and middle-class Congress leaders offered no solution to their problems. The known devil of colonial rulers was perceived to be more tolerable to the untouchables.[62]

This perception of the Dalits still persists despite the affirmative action policies of successive governments. But with the BJP at the helm of power Dalits feel more vulnerable and fear that upper-caste hegemony will deprive them of the gains they have made over the years. This is the reason why every year large crowds gather at Bhima Koregaon: to make a political statement about their valour and special identity. They have devised many ways of fighting back. This obviously is also a fight of secular, democratic forces against the majoritarian, neoliberal Hindutva hegemony controlling the Indian state and its society today.

THE FIGHT TO SAVE THE SECULAR, MULTICULTURAL, INCLUSIVE SOUL OF THE NATION

The idea of India as we understand today was a gradual development that emerged from the independence movement. However, Hindutva forces have been resorting to selective amnesia about the role of minorities and Dalits in India. Where it suits them, the Hindutva ideologues consider certain events relating to the upper castes as nationalistic while other events which involve Dalits and minorities are deemed to be antinational. While upper-caste Peshwas who aligned with the British to defeat the Hindu Marathas were treated as patriotic, Tipu Sultan, a Muslim ruler who fought against the colonial rulers, the British and the French, while at the same time helping to rebuild the Hindu temple ransacked by Hindu Maratha rulers, is considered to be a 'tyrant' and an antinational. This divisive discourse and selective amnesia is deployed to delegitimize the existence, survival and political participation of Dalits and minorities. However, in recent years, some political parties as well as Dalit activist groups have begun to fight back. If the congress government in Karnataka goes ahead with celebrating Tipu's birth anniversary despite threats of violence from Hindutva groups, the Delhi government of Aam Admi Party (AAP) courageously goes ahead with installing Tipu's portrait in the Assembly Hall.[63] In the same manner, many secular organizations, activist organizations, leftists, students and especially Dalit groups have started working together to counter the bigoted, casteist, majoritarian, antisecular Hindutva ideology and the Hindutva state.[64] Multiple sites and other cultural expressions such as social media, cartoons, parody and humour challenge the regressive imposition of memory and 'false' history by the Hindutva forces. This is the war for the soul of secular and inclusive India, visualized by Ambedkar, Gandhi, Nehru and others against the majoritarian, divisive and exclusionary 'Hindu Rashtra' visualized by Savarkar and others of the RSS.[65]

History is a perpetually contested arena in the life of a nation simply because the nations as we know today, though ethnically defined, are constitutive of multiethnic, multireligious, multilinguistic, multicultural and multiracial populations. Most of these nations, being democratic by rule, treat discrimination against any particular group as illegal and against human rights. However, the fight for hegemony over one another will be a perpetual struggle for various groups even in democratic countries. History and memory are two such arenas where this power struggle takes place. In the process of this struggle, violence is often used by certain groups to establish and perpetuate their dominance through contestation and erasure of memories of the rival or subservient groups. In the Indian subcontinent, this process has been going on since the nation was partitioned. In the early decades following independence, with its emphasis on a secular democracy, there was ample space for minorities, Dalits and women to express themselves and live life according to their personal and communitarian choices. However, current Hindutva domination has resulted in a violent enforcement of a majoritarian Hindutva ideology upon these oppressed groups. The current BJP government appears to sanction violence against minorities, Dalits and women to impose the patriarchal Hindutva project. At the same time, realizing the dangers of this ideology as destroying national institutions, communal harmony, human rights, women's rights, Dalit enablement and minority development, many individuals, intellectuals, grassroots organizations, student movements and political formations have begun fighting back for the reinscription of memories of a secular democracy. This could be a long battle for the shaping of history, memory and identity towards retransforming the nation into an inclusive, multicultural secular space.

NOTES

1. Hindutva is a political ideology of some of the conservative, often fundamentalist, Hindu organizations called 'Sangh Parivar' (Family of organizations that contain outfits such as the Vishwa Hindu Parishad (VHP), Bhajrang Dal and a number of local groups which supply foot soldiers for local mobilizations) that promote political and cultural Hinduism, under the ideological mentoring of the RSS (Rashtriya Swayamsevak Sangh—National Volunteer Organization), with the intention of establishing a *Hindu Rastra* (Hindu Nation). In the words of Veer Savarkar, the founder and the chief ideologue of this movement, Hindutva refers to everything Indic. In his view Hindutva is a history and it embraces all the departments of thought and activity of the whole being of the Hindu race. According to Hindutva ideology, in order to be a true Hindu one should satisfy the following three affinities: *pitrbhoo, jati* and *sanskriti*. The first refers to one's affinity by birth with the fatherland the 'Sindhu' nation which refers to the land mass covering areas between river Indus and the two seas (Arabian Sea and Bay of Bengal). The second refers to one's belonging to one of the designated hierarchy of castes within Vedic traditions and the third refers to the requirement of considering India as one's '*punyabhoo*' (holy land), one's cultural affinity. Among the three, the last one is the most important. By corollary, one can say that the Buddhists, the Sikhs and the Jains belong to the Hindu family, while the Muslims and Christians do not because their holy lands are outside India. Hence, one could say that this ideology was built on an ethnic supremacy of Aryan Hindus as well as a racial ideology, and on the mystical conceptions of sacred geography, ethnic affinity and cultural choice. Satish Deshpande, 'Communalising the Nation-Space: Notes on Spatial Strategies of Hindutva,' *Economic & Political Weekly* 30, no. 50 (1995): 3220–27.

2. Anand Teltumbde, 'BJP's Arrogance on Alert,' *Economic & Political Weekly* 53, no. 14 (2018), http://www.epw.in/journal/2018/14/columns/bjps-arrogance-alert.html.

3. Asim Roy, 'High Politics of India's Partition: The Revisionist Perspective', in Hasan Mushirul, ed., *India's Partition: Process, Strategy and Mobilization* (New Delhi: Oxford University Press, 1993).

4. Contrary to the historical myth perpetuated over the years to pin the entire blame on Jinnah and the Muslim League for the Partition of the nation, Ayesha Jalal, through her research, has clearly vindicated the role played by the Congress Party to bring about the situation or force Jinnah to adopt a hardline tactical position that resulted in partition. For a detailed discussion on this revisionist argument, read Ayesha Jalal, *The Sole Spokesman: Jinnah, the Muslim League and the Demand for Pakistan* (Cambridge: Cambridge University Press, 1985).

5. Karan Thapar, 'Why Jinnah's Portrait Hangs in Amu', *Tribune*, 4 May 2018, http://www.tribuneindia.com/news/comment/why-jinnah-s-portrait-hangs-in-amu/583771.html.

6. Akshaya Mukul, *Gita Press and the Making of Hindu India* (New York: HarperCollins, 2015); Gyanendra Pandey, *Remembering Partition* (Cambridge: Cambridge University Press, 2001).

7. Radhika Desai, 'Neoliberalism and Cultural Nationalism: A Danse Macabre', in Dieter Plehwe, Bernhard Walpen and Gisela Neunhöffer, eds., *Neoliberal Hegemony: A Global Critique* (New York: Routledge, 2006); Prabhat Patnaik, 'Neo-Liberalism and Democracy', *Economic & Political Weekly* 49, no. 15 (2014).

8. Dalits are those who are categorized as 'lower castes' within the Hindu caste hierarchy. They are also called 'untouchables' and treated as 'unclean' by the 'upper caste' Hindus. The word 'Dalit' means 'the oppressed'. This term is used by the Dalits themselves and it also is a political category used to identify this section of the Indian population.

9. Ernesto Laclau and Chantal Mouffe, *Hegemony and Socialist Strategy: Towards a Radical Democratic Politics* (New York: Verso, 2001).

10. Jasper Heinzen, 'Graduate Research Essay—"Memory Wars": The Manipulation of History in the Context of Sino-Japanese Relations,' *New Zealand Journal of Asian Studies* 6 (2004): 148–64.

11. Michel-Rolph Trouillot, *Silencing the Past: Power and the Production of History* (Boston: Beacon Press, 1995).

12. Jacques Derrida, *Archive Fever: A Freudian Impression* (University of Chicago Press, 1996); Gyanendra Pandey, 'In Defense of the Fragment: Writing About Hindu–Muslim Riots in India Today', *Representations* 37:27–55; 'Un-Archived Histories: The "Mad" and the "Trifling"', *Economic & Political Weekly* 47, no. 1 (2012): 38–41.

13. Allan Megill, 'History, Memory, Identity', *History of the Human Sciences* 11, no. 3 (1998): 37–62.

14. Ever since Maurice Halbwachs, in *On Collective Memory* (Chicago: University of Chicago Press, 1992), conclusively established the dynamic manner of the social construction of memory, various researchers have argued that memory, along with archived information, is equally important for a democratic and inclusive construction of historical narratives. See, for example, Paul Ricoeur, *Memory, History, Forgetting* (Chicago: University of Chicago Press, 2004). Also, memory is a powerful tool available for marginalized or powerless groups to fight against powers that try to silence or erase the social existence, national contribution and/or cultural identity of such groups. See, for example, Paul Connerton, *The Spirit of Mourning: History, Memory and the Body* (Cambridge: Cambridge University Press, 2011).

15. The Indian Nation Congress (INC) was founded on 28 December 1885 by A. O. Hume, a retired British officer. This was the largest political party that led India's struggle for freedom and still continues to be one of the major political parties today. Indian National Congress, Encyclopaedia Britannica, last Modified on 3 October 2018, https://www.britannica.com/topic/Indian-National-Congress.

16. Akhil Bharatiya Hindu Mahasabha, popularly known as tshe Hindu Mahasabha, is a right-wing Hindu nationalist party in India. It was established in 1915 under the leadership of Madan Mohan Malaviya, who was one of the prominent leaders of the Indian National Congress Party. Akhil Bharatiya Hindu Mahasabha, Wikipedia, last updated on 25 October 2018, https://en.wikipedia.org/wiki/Akhil_Bharatiya_Hindu_Mahasabha#Establishment.

17. The All India Muslim League was a political party founded on 30 December 1906 under the leadership of Syed Ahmed Khan. Initially started as a literary move-

ment it evolved into a political party advocating the interests of Muslims during the preindependence days in British India. All India Muslim League, Wikipedia, last updated on 23 October 2018, https://en.wikipedia.org/wiki/All-India_Muslim_League.

18. Asim Roy, 'High Politics of India's Partition: The Revisionist Perspective', in Hasan Mushirul, ed., *India's Partition: Process, Strategy and Mobilization* (New Delhi: Oxford University Press, 1993).

19. In his recent book *Gita Press and the Making of Hindu India* (New York: HarperCollins, 2015), Akshaya Mukul explains in detail how congressmen such as Madan Mohan Malaviya were responsible for the congress' strong and steadfast Hindu bias. He also explains how a section of the congress was very closely associated with Gita Press and those who wanted to promote Sanatan Dharma as the predominant religion in India. Hence, many of them left the congress, opposing its inclusive approach. Ironically, Madan Mohan Malaviya, who founded the Akhil Bharatiya Hindu Mahasabha, the right-wing Hindu organization, was a two-time president of the Congress Party. Hence, the congress had in its ranks people who were deeply Hindu and did not subscribe to the secular and inclusive approach of the other wing of the congress. According to Ayesha Jalal, it was congress' intransigence and Hindu bias that caused Jinnah's frustration and his embrace of the Muslim League. Her stated view is that Jinnah's unstated intention was a tactical approach to find adequate representation for Muslims in a united country whereas the congress' unstated intention was to alienate Jinnah and the Muslim interests. Hence, the grand narrative propagated by many historians that the congress was secular and the Muslim League was communal was factually incorrect and was a myth perpetrated over the years. Ayesha Jalal, *The Sole Spokesman: Jinnah, the Muslim League and the Demand for Pakistan* (Cambridge: Cambridge University Press, 1985).

20. Jalal, *The Sole Spokesman*.

21. Urvashi Butalia, *The Other Side of Silence: Voices from the Partition of India* (London: Hurst & Co., 2000); Pandey, *Remembering Partition*.

22. As previously discussed (basing on Ayesha Jalal and others' research) the behaviour of the congress during the prepartition days was communal in some sense. But its recent history is also no exception either; for example, its members' open participation in Anti-Sikh riots of 1984 or its tacit approval or looking the other way when Hindutva rioters indulging in communal violence during the destruction of Babri Masjid in 1992, as Professor Ram Puniyani has shown in his article in the online magazine Countercurrents.org, https://www.countercurrents.org/puniyani21210.htm.

23. Gurbir Singh, 'The State Is Using the "Maoist" Label to Muzzle Liberal Criticism', TheWire.in, 28 August 2018, https://thewire.in/rights/the-state-is-using-the-maoist-label-to-muzzle-liberal-criticism.

24. Sai Thakur and Byasa Moharana, 'Bhima Koregaon and Politics of the Subaltern', *Economic & Political Weekly* 53, no. 7 (2018).

25. Ramachandra Guha, 'Patriotism vs Jingoism', *Outlook*, 24 January 2018, https://www.outlookindia.com/magazine/story/patriotism-vs-jingoism/299735; Prabhat Patnaik, 'What It Means to Be "National"', *The Hindu*, 27 February 2016, http://www.thehindu.com/opinion/lead/What-it-means-to-be-%E2%80%98national%E2%80%99/article14101978.ece.

26. Patnaik, 'What It Means to Be "National"'.

27. Hindutva (Hinduness) should not be confused with Hinduism, which is also known as Sanatana-Dharma. It is the dominant religion of the Indian subcontinent with a fusion of various Indian cultures and traditions. In a word, 'Hinduism' is a collection of multiple intellectual or philosophical points of view, including atheism, rather than a rigid, common set of beliefs. It not only contains elements of the historical Vedic religion of Iron Age India, but also contains elements of mesolithic and neolithic cultures of India, such as the religions of the Indus Valley Civilization, Dravidian traditions and the local and tribal religions. Hence, by nature it is open to new streams and was able to take in its stride elements of Islam and Christianity as they arrived in India. Shashi Tharoor, *Why I Am a Hindu* (Oxford University Press, 2018).

28. Though the above kind of nationalism was practiced in the early stages of national development, today most European nations follow multiculturalist and inclusive policies whereas India, under the Hindutva rule, is moving towards the opposite direction of majoritarianism.

29. Guha, 'Patriotism vs Jingoism'.

30. Singh, 'The State Is Using the "Maoist" Label to Muzzle Liberal Criticism'.

31. Sumit Sarkar, 'The Fascism of the Sangh Parivar', *Economic & Political Weekly* 28, no. 5 (1993): 163–67.

32. Patnaik, 'Neo-Liberalism and Democracy'.

33. Radhika Desai, 'Hindutva's Ebbing Tide', in Sanjay Ruparelia, Stuart Corbridge, John Harriss and Sanjaya Reddy, eds., *Understanding India's New Political Economy: A Great Transformation?* (New York: Routledge, 2011).

34. Prabhat Patnaik, 'The State under Neo-Liberalism', *Social Scientist* 35 (1/2): 4.

35. Patnaik, 'Neo-Liberalism and Democracy', 41.

36. Manuel Castells, *The Power of Identity*, second edition (Chichester: Wiley-Blackwell, 2010).

37. According to Prabhat Patnaik, 'identity politics' is a misleading term because it lumps together very dissimilar and even diametrically opposite phenomena under one term. Hence, he distinguishes three distinct phenomena: 'identity resistance politics' such as Dalit movements, women's movements and so on; 'identity bargaining politics' where middle or upper castes, such as Jats, Patidars, Marathas and so forth, that perceive themselves as economically disadvantaged, organizing political resistance or demanding reservation facilities; and the most important and typical 'identity fascist politics', experienced as communal fascism in India, based on particular identity groups, especially of the majoritarian kind, that virulently target other 'identity groups' such as the Dalits, minorities or women. Patnaik, 'Neo-Liberalism and Democracy', 39–44.

38. Desai, 'Hindutva's Ebbing Tide', 414.

39. Ibid., 412–46.

40. Craig Jeffrey, 'Timepass: Youth, Class, and Time among Unemployed Young Men in India', *American Ethnologist* 37, no. 3 (2010): 465–81.

41. Jawaharlal Nehru was the first prime minister of India after independence.

42. The Babri Masjid (translated as Mosque of Babur) was a mosque in the Ayodhya of Faizabad district of India. It was one of the largest mosques in the Uttar Pradesh state and it was built in 1528–1529 CE during the reign of Mughal emperor Babur.

43. Muzaffar Assadi, 'Threats to Syncretic Culture: Baba Budan Giri Incident', *Economic & Political Weekly* 34, no. 13 (1999): 746–48.

44. According to Hindutva ideology, in order to be a true Hindu one should satisfy the following three affinities: *pitrbhoo*, *jati* and *sanskriti*. The first refers to one's affinity by birth with the fatherland, the 'Sindhu' nation, which refers to the land mass covering areas between river Indus and the two seas (Arabian Sea and Bay of Bengal). The second refers to one's belonging to one of the designated hierarchy of castes within Vedic traditions and the third refers to the requirement of considering India as one's '*punyabhoo*' (holy land), one's cultural affinity. Among the three the last one is the most important.

45. Deshpande, 'Communalising the Nation-Space'.

46. Kancha Ilaiah, *Why I Am Not a Hindu: A Sudra Critique of Hindutva Philosophy, Culture and Political Economy* (Kolkata: Bhatkal and Sen, 2005).

47. Vinayak Damodar Savarkar, 'Hindutva: Who Is a Hindu? 1923', *Bombay: Veer Savarkar Prakashan* (1969).

48. Harinder Kaur, 'The Vague "Urban Naxal" Was Invented to Avoid Difficult Questions on Modi's Vikas', *The Print*, 13 June 2018, https://theprint.in/opinion/the-vague-urban-naxal-was-invented-to-avoid-difficult-questions-on-modis-vikaas/69926/.

49. According to the mosque's inscriptions, Babri Masjid was built in 1528–1529 CE (935 AH) during the reign of the Mughal emperor Babur (after whom it is named). Some Hindus believe that the mosque was built by destroying a temple dedicated to Lord Ram from the Indian mythology *Ramayana*. Hindus regard the spot upon which the mosque was built to be the birthplace of Lord Ram. A. G. Noorani, *The Babri Masjid Question, 1528–2003*, vol. 1 (New Delhi: Tulika Books, 2003).

50. Kancha Ilaiah, 'Beef, BJP and Food Rights of People', *Economic & Political Weekly* 31, no. 24 (1996): 1443–45.

51. Sarkar, 'The Fascism of the Sangh Parivar'.

52. Harish Khare, 'Narendra Modi's Assurance to Minorities'. NDTV.com, 10 June 2014, http://www.ndtv.com/article/opinion/narendra-modi-s-assurance-to-minorities-539205?pfrom=home-cheatsheet.

53. Varija Bolar, 'The Role of Islam in Karnatak', *International Journal of Social Sciences and Humanity Studies* 3, no. 2 (2011): 489–98.

54. Ibid.

55. Muzaffar Assadi, 'Tipu Sultan: A Secular Internationalist, Not a Bigot', *The Hindu*, 27 September 2015, http://www.thehindu.com/news/national/karnataka/tipu-sultan-a-secular-internationalist-not-a-bigot/article7692879.ece.

56. Ibid.

57. Ibid.

58. Shraddha Kumbhojkar, 'Contesting Power, Contesting Memories: The History of the Koregaon Memorial,' *Economic & Political Weekly* 47, no. (2012): 103–07.

59. Ibid.

60. Ibid., 104.

61. PTI, 'Pune: Violence Mars Bhima Koregaon Battle Anniversary Event', *Indian Express*, 1 January 2018, https://indianexpress.com/article/india/pune-violence-mars-bhima-koregaon-battle-anniversary-event-mevani-5007857/.

62. Kumbhojkar, 'Contesting Power, Contesting Memories', 105.

63. Scroll staff, 'Delhi: BJP Opposes Inclusion of Tipu Sultan's Portrait in Assembly', Scroll.in, 27 January 2018, https://scroll.in/latest/866623/delhi-bjp-opposes inclusion-of-tipu-sultans-portrait-in-assembly.

64. Arun Ferreira and Vernon Gonsalves, 'Why People's Coalitions Are Uniting against Hindutva—the New Peshwai', DailyO.in, 30 January 2018, https://www.dailyo.in/voices/ambedkar-bhima-koregaon-peshwa-dalits-hindutva-fascism-sangh-parivar/story/1/22069.html.

65. Here one needs to recall how Savarkar had genuflected before the colonial British to gain clemency while other freedom fighters were incarcerated in jails for their fight for freedom. It must also be recalled here that one of the close allies of Savarkar named Nathuram Godse had shot dead Mahatma Gandhi, the father of the nation. Ajaj Ashraf, 'History Revisited: Was Veer Savarkar Really All That Brave?', Scroll.in, 27 May 2016, https://scroll.in/article/808709/the-hollow-myth-of-veer-savarkar.

REFERENCES

Ashraf, Ajaj. 2016. 'History Revisited: Was Veer Savarkar Really All That Brave?'. scroll.in. May 27. https://scroll.in/article/808709/the-hollow-myth-of-veer-savarkar.

Assadi, Muzaffar. 1999. 'Threats to Syncretic Culture: Baba Budan Giri Incident'. *Economic & Political Weekly* 34 (13): 746–48.

———. 2015. 'Tippu Sultan: A Secular Internationalist, Not a Bigot'. *The Hindu*. September 27. http://www.thehindu.com/news/national/karnataka/tipu-sultan-a-secular-internationalist-not-a-bigot/article7692879.ece.

Bolar, Varija. 2011. 'The Role of Islam in Karnatak'. *International Journal of Social Sciences and Humanity Studies* 3 (2): 489–98.

Butalia, Urvashi. 2000. *The Other Side of Silence: Voices from the Partition of India.* London: Hurst & Co.

Castells, Manuel. 2010. *The Power of Identity.* Second edition. Chichester: Wiley-Blackwell.

Connerton, Paul. 2011. *The Spirit of Mourning: History, Memory and the Body*. Cambridge: Cambridge University Press.

Chowdhury, Adrija. 2018. 'Amu and Jinna: A Love-Hate Relationship'. *The Indian Express*. 4 May.

Derrida, Jacques. 1996. *Archive Fever: A Freudian Impression.* University of Chicago Press.

Desai, Radhika. 2006. 'Neoliberalism and Cultural Nationalism: A Danse Macabre'. In *Neoliberal Hegemony: A Global Critique*, edited by Dieter Plehwe, Bernhard Walpen and Gisela Neunhöffer, 222–35. New York: Routledge.

———. 2011. 'Hindutva's Ebbing Tide'. In *Understanding India's New Political Economy: A Great Transformation?*, edited by Sanjay Ruparelia, Stuart Corbridge, John Harriss and Sanjaya Reddy, 172–85. New York: Routledge.

Deshpande, Satish. 1995. 'Communalising the Nation-Space: Notes on Spatial Strategies of Hindutva'. *Economic & Political Weekly* 30 (50): 3220–27.

Ferreira, Arun, and Vernon Gonsalves. 2018. 'Why People's Coalitions Are Uniting against Hindutva—the New Peshwai'. DailyO.in. 30 January. https://www.dailyo.in/voices/ambedkar-bhima-koregaon-peshwa-dalits-hindutva-fascism-sangh-parivar/story/1/22069.html.

Guha, Ramachandra. 2018. 'Patriotism vs Jingoism'. *Outlook*. 24 January. https://www.outlookindia.com/magazine/story/patriotism-vs-jingoism/299735.

Halbwachs, Maurice. 1992. *On Collective Memory*. Chicago: University of Chicago Press.

Heinzen, Jasper. 2004. 'Graduate Research Essay—'Memory Wars': The Manipulation of History in the Context of Sino-Japanese Relations'. *New Zealand Journal of Asian Studies* 6 (2): 148–64.

Ilaiah, Kancha. 1996. 'Beef, BJP and Food Rights of People'. *Economic & Political Weekly* 31 (24): 1443–45.

———. 2005. *Why I Am Not a Hindu: A Sudra Critique of Hindutva Philosophy, Culture and Political Economy*. Kolkata: Bhatkal and Sen.

India, Press Trust of. 2018. 'Pune: Violence Mars Bhima Koregaon Battle Anniversary Event'. The Express Group. *Indian Express*. 1 January. https://indianexpress.com/article/india/pune-violence-mars-bhima-koregaon-battle-anniversary-event-mevani-5007857/.

Jalal, Ayesha. 1985. *The Sole Spokesman: Jinnah, the Muslim League and the Demand for Pakistan*. Cambridge: Cambridge University Press.

Jeffrey, Craig. 2010. 'Timepass: Youth, Class, and Time among Unemployed Young Men in India'. *American Ethnologist* 37 (3): 465–81.

Kaur, Harinder. 2018. 'The Vague "Urban Naxal" Was Invented to Avoid Difficult Questions on Modi's Vikas'. *The Print*. 13 June. https://theprint.in/opinion/the-vague-urban-naxal-was-invented-to-avoid-difficult-questions-on-modis-vikaas/69926/.

Khare, Harish. 2014. 'Narendra Modi's Assurance to Minorities'. NDTV.com. 10 June. http://www.ndtv.com/article/opinion/narendra-modi-s-assurance-to-minorities-539205?pfrom=home-cheatsheet.

Kumbhojkar, Shraddha. 2012. 'Contesting Power, Contesting Memories: The History of the Koregaon Memorial'. *Economic & Political Weekly* 47 (42): 103–07.

Laclau, Ernesto, and Chantal Mouffe. 2001. *Hegemony and Socialist Strategy: Towards a Radical Democratic Politics*. London: Verso.

Megill, Allan. 1998. 'History, Memory, Identity'. *History of the Human Sciences* 11 (3): 37–62.

Mukul, Akshaya. 2015. *Gita Press and the Making of Hindu India*. New York: HarperCollins.

Noorani, A. G. 2003. *The Babri Masjid Question, 1528–2003*. Vol. 1. New Delhi: Tulika Books.

Pandey, Gyanendra. 1992. 'In Defense of the Fragment: Writing About Hindu–Muslim Riots in India Today'. *Representations* 37:27–55.

———. 2001. *Remembering Partition.* Cambridge: Cambridge University Press.

———. 2012. 'Un-Archived Histories: The "Mad" and the "Trifling"'. *Economic & Political Weekly* 47 (1): 38–41.

Patnaik, Prabhat. 2007. 'The State under Neo-Liberalism'. *Social Scientist* 35 (1/2): 4–15.

———. 2014. 'Neo-Liberalism and Democracy'. *Economic & Political Weekly* 49 (15): 39–44.

———. 2016. 'What It Means to Be "National."' *The Hindu*. 27 February. http://www.thehindu.com/opinion/lead/What-it-means-to-be-%E2%80%98national%E2%80%99/article14101978.ece.

PTI. 2018. 'Pune: Violence Mars Bhima Koregaon Battle Anniversary Event'. *Indian Express*. 1 January. https://indianexpress.com/article/india/pune-violence-mars-bhima-koregaon-battle-anniversary-event-mevani-5007857/.

Ricoeur, Paul. 2004. *Memory, History, Forgetting*. Chicago: University of Chicago Press.

Roy, Asim. 1993. 'High Politics of India's Partition: The Revisionist Perspective'. In *India's Partition: Process, Strategy and Mobilization*, edited by Hasan Mushirul. New Delhi: Oxford University Press.

Sarkar, Sumit. 1993. 'The Fascism of the Sangh Parivar'. *Economic & Political Weekly* 28 (5): 163–67.

Savarkar, Vinayak Damodar. 1969. 'Hindutva: Who Is a Hindu? 1923'. *Bombay: Veer Savarkar Prakashan.*

Singh, Gurbir. 2018. 'The State Is Using the "Maoist" Label to Muzzle Liberal Criticism'. TheWire.in. 28 August. https://thewire.in/rights/the-state-is-using-the-maoist-label-to-muzzle-liberal-criticism.

Staff, Scroll. 2018. 'Delhi: BJP Opposes Inclusion of Tippu Sultan's Portrait in Assembly'. Scroll.in. 27 January. https://scroll.in/latest/866623/delhi-bjp-opposes-inclusion-of-tipu-sultans-portrait-in-assembly.

Teltumbde, Anand. 2018. 'BJP's Arrogance on Alert'. *Economic & Political Weekly* 53 (14). http://www.epw.in/journal/2018/14/columns/bjps-arrogance-alert.html.

Thakur, Sai, and Byasa Moharana. 2018. 'Bhima Koregaon and Politics of the Subaltern'. *Economic & Political Weekly* 53 (7).

Thapar, Karan. 2018. 'Why Jinnah's Portrait Hangs in Amu'. *Tribune*. 4 May. http://www.tribuneindia.com/news/comment/why-jinnah-s-portrait-hangs-in-amu/583771.html.

Tharoor, Shashi. 2018. *Why I Am a Hindu.* Oxford: Oxford University Press.

Trouillot, Michel-Rolph. 1995. *Silencing the Past: Power and the Production of History.* Boston: Beacon Press.

Chapter 7

Postpartition Anxieties and the Matter of Authenticity in Ireland

Louise Harrington

> When we say that Ireland is cosmopolitan often we are misrecognising that what we are really celebrating by saying that is exactly the opposite: it's not that we are celebrating what immigrants are bringing to us from their culture, but rather that through their presence we can see ourselves, our conceits of traditional, national identity, in a refreshed and flattering light.
>
> Immigrants, simply by their presence, affirm our way of life, remind us of who we are, of where we've come from, and give legitimacy to what we have now and where we imagine ourselves in the future—affluent and progressive, a global, even cosmopolitan society, but still a moral community, a people with roots, traditions and a coherent collective history.[1]

What constitutes Irish identity has been deliberated and defended through many centuries of colonial rule and the partition of Ireland. Colonization, the independence struggle, partition and the creation of Northern Ireland, the sectarian violence over this territory from the 1960s to the 1990s, the peace agreement in 1998 and the chaos initiated by Brexit in 2016 have all played a role in the ongoing question of what constitutes being Irish or an imagined state of Irishness. But another issue needs to be added to the list and studied alongside the history of British rule and the legacy of partition—the impact of globalization and inward migration. As Kuhling and Keohane suggest in the epigraph, the influx of immigrants to Ireland in the 1990s and the subsequent questions around Irish citizenship led to a reconsideration of identity and the reclaiming of a collective history of oppressed but resilient Irishness, a people that withstood colonial domination and the carving up of the island to emerge as both thoroughly modern and distinctly rooted.

In 2006 the then-President of Ireland, Mary McAleese, declared in her St Patrick's Day speech that Ireland 'today is a vibrant, cosmopolitan' place, cementing the widely held belief that the sociocultural changes which took place in Ireland from the early 1990s onwards led to the country's entry into the coveted space of 'global citizenship'. The aptly named, flourishing Celtic Tiger economy of this period branded the societal transformation in a neat aphorism ripe for export, as previously happened with the wild success of the theatrical show *Riverdance* and the Celtic music of Enya. Furthermore, the euphoria surrounding the period of the Celtic Tiger emphasized in public discourse the seamless integration of inward migrants into the colourful fabric of Irish society as evidence of the country's newfound multiculturalism. This viewpoint, however, problematically elides the elitism of such Celtic cosmopolitanism, which in reality privileged white Irishness, something that was laid bare in the country's 2004 Citizenship Referendum. The conceit of Celtic Tiger terminology around demographic diversity, such as 'nonnational' or 'non-Irish national', also reveals deep insecurities relating to national identity. Through a discussion about these issues alongside an exploration of contemporary migrant literature and migrants in literature, this chapter examines the connection between the anxious discourse around authenticity and belonging in Ireland's recent past which establishes hegemonic control over perceived noncosmopolitan migrant subjects, and the country's colonial past, the struggle for freedom from British rule, and the partition.

Ireland's independence struggle in the nineteenth and twentieth centuries naturally invoked a mythical and imagined collective identity, not unlike other freedom movements against colonialism, such as in India. For instance, Ireland was depicted in popular culture as a suffering woman, Cathleen Ní Houlihan, notably in W. B. Yeats and Lady Gregory's 1902 play of the same name. Mirrored by the figure of Bharat Mata in India, who was also immortalized on the stage, Cathleen or the Sean Bhean Bocht ('poor old woman') represented organic purity and strength in the face of extreme repression, but needed her young men—the sons of the soil—to save her from the colonizers and die for her if necessary. The symbolism of Mother Ireland encouraged nationalist pride and patriotism that would bolster the independence movement, which was already, by the time of W. B. Yeats and Lady Gregory's successful play, well under way. Another historically important purveyor of a collective Irish identity, the Gaelic Athletic Association (GAA), is linked to Gaelic nationalism. In 1884, the GAA was founded to preserve tradition and indigenous sport and culture, yet it is generally accepted that it also aimed to foster nationalism and to shield Irishmen from the influence of the British. Many members of the Irish Republican Brotherhood (an incarnation of the earlier Fenian Movement) belonged to the GAA, and used the sports club to recruit and train young men to fight for the country; it was therefore banned by the British government in 1918, an action that stoked the nationalist fires.

Indeed, the separation of identity politics and cultural pursuits at this time was next to impossible. If something was originally intended to be apolitical, such as *Conradh na Gaeilge* or the Gaelic League for instance, it inevitably became a medium through which Irish nationalism could flourish and counter the invasion of British culture. Set up by Douglas Hyde in 1893 to preserve Irish culture and, particularly, the Irish language, *Conradh na Gaeilge* was instrumental in the Gaelic Revival that followed in the early twentieth century. It is important to note that these movements, while set up to preserve, revive and promote Irish culture, had their origins in 'an ancient Gaelic kingdom' that had been 'usurped by the Protestant invader'.[2] Though the Gaelic Revival is most commonly remembered as the venue for a proliferation of celebrated literary and cultural output, from the likes of J. M. Synge, Sean O'Casey, W. B. Yeats and Lady Gregory, centering on the Abbey Theatre in 1904, it also represented a loyalty to communalism and a deep suspicion of the outsider. During the Revival, 'native ethnicity took on the xenophobic Catholicism of a subjugated peasantry and priesthood', while the Anglo-Irish stratum—fronted by Yeats—asserted indigeneity by invoking kinship with ancient aristocratic Gaelic warriors and worked Irish folklore and legend into its creative output.[3]

It follows that, as in many independence movements across the world, the sustained emphasis on a pure ethnic and national identity was necessarily exclusionary. The success of the revolutionary movement against British imperialism depended on the identification of the majority population with an ancient and precious Irish character that deserved sovereignty. Given the context of the Gaelic Revival, Irish nationalism can be regarded as positively tribal before, and after, independence; as Piaras Mac Éinrí articulates, 'Mainstream Ireland has imagined itself in mono-ethnic, mono-cultural tribal terms since the foundation of the state, even if this never corresponded to the realities'.[4] It is then a logical consequence that the formation of an Irish nation-state invariably cited homogeneity; a white Celtic people, Catholic preferably, standing in opposition to the colonizing powers. This did not embrace nonwhite, non-Celtic people or anyone who could not participate in the collective memory of colonization, of nationalist struggles for self-rule, of the partition of the island and postpartition trauma. The memory of this collective experience, passed down through generations and often as strongly felt by those who were not alive during the early 1900s as those who were, has been and continues to be crucial to 'being Irish'. While Anglo-Irish relations have come a long way in the recent past, as evidenced for instance in the queen's visit to Ireland in 2011, it is interesting how the narrative around 'eight hundred years of oppression', which is popular discourse for British colonial rule and the legacy of it as manifested in the partition of the island, emerges as a glue of sorts that traverses generations and locations, so much so that the Irish American diaspora continue to be fervent proponents of Sinn Féin's nationalist politics. While this collective memory of colonization and the struggle for independence may not develop into active republicanism, it can translate into either a strong desire to see Ireland reunified or an ambivalence to those 'north of the border' who are often not regarded as *Irish* Irish by southerners but rather some version of *British* Irish.

The partition of Ireland in 1922 saw the Irish Free State (the South) leave the Union of Great Britain and Northern Ireland remain as a devolved statelet. The partition was bound with the possession of land and the exercise of power over territory as all partitions tend to be. The negotiations for Home Rule and Irish independence ran in earnest from 1912 to 1920, when the decision was finally made through the Government of Ireland Act that the six predominantly Unionist counties of the northern province Ulster would form Northern Ireland. The three remaining counties of Ulster would join the rest of the island to form the Irish Free State as a result of the two-and-a-half-year Irish War of Independence. It was not a solution that pleased everyone, indeed, the Anglo-Irish Treaty that cemented partition was an unpopular agreement on all sides and many harboured hope that it would be reversed, but the partition of Ireland was seen by the political players as a necessary compromise for both nationalists and unionists. However, the division of the province of Ulster, and the deterritorialization and reterritorialization of the island to accommodate the Catholic, Protestant, Nationalist and Unionist populations, put limits on the imagined space of being Irish. For the south of the country, partition cut off the north and marked it as a place controlled by non-Irish loyalists to the Crown. In Northern Ireland, the space of Irishness was, and remains, more complicated.

Montserrat Guibernau states that 'identity is constructed both through belonging and through exclusion',[5] and for the minority Catholic and majority Protestant populations in Northern Ireland at the time of partition, the matter of belonging and not belonging became the principal concern. The creation of a border across the province of Ulster refocused the concept of Irishness in so far as it magnified the question of whose area of land this was, who could lay claim to it, and who could protect and guard it. The Plantation of Ulster officially dates from 1609 to 1630 and saw Protestant settlers from Scotland and England colonize Ulster and marginalize the native Catholic Irish. Prior to this, Ulster was a stronghold of Gaelic culture ruled by local Catholic chiefs but over years they were dispossessed of their land by the might of the Anglo-Scottish Crown. Therefore, the partition was not a division made to house just one religion or ethnic group, but rather the six counties had to be shared between those who saw themselves as Irish, as British and later as

Northern Irish, by virtue of an ancient claim to the land or based on historical settlement.

The battle over such disputed territory has long been fought, culminating in the violent period of the Troubles from 1968 to 1998.[6] The emphasis during the conflict was always on the right of each opposing side to the land of Northern Ireland; however, this was wholly altered by the 1998 Good Friday Agreement.[7] This agreement was a milestone in the peace process to end the Troubles and was ratified by two referenda, one in Northern Ireland and one in the Republic. The approval of the referendum in the Republic to amend the Constitution of Ireland, based on the terms of the agreement, led to the relinquishing of any territorial claim to the six counties of Northern Ireland. Prior to the agreement, the constitution included a territorial claim to a thirty-two-county Ireland, that is, the twenty-six counties of the Republic plus the six counties of the North, something that nationalists all over the island and, in particular, the nationalist party Sinn Féin held onto tightly. After 1998, however, the erasure of this claim divested nationalists, and anyone hoping for reunification of the island of Ireland, of their right to the land. In Northern Ireland, the terms of the agreement created a devolved legislature at Stormont in Belfast, embraced consociationalism, and formally ended the colonization of Northern Ireland some sixty years after it ended in the Republic of Ireland,[8] because the agreement led to the end of direct rule by Britain, something that had occurred after partition in the South with the creation of the Oireachtas or the legislature of Ireland. While the Good Friday Agreement had positive outcomes for peace in Northern Ireland, it also had the perhaps unforeseen consequence of causing the extensive reimagination and reformulation of Irish identity. Territory was now suddenly less central than it had been for centuries and the matter of Irishness took on a less tangible form, that of a genealogical and imagined Irishness. Given that the Republic of Ireland no longer had a constitutional right to the territory of the six counties, then a claim could instead be made to a collective Irish heritage and an imagined nation state of Irishness that unites the island irrespective of the partition border.

Two issues became especially pertinent at this point in the late 1990s alongside the Good Friday Agreement: a renewed focus on the integrality of the Irish diaspora and the idea of blood ties. Mary McAleese often spoke of the diaspora during her tenure as President of Ireland from 1997 to 2011, but it was her predecessor Mary Robinson who first realized the importance of the symbolism of emigration. In a famed address, she said:

> Irishness is not simply territorial. In fact, Irishness as a concept seems to me at its strongest when it reaches out to everyone on this island and shows itself capable of honouring and listening to those whose sense of identity, and whose

> cultural values, may be more British than Irish. It can be strengthened again if we turn with open minds and hearts to the array of people outside Ireland for whom this island is a place of origin.[9]

Robinson spoke to the vast Irish diasporic community and stressed the existence of a global Irish family, scattered across the world but all belonging to one Ireland. Building on these kinds of pronouncements, a discourse of kinship flourished in Ireland in the early 2000s; one that took into account the existence of state and international borders but transcended them to affirm the innate connection of Irish people wherever they might reside. The attention given to this topic has not subsided over the years; if anything it has become a key agenda item for the Irish government, evidenced by the issuing of a Diaspora Policy called 'Global Irish' in 2015. Part of this policy is a new commitment to the Certificate of Irish Heritage, first introduced in 2011, which is available for a fee to those not born on the island of Ireland but who are of Irish descent. This ties into the second point mentioned above: the concept of the Irish as a community of blood. In a post–Good Friday Agreement world, the vitality of kinship was reinstated. To accommodate those in Northern Ireland who saw themselves as Irish rather than British or even Northern Irish, and in light of the absence of a territorial claim to the six counties, blood could be invoked in order to participate in Irishness. This tribal resonance dispensed with the details of which county or country someone was born in because identity and belonging in Ireland became a matter of *jus sanguine*, or citizenship defined by blood relationships.

The final event in the current trajectory of perceived Irishness occurred in the aftermath of the Celtic Tiger, a moniker applied by economists to the boom years of the mid to late 1990s. This time of growth and prosperity ripped through the country for better or for worse, irrevocably altering its physical and social landscape, before collapsing into an economic recession in 2008. One outcome of this period was that half a million migrants, many from previously little or unrepresented countries and ethnicities, settled in Ireland. The unanticipated influx of people proved problematic for the government, who were blatantly unequipped legally (in terms of policy), socially, culturally and in almost every other way to deal with the inward migration in a fair, timely and compassionate manner. The foremost instance of this ineptitude is the 2004 Citizenship Referendum, which formulated and standardized a concept of Irishness that was essentially monoethnic. Before the referendum, anyone born on the island of Ireland, so as to include people from Northern Ireland as asserted by the Good Friday Agreement, was entitled to Irish citizenship, but after the referendum an Irish-born child of non-Irish-born parents could be regarded as a 'nonnational'. This referendum transpired largely due to racialized rhetoric about 'citizenship tourism' that incited a panicked response from the Irish public to the perceived increasing numbers of (non-white) female immigrants giving birth to children in Ireland, which according to pre-2004 referendum law immediately entitled the child to Irish citizenship. An emphatic vote to radically alter the parameters of this situation led to a result that officially favours blood over the soil. The outcome of the referendum not only revealed the new power of globalization, the inclusion of the Irish diasporic community, but also suggested an acceptance of partition and a move away from irredentist ideologies, echoing the deterritorialization inherent in the Good Friday Agreement where 'the unilateral claim over Northern Irish territory was abandoned [by the Republic of Ireland] along with the definition of the national territory as congruent only with the whole island of Ireland'.[10] As I have already outlined in this chapter, ancestry and bloodline have long been features of an accepted or sanctioned Irishness, but it was not until 2004 that this inclination was certified.

The inequities of the Citizenship Referendum have been represented most directly in just one cultural form thus far—the novel *Flight* by Oona Frawley. Published in 2014, this book captures the impact of the vote on a female migrant, Sandrine, from Zimbabwe, who is pregnant upon arrival in Ireland and gives birth to her daughter in Dublin before she is deported for violating the terms of her visa. The concept of 'birth tourism' or 'citizenship tourism' is openly portrayed in the novel; this is not a background issue, but it is framed against Sandrine's somewhat accidental position as a carer for an elderly couple who are suffering from dementia. Their daughter, Elizabeth, acts as Sandrine's analogue, except that she is white Irish and unable to have children. Sandrine's pregnancy, which she keeps a secret for as long as she can, is the centre of attention from the first pages when she takes a flight from Harare to Dublin via London. On the short journey from London to Dublin, a very perceptive woman warns Sandrine not to go to Ireland because 'they kick you out for being pregnant'.[11] Simultaneously, Sandrine becomes aware of her skin colour for the first time, noticing that she is the only black person on the plane and is the focus of many gazes, described as not unkind, but not friendly, rather greedy in a desire to know 'what her skin meant'.[12] In a way, this scene sets up an odd reversal where Sandrine is the supposed 'citizenship tourist' to Ireland but the passengers on board the Aer Lingus flight are depicted as voyeuristically wanting to consume this black-skinned foreigner. Once she is in Ireland, incidents of overt racism ensue; first, in the benign form of Deirdre, who takes in immigrants temporarily in her bed and breakfast in Co. Wicklow. Deirdre is fascinated by how well Sandrine speaks English and is delighted to be seen about the town with such an exotic creature. As the novel progresses, however, overt discriminatory acts occur: 'People stare, snigger, or turn away.

At worst—at least, so far, this has been the worst—there is the cursing, the spitting, the murmuring, the feeling she has of being threatened when certain people pass her in the streets. They deny her, and she feels it'.[13] Taking place in the run-up to the referendum in 2004, this racist behavior intimates what the outcome of the vote will later be.

The racism escalates as the referendum nears, culminating in a repulsive incident just as Sandrine has found her feet, feels less lonely and more familiar with Dublin life. While passing two men in the street, with her obviously pregnant belly, 'One of the men spat on the ground as he strode past and said something to his friend that Sandrine did not catch immediately but heard in afterthought: *fucking asylum-seeking nigger*. The shock of it. Tears started to her eyes in an instant. It turned her stomach and left her unable to speak'.[14] Here, it is not simply that she is not white, but she is pregnant, and therefore symbolic of all the asylum-seekers, foreigners, nonnationals, Africans and Chinese who are apparently using devious means to gain the right to remain in Ireland. Sandrine literally embodies the foreign alien trying to penetrate the pure, white Irish bloodline that represents the country. Her expectant state connotes sex and reproduction; an unborn black child who is waiting to gain Irish citizenship, the very thing that the many supporters of the Yes vote in the Citizenship Referendum warned so vehemently against. For Sandrine, the hotlines set up for unexpected or unwanted pregnancies, to provide support to women who might not have anywhere to turn, are not available. She knows that they 'had not been set up for her'[15] and instead feels embarrassed and isolated by both the colour of her skin and her pregnancy. Her conclusion is that being pregnant in Ireland is in fact dangerous at such a time that a woman's body is so politicized, and she resolves: 'It was no good calling anyone or doing anything about it. No good could come of it, not here, not when the country was debating who belonged, who was Irish, who could become *new Irish*'.[16]

The omniscient narrator of the novel uses Sandrine's bewildered but growing understanding of how the *new Irish* might be treated in Ireland to comment on the inequity of the referendum and the racism rife in society. For instance, the complicity of the media and the press in normalizing racist attitudes is addressed when Sandrine observes the way in which all migrants, whether Filipino, Nigerian or Romanian, white or nonwhite, are homogenized as job-grabbers or criminals. The fact that their Irish-born children speak together in English and Irish outside the school gates is somehow ignored by the newspapers. This observation is astute in so far as it gets at the entrenched racial rhetoric around migrants, belonging and national identity. In the aftermath of the Citizenship Referendum and in much of the academic scholarship since, the change the referendum result initiated—from *jus soli*, citizenship defined by birthplace, to *jus sanguine*, blood relationships—has been stressed. Bryan Fanning, a scholar of migration and social policy, responded to the amendment of the Constitution by observing that 'the immigrant can never become Irish because he or she does not have Irish blood and is not part of the Irish 'race'. There is no melting pot'.[17] This privileging of a community-of-descent rather than of residence has an immeasurable impact on Ireland's immigrant population, and not only in practical matters, but in countless intangible ways which ideologically place them in the realm of 'guest'.[18] In this way, 'guests', or in official and popular terminology 'non-Irish nationals', are racialized, excluded and unable to participate in the imagined state of ancient Irishness that to a large extent drives the national memory of independence and identity. In their fervent critique of state practices, Ronit Lentin and Robbie McVeigh describe modern Ireland postreferendum as a racist state. They argue that Ireland is a 'gated community' in the age of globalization and that the state protects racial hierarchies by 'strictly controlling the conditions of access for non-citizens. Their labour power remains desirable, nay absolutely necessary. . . . But they are to be regulated and policed in new ways; they are—definitively—*not to be citizens*'.[19]

Problematically, of course, Ireland is not, nor has it ever been, the homogenous white, Catholic, Celtic society that it is imagined to be. It has always been a place of minorities; of Protestants, Jews, Travellers and Chinese for example, but this has not stopped the invocation of the 'pure Irish' myth. Many nations have been built on and shaped by their perception of themselves as an identifiable monocultural, monoracial unit, and the connection of this to a history of colonization, as well as the legacy of partition, is not difficult to recognize. Geraldine Moane's work on the psychological impact of the past on Celtic Tiger–era and contemporary Ireland illuminates the complex reality of life in a postcolonial and postpartition society. The 'repeated occurrence of trauma, dispossession, loss and defeat', whether through natural disasters such as famine, the domination of colonial forces, the partition of the island or the powerful influence of the Catholic Church, have fundamentally shaped Ireland's present state. The enduring influence is not easily shaken and, even in light of recent periods of prosperity and radical development, 'a decade of transformation cannot undo historical legacies'.[20] Some of the effects of colonial trauma that Moane identifies are inferiority, guilt, shame and denial, which manifest in various 'cultural pathologies' including alcoholism, social irresponsibility and racism in the form of 'horizontal hostility' or anger that is displaced from the colonizer onto peers or those subordinate.[21] Within this context, the results of the 2004 Citizenship Referendum expose the scars of the past, as structures of domination and control around citizenship were approved and enforced. Furthermore, the internalization of suffering and the long-held reticence in Ireland on aspects of the traumatic past have produced a culture of 'historical forgetting', which means that 'Irish multicultural policy is characterized by an assimilationist approach, rather than one based on cultural pluralism'.[22] The importance of assimilation in state policy and in popular opinion is what Bryan Fanning calls 'weak multiculturalism'.[23] In this formulation, an emphasis is placed on the united Irishness of Ireland, a country that is prepared to resist invasion and defeat oppressors, a country that will not be colonized or divided as in the past, and a people that will not be subjugated. In this light, the multitude of 'true Irish' protects their heritage and their glorious Gaelic culture.

Against this background, it is no wonder that migrant writers, or nonwhite writers or anyone who does not fit into an exclusive, blood-based group, might feel that there are ethnic boundaries in Irish literature. It was for this reason that the Women Writers in the New Ireland Network was set up in 2007 by some academics working on migration and citizenship in Ireland. In this initiative, they sought to counter 'the bleak centrality of a hegemonic and mythical ethnic genealogy' that is grounded in history, the prior pursuit of an authentic Irishness, and actively excludes that which unsettles the normative definition of Irishness.[24] Working with women writers from twenty-five countries and learning from their experiences of living and writing in Ireland, the founders discovered that these women were largely excluded from the literary spaces that the 'native' Irish enjoyed because, even in the cultural landscape, '"Irishness" is reinscribed as a spiritual quantity; it is a kind of religion to which the "stranger" can be converted or recruited; it acquires an atemporal quality as that which endures unchanged while the diversity of "identifications" and "subcultures" comes and goes, dissolved by its elemental force that yet remains essentially untouched by that which it assimilates'.[25] In this tangible elitism, the 'stranger' must struggle to find his or her place, both in society and in the colossus that is the Irish literary sphere. For instance, one writer who joined the group, Thabi Madide from South Africa, remarked that even after a decade living in Ireland she continued to feel like an outsider, excluded from a privileged state of Irishness, but in the network she could feel a connection to other 'out-of-place' writers.

The lives of 'strangers' in Ireland has not been entirely overlooked in Irish literary circles. In addition to the novel *Flight*, discussed earlier, the most well-known depiction of the immigrant experience in Ireland is Roddy Doyle's serialized short stories, collected in *The Deportees* (2007). Doyle is of course a heavyweight in contemporary Irish literature and his suitably frank depiction of a changing Irish society post–Celtic Tiger is a much-needed addition to the negligible literary canon that deals with multiculturalism in Ireland and shifting concepts of Irishness. His various sketches, originally published in the multicultural newspaper *Metro Éireann*, are a welcome contrast to the conventional feel-good rhetoric of the state on the integrated diversity and model tolerance of Irish society. Doyle offers a more candid glimpse into the frequently complex and harsh world navigated by Ireland's many migrants, with particular reference to Africans and Eastern Europeans. However, the fact that Roddy Doyle is a white Irishman cannot be ignored and, while he provides a valuable perspective on minorities in his short stories, it is ultimately his own voice that is heard, speaking from the point of view of the host society. *The Deportees* is an account of migrancy in which, in the words of Maureen T. Reddy, 'White Irish . . . remain firmly in charge of the racial discourse'.[26] As Reddy goes on to argue, Doyle's 'stories succeed best at explaining Irish racial attitudes to immigrants' rather than offering any real insight into what it is actually like to be African or Eastern European in Ireland.[27]

Similarly, in *Flight* ventriloquism is evident in so far as a white Irish-American writer imagines the experience of Zimbabwean immigrant Sandrine. *Flight* may not flinch from taking a critical stance on the Citizenship Referendum and the propaganda around 'birth tourism', but Frawley also represents Sandrine's experience as a black pregnant woman in Ireland. She is characterized largely in relation to the white Irish family that she comes to serve as a carer; that is, what the elderly couple, Tom and Clare, think of her in their advancing stages of dementia, and how her relationship evolves with their daughter Elizabeth, who problematically becomes something of a savior to Sandrine. As Elizabeth warms to Sandrine, and confides in her, she helps Sandrine navigate the legal repercussions of violating her student visa and is her companion through the first three months of her baby's life. Elizabeth even suggests that she could keep the child and look after it in Ireland to give her a better life, an offer that is declined by Sandrine. The figure of the kind, barren white woman who 'rescues' the pregnant black migrant overshadows Sandrine's experience towards the end of the novel as she fades away back to Zimbabwe. An earlier section of the book, perhaps coincidentally, sums up the whole tale when the narrator states that, in Ireland, Sandrine 'has no story'. Furthermore, 'When she arrived in Ireland, Sandrine had thought that some story of hers was beginning. . . . But in the reality of Ireland, the reality of a foreign land, that was not possible, not immediately. The story was not yet hers'.[28] On a broader scale, the story, or the voice, belongs to the migrant in neither *Flight* nor *The Deportees*, instead it belongs to those the migrant is presented in relation to, those who are reacting to their presence: the white, indigenous Irish. This is not to suggest that these books are unimportant contributions to the negligible output by Irish fiction writers that include nonwhite or migrant characters in their central focus, but there needs to be an awareness of who is speaking for whom. In another example, when Kevin Curran, the author of *Beatsploitation* (2013), suggests that his writing of a black character breaks pioneering new ground, questions must be raised about agency. In a triumphantly written newspaper article promoting his novel, Curran states, 'The white Irish voice is the eyes and ears and mouth of the novel, but Kembo Pereira, a fifteen-year-old Angolan refugee, is the soul of the piece. *Our* hero. A black hero in a national literature which has yet to find one' (emphasis added).[29] A more critical understanding of the ways in which it is problematic that a white Irish voice might be 'the eyes and ears and mouth' of a black African would not go astray here, especially when *our* hero is to be consumed by *our* nation and inserted into the dominantly white national literature. Caution should also be exercised against the propagation of using other cultures and ethnic groups, migrants, refugees and asylum seekers in a modern form of Gramsci's concept of imperial cosmopolitanism whereby 'the periphery is cultural fodder for the centre'.[30]

Pilar Villar-Argáiz's important edited volume *Literary Visions of Multicultural Ireland: The Immigrant in Contemporary Irish Literature* is a comprehensive study of race and ethnicity in Irish literature but recognizes its 'one-dimensional nature' as it is framed from the perspective of how 'native' Irish writers portray immigrants.[31] In so doing, however, it gets at important questions about othering and how Irish writers represent minorities such as the Polish, Chinese and Africans in Ireland. Beyond literature, Villar-Argáiz's article 'The Representation of Non-Irish Immigrants in Recent Irish Films' discusses the ways in which cinema by Irish directors and producers depicts immigrants from Eastern Europe and further afield as variously marginalized and othered. Being white or from Europe does not exempt the migrant from being othered as a result of the basic principle of not being *really* Irish, although the colour of one's skin, not being white, does contribute to the degree of othering that is exercised by the mainstream Irish characters and protagonists.[32] The perspective of the 'privileged majority'[33] is no doubt a useful starting point to develop the conversation around diversity, integration and interculturalism in Ireland, but serving as an antidote to appropriation and essentializing there are migrant voices who speak for themselves without an insider interlocutor and who give a glimpse into the lives of those excluded from protected and privileged cultural and social spheres because they cannot claim to belong to a pure Irish bloodline.[34] Issues of integration and assimilation, racism and discrimination, diasporic life and transnationalism are strong features of this literature, forming a small collection of migrant writing in Ireland and offering a refreshing counterpoint to the wealth of literature about the Irish themselves as migrants in the world, in the United States and the United Kingdom for instance. Included in this canon are Indian-born Cauvery Madhavan's novel *Paddy Indian* (2001), Iranian-born Marsha Mehran's novel *Pomegranate Soup* (2005), Nigerian-born Olutoyin Pamela Akinjobi's *HerStory: Migration Stories of African Women in Ireland* (2006), Polish-born Natalia Kostrzewa's play *More Light* (2007) and Polish-born Daniel Zuchowski's collection of short stories *The New Dubliners* (2014). Two other writers, Nita Mishra and Ursula Rani Sarma, deal with the topic of belonging in Irish society in particularly effective, though very different, ways.

Mishra, a poet who moved to Ireland from India with her family in the mid-2000s, has published work depicting the migrant's experience in Ireland in the 2012 anthology *Embers of Words: An Irish Anthology of Migrant Poetry.* In the poem 'Aching Bones', Mishra considers how different life in India is, where having home help—cleaners and cooks—is normal for most middle- and upper-class families. While this is a simple difference it exposes a deeper cultural divide between Ireland and India that speaks to not just variations in social norms pertaining to home and family, but also to gender roles. The distinction between family life in the two countries is again emphasized in another of Mishra's poems, called 'The Son of God', which simply but effectively portrays the difficulty of raising Hindu children in a Catholic country. Here, the poet addresses the challenging issue of religious diversity in Ireland and particularly how schools are ill-equipped to deal with the increasing numbers of children who are not Catholic or Christian. It raises the point that many children in Ireland are now part of a minority ethnic or religious group but receive education that is tailored to the majority Catholic population. Thus, when the child in the poem asks his mother, 'if the son of god/Lives in a church/Where does god live?', to which she answers, 'God lives in the temples/Back home'.[35] The suggestion is that there is no place for non-Irish gods in Ireland; Hindus can live there but their religion belongs elsewhere.

In the poem 'Tom's Exotic Princess', Mishra offers an amusing but meaningful illustration of white Irish people's reactions to meeting an Indian. She refers to being seen as a 'brown woman', being judged or sized up immediately because of the colour of her skin as people try to figure out where she might be from, which only exposes their lack of knowledge, as she says, 'Even before I speak/Your mind races across continents'.[36] Mishra further highlights the ignorance she meets in Ireland when she describes how people are surprised at her language ability, saying 'Oh, she speaks English', and later, 'Must be an aberration, *whhhaat*?!/Pays taxes as well!/Jaysus!'[37] The fact that people assume she is a tax-evading refugee who does not speak English well, or that she is simply the exotic girlfriend of Tom, lays bare the realities of being a migrant in Ireland for this poet. In 2017, the governmental Irish Naturalisation and Immigration Service published a report called 'Language and Migration in Ireland', which was compiled by language and literature academics at NUI Galway. This document includes two of Mishra's poems that speak specifically to the migrant experience in Ireland. In 'Migrants' she focuses on the assimilation required to become Irish, such as the correct use of the English language and 'foreign' accents that may not fade. She writes:

> Over the years
> A slow realisation dawns
> Upon them, that
> They are still
> Different, migrants
> Foreigners
> And the colour of the skin
> Hasn't paled
> Even a wee bit[38]

Nita Mishra provides a valuable insight into the migrant experience through her poems, speaking openly about racist attitudes and prejudices against those who do not look or sound natively Irish and the everyday obstacles facing Ireland's nonwhite migrants, as well as white migrants perhaps. Moreover, the poems draw attention to the implications of being an increasingly culturally and religiously diverse society where state policy and procedures need to catch up with the changing demographic landscape, for instance in the education system, which is deeply tied to the Catholic Church.

Another writer, Ursula Rani Sarma, represents a remarkable interpretation of Ireland. A successful playwright, screenwriter and poet, Sarma describes herself as 'multicultural Irish' since her mother is Irish and her father is Indian. She was born in Canada, grew up in the West of Ireland, and now resides in London. Interestingly, however, Sarma's plays do not engage specifically with India or migrants in Ireland and she has revealed that she does not feel obliged to portray these things in her work. In response to a question on this matter in an interview, Sarma replied, 'I don't believe I have a duty to represent any community or gender but my identity and experiences automatically become part of the tapestry of the work'.[39] Her play *A Tiny Light in the Darkness* (2006) is set in London in a Tube carriage and deals with multiethnic society, but her Irish plays are instead preoccupied with issues of home and belonging, of exile and alienation; key tropes of transnational identity. Growing up in Ireland, Sarma has described that she could not escape her hybrid identity, being one of only two mixed-race families at her school. She further explains that her Indian-ness was a source of great interest to those around her and she noticed society's apprehension at the demographic changes taking place in society in the 1990s.[40] But rather than a focused depiction of this in her plays, Sarma clarifies, 'my dual heritage has meant that

I am very interested in the concept of home and what it means to belong. This theme recurs in my work'.[41]

Consequently, Sarma's is among the most vibrant and exciting theatre to depict modern Ireland, influenced as it is by the aforementioned tropes of transnationalism and offering a perspective from someone who does not belong to a restricted insider group. Her plays do not shy away from addressing some of the more unpleasant aspects of the economic boom years, including drug culture and the rural–urban divide. Her alienated characters seem to symbolize every young man and every young woman grappling with the fast-paced changes brought about by the Celtic Tiger. This can be clearly seen for instance in her 1999 play, called . . . *touched* . . . , which vividly depicts the vagaries of belonging as it centers around the flight of a brother and sister from the Irish countryside to Dublin city. For these teenage siblings, Dublin represents an idealized but necessary escape, particularly for the female protagonist, Cora, who has been continually sexually abused by the local doctor. Yet, Dublin is far from the paradise they envision and they find it to be a dark and dangerous place, leaving Cora to cry, 'I don't like Dublin, I want to go home . . . I just want to go home'.[42] The question of where home is, where to belong, also permeates another of Sarma's plays, *Blue*, which was first performed in the year 2000 and portrays three childhood friends on the brink of adulthood in a small village in the West of Ireland. The oppression of the rural surroundings and the lure of urban life are again central as the protagonists feel unbearably trapped in their community and long to escape to a foreign country. One character in particular, Danny, dreams of being exiled as if it were an ideal condition; to belong somewhere else, other than 'here'. Therefore, while not speaking directly to her own experience of belonging in Ireland, Sarma's catalogue of work is stimulating and pioneering in its portrayal of the country from the perspective of an Irish Indian woman. As Charlotte McIvor has written, Sarma, from her position as a minority-ethnic playwright in Ireland, unapologetically presents an 'ethically bankrupt and alienated post-Celtic Tiger Ireland' which 'forces a reckoning with Irish futures'.[43] Sarma's work demands a reconsideration of the ethics of embodied representation and the importance of listening to transnational voices that might not directly address the issue of migrants but pursue new directions in the illustration of contemporary Ireland and of Irishness.

In a 2009 interview, the Irish writer and academic Barry McCrea states, 'I do wish there was less celebration of Irishness around, and more realistic depictions of it'.[44] Contrary to this plea, the numerous and elaborate centenary commemorations of the 1916 Rising, as well as the government's 'Decade of Centenaries' programme for example, lay bare the recurrent tendencies to dedicatedly celebrate Irishness and emphasize the historical lineage of the nation today. The legacy of historical trauma and oppression has fed into a present that privileges white Irishness and belonging to the soil, and remains wary of the dilution of a small island population. The matter of authenticity is very important in Ireland's postcolonial context, indeed 'The nation's very reason for being, its logic of existence is its claim to an undeniable authenticity as a pure expression of the "real", the obvious, the natural'.[45] A strong belief in the importance of the Irish language and Gaelic culture, as distinct from English or British, and regardless of how malnourished these things are in the everyday life of the average citizen, also contributes to the protectionist attitude towards all things Irish, including who might be accepted to really belong to the country. The revival and promotion of a single unified national identity was, as I have illustrated, instrumental in fighting British colonial domination; and the sustained protection of Irish culture is without question vital, but exclusionary policies and politics should not be excused as some kind of inevitability of the legacy of colonization and partition. There are a number of borders apparent in this conversation, but the two most significant are the one between the Irish people and its migrant population, and that between the Republic of Ireland and Northern Ireland. The rise and development of the latter has shaped the reality of the former.[46] A partition does nothing if not draw lines on the ground—on a map—to include and exclude, to segregate. The Irish borderlands may look considerably different today than forty years ago during the Troubles, or ninety years ago after the division of the island, but the partition of the country has resonated in ways unforeseen and unresolved.

The success of the Leave campaign in the 2016 Brexit referendum in the United Kingdom reignited the discussion about the state and fate of the Republic of Ireland/Northern Ireland border, or what will become the only land border between the United Kingdom and the rest of the European Union. For those interested in border studies with respect to Ireland, the legacy of the Troubles, the fragility of the peace process, the rise of Sinn Féin in the political sphere, the contemporary incarnations of IRA factions or the slow and steady positive development of cross-border relations in trade, education or culture—for instance, the sudden possibility of the island being 'rebordered' as a result of a hard Brexit—is both shocking and worrying. A hard Brexit would involve, amongst other things, the reintroduction of security installations and customs checks at the partition line. Therefore, in the wake of the vote to leave the European Union, politicians and social commentators were out in force to put forward various theories, predictions and warnings for Northern Ireland given the precarity of the border. Given that 56 per cent of the electorate in Northern Ireland voted to remain in the European Union, the victory for the Leave campaign, according to the Ulster Unionist leader Mike Nesbitt, has provoked an increase in Irish nationalist sentiment. It has reopened 'the constitutional question and we now have people who were content in Northern Ireland last week thinking again about a united Ireland'.[47] Under the terms of the Good Friday Agreement of 1998, anyone born in Northern Ireland has the right to be a citizen of the United Kingdom, of Ireland or of both. Thus, Brexit has direct and complicated consequences for the constitutional rights of those in Northern Ireland; can some citizens belong to European Union and some not?

In addition to the identity politics and potential constitutional predicament, what happens to the physical, now porous, border is a serious question. Fintan O'Toole, writing in *The Guardian* newspaper, suggests:

> What will now happen is not that the old border will come back. It's much worse than that. The old border marked the line between neighbouring polities that had a common travel area and an intimate, if often fraught, relationship. It was a customs barrier. The new border will be the most westerly land frontier of a vast entity of more than 400 million people, and it will be an immigration (as well as a customs) barrier.[48]

While numerous politicians maintain that the border situation will remain unchanged, it is difficult to see how this would work on a practical level and some changes to the border will surely need to be put in place. What exactly this will look like is anyone's guess at the time of writing, but beyond the requirement to control the movement of non-EU citizens in and out of EU countries, the fact is that Brexit has led to a reimagining of what Ireland could look like, especially from the perspective of Sinn Féin and all those who might support reunification of Northern Ireland and the Republic of Ireland. Even before the Brexit referendum, Gerry Adams, the longstanding leader of Sinn Féin until February 2018, was clear that he thought the whole island of Ireland should be the primary concern for Northern Irish voters because what happens on one side of the border will inevitably affect the other side. In the aftermath of the Leave vote, he argued that because the majority of Northern Ireland voted to remain in the European Union, this should be upheld rather than superseded by the votes of England and Wales where the majority voted to leave. His successor, Mary Lou McDonald, upholds Adams' view and also suggests that Brexit might lead to significant changes in the existence of the border: 'the planned imposition of Brexit in Ireland has again demonstrated the failure of partition, and exposed further the gaping democratic deficit inherent in a partitioned Ireland. In this vein, Brexit has cast the project for Irish unity as an urgent, desirable and realisable political objective'.[49] Whether a referendum on the reunification of Ireland will ever take place remains to be seen, but the everyday practicalities of and the shifting ideological positions on a partitioned Ireland post-Brexit are unavoidable and alarming concerns.

The partition of Ireland has had many repercussions, from the minor and mild to the immense and violent. One that does not always garner attention due to its subtle pervasiveness is the existence of a strong border consciousness on both sides of the dividing line. In the context of Northern Ireland, Jon Curley observes that 'partitions are proliferating entities rather than fixed division zones',[50] which could be applied to the land south of the border as much as north of it, though not with quite the same intense meaning given the violence of the Troubles and its aftermath. The act of partition brings to the fore the reality that there are places to which some people belong and places to which they do not. This belonging is not necessarily their choice but it is decreed by political agreements and therefore must be obeyed. In this way, belonging and the matter of being 'in place' is not to be trifled with, but rather protected, because it is only by safeguarding one's place that the person or the place can survive future conflict; on a small island such as Ireland the impact of partition is strongly felt, it is part of the psyche, and its effects linger in ways that cannot necessarily be seen or quantified in the twenty-first century when it is held up as a success story for other ethno-religio-national conflicts to learn from. No amount of perceived postpartition, postconflict stability can undo the formation and cementation of insider-outsider divisions, nor eliminate the collective anxieties around territory and belonging, nor stem the desire to maintain a carefully bordered authenticity that binds the people to the land.

NOTES

1. Carmen Kuhling and Kieran Keohane, *Cosmopolitan Ireland: Globalisation and Quality of Life* (London: Pluto Press, 2007), 68.
2. John Hutchinson, *The Dynamics of Cultural Nationalism: Gaelic Revival and the Creation of the Irish Nation State* (London: Allen and Unwin, 1987), 214.
3. Ibid., 214–16.
4. Piaras Mac Éinrí, 'If I Wanted to Go There I Wouldn't Start from Here: Re-Imagining a Multi-Ethnic Ireland', in Debbie Ging, Michael Cronin and Peadar Kirby, eds., *Transforming Ireland* (Manchester: Manchester University Press, 2009), 38–51.
5. Montserrat Guibernau, *Belonging: Solidarity and Division in Modern Societies* (Cambridge: Polity, 2013), 2.
6. 'The Troubles' is the term euphemistically applied to describe the period of most intense sectarian violence in Northern Ireland. It is regarded as having come to an end in 1998 with the signing of the Good Friday Agreement.

7. Also known as the Belfast Agreement, the Good Friday Agreement was signed in Belfast on 10 April 1998 (Good Friday). In it the governments of Ireland and Britain along with all the major political parties reached an agreement on a number of major issues, including a devolved government in Northern Ireland known as the Assembly, power-sharing between nationalists and unionists, also known as the consociational model, and the decommissioning of paramilitary weapons, notably by the IRA (Irish Republican Army) and the UDF (Ulster Defence Force).

8. Brendan O'Leary, 'The Shackles of the State and Hereditary Animosities: Colonialism in the Interpretation of Irish History', *Field Day Review* 10 (2014): 164.

9. Mary Robinson, 'Cherishing the Irish Diaspora', address by Uachtarán na hÉireann to Joint Sitting of the Houses of the Oireachtas. Dublin, Ireland, February 1995.

10. Philippe Cauvet, 'Deterritorialisation, Reterritorialization, Nations and States: Irish Nationalist Discourses on Nation and Territory Before and After the Good Friday Agreement', *GeoJournal* 76 (2011): 78.

11. Oona Frawley, *Flight* (Dublin: Tramp Press, 2014), 11.

12. Ibid., 11–12.

13. Ibid., 112.

14. Ibid., 124.

15. Ibid., 156.

16. Ibid., 158.

17. Bryan Fanning, *New Guests of the Irish Nation* (Dublin: Irish Academic Press, 2009), 95.

18. Ibid., 105.

19. Ronit Lentin and Robbie McVeigh, *After Optimism? Ireland, Racism and Globalisation* (Dublin: Metro Éireann Publications, 2006), 28.

20. Geraldine Moane, 'Colonialism and the Celtic Tiger: Legacies of History and the Quest for Vision', in Peadar Kirby, Luke Gibbons and Michael Cronin, eds., *Reinventing Ireland: Culture, Society and the Global Economy* (London: Pluto Press, 2002), 113–14.

21. Ibid., 119. It is also worth noting that Moane identifies some cultural strengths that emerge in the psychosocial legacy of colonialism, such as creativity, spirituality and solidarity, but these can only thrive if the postcolonial nation avoids slipping into 'dominator mode'.

22. Kuhling and Keohane, *Cosmopolitan Ireland*, 67.

23. Bryan Fanning, *Racism and Social Change in the Republic of Ireland* (Manchester: Manchester University Press, 2002), 178.

24. Alice Feldman and Anne Mulhall, 'Towing the Line: Migrant Women Writers and the Space of Irish Writing', *Eire-Ireland* 47 (Spring/Summer 2012): 218.

25. Ibid., 216.

26. Maureen T. Reddy, 'Reading and Writing Race in Ireland: Roddy Doyle and *Metro Eireann*', in Wanda Balzano, Anne Mulhall and Moynagh Sullivan, eds., *Irish Postmodernisms and Popular Culture* (Basingstoke: Palgrave Macmillan, 2007), 23.

27. Ibid., 23.

28. Frawley, *Flight*, 118.

29. Kevin Curran, 'Kevin Curran on Why He Wrote Irish Literature's First Black Hero', *Irish Times*, 24 May 2015, http://www.irishtimes.com/culture/books/kevin-curran-on-why-he-wrote-irish-literature-s-first-black-hero-1.2223676.

30. Kuhling and Keohane, *Cosmopolitan Ireland*, 63.

31. Pilar Villar-Argáiz, ed., *Literary Visions of Multicultural Ireland: The Immigrant in Contemporary Irish Literature* (Manchester: Manchester University Press, 2014), 15.

32. Pilar Villar-Argáiz, 'The Representation of Non-Irish Immigrants in Recent Irish Films', *Irish Studies Review* 22, no. 4 (2014): 466–86.

33. Villar-Argáiz, *Literary Visions*, 15.

34. There are a number of scholarly publications that deal with the lives of migrants and refugees in Ireland, such as Luz Mar Gonzáles Arias et al. "The New Irish: Towards a Multicultural Literature in Ireland?" In *In the Wake of the Celtic Tiger: Irish Studies in the Twenty-First Century*, edited by David Clark and Rubén Jarazo Álvarez, 157–81 (Coruña: Instituto Universitario de Estudios Irlandeses 'Amergin', 2010) and Borbála Faragó and Moynagh Sullivan, eds., *Facing the Other: Interdisciplinary Essays on Race, Gender and Social Justice in Contemporary Ireland* (Newcastle: Cambridge Scholars Publishing, 2008), while collections such as Charlotte McIvor and Matthew Spangler, eds., *Staging Intercultural Ireland: New Plays and Practitioner Perspectives* (Cork: Cork University Press, 2014), Jody Allen Randolph, ed. *Close to the Next Moment: Interviews from a Changing Ireland* (Manchester: Carcanet Press, 2010) and Susan Knight, *Where the Grass is Greener: Voices of Immigrant Women in Ireland* (Cork: Oak Tree Press, 2001). offer interviews with migrant writers in Ireland.

35. Nita Mishra, 'The Son of God', in Theophilus Ejorh, ed., *Embers of Words: An Irish Anthology of Migrant Poetry* (Drogheda: Choice Publishing, 2012), 58–59.

36. Mishra, 'Tom's Exotic Princess', in *Embers of Words*, ed. Ejorh, 55.

37. Ibid.

38. Nita Mishra, 'Migrants', in 'Language and Migration in Ireland', report written by Anne O'Connor and Andrea Ciribuco (Immigrant Council of Ireland, 2017), 35. https://www.immigrantcouncil.ie/sites/default/files/files/Language%20and%20Migration%20in%20Ireland.pdf.

39. Ursula Rani Sarma, 'To Try for Something Extraordinary', interview by Fintan Walsh, *Irish Theatre Magazine*, 26 June 2012, http://itmarchive.ie/web/Features/Current/To-try-for-something-extraordinary.html.

40. Ursula Rani Sarma, in *Close to the Next Moment: Interviews from a Changing Ireland*, edited and interview by Jody Allen Randolph (Manchester: Carcanet Press, 2010), 43.

41. Sarma, 'Something Extraordinary'.

42. Ursula Rani Sarma, *Blue; . . . Touched . . .* (London: Oberon, 2002).

43. Charlotte McIvor, 'Staging the 'New Irish': Interculturalism and the Future of the Post-Celtic Tiger Irish Theatre', *Modern Drama* 53, no. 3 (2011): 236.

44. Barry McCrea, in *Close to the Next Moment: Interviews from a Changing Ireland*, edited and interview by Jody Allen Randolph (Manchester: Carcanet Press, 2010), 76.

45. Colin Graham, '"Blame it on Maureen O'Hara": Ireland and the Trope of Authenticity', *Cultural Studies* 15, no. 1 (2001): 60.

46. The journalist Fintan O'Toole makes an astute connection in his *Irish Times* article 'No Integration Please, We're Irish' between the reticence around religion in Irish society, specifically about Catholicism as a marker of belonging in Ireland, and the failure of integration regarding Ireland's migrant population. I would argue further that the inability to really talk about religion and to move meaningfully towards a secular society is tied to the events of partition and the perceived inherence of Catholicism to the identity of the Republic and Protestantism to Northern Ireland, as this binary is the basis of sectarianism. *Irish Times*, 17 February 2018. https://www.irishtimes.com/opinion/fintan-o-toole-no-integration-please-we-re-irish-1.3393435.

47. John Manley, 'Irish Nationalism Reawakened by Brexit Vote, Says Mike Nesbitt', *The Irish News*, 27 June 2016, http://www.irishnews.com/news/northernirelandnews/2016/06/27/news/nesbitt-says-irish-nationalism-reawakened-in-north-by-brexit-vote-580533/.

48. Fintan O'Toole, 'The English Have Placed a Bomb Under the Irish Peace Process', *Guardian*, 25 June 2016, https://www.theguardian.com/commentisfree/2016/jun/24/northern-irish-peace-sacrificed-english-nationalism.

49. Mary Lou McDonald, 'This DUP-Tory Pact Will Fall Apart, But We'll Have to Live with Its Toxic Legacy', *Guardian*, 16 March 2018, https://www.theguardian.com/commentisfree/2018/mar/16/dup-tory-pact-ireland-good-friday-agreement-sinn-fein.

50. Jon Curley, *Poets and Partitions: Confronting Communal Identities in Northern Ireland* (Brighton: Sussex Academic, 2011), 11.

REFERENCES

Cauvet, Philippe. 2011. 'Deterritorialisation, Reterritorialization, Nations and States: Irish Nationalist Discourses on Nation and Territory Before and After the Good Friday Agreement'. *GeoJournal* 76 (1): 77–91.

Curley, Jon. 2011. *Poets and Partitions: Confronting Communal Identities in Northern Ireland*. Brighton: Sussex Academic.

Curran, Kevin. 2015. 'Kevin Curran on Why He Wrote Irish Literature's First Black Hero'. *Irish Times*. 24 May. http://www.irishtimes.com/culture/books/kevin-curran-on-why-he-wrote-irish-literature-s-first-black-hero-1.2223676.

Doyle, Roddy. 2007. *The Deportees and Other Stories*. London: Jonathan Cape.

Ejorh, Theophilus, ed. 2012. *Embers of Words: An Irish Anthology of Migrant Poetry*. Drogheda: Choice Publishing.

Fanning, Bryan. 2002. *Racism and Social Change in the Republic of Ireland*. Manchester: Manchester University Press.

———. 2009. *New Guests of the Irish Nation*. Dublin: Irish Academic Press.

Faragó, Borbála, and Moynagh Sullivan, eds. 2008. *Facing the Other: Interdisciplinary Essays on Race, Gender and Social Justice in Contemporary Ireland*. Newcastle: Cambridge Scholars Publishing.

Feldman, Alice, and Anne Mulhall. 2012. 'Towing the Line: Migrant Women Writers and the Space of Irish Writing'. *Eire-Ireland* 47: 201–20.

Frawley, Oona. 2014. *Flight*. Dublin: Tramp Press.

'Global Irish: Ireland's Diaspora Policy'. 2015. Department of Foreign Affairs and Trade. https://www.dfa.ie/media/globalirish/global-irish-irelands-diaspora-policy.pdf.

Gonzáles, Arias, Marisol Morales Ladrón and Asier Altuna-García de Salazar. 2010. 'The New Irish: Towards a Multicultural Literature in Ireland?' In *In the Wake of the Celtic Tiger: Irish Studies in the Twenty-First Century*, edited by David Clark and Rubén Jarazo Álvarez, 157–81. Coruña: Instituto Universitario de Estudios Irlandeses 'Amergin'.

Graham, Colin. 2001. '"Blame it on Maureen O'Hara": Ireland and the Trope of Authenticity'. *Cultural Studies* 15 (1): 58–75. doi:10.1080/09502380010006754.

Guibernau, Montserrat. 2013. *Belonging: Solidarity and Division in Modern Societies*. Cambridge: Polity.

Hutchinson, John. 1987. *The Dynamics of Cultural Nationalism: Gaelic Revival and the Creation of the Irish Nation State*. London: Allen and Unwin.

Knight, Susan. 2001. *Where the Grass is Greener: Voices of Immigrant Women in Ireland*. Cork: Oak Tree Press.

Kuhling, Carmen, and Kieran Keohane. 2007. *Cosmopolitan Ireland: Globalisation and Quality of Life*. London: Pluto Press.

Lentin, Ronit, and Robbie McVeigh. 2006. *After Optimism? Ireland, Racism and Globalisation*. Dublin: Metro Éireann Publications.

Mac Éinrí, Piaras. 2009. 'If I Wanted to Go There I Wouldn't Start from Here: Re-Imagining a Multi Ethnic Ireland'. In *Transforming Ireland*, edited by Debbie Ging, Michael Cronin and Peadar Kirby, 38–51. Manchester: Manchester University Press.

Manley, John. 2016. 'Irish Nationalism Reawakened by Brexit Vote, Says Mike Nesbitt'. *Irish News*. 27 June. http://www.irishnews.com/news/northernireland-news/2016/06/27/news/nesbitt-says-irish-nationalism-reawakened-in-north-by-brexit-vote-580533/.

McDonald, Mary Lou. 2018. 'This DUP-Tory Pact Will Fall Apart, But We'll Have to Live with Its Toxic Legacy'. *Guardian*. 16 March. https://www.theguardian.com/commentisfree/2018/mar/16/dup-tory-pact-ireland-good-friday-agreement-sinn-fein.

McIvor, Charlotte. 2011. 'Staging the 'New Irish': Interculturalism and the Future of the Post-Celtic Tiger Irish Theatre'. *Modern Drama* 53 (3): 310–32.

McIvor, Charlotte, and Matthew Spangler, eds. 2014. *Staging Intercultural Ireland: New Plays and Practitioner Perspectives*. Cork: Cork University Press.

Mishra, Nita. 2017. 'Migrants'. In report written by Anne O'Connor and Andrea Ciribuco, 'Language and Migration in Ireland'. Immigrant Council of Ireland. https://www.immigrantcouncil.ie/sites/default/files/files/Language%20and%20Migration%20in%20Ireland.pdf.

Moane, Geraldine. 2002. 'Colonialism and the Celtic Tiger: Legacies of History and the Quest for Vision'. In *Reinventing Ireland: Culture, Society and the Global*

Economy, edited by Peadar Kirby, Luke Gibbons and Michael Cronin, 109–23. London: Pluto Press.

O'Leary, Brendan. 2014. 'The Shackles of the State and Hereditary Animosities: Colonialism in the Interpretation of Irish History'. *Field Day Review* 10:148–85. http://www.jstor.org.login.ezproxy.library.ualberta.ca/stable/43054897.

O'Toole, Fintan. 2016. 'The English Have Placed a Bomb Under the Irish Peace Process'. *Guardian*. 25 June. https://www.theguardian.com/commentisfree/2016/jun/24/northern-irish-peace-sacrificed-english-nationalism.

———. 2018. 'No Integration Please, We're Irish'. *Irish Times*. 17 February. https://www.irishtimes.com/opinion/fintan-o-toole-no-integration-please-we-re-irish-1.3393435.

Randolph, Jody Allen, ed. 2010. *Close to the Next Moment: Interviews from a Changing Ireland*. Manchester: Carcanet Press.

Reddy, Maureen T. 2007. 'Reading and Writing Race in Ireland: Roddy Doyle and *Metro Eireann*'. In *Irish Postmodernisms and Popular Culture*, edited by Wanda Balzano, Anne Mulhall and Moynagh Sullivan, 15–25. Basingstoke: Palgrave Macmillan.

Robinson, Mary. 1995. 'Cherishing the Irish Diaspora'. Address by Uachtarán na hÉireann to Joint Sitting of the Houses of the Oireachtas. Dublin, Ireland. February. https://www.gpo.gov/fdsys/pkg/CREC-1995-02-27/pdf/CREC-1995-02-27-pt1-PgS3145.pdf.

Sarma, Ursula Rani. 2002. *Blue; . . . Touched . . .* London: Oberon.

———. 2012. 'To Try for Something Extraordinary'. Interview by Fintan Walsh, *Irish Theatre Magazine*. 26 June. http://itmarchive.ie/web/Features/Current/To-try-for-something-extraordinary.html.

Villar-Argáiz, Pilar. 2014a. 'The Representation of Non-Irish Immigrants in Recent Irish Films'. *Irish Studies Review* 22 (4): 466–86.

———, ed. 2014b. *Literary Visions of Multicultural Ireland: The Immigrant in Contemporary Irish Literature*. Manchester: Manchester University Press.

Chapter 8

Drawing Partition and Its Violence

Joe Sacco's *Palestine* and Vishwajyoti Ghosh's *This Side, That Side*

Vedita Cowaloosur

The end of World War II saw the violent births of a number of new nations, following partitioning of land, resources and people. Among these were the partitions of the Indian subcontinent (into India and East and West Pakistan in 1947, and Bangladesh and Pakistan in 1971) and the 'partition' of Israel and Palestine. I use the word partition between inverted commas at first instance since the Green Line drawn to demarcate the Israeli-occupied territories within and across Palestine was not set up as a permanent border, in the way that it was drawn for India, Pakistan and Bangladesh. Indeed, the boundaries are still shifting and there is no national or international consensus on the lines segregating Israel and Palestine. While borders continue to be redefined and shifted around, this ongoing issue increasingly divides global opinion and support. In the case of India and Pakistan (East and West), and later Bangladesh and Pakistan, partition violence often forms part of a narrative that is buried deep beneath the celebratory accounts of independence, decolonization and freedom, which gained more attention in global and national reportage than the stories of loss and violence that ensued in these partitions. The likenesses between these contested partitioned borders are therefore not always obvious. But despite their deep-seated political differences, the centrality of violence ties the partitions of India, Pakistan, Bangladesh and Israel and Palestine together. While, in almost all these cases, partition was officially projected as a political attempt to impose peace on a riotous people by segregating those who could not be imagined to live together peacefully (Hindus and Muslims, Muslims and Jews . . .), partitions have invariably given way to more violence in their aftermath, as the public violence of warring political parties intrudes into the private and domestic spheres of the inhabitants of the land—the primary victims of the drawn lines.

In their books, including *The Other Side of Silence* (2000), *Remembering Partition: Violence, Nationalism and History in India* (2001), and *Literature, Partition and the Nation State* (2002), Urvashi Butalia, Joe Cleary and Gyanendra Pandey have extensively explored and analyzed the relationship between partitions and violence. The authors discuss how partition revealed a theatre of violence that engulfed entire populations. If displacement, loss of land and home and forceful migration were some of the immediate and visible violent repercussions of partition, there were numerous other forms of violence that remained less visible and immediate. For example, as it emerges in their various analyses, violence was not just perpetrated by the 'enemy' on one's community, but was also performed by communities on their own kin, both voluntarily and involuntarily. They also explore how the victims of partition include a far wider range than those directly affected, and how partition narrative is no longer just the victim's narrative but also percolates downwards across generations and spaces, inherited as part of a traumatic legacy.

Given the groundwork that has already been done, I am not going to dwell on constructing and establishing the link between violence and partitions here. What I do want to dwell on is the choice of texts about partition that are used to illustrate and bring out the inherence of violence to partition. Butalia, Cleary and Pandey have written about the various ways violence accompanies partitions by consulting memoirs, political treatises, official charters and fiction that narrate these events. There is also a plethora of cinematic and literary texts that have lent themselves to this analysis, notably by Ritu Menon and Kamla Bhasin, among others. Menon and Bhasin, especially, make a case for the significance of cinematic and literary texts in recording the 'full horror'[1] of partition in their book *Borders and Boundaries* (1998). They argue that official documentations and political treatises on partition do not come close to doing justice in conveying the extent and expanse of partition violence. There is, however, very little on a medium that I consider effective and conducive to representing the 'full horror' of partition. That medium is the comic form.

The comic form is a unique instrument that can combine visual and narrative mediums—in whatever measure that the artist chooses—to render a story poignant. Everything 'speaks out' the story in a comic: whether it is an image, a word, a line, a colour, a photograph, or even the lack of any of these. If a panel crammed with drawings, words, figures, text boxes and thought balloons advances the story through what it says/shows as much as through its form, empty panels and blank spaces are just as meaningful in their formal and technical silence. Like in cinema, comic artists have the freedom to focus on the tiniest of details through close-up drawings, or take a bird's-eye view on the depiction of their subject via long-shot images—depending on what point they may want to make. But unlike cinema, the comic artist is not bound by camera angles and optical flows. A film cannot change focus without having the camera follow its movement, but comic artists have the liberty and ability to juxtapose panels without having to create that flow. Panels showing interiors can sequentially follow panels depicting exteriors. Two or more narrative subjects can be placed side by side, in concurrent panels. Panels do not need to be of a standard size or shape. A full-page panel can be followed by another page that is broken into a series of single frames. Panels can have borders, or none at all. Eventually, each of these features contributes equally to meaning-making in comics.

When telling the story of partition violence, the various freedoms of the comic form become particularly significant. Firstly, the scatteredness of its form—divided into panels, borders and pages—is apt to emulate the brokenness and divisiveness of partition itself. How certain perspectives and voices gained more credence than others, how certain stories and personal histories were overshadowed by others, how people and places were segregated from each other following the erection of national boundaries . . . can all be replicated through the arrangements, design and layout of comic panels. Like the narrative of partition itself, which cannot be reconstructed single-handedly, multiple panels reconstruct the narratives of partition and its violence. The comic artists' liberty to choose the subject and focus for each panel also helps in drawing a more extensive picture of violence of all kinds, bringing home the everydayness of violence in the stories and histories of partition, for the comic form is also the medium through which some of the overshadowed figures of partition can be recovered. This is enabled, for example, by comic narratives' ability to foreground the personal and marginal stories over the official accounts that are preserved in official treatises. And nowhere is this attempt at reporting, recording, and safekeeping the violence of partition and recalling its harrowing history more obvious than in Joe Sacco's *Palestine* (1996) and Vishwajyoti Ghosh's anthology, *This Side, That Side* (2013), where the comic form is used effectively to tell the longer story of partition.

Sacco's *Palestine* is an eyewitness account of the artist's sojourn in the West Bank and the Gaza Strip, where he meets Palestinians, talks to them about their everyday lives and listens to them as they reminisce about their expulsion from their land, the first Intifada and the Gulf War. Most of Sacco's respondents talk about their experiences firsthand, corroborating their narratives with the stories of other Palestinians who have been through similar situations. In most cases, Sacco gives his interlocutors the narrative voice and inserts their stories as flashbacks, without removing himself as the listener and receiver of these narratives. The narrative is therefore at once his, and not his. He is conscious that he is telling a story that is not his own. He is conscious of injecting himself as the ‘outsider’—the American who goes to the Middle East to find out what is really happening there, and thereafter write to enlighten the West about Palestine. Though Sacco does not explicitly participate in any known progressive alliances against the Israeli state, or their activities in the Gaza Strip and the West Bank (he is remarkably nonaligned in the way that he catalogues, writes down and records the versions of everyone he meets on his travels: from Palestinian militants, refugees and detainees, to displaced children and old people, social activists, Israeli soldiers and citizens, American tourists—among many others), the motivation behind his conception of the book already reveals his involvement with resistance to Israeli occupation of the Gaza strip and the West Bank. Sacco admits, in the comics, that what led him to Gaza was a feeling that he had not heard the ‘whole’ story, because the narratives floating around in the Western media did not cover the Palestinian side in nearly enough depth. His self-appointed task to bring out the ‘other’ version therefore seeks to resist some of the simplified narratives of the occupied Palestinian territories. This is a feature that he emphasizes often through self-mockery and self-deprecating humour in various panels. In one such instance, a Palestinian’s sincere thanks, and his request to Sacco that he ‘write something about us? I showed you, you saw! You tell about us?’ receives the following reaction (recorded in textboxes):

> Now he’s thanking my ass! He’s touched! I’ve come all this way! [. . .] Of course of course! I’m off to fill my notebook! I will alert the world to your suffering! Watch your local comic-book store . . .[2]

Sacco’s drawings reflect this self-awareness of the ethical problem in narrating and narrativizing a struggle with which he may sympathize, but that is eventually not his own. The self-mocking words that he uses for himself address precisely this dilemma: the ethnographic task he has undertaken is necessarily exploitative, and yet necessary for revealing the plight of Palestinians to his readers.

On the other hand, Ghosh’s anthology does not have as many individual interactions and accounts, though—both by virtue of being a collection, and due to the different techniques used for each story—it has more narrative voices than Sacco. Ghosh brings together artists from across borders to collaborate on restoring tales of partition that have often been relegated to the realms of memory. Writers and artists are set to task to dig into memory and story galleries, and revive personal tales of partition, though the conditions for doing so are that people with different experiences of the same history have to work together. Hence, Pakistanis, Indians and Bangladeshis—in interchangeable pairings and groupings—collaborate on a single story. Most of the time, the stories are not as personal as Sacco’s interlocutors: they ‘belong’ to (either of) the contributors’ grandparents, great-grandparents, or form part of an inherited folklore among those whose ancestors lived through partition. But given how the comic artist and storywriter work together on the story, the authorial persona has to be reworked in order to accommodate the different viewpoints. Any of the stories necessarily has greater resonances with either of the collaborators, more than the other. For example, 'The Exit Plan', a story about Bengali-speakers escaping from Pakistan in the aftermath of the Bangladesh war of independence in 1971, is ostensibly more Khademul Islam's (the author) than Sarbajit Sen's (artist), since the story is based on Islam's family's lived experiences. However, the authorial voice is in consonance with the images in 'The Exit Plan', so that the narrative of this story—as with all the other stories in *This Side, That Side*—is polyphonic.

Formally and stylistically, therefore, Sacco and Ghosh's projects are quite different. What I seek to do by comparing these two unlikely comic books is to take on the challenge posed by Edward Said in which he said:

> [T]he intellectual task is explicitly to universalize the crisis, to give greater human scope to what a particular race or nation suffered, to associate that experience with the suffering of others. . . . This does not at all mean a loss in historical specificity, but rather it guards against the possibility that a lesson learnt about oppression in one place will be forgotten or violated in another place or time.[3]

Up to a point, the authors embody Said's philosophy already through the collaborative and multifaceted nature of their projects. For my part, I base my analysis of the violence depicted in Ghosh's and Sacco's books on Said's hypothesis, in order to see how the two authors reveal a map of a bleak, shared past in which violence is repeatedly shown to only beget violence across boundaries, eras and communities. I also seek to illustrate that, through their nonintrusive—even nonjudgmental—tales of violence, Sacco and Ghosh create a manifesto for a hopeful, nonviolent future in their respective oeuvres.

THE SHAPE OF VIOLENCE

I have said above that violence is the lens that records the trauma of partition across these two contexts, so that all the artists in both comic books foreground violence to depict partition. Violence, in both *Palestine* and *This Side, That Side*, is given a context, a shape, sometimes even a face and a name. Scenes of violence are not inserted just for descriptive and engaging purposes—unlike in superhero comics such as *Deadpool*, *Batman* or *X-Men*, for example, which have often sought to aestheticize violence in order to excite and titillate readers. Here, violence forms an elemental part of the plot, shedding light on situations, events and people's psyches—denouncing and explaining the urge and drive behind the violence (without necessarily sympathizing), and hence advancing the storyline from one issue to another. The violence depicted is therefore not as glittering as in *Deadpool* or *Batman*, for example. It is understated. It is also not momentous or cathartic, unlike in the superhero comics where superheroes, who stand for the values of justice, fairness and humanity, use violence as unthinkingly and unsparingly as the villains, making the use of violence appear justifiable, even desirable.[4] Instead, Sacco's illustrations of routine horror and daily-lived realities, and the narratives of memorialization of partition by Ghosh are stories in which violence is not instantaneous but prolonged and impactful. The depiction of violence in these two books helps in constructing and preserving the stories of partition's victims in two principal ways:

1. By drawing the repercussions of the violence of political decisions on ground realities (resulting in such effects such as deterritorialization, migration and segregation), and
2. Through accounting for partition violence in real human terms by foregrounding personal histories, memoirs and oral narratives that have survived a generation or two.

It would be deceptive to assume that the lightness, humour and satire associated with the very form of the comic falls short in conveying the violence and horror of partition. Part of my task in this chapter is to analyze the ways in which the artists take up this challenge, formally and theoretically. Does the wit and dry humour of many of these stories lessen the violent impact of these events? I also explore how—if at all—the retelling of stories of partition from a temporal or physical distance or as an outsider bring objectivity and neutrality in portraying the violence of partition. In many cases, victims of oppression also resort to violence. How does one then tabulate this violence? Is violence still violence when it is the violence of the violated? Jean Paul Sartre, in his essay on the Vietnam War, talks of an ethics of violence that differentiates the violence of the oppressed and that of the oppressor:

> During the Algerian War, I always refused to make a parallel between the terrorist use of bombs, the only weapon available to the Algerians, and the actions and extortions of a rich army of half a million, which occupied the entire country. It is the same in Vietnam.[5]

Following Sartre, I also explore whether the demarcation between the violence of the oppressed and that of the oppressor is made any clearer through the comic form.

'THIS CAN'T BE HOW NATIONS ARE MADE'

Contradictory as this may sound, Ghosh and Sacco rarely include stark illustrations of violence in action, or in abundance. Despite the fact that violence is the running thread that binds these multiple stories of partition, there are few scenes of fighting, or gore and grime depicted. Violence almost resides in melancholia. We *hear* and *read* of violence constantly: it is omnipresent in the tales of Sacco's respondents as they recount to him their stories of territorial dispossession, unlawful imprisonments, torture at the hands of the Israeli authorities, and usurpation of their identities and rights. It resides in Ghosh's stories about forceful evacuations, mass migration, lost homes, friends and families, and reinsertions into new spaces where they are not always made welcome. In fact, as it emerges from each tale that Sacco and Ghosh foreground, every story of partition is violent by its very nature, not just because of the traumatic events that accompanied the moment of partition, but also because of whatever remains (or not!) of the people, their relations and their livelihoods once land has been divided.

I will push this further and argue that we perhaps learn *more* about partition violence in these two books than we do from many written narratives about partition, in which the hagiographic portrayal of the 'victim'[6] of partition often ends up suppressing the violence meted out by the victims themselves—especially on members of their own victimized community. Pandey explains how narratives of partition have traditionally suppressed tales of community-led violence on their own community by classifying violence as criminal, martyrdom or revenge:

> Violence marks the limits of the community, that is to say, violence can occur only at or beyond that limit. By the same token, what occurs within the boundaries of the community is, by definition, not violence.[7]

However, this form of violence does not remain silent in Sacco and Ghosh's works. They include tales and anecdotes about violence perpetuated by communities on their own members—and not just the violence of the 'enemy' on their opponents.

In some stories in Ghosh's anthology, such as Maria M. Litwa's 'Welcome to Geneva Camp', for example, we read of how being a refugee affects those who move across borders and are rejected by the very people with whom they seek national and communal affiliation and identification. These include Muslim Urdu speakers, primarily from the region of Bihar, who moved to East Pakistan after the 1947 partition, but have remained stateless ever since the inception of Bangladesh, following its separation from Pakistan in 1971. Bengali-speaking (also primarily Muslim) Bangladeshis would view the

Urdu-speaking Muslims as unfit for the country, since they were linguistically different.[8] And yet, Pakistan would not accommodate them either, because of a perceived clash in the culture of Biharis and that of Pakistanis—in terms of cuisine, clothing, lifestyle and especially, history. Consequently, the Urdu-speaking community in Bangladesh ended up in a state of limbo, living in temporary settlements and ghettos. They would not be allowed to apply for the national ID card of Bangladesh until 2008. Stylistically, this silence is broken by Litwa through photographs that speak of the reality of being disinherited and disowned by the state and one's community, including close-up shots of people's despondent faces, interiors of barely furnished houses crammed with people, the dinginess of the camp and other shots showing the everyday lives of the refugees. Even the happy faces of children reveal the state of violence in which they live, as their hopeful faces makes a telling contrast against the squalor of their environment. The first panel of this story is a photo of mud and corrugated iron-sheet shacks—Geneva Camp—against a background of high-rise concrete buildings—the Bangladesh from which the Urdu-speaking Muslims are banned. The accompanying text[9] is not a commentary on the photograph but, in the light of the story that emerges, this photograph alone denounces the silent victimization of a group whose only crime was to move to the space where they felt they would be safer and have a closer bond with the community that lived there.

Other disinherited groups subjected to the violence of their own community include people who are in the kind of situation as the various characters in Sonya Fatah and Archana Sreenivasan's story, 'Karachi-Delhi Katha'. For the characters in this comic story, the idea of home is always elsewhere, and they therefore never quite belong to the nation or community where they are situated. Sonya, a Muslim, moves to India from Pakistan, leaving her mother behind in the care of Paro and Hemu—Hindus, who are on the lookout for opportunities to move to India, due to the persecution of minority communities in Pakistan. Sonya keeps flitting between India and Pakistan, never answering definitely to whether she feels a closer bond to either space. Meanwhile, in Delhi, Sonya is served by Vimla, whose real name is Syeda, and who is an illegal migrant from Bangladesh. Syeda/Vimla camouflages her identity as a Muslim and a Bangladeshi in order to be accepted in the country that she has embraced. While Sonya has the prerogative of class ('a relative bastion of elitism'[10] as she calls it) to live and be recognized—if not accepted—as a Muslim in India, Syeda is subjected to violence on various counts: her minority status, her gender and her class. While the gender and class violence is something she would undoubtedly have experienced even in Bangladesh (possibly one of the factors that pushed her to migrate in the first place), the community that she adopts subjects her to violence too. This is the violence of conformity, which is here a condition for acceptance in her new surrounding and includes a cam-

ouflaging of her minority status through such acts as wearing *bindis* and sarees, participating in Hindu festival preparations despite her 'not feeling right about it', and so forth. Concurrently, Paro in Pakistan has to forego her *bindis* for the exact same reason, namely acceptance and absorption into the local community—even as she continues to resist her sister's attempt at radicalizing her by giving up meat, going to the Hindu temple, and greeting by chanting the name of Hindu gods,[11] to adopt a more definite Hindu identity. In all these cases, violence resides in the strictures of the community, the need to be made acceptable to one's community. The artist and writer represent this violence through subtle techniques that denounce the silence around it. Syeda's face is blurred in the panels, until the moment when she announces that she now has an Indian ration card: 'Everything is possible here! I just got my ration card! I'm happy! Nothing to worry about! From today, my existence is legal!'[12] Her facial features become visible after this. Obliterating her 'real' identity as a Bangladeshi Muslim and taking on an Indian Hindu identity opens her up to the world. Through these stylistic choices, Fatah and Sreenivasan seem to encourage readers to reflect on the nature of the violence that grants equal humanity only when someone is 'one of us'. Community violence is rendered real, despite the absence of any bloodshed or scenes of crime. This is unique, since violence of this kind has not often found a place in many political, historical or social narratives about partition, given their frequent perception of partition violence as 'temporary madness'.[13]

Violence against women, in particular, has often been silenced in narratives of partition, and both Sacco and Ghosh take up the task of penetrating, understanding and breaking this silence in their works. Sacco's encounter with two representatives of the Palestinian Federation of Women's Action Committees reveals how women are doubly violated and victimized under the Israeli occupation: they are not only subjected to the oppression of the Israeli administration, but are also disregarded by their own community, who relegate the question of their rights to the status of a minor concern, disregarding the injustice meted to them, and hence perpetuating the violence to which they have been exposed. One of them admits to him: 'We're [that is, Palestinian women] attached to the National Movement. . . . Any regression in the National Movement and we're the hardest hit people. . . . The Intifada isn't over . . . but people figure, "if we lose Palestine, why worry about women"'[14]—revealing how violence against women is often banished into the realms of silence, due to presumed urgency over a greater cause.

Deepa Narsimhan-Madhavan explains the silence around violence against women during the Indian partition thus:

> While August 15, 1947 marked the division of India and the birth of Pakistan it also marked the worst communal violence in India's history. The threats to

> family, religion, national status and security during the partition magnified the tension over ownership and honour in female sexuality, leading to terrible violence inflicted against the women of both societies. This violence, in turn became a very powerful tool against the men of the attacked society. Through the violence, the female body became the very territory that both communities were fighting over. She symbolically represented land that was to be claimed, reclaimed, desecrated or conquered.[15]

Violence perpetuated by members of one's community in order to restore what has been defiled (or to sometimes preemptively save their community from defilement by killing their women, or abetting them to do so themselves) is unspoken and unstated because it directly references male honour and prestige. It is in the interest of preserving this 'honour' that stories of rape and abduction are never revealed.

This violence is a recurrent feature in many of the tales that are curated by Ghosh. Ankur Ahuja, in 'The Red Ledger', explores how violence against women during partition was perhaps even more heinous because of how rarely it was recognized or compensated. The abduction, rape and forceful conversions of women by members of the 'other' community[16] are often buried under layers of lies or downright refusal to be acknowledged. This silent violence by a family upon one of their own members is a particularly haunting element of Ahuja's comic story about homelessness, in which the disappearance—and then reappearance—of a female relative is glossed in this way: 'One of his sisters was abducted during the journey from Bahawalpur to Delhi. She found her way back much later but my grandmother refused to discuss what had happened to her'.[17] Butalia has documented the silence that surrounds the fate of women who are kidnapped during partition extensively. She explains how many of the women who were kidnapped were often raped, and/or sometimes forced to marry the men of the other community. In some cases, the women managed to escape—or were sometimes brought back (voluntarily or involuntarily) due to a recovery and rehabilitation programme (the Central Recovery Operation) started by the respective governments to 'return' the abducted women to their families. However, in several cases, families would refuse to reintegrate these women back in their midst, due to the complex understanding of honour which was tied to women's sexuality. The relations that some of these women would have maintained with the men of the other community meant that families would often see the women as having been tarnished and defiled, and would therefore refuse to accept them. Unfortunately, not many of these women found a platform to contest this violence since even the government program would not ask for their will, but merely used them as a symbol to represent their own goodwill.[18]

In the case of women who do speak up and against violence and oppression directed at them, they are quickly ostracized—as is the case with Lily in Malini Gupta's and Dyuti Mittal's story 'The Taboo', in which Lily (who leaves her fellow-refugee husband because he hits her) becomes a subject of scorn, not admiration. Only some of the women in the refugee camp look up to her as a role model, though few dare to emulate her. The men mostly reject what Lily and her independence represent, hence revealing how—for them—Lily should rather silently have accepted violence as her lot and her way of life. In several ways, 'The Taboo' reads as a retrospective reimagination of independence in view of the violence that follows it. Gupta and Mittal explore the meaning of independence, pushing us to question whether independence comes at the cost of violence, and whether the desire to eschew violence is mutually incompatible with independence.

There are numerous other such instances where it emerges how coherently violence is tangible everywhere in the very storylines of partition. However, to revert to the point I made above, not much of this violence is *visualized* in the comics. It rarely forms part of the panels and strips—and this applies both to the violence of the oppressor and that of the oppressed. Violence remains unseen—or *hors champ*, to use the technical French word that designates what does not appear inside the frame of any given panel. Violence is what occurs in the 'virtual supposed space outside the form of a certain panel'.[19] Hence, for example, we read of explosions, murders, beatings and even rape, but they are rarely drawn. This is also true of Sacco. Even in instances where Sacco is present in the scene, it is mostly his reaction that hints at the violence unfolding outside our realm of vision around him, rather than the depiction of the violence itself. In the case of Ghosh's anthology, the styles and approaches of each comic artist and writer is varied and unique, but even across these various stories, violence is not so much drawn as evoked through references, anecdotes and in conversations with those who have either lived through partition, or heard of it from others.

It is perhaps ironic that among the most turbulent images depicted in both books are scenes of commotion among the victims of violence. Nina Sabnani's 'Know Directions Home?' is a comic story entirely built on the confusion created by the movement of migrants across borders—evoking a semblance of disorder and tumult throughout. The involvement of the Indian authorities who trigger this violence is itself lost in the larger depiction of the ruckus among the displaced refugees in an attempt to seek a place to call home. This story has few distinct panels. Each page is packed and crammed with images of bodies, vehicles, cattle, tents and houses strewn all over the page. Even the speech bubbles are interspersed in the spaces between the images, inducing a sense of claustrophobia. Dotted lines and arrows run in straight lines, loops, and zigzag across all the pages, echoing the sense of loss of directions. The pages cannot be taken in with a single glance because of the amount of information and material they carry. The artists deliberately draw them in such a way that they are made uncomfortable and jarring reading experiences, and reflective of the violence of the refugees' lived reality.

In Sacco, the crowd scenes during anti-Israeli protests and demonstrations for peace by Palestinians and the unsteadiness and unhappiness in the refugee camps appear more tempestuous in the drawings and sketches than the panels in which the artist mentions floggings and firings. These panels usually consist of crowds, angry faces with bared teeth that are exaggeratedly enlarged, banners protesting the Israeli occupation, speech bubbles revealing the slogans being chanted and often textboxes with Sacco's sarcastic ruminations on the validity of all this anger and commotion. He, for example, describes an antisettlement march as follows: 'A mini-demonstration! Maybe 50 people some kids, some women. They march a few dozen yards . . . chanting their heads off . . . raising more decibels in the two minutes than I have heard all afternoon . . . I mean, they're screaming like their lives depended on it!'[20] Elsewhere, Sacco's panel on being caught in the middle of another demonstration against the violent armed presence of Israeli occupation and surveillance in the West Bank reserves for the reader a perspective that makes them aware that they are situated in a space where unrest and violence is a way of life. But Sacco also strategizes his panel in such a way that confuses the reader. While it is clear that Sacco seeks to tell the Palestinian tale of oppression and resistance, the vivid images of the antisettlement demonstrations brings out the chaos and complexity of a society subjected to violence. Sartre demarcates between the violence of the oppressor and the violence of the oppressed, but this demarcation is difficult to map onto images in which the journalist, who is clearly on the side of the Palestinians (without glorifying them or treating them as sacrosanct), is seen trembling like a leaf on the peripheries of demonstrations for restoration of peace and order in Palestine. How do artists live up to the challenge of drawing the difference between the violence of the oppressor and the violence of the oppressed, when the oppressor and the oppressed are both capable of generating violence to the extent of alienating even those who support their cause? In the rest of this chapter, I am going to explore how this difference pivots around the use of symbols, and different stylistic and technical choices.

SYMBOLS

Partition stories from each of the countries involved often reveal the fracturing of the same truth—the oppressor and the oppressed are often interchangeable, and the identity of one constitutes the other. To set these identities apart from each other, the comic artists therefore resort to playing with diegetic focus, framing devices and other techniques. Comic artists have the unique ability and liberty to modify physical traits, bodily proportions and other visual factors that differ from actual facts to correspond to the narrative progress of their story. To their credit, neither Sacco nor Ghosh's artists indulge in the cheap mechanism of stereotyping and exaggerating facial features to achieve the possibility of demarcating and discrediting the oppressor. In fact, if features are at all exaggerated, then they are exaggerated for everyone—and none more so than for Sacco himself, as he indulges in mocking his discernible presence ('Japanese?'[21] he is asked, several times) in the landscape wrought by violence and deprivation. Instead, the artists accentuate certain symbols that speak of the violence of oppression.

Guns, even when they are not being fired, are one such obvious and potent symbol. In *Palestine* especially, guns symbolize the Israeli settlers. Palestinian resistance is neither allowed, nor are they able to afford guns. Their weapons (to resist or to attack) are rocks and Molotov cocktails, which do not usually figure in many panels. Israeli authorities, however, rarely appear without a gun in hand. Guns often overshadow the soldiers themselves in the sketches, as Sacco paints the guns an ominously darker shade to make them stand out, or draws the scene from a point of view that foregrounds the guns prominently. Ironically, while Palestinians (including youth and children) often get attacked, jailed and tortured for pelting rocks or throwing Molotov cocktails at Israeli soldiers, the guns themselves are used without any significant retributive consequence. The guns are almost inviolable in their might, firmly establishing them as a symbol of tyranny.

The Western Wall is another obvious symbol of Israeli occupation and ownership of land and space in the West Bank. The first time Sacco introduces his readers to Israeli occupation in Jerusalem is through the Western Wall, which—though it carries holy significance in Judaism—is here used as a prop by Sacco to outline the story of how Israel came into existence by encroaching on Palestinian land and displacing Palestinians. It is atop the Western Wall that the two Israeli girls whom Sacco befriends justify Israeli occupation. Talking about her time in the army service when she was based in the West Bank, Paula says: 'When I was there [that is, in the West Bank], I understood the danger of giving the land back to the Arabs'.[22] Their positioning is particularly interesting: they are standing on top of the wall, overlooking the Israeli settlement, as they argue for the rationale behind Israeli presence in Gaza and the West Bank, so that their stance enacts the quasicolonial encroachment of the land that they are discussing.

In all the scenes set in Jerusalem, the Western Wall often lurks in the background, acting as a reminder of the expropriation of Palestinians from their homes. Israelis, however, have the exact opposite association about the wall and the significance of home. Dave the American Jew's realization that his trip to Israel is in fact his homecoming (following the Law of Return that enables any person of Jewish descendent to get full Israeli citizenship if they so want, regardless of whether or not they have lived in Israel before) occurs by the wall too. Looking at the wall, Dave ruminates: 'Kinda funny being here at the Western Wall getting into my heritage'.[23] What for Palestinians who used to live in the Gaza Strip is a reminder of dispossession, displacement and refugeeism is for Dave a symbol of his heritage. In several ways, the Western Wall then acts as a parameter for demarcating the oppressor from the oppressed, because of the different relationships that they maintain to the wall.

Walls have an equally symbolic function in the stories in Ghosh's anthology. Images of cracks in walls often stand in for partition and its rippling effect that causes yet more fissures. Ravish Kumar and Ikroop Sandhu's 'Which Side?', for example, features an image of a hole in a wall that opens up more cracks, eventually filling up the whole page. It is not difficult to see how the wall is symbolic of the nation, and how the gashes created by the fracture at the centre of the wall stand in for the overbearing and pervasive nature of violence and oppression. The wound that is created in its wake cannot remain isolated. It has a knock-on effect around it, so that the whole wall eventually succumbs to the force of violence and begins to crumble.

Irfan Master and Prabha Mallya's 'Fault Lines' also exploits images of walls to connote oppression and violence. The walls of the prison become, for the prisoners from different religious and ethnic communities caught between 'no man's land', a bearer of their torture and agony. In this Manto-esque story, two prisoners, separated from each other by a cell wall, seek to while away their time in prison—as they wait for more information on whether they are now situated in India or Pakistan—by scribbling on the walls. While it is easy to read this scribbling as an attempt to vent their frustration, it is meaningful that it is the wall that separates the two onto which this frustration is inscribed. If partition was interpreted as a hole created in a solid wall to provoke the disintegration of the nation/wall in 'Which Side?', Master and Mallya's story represents the act of partitioning itself as the erection of a wall to divide one fellow human from the other. This is why the wall has to bear the brunt of the prisoners' frustrations: its oppressive presence is a symbol of the violence dictated by national leaders on both nations. Muhammad Ali Jinnah's and the Muslim League's demand for a separate homeland for Muslims, and Jawaharlal Nehru's and the Indian National Congress's vote in favor of the division, all led to the creation of a wall of violence that would affect people's lives in ways that none of the leaders had foreseen in their negotiations.

There are several other discernible symbols that speak of the violence of oppression in both books, such as refugee camps set up for the temporary relief of the disinherited which turn into permanent abodes with a less-than-satisfactory quality of life, rubbles and remnants of destroyed homes and lives, lines drawn on the floor that emulate the arbitrariness and randomness of the decision to separate people from land, and land from people. There is one recurring symbol in *Palestine* though that denotes violence and oppression more potently than any of the other representations. For a book set in the Occupied Territories, where instances of militancy and torture abound, the starkest visuals of partition and its violence are, surprisingly, drawings of mud. Mud—land in a semifluid state—runs like a thread and acts as a backdrop to the stories of horror that Sacco's interviewees reveal to him. Sacco often leaves mud to do the talking and to fill in the gaps about Palestinian experiences. A chapter called 'One Shekel to Gaza Town' that follows a tragic encounter with Palestinians deprived of their means of livelihood due to Israeli occupation rules, sees a full page of pencil drawings of mud, without a single line explaining the image. Another chapter, 'Refugeeland', also features two full pages of sketches of mud—and of people wading around in the mud—without any writing. Mud is also primed on the cover of the book—suggesting that 'mud' fills in the impasses left by Israeli occupation—and becomes a symbol of their daily, infernal, violent, lived reality. In the way that he chooses to concentrate on a symbol as mundane as mud, Sacco broadens the narratives about violence and its repercussions. Violence is shown as being present in the everyday, and not just as conflict and armed struggle. It is not the question of just one Intifada. Violence is a continual state of affairs until a permanent solution to the Israeli presence in the West Bank and Gaza Strip is found.

TECHNIQUE

Faces play an important role in keeping count of violence in both books. Sacco often depicts close-up images of human faces and expressions in the midst of narrations about stories of violence and dispossession. In films, scenes in which characters open up about past experiences would often see the camera panning out to depict the narrated scenes—as flashbacks. Sacco does not indulge in this, but adopts other cinematic techniques, in terms of mise-en-scènes, angles and viewing positions. An old woman's account of her son's arrest, for example, is drawn from a high angle that looks down on the old woman, making her look vulnerable, small and lonely in a relatively bare room in which her worldly possessions amount to some furniture—as she talks about losing her son to the struggle against oppression. The more frequent technique of leaving the focus on the respondents' faces on an eye-level is, however, particularly potent, for it reveals an attempt to have Palestinian dispossession and the violence meted to them accounted for in human terms—resisting the knack of the reporter or journalist to record them in terms of length of news and national losses. In fact, this focus on faces and physiques does more than just giving a face to the victims of violence. It is per se a more humane reflection on the national state of affairs in an oppressive setting. Gita Viswanath and Salma Malik explain that personal stories about national events are not just exclusive to the narrator or protagonist, for, 'more often than not, the private sphere is a stand-in for the larger public categories of nation and state'.[24] Arguably, the pathos of violence is therefore reflected more effectively in the somehow exaggerated sketches of the impoverished settings, drab clothes, baggy eyes, wrinkled faces, falling teeth, angry frowns and sometimes brave, feigned smiles than it would have in a drawing depicting this scene in flashback.

The scarcity of violent sketches in both comic books is an effective technique in itself. By complementing their violent anecdotes and stories with the depiction of the enthusiasm and frequency with which Sacco is welcomed into the homes of those he meets—to learn about their lives, see their wounds, record their stories, drink endless cups of tea and share whatever hospitality they are able to provide—underlines the despondency of the people he encounters: they seem to have given up all hope on political promises and negotiations and are instead hopeful that it is a stranger who writes comic books who will 'alert the world of [their] suffering'.

The same technique is used efficiently in Ghosh too. In Arif Ayaz Parrey and Wasim Helal's 'Tamasha-e-Tetwal', the decision of a deaf old man to take off his ear piece—rather than listen to propaganda blaring out from loudspeakers justifying the involvement of armed forces in Kashmir—makes the point about how wretched and confounded their everyday reality is more powerfully than depictions of gunshots and explosions. Interestingly, the old man himself, a Kashmiri Hindu (as apparent through his style of dressing and the fact that people address him as 'Pandit'), continues to maintain his friendship with a Kashmiri Muslim (the other old person, wearing a skullcap in the image). These friendships are overheard and overseen by the Indian and Pakistani authorities who are keen to create camps and divides among the various religious communities through constant, loud, all-pervasive propaganda, in order to garner more support for the separate states. Thus, deafness here becomes at once a fruit of this violence, and a sign of resistance to it.

Neither Sacco's narrative nor Ghosh's project dabble in any kind of rhetoric of disillusion. Both books are almost apolitical in setting up who is in the 'right' and who is in the 'wrong'. Sacco, for example, does not glorify the Palestinians. He includes stories of being conned by Palestinian children, sometimes expresses suspicion at his interlocutors, and often anguish and fear when he finds himself in the midst of demonstrations and unrest. By his own admission:

> I don't sugarcoat the Palestinians. I don't sugarcoat their anger, their vitriol. I don't sugarcoat acts they commit that as far as I'm concerned don't help their cause. I lay it out.

There is also no buildup of melodrama in either of the books. The comic artists often diffuse tension and tragedy through seemingly vapid asides. Harrowing tales of settlers attacking villages, houses being demolished and Palestinians being killed are frequently intercepted by seemingly insipid references to how much tea Sacco has been drinking and ensuing concern for the state of his bladder. In 'I Too Have Seen Lahore', an old man's tale of his journey, as a young boy, from Lahore to Jalandhar amidst a sea of unrest and attacks, ends with him stating his lasting memory of his ancestral land, Lahore, is that of a visit to the zoo, where he remembers seeing a frog in an aquarium trying to swim to the top unsuccessfully. The old man, Darshan Singh, then laughs like a child—and that is the memory that remains with the artist, despite all the harrowing tales that Darshan Singh tells him about how he and his companions saw corpses being strewn all the way along their journey across the border. This lack of melodrama, the dry humor, is eventually able to convey the poignancy of violence more effectively than any elaborate moving depiction of violence in action might have been able to.

MANIFESTO AGAINST VIOLENCE

At the beginning of this chapter, I called *Palestine* and *This Side, That Side* projects that can act as manifestoes against violence. In Sacco's case, it is his solidarity for the Palestinian cause that becomes his hope for a nonviolent future, as well as his message of resistance against violence. Sacco has been called 'the moral draughtsman' by Christopher Hitchens for the way in which he treats the subject of the human costs of the political turmoil over the Gaza Strip and the West Bank. The morality, however, is not just tied to ethics, but is also part of his political action. Sacco's morality is in fact his very act of resistance to violence.

As for Ghosh, his message against violence is in the very form and arrangement of his anthology. The juxtaposition of a Pakistani story alongside an Indian and a Bangladeshi one means that it is harder to distinguish the 'us' and the 'other'. Audiences are encouraged to seek and create their own identification, as the creators erase any overt national, cultural or communal appurtenances. The erasure of these categories means that violence perpetrated by communities on their own is finally divested of the sheen of martyrdom and shown to be what it is—and thus gives a voice to the victims of partition who were silenced in the national stories representing the history of partition and its violence. Women, refugees, non-Indians, ex-Indians . . . among others, all find a space to open up about the violence of partition.

The wars, the confrontations and the slaughter might have run their course, but, as it emerges from both Sacco and Ghosh's tales, partition violence can hardly be dismissed as temporary madness. Mehreen Murtuza's 'Bastards of Utopia' perhaps best summarizes the message of the comic artists who figure in both these books, in which the end of the world is depicted as being, in actual fact, the projection of an internal catastrophe. The metaphor of Siamese twins that Murtuza uses helps visualize the abnormality, disorder and loss of this divisive act, as two faces—mirroring each other—appear to rise out of the sea and form a whole on a page divided into day and night. The message is clear: in the process of partitioning ourselves—which is here a metaphor for partitioning countries, of course—the pain and violence that will ensue will not spare anyone. The hurt *will* be universal, and *each* will be a victim as well as aggressor.

NOTES

1. Kamla Bhasin and Ritu Menon, *Borders and Boundaries: Women in India's Partition* (New Brunswick, NJ: Rutgers University Press, 1998), 6.
2. Joe Sacco, *Palestine* (Seattle: Fantagraphic Books), 10.
3. Edward Said, *Representations of the Intellectual: The 1993 Reith Lectures* (London: Vintage, 1996), 43–44.
4. For example, the demise of antiheroes at the hands of the superheroes—be it Lex Luthor in *Batman* or any of the villains in *Punisher Max*—calls for glorified violence that matches that of the antiheroes themselves in their unlawful and evil pursuits, hence blurring the line between the principled and the unprincipled, the ethical and the unethical.
5. Jean Paul Sartre, *Situations III* [1949] (Paris: Gallimard, 1972), 34–35.
6. I use the term 'victim' in inverted commas here because the ascription of victimhood largely depends on who is doing the telling.
7. Gyanendra Pandey, 'Community and Violence: Recalling Partition', *Economic & Political Weekly* 32 (32): 2037.
8. Urdu was, crucially, also the official language of Pakistan. The (West) Pakistani government administration sought to impose Urdu as the only official language of Bangladesh (then East Pakistan), in vain. Bangladesh's separation from Pakistan also

pivots on the question of language dominantly, though there are some more cultural and historical factors involved.

9. The textbox reads: 'The biggest exodus in human history came with the Partition of India in 1947. The bloody clashes of faiths, belongings, identities, and even languages made the partition an ongoing narrative. Fearing prosecution and danger in India because of their religion, thousands of Urdu-speaking Muslims from Bihar and other states moved to East Pakistan, today's Bangladesh'. Maria M. Litwa, 'Welcome to Geneva Camp', in Vishwajyoti Ghosh, ed., *This Side, That Side: Restorying Partition* (New Delhi: Yoda Press, 2013), 250.

10. Sonya Fatah and Archana Sreenivasan, 'Karachi-Delhi Katha', in Ghosh, *This Side, That Side*, 204.

11. Ibid., 193.

12. Ibid., 198.

13. The reference to partition violence as 'temporary madness' is recurrent in many colonial and government records, which ascribed violence as being propelled by hooligans.

14. Sacco, *Palestine*, 136.

15. Deepa Narasimhan-Madhavan, 'Gender, Sexuality and Violence: Permissible Violence against Women during the Partition of India and Pakistan', *Hawwa: Journal of Women of the Middle East and the Islamic World* 4 (2006): 400.

16. Hindu, in the case of a Muslim victim, or Muslim in the case of a Hindu victim.

17. Ankur Ahuja, 'The Red Ledger', in Ghosh, *This Side, That Side*, 174.

18. Butalia has an extensive analysis of the Central Recovery Operation and its limitations in her book.

19. Pascal Lefèvre, 'The Construction of Space in Comics', in Jeet Heer and Kent Worchester, eds., *A Comics Studies Reader* (Jackson: University Press of Mississippi, 2009): 158.

20. Sacco, *Palestine*, 20.

21. Ibid., 29

22. Ibid., 255.

23. Ibid., 15.

24. Gita Viswanath and Salma Malik, 'Revisiting 1947 through Popular Cinema: A Comparative Study of India and Pakistan', *Economic & Political Weekly* 44, no. 36 (2009): 69.

REFERENCES

Butalia, Urvashi. 2000. *The Other Side of Silence: Voices from the Partition of India.* Durham, NC: Duke University Press.

Ghosh, Vishwajyoti, ed. 2013. *This Side, That Side: Restorying Partition.* New Delhi: Yoda Press.

Lefèvre, Pascal. 2009. 'The Construction of Space in Comics', In *A Comics Studies Reader*, edited by Jeet Heer and Kent Worchester, 152–62. Jackson: University Press of Mississippi.

Menon, Ritu, and Kamla Bhasin. 1998. *Borders and Boundaries: Women in India's Partition*. New Brunswick, NJ: Rutgers University Press.
Morales, Xavier. 2003. '*Kill Bill*: Beauty and Violence'. *The Harvard Law Record.* 16 October. http://hlrecord.org/2003/10/kill-bill-beauty-and-violence/ (accessed 30 June 2016).
Narasimhan-Madhavan, Deepa. 2006. 'Gender, Sexuality and Violence: Permissible Violence against Women during the Partition of India and Pakistan'. *Hawwa: Journal of Women of the Middle East and the Islamic World* 4: 396–416.
Pandey, Gyanendra. 1997. 'Community and Violence: Recalling Partition'. *Economic & Political Weekly* 32 (32): 2037–45.
Sacco, Joe. 1996. *Palestine*. Seattle: Fantagraphic Books.
Said, Edward. 1996. *Representations of the Intellectual: The 1993 Reith Lectures.* London: Vintage.
Sartre, Jean Paul. 1972. *Situations III*. Paris: Gallimard.
Viswanath, Gita, and Salma Malik. 2009. 'Revisiting 1947 through Popular Cinema: A Comparative Study of India and Pakistan'. *Economic & Political Weekly* 44 (36): 61–69.

Chapter 9

Advertising (Across) Borders

Fetishizing Humanism and the 'Magic' of Capitalism

Anindya Raychaudhuri

While the way borders are imagined, reimagined, configured and reconfigured through cultural representation has long been of interest to scholars of literary and cultural studies, there has been, to date, little or no work done on the way borders feature in advertising.[1] This is unfortunate not least because advertising has arguably been of central importance in the ways in which globalized capitalism has apparently elided national borders in the second half of the twentieth century and since. It remains surprising to me how rarely academics from literary, film studies or cultural studies backgrounds actively engage in the study of advertising. Its presence in the contemporary world has become so naturalized that we most often don't notice it; indeed, we often reinforce the illusion that advertising is marginal to our lives by fast-forwarding through the ad-breaks when watching recorded TV. We almost never know the individuals or companies who design the adverts, yet we almost always remember particularly effective adverts for much, much longer than we do the actual programmes we were watching at the time. No other genre is at once more influential, more anonymous and more critically neglected than advertising. Advertising remains a minority presence in the study of cultural production, in a way that is both remarkable and remarkably unfortunate.

In this chapter, I will begin to address this gap by focussing on a selection of advertisements that might be said to constitute a bit of a tradition. Over the last thirty years there have been at least a dozen advertising campaigns for various companies and various products, as well as some public service advertising commissioned by governments but produced by commercial advertising agencies, that use borders, partitions and reunifications as themes and motifs. Critically analysing the ways in which partitions and national borders, 'real' or imaginary, are used to sell consumer products will, I believe, help us to better understand the culturally held conceptions of national borders, and the acts of partition that create them. An analysis of how borders are represented in advertisements will not just provide insight into hegemonic notions of borders, but also help to illuminate the structures of advertising, and the processes through which they work.

The first significant year in the history of border-related advertising is, perhaps unsurprisingly, 1989. The year that saw the fall of the Berlin Wall also saw at least three corporations (AT&T, Pepsi and Quintessence fragrance) releasing commercials which invoked that seismic event. That same year, the *Philadelphia Daily News* predicted that 'in a business that treasures the bandwagon, there are sure to be more Berlin Wall-like ads from US advertisers on the way'.[2]

Around the same time that the Berlin Wall adverts were hitting the television sets in the United States, the Northern Ireland Office of the British Government launched a series of advertisements promoting its confidential hotline, which people were being encouraged to use to pass on information that could help the police and the armed forces combat the sectarian violence that became euphemistically known as 'the Troubles'. These adverts, in various forms with various messages, would be broadcast for a decade, till the ratification of the Good Friday Agreement in 1998. While very different in terms of their intended effect, these public information films do, as I hope to show below, share much with the commercial adverts in the way they are produced, and in the unspoken and unquestioned assumptions that lie behind the politics of representation and discourse that they perform.

In the first two decades of the twenty-first century, there would be more adverts featuring borders and partitions of various kinds. Israeli telecommunications company Cellcom used the Israel/Palestine wall, while Indian telecommunications company Airtel has used various real and imaginary borders in their advertisements as well. There have been a number of adverts for Coca-Cola that have also used real and imaginary borders, culminating most famously in the 2013 *Small World Machines* campaign, featuring the India/Pakistan partition. That same year, Google launched its hugely successful *Reunion* campaign, also featuring the India/Pakistan partition.

In 1989, AT&T connected its use of the Berlin Wall to its long-running and phenomenally successful *Reach Out and Touch Someone* campaign that had been launched in the 1970s. Around one minute long, the advert opened with archive footage of the militarized border represented by the Berlin Wall. A man, standing in front of the remnants of the wall says: 'It was like an operation in the heart of Berlin. And the heart was divided'. The soundtrack is replaced with Louis Armstrong's 'What a Wonderful World' as the audience is shown footage of the wall being demolished. A woman says, 'I thought it was beautiful, everybody is free now'. There are shots of people standing in front of a phone booth, as a male voice says: 'Then I called my sister in East Germany, and she can't believe it, she hadn't heard on the TV, not radio, nothing'. There is a sound collage of various voices talking about calling friends and family across the border, and giving them the news. 'I ran right away to the phone and called my mother in Germany and she was happy'. The screen blacks out, as the words 'Reach out and touch someone' appears, followed by the AT&T logo.[3]

Pepsi's effort to invoke the fall of the Berlin Wall covered similar ground. Like the AT&T advert, this, too, was formed of a collage of footage of the wall coming down, and people celebrating. Pepsi's choice of rousing celebratory music is the Hallelujah chorus from Handel's 'Messiah'. Shots of armed guards are juxtaposed with shots of people attacking the wall with hammers, and children celebrating. In one particularly memorable shot, a child is shown handing a rose to a man in an army uniform. The voiceover intones, 'In this, the season of giving, the gift of freedom is the greatest gift of all'. The final shot is an image of the soldier attaching the rose to his uniform, as the Pepsi logo appears on screen, accompanied with the words, 'Peace on Earth'.[4] Interviewed in the *San Bernardino County Sun*, Pepsi spokesperson Todd MacKenzie was quoted as saying that they tried to 'capture genuine, unscripted moments that exemplified the joys of freedom' and that the advert 'continues the tradition of building bridges between East and West'.[5]

Perhaps unsurprisingly, the commonest and most powerful narrative is that of communication and reconciliation. Again and again, these adverts extol the possibilities of overcoming barriers by emphasizing commonalities over difference. In the AT&T advert, then, the yellow German phone box that can now allow communication between East and West Germany becomes a symbol for communication in general, a symbol with which AT&T can associate itself, so that it comes to represent communication and reconciliation, just as securely as the Berlin Wall represents conflict and division. A similar discursive strategy can be seen in Indian telecommunications company Airtel's 2006 *Express Yourself* advert that claimed to celebrate 'the power of human expression'. In a revealing juxtaposition, the producers included footage of Pakistani singer Nusrat Fateh Ali Khan with the caption 'Some can dissolve boundaries', followed by footage of the dismantling of the Berlin Wall with the caption, 'One act of defiance can spark a revolution'.[6] Much like AT&T and Pepsi did in the 1980s, Airtel here is aligning itself with a narrative of transcending differences, first explicitly extolling the power of communication in order to overcome boundaries, and then, more implicitly, more subtly, but just as powerfully, connecting itself as a corporation with this assumed power of human communication.

Airtel continued this same pattern the following year with its next major advertising campaign to use borders, using the slogan, 'No more boundaries'. The advert opens on a young boy eating at the family dinner table, as an older woman (presumably his mother) cooks with her back to the camera, and to the child. The child sees a football bouncing outside the window. He goes outside into a semi-arid landscape, in which the most visible landmark is a barbed-wire fence. There is another boy standing on the other side of the fence, clearly asking him to kick the ball back. After a few such requests, the first boy kicks the ball back, and then the second boy asks him to cross the fence, so they can play together. They discover a hole in the fence, and as the boy crosses over, the extremely recognisable Airtel jingle starts playing. A voiceover says, 'There is no wall, no barrier, that can keep us apart, if only we talk to each other'. Apart from the voiceover, all the other communication takes place in a language that is evidently not south Asian.[7] As Irshad Daftari put it in the *Economic Times*,

> Everything about the film is foreign. The two protagonists aren't professional actors; they were hand-picked from the streets of Morocco. The language they speak is a local dialect of French.[8]

When asked why the original plan, which was apparently to 'set the ad at the Wagah Border, and get Indian and Pakistani soldiers to start a football game together, quite spontaneously' was changed, K. S. Chakravarthy of advertising agency Rediffusion DY&R argued that 'We wanted to make our idea more universal, more human. After all, the brand is about regular people'.[9]

This strategy is undeniably powerful in its depiction of childhood innocence as representative of universal human emotions. It is not surprising, then, to see that it is one that has been used in partition-related advertising before. In July 1995, the Northern Ireland Office (NIO) of the British Government commissioned the latest of a series of public information commercials to change public attitudes about sectarian violence, and to promote the developing peace process and the still-fragile ceasefire. Called *Boys*, it was filmed in Portballintrae, County Antrim, and, like the Airtel advert, featured two young boys. The minute-long advert shows the two boys running along the beach, tumbling down a sand dune, chasing sheep and playing in the water. The soundtrack is perhaps the most iconic aural symbol of the Northern Irish peace process, Van Morrison's song 'Days like This'. The final message that appears at the end of the advert is 'Wouldn't it be great if it was like this all the time?' While it is not coded quite as 'foreign' as the Airtel advert, its political specificity is underplayed, to say the least. The only clue that these two boys represent the Protestant and Catholic communities of Northern

Ireland comes from a couple of shots, in which they are shown exchanging badges. One of them has an orange badge with a picture of King William, and the other has a green Gaelic Athletic Association (GAA) badge—the only two moments that give any indication of political specificity at all. The two badges, and the message of reconciliation that is implied through them, is an example of what Roland Barthes described as a message without a code. The knowledge required to decipher this message is 'a matter of an almost anthropological knowledge'[10]—the knowledge that the names 'King William' and 'GAA' and their respective colours orange and green stand in for the two sides of the sectarian violence in Northern Ireland. The haste with which the camera passes on from the badges, however, suggests that this advert, described by advertising executive David Lyle as 'one of the most compelling stories of that series of ads',[11] rests on a set of symbols and associations that are beyond the political significance of the green and orange colours in the context of Northern Ireland.

The simple truth is that, as the producers of the Airtel advert also realized, the power of two children playing together can be powerfully and easily harnessed to tell a story of commonality. The image of the innocent *tabula rasa* of a child, who is prepared to play with a child of the 'other' community because he or she knows no different, becomes a powerful tool for the humanistic message that is at the heart of all of these advertising campaigns.

Children are useful for this message, but they are certainly not essential. Coca-Cola's 2011 advert called 'Border' shows two dedicated patrol officers guarding each side of a remote border outpost. They are dressed in a rather odd collection of 'period' costume that takes great care not to reflect any historic or geographic specificity. They are shown patrolling in parallel to this unnamed border. One of them opens a bottle of Coke, and clearly registers the other's desire for it. The first guard places it on the ground, and uses his sword to redraw the border, so that the second guard can pick it up without having technically crossed the border. Neither of them speak at all, as the producers have been careful to not allow any linguistic or visual clue towards any particular partition, or any particular border.[12] The point is not to depict a particular example of political conflict, but rather the general concept of conflict and division, which Coke can then help to transcend. Like the Airtel advert, this too was shot in Morocco because, according to Erika Madison, one of the producers with advertising agency Wieden & Kennedy, 'We considered filming outside Los Angeles in the Palmdale region, but ultimately chose Morocco . . . to further enhance the international, unidentifiable and timeless look of the spot'.[13]

These three adverts are performing the same discursive gesture—suppressing all evidence of historic or geographic specificity while extolling a generic, unspecified and abstracted notion of commonality across apparently divided communities. The specific political context in all of these adverts is coded as divisive and contentious—in other words as dangerously and unacceptably political, while the generalized and abstracted narrative of commonality is coded through the apparently apolitical and universally acceptable symbols of children playing, or two men sharing a drink.

This imperative to make it more universal by removing all context is reminiscent of Roland Barthes's acute analysis of the photographic exhibition *The Family of Man*. Many of the adverts I am looking at here follow the process that Barthes identified remarkably closely:

> This myth of the human 'condition' rests on a very old mystification, which always consists in placing Nature at the bottom of History. Any classic humanism postulates that in scratching the history of men a little, the relativity of their institutions or the superficial diversity of their skins . . . one very quickly reaches the solid rock of a universal human nature.[14]

Barthes demonstrates the way in which the myth of humanism is constructed through the portrayal of facts without any context:

> if one removes History, there is nothing more to be said about them: any comment about them becomes purely tautological . . . to reproduce death or birth tells us, literally nothing.[15]

It seems to me that these adverts are performing a very similar role to the photographs in the Paris exhibition. By removing any specificity of historical or geo-political context, the adverts merely reproduce the fact of borders and are, in this sense, simply tautological.

In other words, what Barthes identifies as History, what we may as well call the political, and what is missing or underplayed from both the photographs that Barthes is studying and the advertisements that I am studying, is an acknowledgement of hierarchy. The advertisements are attempting to create a nonhierarchical, universal, egalitarian and all-inclusive notion of the human, which can then be unproblematically associated with Airtel or Coke or, indeed, the Northern Irish peace process.

At this point it is important to clarify the relationship between the commercial adverts I am looking at on the one hand, and the public information broadcasts commissioned by the NIO of the British Government on the other. The respective goals of these two groups of adverts are so different that it might be asked whether it is fair to examine them together. While the adverts were indeed commissioned in the public interest by the NIO, they were produced by the multinational commercial advertising agency McCann

Erickson. Speaking in 2018 of what she saw as the success of the campaign, executive creative director Julie Anne Bailie made explicit the connection between these various forms of advertising:

> There was a 729% increase in useful or genuine calls to the confidential telephone. Imagine a brand manager for any big brand like Coca-Cola or Adidas, got any kind of response like that. It was overwhelming.[16]

Thus, while on one level an advert promoting a government hotline is doing something different from one that is attempting to sell a mobile phone network or a soft drink, structurally and formally, these two groups of adverts are very similar. The ways they were put together, the interests and methods of the producers, and the technologies used to generate audience interest are all very similar. As Raymond Williams pointed out in connection with the recruitment campaigns for World War I, 'the needs of the war' and 'the needs of the economic system' are not all that different, and the system of images used to control and organize a nation is not all that different from the one used to control and organise a market.[17]

The NIO's decade-long campaign was conceived as a governmental effort to promote and publicize the confidential telephone line, using which people could report any information they had about sectarian violence to the police and army. It began with 'A Future' from January 1988, which tells the story of an unnamed young man who admits his apathetic reaction to the violence that has engulfed his streets because he would do 'anything for a quiet life'. The advert takes great care to not specify which community he belongs to, and while it does not shy away from depicting extreme grisly violence (including perhaps the first mainstream televisual depiction of knee-capping), the violent offenders are equally clearly not identified in terms of their community background. While the advert is clearly rooted in the context of Northern Ireland, there is an equally clear attempt to undermine any specific political context behind the violence, and instead to promote it as an apolitical and criminal activity. The British authorities thus emerge as neutral and objective, and the telephone hotline which represents the connection between the 'ordinary' civilian and the neutral government can play the same role as Airtel and Coke does in their adverts—transcending political differences, in this case that between Protestant and Catholic, and helping to bring the community as a whole together, as part of an undifferentiated, nonhierarchical humanity.

The humanist ideology of the campaign becomes even clearer in *Eye Shutter* from December 1992. Over footage of buildings on fire and of sectarian violence, a voiceover proclaims: 'Last year, they killed, and killed, and killed again. Together we can all help to stop them'. The phrase 'we' is here being used to interpellate a united community of civilians, Protestant and Catholic, who had been identified, in the words of the audience research carried out by McCann Erickson, as 'mainstream decent people', or, in the words of David Lyle, 'the vast majority of the population, both Protestant and Catholic, who were totally disapproving of all paramilitary organisations'.[18] My point here is not to quibble with the accuracy or otherwise of this statement, but rather to argue that, in line with many of the other adverts I am studying here, its discursive strategy is to portray politics as messy, conflict-ridden and almost inherently violent, while simultaneously attempting to create a nonpolitical, nonhierarchical community of human beings who can be evoked in order to demonstrate the artificiality of politics, in opposition to the natural, decent, apolitical world that apparently correctly describes most of the population.

In using their advertising campaign to interpellate the majority of the population into this body of acquiescent 'mainstream decent people', the NIO and McCann Erickson was following the precepts of propagandist newsreels that Walter Benjamin identified:

> Mass reproduction is aided especially by the reproduction of masses. In big parades and monster rallies, in sports events, and in war, all of which nowadays are captured by camera and sound recording, the masses are brought face to face with themselves.[19]

This process of interpellation posits the newly created body of 'mainstream decent people' as the antidote to sectarian violence and accords them the power of being able to overcome the brutality of sectarian violence by cooperating with the neutral arbiters of justice—the British Government.

Invoking the power of such ordinary, decent people to overcome histories of political conflict also underlies Coca-Cola's 2013 advertising campaign *Small World Machines*—which included multiple videos on sites like YouTube[20] and Vimeo (which have had more than three million hits), a flurry of articles on Coke's own website, as well as online polls, and a live chat on Twitter which apparently included over seven million users. In May 2013, Coke installed customized, high-tech vending machines in The Mall of Lahore in Pakistan, and the MGF Mall in Gurgaon, India. These machines allowed people to see and communicate with those across the border. The machines asked the users to copy each other's gestures—dancing, waving at each other, joining hands and tracing a peace symbol. Successfully shared gestures would be rewarded with cans of coke. These machines and the ways in which people interacted with them on either side of the border was turned into a three-minute video which was always designed for online as opposed to TV advertising and, as it happens, it immediately went viral and elicited widespread discussion on Facebook, Twitter and other social network spaces. The general consensus seemed to be that the heart-warming, positive message of the advert meant that Coke was to be applauded for a job well done. Writing for designtaxi.com, Erwan Xiao argued that 'Coca-Cola's heart-warming video shows that it's a small world after all'[21] while in *First Post*, Animesh Das claimed that this latest campaign 'had everyone smiling in appreciation'.[22]

Unsurprisingly, publicity material from Coke itself reinforced this narrative of happiness. Articles written by the various people who worked on the project highlighted this feel-good factor as well. Moiz Syed and Saad Pall from Coca-Cola Pakistan wrote about how the experience made the people realize that 'what united them was stronger than what set them apart'.[23] Ajay Naqvi from the Coca-Cola India team referred to: 'the sweet sip of the genuine epitome of happiness on both sides of the border'[24] while the project leader Jackie Jantos Tulloch cites an anonymous teammate's reaction when the connection was first made: 'A teammate told me he felt the same way as when his wife told him she was pregnant'.[25]

As Rahul Gairola has astutely pointed out, the video demonstrates, among other things, the coercive and neoliberal power of happiness. After a montage of various 'ordinary' people on both sides of the border talking about the relations between the two nations, the screen fades to show text in Coke's livery of red and white: 'A moment of happiness has the power to bring the world closer together'. What is happening here, however, is not just, as Gairola demonstrates, the co-opting of happiness in order to maximize profits, but also, and as the previous adverts I have looked at have also done, to deploy this same happiness in constructing an apparently apolitical and commonsensical humanism. Interviews with 'ordinary' Indians and Pakistanis reflect this attempt to construct a nonhierarchical narrative of humanism, a narrative which can then be used to apparently challenge the hegemony of borders and partitions: 'They have this perception that has been engrained in their heads as the bad guy but when they actually meet them they realise, "you know what, you're just like me"'. As another interviewee puts it, the main problem is that there is no communication: 'And it's sad, because together I think we would do wonders'.

Gairola has argued that the *Small World Machines* campaign targets 'upper-middle class Indians and Pakistanis';[26] it is certainly true that the film features an overrepresentation of upper-middle-class south Asian consumers, but I don't believe that this is the film's target audience. What seems more convincing to me, from both the actual video and the discourse surrounding it, is that the campaign was never targeted at Indians or Pakistanis, and, so, in a very real sense, was never about India–Pakistan relations at all. It was, rather, a sophisticated and generally successful attempt to construct a link between Coke-the-product, and the positive images of people who are known to be in conflict coming together. What Coke is attempting to do is to interpellate its global audience into the role of ordinary decent people who can affirm their status as sovereign consumers who are able to communicate across division, and then, in recognizing themselves as such economic agents, are able to associate this with the act of buying and drinking Coke. The global nature of Coke's target audience is demonstrated by the fact that the video is clearly targeting an audience for whom Indo-Pak relations are not a part of everyday life—some of the people Coke interviews say, 'The relationship between India and Pakistan is one that has seen a lot of loss. It's stressful, it's tense, it seems that it is not improving and it's getting worse. . . . It saddens me that we have this neighbour that we can't even go visit. . . . They're near us but we have no access to them'. Taking place entirely in English (with no subtitles in any South Asian language), hosted mainly on YouTube (a medium that is officially banned in Pakistan), Coca-Cola clearly does not intend this campaign to radically alter sales in the subcontinent. To say this is not, of course, to say that Indians and Pakistanis did not watch and comment on the videos, but that the impetus was always of a multinational company, with a team largely dominated by outsiders, bringing the machines into India and Pakistan in order to capture their reactions. The main video itself prominently features the packing boxes labelled 'India' and 'Pakistan'—as if reminiscent of aid packages sent across borders. Coke produced another video showing the design and manufacture of the 'Small World Machines'. Set mostly outside the subcontinent, this video is captioned: 'This year, two countries will show that what unites us is stronger than what sets us apart, and come together to share a Coca-Cola'—showing clearly that the message is much more for 'us' than it is for the 'two countries'.[27] Like the NIO commissioned adverts like *Eye Shutter*, Coke here is attempting to construct and maintain a carefully manufactured notion of a 'we', which is presented as all-inclusive, but which in reality is hiding a silenced and often invisible 'them'.

As if to highlight the ways in which Indians and Pakistanis remain alienated from the entire campaign, Gabe Aldridge, in his account of the technical challenges, wrote about the 'surprise and intrigue' the 'stylish red beauties' generated among the locals who were 'not overly familiar with Coke machines to begin with'.[28] The associated articles on Coke's own website reinforce this denial of agency to actual Indians and Pakistanis. The producers write about the challenges they had to overcome to complete the project. These challenges include 'time differences, language barriers and cultural sensitivities', 'broadband speeds', 'the mountain of regulations' and 'greater security challenges'—all of which apparently allowed Coca-Cola to think of itself as 'the little engine that could'.[29] The challenges were worth overcoming, however, as *Small World Machines* was 'a life-altering project that change[s] you for the better'.[30]

In a logical extension of this campaign, Coke launched a Twitter poll asking users to suggest other places where the *Small World Machines* could travel to next. Suggestions included Afghanistan, Israel/Palestine, and, perhaps more tongue-in-cheek, Yankee Stadium and Fenway Park. The *Small World Machines* really do become an aid package that can be transported across borders to magically reunite warring communities. The specific political context behind the conflict becomes irrelevant, because Coke can always perform its magic. The specific people being depicted become helplessly mired in their conflict, coming to depend on Coke in order to transcend their petty divisions. Through the discursive magic that Coke wields, this transcending of division takes the form of eliding political hierarchies in order to apparently create an inclusive, nonhierarchical, egalitarian form of humanity whose members can be defined in terms of their desire for unity, and their ability as sovereign economic agents to buy and consume Coke.

There is, then, a central contradiction here. On the one hand, Coke is attempting to depict the agency that 'ordinary' people have to transcend difference through the simple act of communication. This ability to communicate is co-opted in order to construct an undifferentiated, inclusive and above all natural model of humanity, to contrast with and undermine the unnatural act of partition. For the message to work, the Indians and Pakistanis depicted in Coke's videos need to be portrayed as agents who are able to cross borders. On the other hand, in using the India–Pakistan conflict to sell a message of humanity to its global audience, Coke is also effectively denying the same agency that it is apparently ascribing. Indians and Pakistanis aren't used to connecting with each other, and they need the magic of Coke to be able to do so. Coke is on the one hand constructing an undifferentiated and inclusive model of humanity, while effectively relegating the actual human beings it is depicting to an inferior position.

Insofar as Coke can have it both ways, it is little wonder that in their publicity, Coke has repeatedly described the machines and what they do as 'magic'. Gabe Aldridge describes the process of creating the 'magic machines', and how they wanted the Indians and Pakistanis to 'ignore the wizardry and magic, and to just share the wonderful experience'.[31]

Of course, the real magic, as Raymond Williams long ago noted, is not the technology that allows vending machines to link up together, but the discourse that is able to construct such apparently inextricable links between a sugar-based, aerated soft-drink and communal happiness and harmony. As Williams argued in his famous essay 'Advertising: The Magic System':

> it is clear that we have a cultural pattern in which the objects are not enough but must be validated, if only in fantasy, by association with social and personal

> meanings which in a different cultural pattern might be more directly available. The short description of the pattern we have is *magic*.[32]

Williams correctly identifies that far from advertising being evidence 'that our society is too materialist', the 'crucial cultural quality' of advertising is the precise fact that 'the material object being sold is never enough'. In the words of Irshad Daftari, the producers of the Airtel border advert realized that 'network quality' was not an effective selling point because 'a functional differentiator simply didn't cut ice with the consumer. So the consumer connect had to be at an emotional level'.[33] The material qualities of Pepsi or Airtel or Coca-Cola becomes irrelevant to the process of promoting the product and attracting consumers. When Coke can no longer sell itself as superior to Pepsi, it needs to resort to an elaborate narrative of feel-good humanism in order to achieve a connection with its consumer.

Effects of this approach can be seen particularly in Google's spectacularly successful *Reunion* campaign—by far the most popular of the adverts under discussion here. Also released mainly on YouTube (which, not incidentally, is also owned by Google) this video has received more than fourteen million hits. *Reunion* opens with Baldev, an elderly man living in Delhi, telling his granddaughter stories about his childhood friend Yusuf, whom he knew when he lived in Lahore, before partition. He tells her about their childhood games in a park near the oldest gate in Lahore, and how they used to steal and eat 'jhajhariya', a kind of sweet from Yusuf's father's sweetshop. The granddaughter uses these details, and the connectivity of Google, to get in touch with Yusuf and his grandson. Together they manage to bring Yusuf to Delhi, to surprise Baldev on his birthday. The final shot of the advert shows the two old men happily sitting and chatting in the rain.[34]

In certain formal ways, this is very different from both the Airtel and the Coke campaigns—its target audience is the one that was partitioned—the video is in Hindi/Urdu and Punjabi, without subtitles, people wear non-Western clothes, drive in non-Western cars and never speak English. Far from seeking to escape the possible political consequences of using a sensitive topic such as partition, Google apparently embraced it willingly. Abhijit Avasthi, head of the Ogilvy India team that developed the ad, was quoted as saying:

> Yes, this is a sensitive topic, a part of history with bitter memories. But that was the whole point, which is to tell people that those memories are in the past, that there is a way to revive your connection with your lost ones.[35]

Baldev is shown crying at the pain of partition, as the young people in both countries struggle to understand the true impact of partition on the lives of their family. By making the advertisement so visually non-Western, Google was very cleverly able to position itself as virtually the only nonindigenous product in the video, and therefore achieve a greater visual prominence. Like the Airtel and Coke adverts, however, the narrative does not emphasize the superiority of the product in comparison with its competitors—rather, the emphasis is on the emotional consequences of successful contact. The underlying message, then, is the same in all of these adverts. Human beings are essentially the same around the world, and the act of putting up borders and partitions is an unnatural act that forces us to forget our essential commonality. Google helps them find people on the other side of the border, helps them research the visa-application process, check on the status of flights and the weather—in short, it is thanks to Google that these two friends can finally cross the border (though the actual border is never shown) and reunite—thus demonstrating for each other, and for Google's target audience, the commonality of all of us, whichever side of any border we happen to be on. This commonality is then, to use Williams' formulation, magically connected either to the connective powers of Google or Airtel, or to the apparent social lubricant that is Coke or Pepsi.

It is not just the connection between the myth and the product that is magical, but the myth itself. *Reunion* makes no mention of the many bureaucratic hoops that must be jumped through before a Pakistani can get a visa to India, even assuming that such visas are being issued at all. Airtel makes no mention of the fact that even phone calls between India and Pakistan are not always easy, or even necessarily possible. When *Small World Machines* features an anonymous Pakistani saying 'If I have any opportunity to go to India, I'll surely go there', the joyousness of an apparently magical connection belies the inconvenient truth that such opportunities are incredibly rare and are dependent on a whole range of other privileges.

All of this suggests a level of magic beyond what Williams identified in his analysis. What is being magicked into existence is not so much a fantastical relationship between a particular product and a particular value system, but actually the very value system itself—the myth of the human community. Interestingly, in his outline of how the myth of humanism is constructed, Barthes, like Williams, also refers to the metaphor of magic: 'a type of unity is magically produced: man is born, works, laughs and dies everywhere in the same way'.[36]

What is ultimately magical about the myth of humanism, and the ways in which these adverts help construct this narrative, is the way they can actively erase so many hierarchies while extolling the apparent commonality and universality of the concept of the human. This erasure was noted by Barthes in his account of the *Family of Man* photographic exhibition, and his point about the necessity of engaging with and examining the material hierarchies that are the cause behind conflict remains relevant to this study of advertising:

> True, children are always born: but in the whole mass of the human problem, what does the 'essence' of this process matter to us, compared to its modes which, as for them, are perfectly historical? Whether or not the child is born with ease or difficulty, whether or not his birth causes suffering to his mother, whether or not he is threatened by a high mortality rate, whether or not such and such a type of future is open to him: this is what your Exhibitions should be telling people, instead of an eternal lyricism of birth.[37]

Thus, while *Reunion* and *Small World Machines* celebrate the commonality of Indians and Pakistanis across the national border (and therefore render the material border unnatural), they deliberately elide all existing material differences between those Indians and Pakistanis who can afford to buy Coke and use Google, and those who cannot. When the NIO advertising campaign promises that 'Together we can all help to stop them', the hierarchy between the 'us' and the 'them' is so subtle that it is almost invisible. If the 'we' that can work 'together' to stop 'them' consists of mainstream decent people—human beings, in other words, the visual depiction of brutal violence strongly suggests the 'they' that must be stopped constitute something other than human.

There are more immediate hierarchies that are either actively reinforced or left unchallenged by the NIO campaign as well. Watching *A Future* for *Ads on the Frontline*, one of the viewers observed that she always thought the man depicted was a Protestant because he was depicted as having a job: 'We [the Catholics] didn't really have any jobs to lose, to be honest'. Again and again, these adverts characterize the Troubles as working-class and male in origin. *Lady* from July 1993 presents a Protestant woman and Catholic woman, both rendered victims because the husband of one of them is in prison for having killed the other. The caption reinforces the masculine nature of the violence and renders the women of the community as helpless victims: 'Two women, two traditions, two tragedies. One married to a victim of violence, one married to a prisoner of violence'. The narrative of all-inclusive humanism is clearly based on a reinforcing of the gendered nature of the Troubles, a view in which women are given little agency or investment in the conflict. Perhaps most memorably, *I Want To Be Like You, Dad* tells a story of violence being passed on from father to son, in a patrilineal tradition within which women are nothing more than victims, to the soundtrack of 'Cats in the Cradle' by Harry Chapin.[38] The sites of violence in these adverts are usually pubs, shops and supermarkets, working-class houses, estates and communities—spaces that are coded as working class. Behind the deliberate ambiguity about whether these adverts were depicting the Catholic or Protestant communities is the even bigger silence about the fact that they were clearly and unambiguously constructing a narrative of the Troubles as emphatically working-class in origin. Far from a narrative of universal humanism, these adverts can be more accurately seen as an upper-class and patrician government attempting to exercise social control over the working-class people it sees as being under its control.

These elisions of material hierarchy in the construction of a narrative of humanism can be seen in another advertising campaign—this time for Israeli telecommunications company Cellcom, also produced by McCann Erickson. The advert shows a military jeep belonging to the Israeli Defence Force patrolling along the Israel–Palestine wall. A football appears from behind the wall and lands on the bonnet of the jeep. The soldiers initially think they are under attack. When they realise it is a football, one of them says, 'Pass them the ball, go ahead'. They are about to move on, when the ball is returned. Music starts, as one of them calls the rest of their platoon over on the walkie-talkie, and they start playing a game of football across the wall. The voice-over says: 'What do we want? We just want to have fun'.[39] At no point does the camera venture onto the 'other', Palestinian side of the wall, nor do we ever actually see any Palestinians. Their existence is deduced only from the fact that the ball keeps getting returned.[40]

It is probably a coincidence that this advert was produced by the Israeli office of the same multinational that was, through its Belfast office, commissioned to create the NIO adverts throughout the 1980s and the 1990s. Either way, however, it is clear from discourse surrounding this advert that the attempt to construct a narrative of humanism is equally powerful here. Faced with criticism of its approach towards the Israeli–Palestinian conflict, the directors at McCann Erickson claimed that:

> We are pleased with the great interest that this clip has generated in Israel and in the world. The only inspiration for the commercial was the fence, in an effort to reflect the connection between opposite ends, without regard to religion, race or gender.[41]

McCann Erickson are still able to claim the narrative of humanism for themselves, even though they are depicting the IDF as just wanting to have fun. As Seth Freedman has put it,

> the message is rammed home loud and clear: in a militarised version of a Cyndi Lauper number, we learn that troops just wanna have fun, whether at home, on the beach, or patrolling a stretch of one of the most contentious walls on earth.[42]

The Cellcom advert, especially because of the controversy it has generated, might seem very different from the Airtel or the Coke adverts, but the underlying logic is exactly the same. The boys playing football in Airtel's advert, or the Indians and Pakistanis joining hands across the border through the *Small World Machines* are performing exactly the same gesture as the soldiers here—a gesture of apolitical, acquiescent (and therefore happy) human commonality.

The conflict between East and West Berlin, between Protestants and Catholics in Northern Ireland, between Indians and Pakistanis or between Israelis and Palestinians is, in one fell swoop, silenced underneath this overarching myth of connected humanity. It is almost as if the myth of humanism, once constructed by and through these adverts, then assumes agency and force of its own—force that can be used not just to sell more phones and soft drinks, but also a discursive force that can be used to reinforce one's own credentials as members of the mainstream decent (human) community. Humanism becomes a sort of self-fulfilling prophecy—one can invoke it in order to make one's case (promote one's product) and then use this invocation to demonstrate one's decency in a circle that is self-perpetuating. As Devina Joshi wrote in her survey of the Airtel advert, 'The world would be a better place if only we all talked to each other'.[43] Preferably only on Airtel mobiles, though.

The entire apparatus that constructs, reinforces and reproduces this myth of humanism is reminiscent of Marx's analysis of commodity fetishism. There, too, we find the use of magic, mystery and religion as a metaphor for the fantastic ways in which capitalism ascribes values to products:

> There it is a definite social relation between men, that assumes, in their eyes, the fantastic form of a relation between things. In order, therefore, to find an analogy, we must have recourse to the mist-enveloped regions of the religious world. In that world the productions of the human brain appear as independent beings endowed with life, and entering into relation both with one another and the human race. So it is in the world of commodities with the products of men's hands. This I call the Fetishism which attaches itself to the products of labour, so soon as they are produced as commodities, and which is therefore inseparable from the production of commodities.[44]

It is my contention that, in and through these adverts, humanism and the myth of commonality itself becomes a commodity that needs to be fetishized as something 'abounding in metaphysical subtleties and theological niceties',[45] to use Marx's phrase. In this form of capitalism, where the use-value of a product becomes so naturalized that it ceases to be a selling point, when Coke and Airtel can no longer sell themselves based on their superiority compared to their competitors, humanism itself becomes a commodity that can be marketed and sold through multimedia advertising.

I have been describing the narrative of humanism that these adverts are constructing as mythical in Roland Barthes' sense, as discourse that 'has the task of giving an historical intention a natural justification, and making contingency appear eternal'. In other words, myth consists of taking 'an historic reality' (like the visual force of the innocence of children at play, or two old friends meeting after many years) and turning it into 'a natural truth':

> Myth does not deny things, on the contrary, its function is to talk about them; simply, it purifies them, it makes them innocent, it gives them a natural and eternal justification, it gives them a clarity which is not that of an explanation but that of a statement of fact.[46]

By abolishing what Barthes calls 'the complexity of human acts' and reducing them to 'the simplicity of essences', the advertisers return the narrative of humanism as that of a natural fact that 'goes without saying'. The emotional connection we feel when watching two children happily chasing each other along a beach, or two elderly men sitting together, happily getting wet in the rain, is here being presented to us as natural truths that do not need explaining or justifying. The true sleight-of-hand of the adverts, of course, is then to magically but unambiguously associate the product that is being sold—a government-managed peace process, or a multinational communications company, with the natural warmth and joy of the images that are presented to us.

Of course, the corollary of the naturalness of human desire for communication is that partition, borders, division, hierarchies—all of these are presented as counterintuitive and unnatural. The presence of a national border, whether in Germany or Ireland or Palestine or India, irrespective and independent of any political analysis, can be presented as unnatural and coercive. The symbol of a fence, or a wall or a barbed-wire is immediately understandable by most of the audience—it is the relic of a violent, top-down and authoritarian reordering of space that also leads to an equally violent and unnatural separation of people. If a literal or a metaphorical act of crossing a border is to be awarded such emotional significance so that it can be used to sell products, the border itself needs to be depicted as an aberration—an unnatural and dehumanizing object that, in an ideal world, would no longer exist to impede the flow of humanity, but also therefore the flow of resources, labour and capital.

In other words, for all of the appropriation of borders and partitions in and through advertising, the borders in these adverts are little more than functional objects which are there precisely so they can be transcended into oblivion. At the risk of stating the obvious, Coke, Google, Airtel and Cellcom are depicting borders in the way they are, not because they are ideologically committed to this naturalized narrative of humanism, nor because they are necessarily invested in a borderless world, but because it is easy for them to profitably associate themselves with this myth. In times and places where this is not the case, these companies have no hesitation at all in attempting to construct a very different narrative.

In December 2013, I visited the Indian side of the Wagah-Atari border, undoubtedly the most famous point of one of the most famous national borders around the world. I was there, along with thousands of others, to watch the ritualized ceremony of the lowering of the flag—the famous vehicle through which both nations perform their military strength and identity at this, the limit-point of each country. I passed a series of billboards, featuring photographs of the ceremony—Indian and Pakistani soldiers with raised fists, standing off against each other with a mock aggression that belies the very real enmity that characterises the relationship between the two countries. Accompanied with patriotic messages, presumably to congratulate the 'mainstream decent people' who were there to support their armed forces, these billboards were emblazoned with the legend and logo of Coca-Cola. Around the world, on YouTube and Vimeo, and on its website, it suits the company to associate itself with a humanising message of cooperation and communication across the border. Here, at ground zero of the bilateral conflict that is the painful legacy of the 1947 partition, however, rendering the border unnatural and counterintuitive does not work as a marketing strategy. For this, much smaller, and much less popular advertising campaign, it is much more convenient for Coke to associate itself with the kind of jingoistic, nationalist and militaristic fervour that characterizes the daily flag-lowering ceremony. Inclusive humanism and exclusive nationalism are, thus, both equally open to appropriation by the irresistible force of market-driven advertising. Capitalism remains, then, infinitely adaptable, and the presence or absence of borders, acts of partition or reunification, can never seriously challenge the ultimate hegemony of capital.

NOTES

1. A recent example of scholarship that does look at partitions and borders in advertising is Rahul Gairola, 'Migrations in Absentia: Multinational Digital Advertising and Manipulation of Partition Trauma', in Amritjit Singh, Nalini Iyer and Rahul Gairola, eds., *Revisiting India's Partition: New Essays on Memory, Culture and Politics* (Lanham, MD: Lexington Books, 2016), 53–69. I will engage with Gairola's work later on in this chapter, but for the moment, it is enough to note that because Gairola concentrates only on two advertising campaigns featuring the India/Pakistan partition, he is unable to look at representation of borders in advertising more generally.

2. Daily News Wire Services, 'Taking Advantage of the Fall of the Wall: Freedom Rings for Das Kapitalists', *Philadelphia Daily News*, 7 December 1989.

3. 'AT&T Ad—Fall of Berlin Wall—1989', https://www.youtube.com/watch?v=FXY1BL8hqNo (accessed 10 June 2018).

4. 'Pepsi Christmas Commercial about Berlin Wall', https://www.youtube.com/watch?v=FuBPw5lvnM8 (accessed 10 June 2018).

5. 'Berlin Wall Gets Role in Commercials', *San Bernardino County Sun*, 11 December 1989, 35.

6. 'Airtel Express Yourself 2', https://www.youtube.com/watch?v=C3ZHg3tnXZI (accessed 10 June 2018).

7. 'AirTel | Two Boys Playing Football at Border | Music by ARR', https://www.youtube.com/watch?v=hlAnf_VBOSY (accessed 10 June 2018).

8. Irshad Daftari, 'Airtel Eyeing "Iconic" Brand Status', *Economic Times*, 8 December 2007, https://economictimes.indiatimes.com/industry/telecom/airtel-eyeing-iconic-brand-status/articleshow/2605985.cms (accessed 10 June 2018).

9. Cited in Devina Joshi, 'Airtel Breaks Barriers to Break the Clutter', afaqs.com, 3 January 2008, http://www.afaqs.com/news/story/20051_Airtel-breaks-barriers-to-break-the-clutter (accessed 10 June 2018).

10. Roland Barthes, *Image Music Text* (London: Fontana Press, 1977), 36.

11. Cited in *Ads on the Frontline*, broadcast on 23 May 2018 on BBC One Northern Ireland.

12. 'SUPER BOWL 2011: Desert Border Patrol / Coca Cola,' https://www.youtube.com/watch?v=Rj4xhzdVxIo (accessed 10 June 2018).

13. Cited in 'Coca-Cola Films Comedy Border Spot on Location in Morocco', 1 March 2011, http://www.thelocationguide.com/2011/03/coca-cola-films-comedy-border-spot-on-location-in-morocco/ (accessed 10 June 2018).

14. Roland Barthes, *Mythologies* (New York: Noonday Press, 1972), 101.

15. Ibid.

16. Cited in *Ads on the Frontline*, broadcast on 23 May 2018 on BBC One Northern Ireland.

17. Raymond Williams, *Culture and Materialism* (London: Verso, 2005), 180.

18. Cited in *Ads on the Frontline*, broadcast on 23 May 2018 on BBC One Northern Ireland.

19. Walter Benjamin, *Illuminations* (New York: Schocken Books, 2007), 251.

20. 'Coca-Cola Small World Machines—Bringing India and Pakistan Together', https://www.youtube.com/watch?v=ts_4vOUDImE (accessed 10 June 2018).

21. Erwan Xiao, 'Coca-Cola's Heart-Warming Video Shows That It's a Small World After All', designtaxi.com, 21 May 2013 http://designtaxi.com/news/357742/Coca-Cola-s-Heart-Warming-Video-Shows-That-It-s-A-Small-World-After-All/ (accessed 10 June 2018).

22. Animesh Das, 'Coca-Cola: "Small World Vending Machines"', *First Post*, 21 December 2014, https://www.firstpost.com/brands/coca-cola-small-world-vending-machines-833283.html (accessed 10 June 2018).

23. Moiz Syed and Saad Pall, 'Coke's *Small World Machines*: From Pakistan, With Love', 19 June 2013, https://www.coca-colacompany.com/stories/migrated-un

bottled-posts/2013/cokes-small-world-machines-from-pakistan-with-love (accessed 10 June 2018).

24. Ajay Naqvi, 'A *Small World* Perspective from Coca-Cola India: Deep Down, We Know That to Co-exist Is to Exist', 20 June 2013, https://www.coca-colacompany.com/stories/a-small-world-perspective-from-coca-cola-india-deep-down-we-know-that-to-co-exist-is-to-exist (accessed 10 June 2018).

25. Jackie Jantos Tulloch, 'My Own Special #smallworldmachines Story (Twitter Chat Recap)', 20 May 2013, https://www.coca-colacompany.com/stories/my-own-special-smallworldmachines-story (accessed 10 June 2018).

26. Gairola, 'Migrants in Absentia', 55.

27. 'Coca Cola Small World Machines', https://www.youtube.com/watch?v=7AWGbz119_s (accessed 10 June 2018).

28. Gabe Aldridge, 'The Big Story Behind Coke's *Small World Machines*', 7 June 2013, https://www.coca-colacompany.com/stories/the-big-story-behind-cokes-small-world-machines (accessed 10 June 2018).

29. Jay Moye, 'Happiness Without Borders', 20 May 2013, https://www.coca-colacompany.com/stories/happiness-without-borders (accessed 10 June 2018).

30. Aldridge, 'The Big Story Behind Coke's *Small World Machines*'.

31. Ibid.

32. Williams, *Culture and Materialism*, 185.

33. Daftari, 'Airtel Eyeing "Iconic" Brand Status'.

34. 'Google Search: Reunion', https://www.youtube.com/watch?v=gHGDN9-oFJE (accessed 10 June 2018).

35. Cited in Krishnadev Calamur, 'Google's India Strategy: One Teardrop At A Time?', *NPR*, 15 November 2013, https://www.npr.org/sections/parallels/2013/11/15/245435210/googles-india-strategy-one-teardrop-at-a-time (accessed 10 June 2018).

36. Barthes, *Mythologies*, 100.

37. Ibid., 102.

38. 'Cats in the Cradle Northern Ireland TV Advert', https://www.youtube.com/watch?v=NswpCTliqxo (accessed 10 June 2018).

39. I am grateful to Dr Marcelo Svirsky for translating the script of this video for me.

40. 'Cellcom Commercial Israel', https://www.youtube.com/watch?v=5bhCUhsuGvs (accessed 10 June 2018).

41. Cited in Ofri Ilany, 'Did Cellcom Steal Idea for Ad Showing Soldiers Playing Soccer at West Bank Fence?', haaretz.com, 1 January 2009, https://www.haaretz.com/1.5056195 (accessed 10 June 2018).

42. Seth Freedman, 'Cellcom's Cynical Commercial', *Guardian*, 20 July 2009, https://www.theguardian.com/commentisfree/2009/jul/20/cellcom-advert-israel-palestinians (accessed 10 June 2018).

43. Joshi, 'Airtel Breaks Barriers to Break the Clutter'.

44. Karl Marx, *Capital,* Vol. 1, in Karl Marx and Frederick Engels, *The Collected Works of Karl Marx and Frederick Engels* (London: Lawrence and Wishart, 1975), 35–83.

45. Ibid., 81.
46. Barthes, *Mythologies*, 143.

REFERENCES

Aldridge, Gabe. 2013. 'The Big Story Behind Coke's *Small World Machines*'. 7 June. https://www.coca-colacompany.com/stories/the-big-story-behind-cokes-small-world-machines (accessed 10 June 2018).

Barthes, Roland. 1972. *Mythologies*. New York: Noonday Press.

———. 1977. *Image Music Text*. London: Fontana Press.

Benjamin, Walter. 2007. *Illuminations*. New York: Schocken Books.

Calamur, Krishnadev. 2013. 'Google's India Strategy: One Teardrop at a Time?'. *NPR*. 15 November. https://www.npr.org/sections/parallels/2013/11/15/245435210/googles-india-strategy-one-teardrop-at-a-time (accessed 10 June 2018).

Daftari, Irshad. 2007. 'Airtel Eyeing 'Iconic' Brand Status'. *Economic Times*. 8 December. https://economictimes.indiatimes.com/industry/telecom/airtel-eyeing-iconic-brand-status/articleshow/2605985.cms (accessed 10 June 2018).

Das, Animesh. 2014. 'Coca-Cola: "Small World Vending Machines"'. *First Post*. 21 December. https://www.firstpost.com/brands/coca-cola-small-world-vending-machines-833283.html (accessed 10 June 2018).

Freedman, Seth. 2009. 'Cellcom's Cynical Commercial'. *Guardian*. 20 July. https://www.theguardian.com/commentisfree/2009/jul/20/cellcom-advert-israel-palestinians (accessed 10 June 2018).

Gairola, Rahul. 2016. 'Migrations in Absentia: Multinational Digital Advertising and Manipulation of Partition Trauma'. In *Revisiting India's Partition: New Essays on Memory, Culture and Politics*, edited by Amritjit Singh, Nalini Iyer and Rahul Gairola, 53–69. Lanham, MD: Lexington Books.

Ilany, Ofri. 2009. 'Did Cellcom Steal Idea for Ad Showing Soldiers Playing Soccer at West Bank Fence?'. haaretz.com. 1 January. https://www.haaretz.com/1.5056195 (accessed 10 June 2018).

Jantos Tulloch, Jackie. 2013. 'My Own Special #smallworldmachines Story (Twitter Chat Recap)'. 30 May. https://www.coca-colacompany.com/stories/my-own-special-smallworldmachines-story (accessed 10 June 2018).

Joshi, Devina. 2008. 'Airtel Breaks Barriers to Break the Clutter'. afaqs.com. 3 January. http://www.afaqs.com/news/story/20051_Airtel-breaks-barriers-to-break-the-clutter (accessed 10 June 2018).

Marx, Karl, and Frederick Engels. 1975. *The Collected Works of Karl Marx and Frederick Engels*. London: Lawrence and Wishart.

Moye, Jay. 2013. 'Happiness Without Borders'. 20 May. https://www.coca-colacompany.com/stories/happiness-without-borders (accessed 10 June 2018).

Naqvi, Ajay. 2013. 'A *Small World* Perspective from Coca-Cola India: Deep Down, We Know That to Co-exist Is to Exist'. 20 June. https://www.coca-colacompany.com/stories/a-small-world-perspective-from-coca-cola-india-deep-down-we-know-that-to-co-exist-is-to-exist (accessed 10 June 2018).

Syed, Moiz, and Pall, Saad. 2013. 'Coke's *Small World Machines*: From Pakistan, With Love'. 19 June. https://www.coca-colacompany.com/stories/migrated-unbottled-posts/2013/cokes-small-world-machines-from-pakistan-with-love (accessed 10 June 2018).

Williams, Raymond. 2005. *Culture and Materialism*. London: Verso.

Xiao, Erwan. 2013. 'Coca-Cola's Heart-Warming Video Shows That It's a Small World After All'. designtaxi.com. 21 May. http://designtaxi.com/news/357742/Coca-Cola-s-Heart-Warming-Video-Shows-That-It-s-A-Small-World-After-All/ (accessed 10 June 2018).

Chapter 10

Following a Theory of Partition

Jennifer Yusin

In this chapter, I explore the question of a theory of partition—that is, of the possibility of founding something that functions as partition theory. Regardless of the disciplinary approach one takes to the study of partition, or if one advances in their research from a theoretical or empirical vantage, the field makes it necessary to specify what it means by partition. This does not go without the necessity of establishing an intrication between a theoretical and practical approach to partition that is more consistent and which goes beyond a hermeneutics of the subject.

By and large, the object of study that defines the field of partition studies is the 1947 partition of British India, which does not go without implying the 1905 partition of Bengal and the 1971 Liberation war of Bangladesh. No matter the disciplinary domains that situate a particular study of partition, what is called partition is consistently linked to the movements of the subject (whoever or whatever the subject may be) who seeks understanding and meaning in being based on the play of objective knowledge. That is, the function of partition in current research programs of any kind is specified as mnemic transmissible knowledge that is totalizable (even if it's to say that some knowledge eludes our grasp), and thus as what makes it possible to know partition as this or that type of experience, as a phenomenal event, or this or that form of political deorganization/organization. For example, this can be observed in critical analyses that aim to elaborate the ways the desires for a missing place (i.e., India, Pakistan, Kashmir) constitute imaginary places as the wellspring of phantasies of nationhood and nationhood as phantasy. Or it can be observed in studies that, in the style of Foucault's methodology, conceive of partition in terms of systems of power and sets of behaviors in order to demonstrate how it was a traumatic event, a gendered type of violence, or a continuation of the haunting legacies of colonial rule.

For all that such approaches contribute to our thinking of partition, they nonetheless designate an objective genitive. In a rather Kantian way, the field of partition studies currently grounds itself in making the concept of partition into a synthetic function that brings with it the function of the norm to be understood as a universal rule. The problem here has to do with the fact that the subject is necessarily an identity that always finds its correspondence in external objects. What is extremely difficult to think is partition qua subject not as identity, but as a function of variables likely to take on signifying values. I will explore partition as this hypothesis, which, as I will also try to show, can be written on the structure of its spatiality.

In this chapter, then, I try to make an advance in the consistency of this hypothesis by showing the neighboring (sameness and difference) between the proposed concepts of partition and the critical formulations from their theoretical and empirical references. This cannot go without noting the philosophical points that such a hypothesis involves. Indeed, the question of partition theory and its possibilities rest on the continuous production of knowledge that functions to establish a deeper consistency that is differentiated from the objective knowledge of reality.

Let's begin with a brief meditation on the title of this collection, *Partitions and Their Afterlives*.

First of all, *afterlife* means a life *after* death, a life continuously haunted by the eternal return of the spectre—like a shadow that stalks a life that runs after its death. Next it means a form of posterity that is later, *afterwards*, like offspring. In both senses, we can hear a double game of activity and of passivity of a renewability and production in *generation*, evoking, once more, the motif of *partition*, the phenomenon—the phantom of separation, of division, of difference—that arrives to interrupt the order of succession. It is life splitting from itself.

We cannot ignore that afterlife is a rather strange form of filiation bound to the word *partitions* by *their*. In English, between *their*, as the plural form of the possessive pronoun (they), and *there*, the demonstrative adverb expressing position, there is an inaudible difference; it can only be read. Whether the terms of the difference between the two words are marked out in speech or in text, a contradictory sense of belonging, at once a relation that is a determining cause and a relation that is the effect of a cause, nevertheless reverberates. For both *their* and *there* belong to the same *matter*: partition. Partition designates the character of a specific relation that gives both form and content to the after that follows. The afterlife following thereby entices a reflection not only on what it might mean to partition, but also on the formation of partition by its afterlife, its progeny. What, then, is partition? What is it to come after, to follow (a) partition?

Partition (*partage*), from the Latin *partītiō*, means the dividing of something whole in two contradictory senses. In the first instance, it can characterize the process of dividing into separated portions as a giving of allocated shares, a distribution among a number. One thus speaks of partition as a certain type of gain. In the second instance, partition as dividing refers to a parting of shares from a common source that brings about a division and henceforth keeps each part and portion out of range of the other. One therefore also speaks of partition as a particular type of loss, a privation. In both senses, another opposition is evoked. In the third instance, then, partition refers at once to a constructed, physical boundary, like a wall or a thin membrane that stabilizes the structure of a living organism, such as a septum in a plant, and to an immaterial division between nonphysical things. One therefore speaks of partition as a structural matter *of separation* (regimes of division, distinction and differentiation), *of exchange* (systems of inheritance and transference) and *of formation* (processes of education, of engendering and of constituting the form of filiation). As these tightly knotted references contained in the word indicate, partition involves a rather strange, yet consistent matter: that of its own continual parting in and by which partition as such is both the subject of the object of making distinctions and the subject of new divisions. Another way of phrasing the matter at hand is that partition consists in putting into place the general form of the structure of the subject and the subjectivity of the structure.

The intersection between contemporary critical theories and Western philosophy bears witness to the fact that traditionally speaking, partition as such is quite familiar. For it names the formal structure of the subject and the means by which it maintains its unique traits. Like an ontological entity, partition becomes a source of sense for the subject. In this regard, we can say that partition functions to designate the very subject of thought and the meanings produced by the determined movements of the thinking being. According to the law of the old house (*oikonomia*), partition installs itself as a telos, or else as an effective regime of causality that installs the condition of subject as a subject supposed to know by being itself, qua subject.[1] As it thus concerns the economy of the relation between the structure of the subject and subjective structures, the age-old custom consists in splitting and dividing the living being in order to make difference and, at the same time, make sense of the differences by taking part in discourse. It is thanks to the simple fact that the subject is already, in one way or another, taken to be *partitioned* in itself, which implies the impetus for metaphor to say what is felt in human experience, to say that the subject *is* partition. Partition is presumed to designate a subjective origin that constitutes the source of all subjectivity.

The sense of this opposition allows us to grasp something of the structure of discourse (qua signifying chain already participating in the generation of meaning), which is the experience of a lack in the form of there being no universal discourse. Such grasping is a way of accounting for this lack (of trying to make it good) by expressing it in terms of affective attachments that, *in being felt through the body*, reveal the irreducibly unique positions of lived, subjective realities and all that they imply in terms of diversity. This mode of affective accounting works to refer subjective origin to the memory of a discourse that funds the epistemological drive, the have-to-know the subject's objective genealogy as an artefact of discourse. For all that they express with respect to renewals of what is involved in discourse, affects imply that one moves around, not simply in terms of escaping experience and discursive oppositions per se, but in terms of *diversion*.

In the tradition of critical thinking, the situation of partition is thus paradoxical. It creates and guarantees the divisions that the subject (qua partition) needs for its own validity as an autonomous body by generating itself as the condition of possibility of the subject of the living being and along with it, the very meaning of being a living being. According to this perspective, there is a locus we can call partition because the human being is the living being who, as a speaking being already in language, separates and opposes himself while simultaneously maintaining himself in producing the object and subject of partition, and moreover, in reproducing partition as the originary form of relation and the general structure of experience. Partition customarily functions as a kind of explanation that in one way or another presumes to be able to say everything about the subject as a form of identity, even if it expresses the subject as what has already been erased.

Not by chance then, partition appears as an evocation of the motif of borders—the limit, the margin, the end, the outline, the frontier, figures of aporia and the gap. The rhetoric of this motif formulates, to borrow a phrase from Homi Bhabha's seminal work on the locations of cultures, 'the border of our times' as a cloven structure, a presumed contradictory unity that accomplishes itself according to its own concept.[2] A double, opposing meaning is found in the border: at once an accomplishment and a disappearance. Whether we speak of the border as that which separates territories, nations and cultures, or of the form of the border that separates terms and concepts, the subject is what repeats itself out of its self-negation. The border is what succeeds itself not simply in the act of tracing boundaries, but also in the cancellation of a limit (in the twofold sense of principle and end) between concepts. Cancellation, or else negation, is their constitutive act—let us say both the constituting and constitutional power of borders. The subject, then, is what must, together with its opposite, negate itself in order to be. Such is the process—in which partition and the problems that issue from it present themselves as no longer an object but as the very subjects of a political power—expressed in and by the border as that which at once establishes, names and makes the limit felt. In this way, partition is situated in a symmetrical position with the border, with which it forms a system (juridical, political, geographic and so forth). The border expresses the interior/exterior bonding of the place to which a thing is subject because of the fact of being in language, that is, of being specified and of designating what is at once inside and outside itself.

If this is true, then what, after all, is the afterlife of partition? What is *a partition* that survives *a history* in, let us say, the history of a national body's passage from being colonized to being a sovereign nation? The word 'nation', which etymologically derives from the Latin *nāscere*, which means to be born and to sprout, signals at once the coming into existence of a new growth and the beginning of growing. Is partition only a common law for all to emerge? Is partition a metaphor of the law as the power of creative separation that consists in its capacity to maintain itself as such persistently regenerating an external object to which the subject may newly identify? In situating the birth of the new, independent subject—supposedly endowed with the power to establish for itself a new governing body—what finally is partition's afterlife if not that which gives support to the subject's desire to correspond to external objects? Is the life of partition only the very form of law that, by means of a play of forces, is the name that refers to historical, cultural, political and social variations of diverse experiences or a structural phenomenon concerning spaces of localization where we find old and new attachments to be hauntingly inseparable? Is partition ultimately what defines the political subject as continual syntheses with external and externalized objects?

Following along these lines, which are situated in the order of a 'theoretical' knowledge, does not go without involving the concept of partition. Its references to actual processes of dividing a territory moves us to describe something like the thought of catastrophe, that is, an initiatory reversal that consists in the *completion* of the order of succession. From the Latin, *complētiōn*, completion means the process of bringing about an accomplishment, a fulfillment of a wish, promise or expectation and the condition of being perfected and of being a perfection. As the historian Gyanendra Pandey succinctly explains in the context of the 1947 Partition of British India in his text *Remembering Partition*, partition describes a 'moment of rupture' which marks 'the termination of one regime and the inauguration of two new ones'.[3] As that which finally happens, partition presents us with the very figure of itself precisely by inscribing this element of rupture in the very heart of the processes by which the old regime is transformed, by means of its end, into the birth of new, independent political bodies. Partition is thereby theoretically and practically invested with the authority of law and causal character. In being the appropriating event, it constitutes both the regime and the case of its law, or if one prefers, it designates a specific form of causality and regime of events by establishing the sphere of its own reference in reality and making that reference regular.

Indeed, as Pandey's saying makes clear, the splitting of British India into India and Pakistan is a clear example of this rule. Yet the validity of partition's rule does not simply coincide with its applicability to the individual case of the inauguration of India and Pakistan as sovereign, independent nations. At stake in Pandey's thought of the Partition of British India as a 'moment of rupture' is nothing less than the traditional thought of human history as presupposing a stable agent and locus of change that predetermines the course of human development and transformation. Against the tendency of the discipline of history to proceed 'on the assumption of a fixed subject', Pandey takes up the historical case of the Partition of British India as an 'opportunity for an unusual exploration of the representation and language of violence'.[4] The course of his analysis shows the ways violence 'becomes a language that constitutes—and reconstitutes—the subject'.[5] Certainly, Pandey here takes up the task of showing the very structure of historiography and historical discourse as essentially proximal to the structure of human language. In gathering together and examining the facts that constitute the passage from the end of the royal sovereign power of British imperial rule into the inauguration of a modern national sovereignty, Pandey's analysis is a matter of discovering in a particular case (here the case of the 1947 Partition of India) the differential feature of the theory of partition, which is inscribed in what already appears as a tradition. For all that it wants by way of trying to break from being a historiography that reinstitutes the inherent problems of epistemological productions, the analysis finally pivots on the relation between violence and language as what sanctions how the new national subject can take off. Thus we are, as the text's titular term helps to remind us, made to remember partition as firstly what refers to the figure of the law of sovereignty in the era of the fulfillment of human history. In this way, Pandey's historiography ultimately serves to confirm and declare its own allegiance to the essential structure of the metaphysical tradition and its classical concept of human life.[6] It designates for us the pregnant moment of a differential feature which was only to be expected.

Even if one begins to approach the study of partition in its different milieus, and decisively not from a set of theoretical structures, partition nonetheless presents the difficult problem of containing its own virtual rupture in the birth of a national body that not only becomes the nation in the form of a sovereign nation-state, but also is one that pronounces the differential character of what the nation-state should be and in what it should consist. This has to do with the extreme difficulty—if not impossibility—in conceiving of the subject of partition or the partition as a subject, as not necessarily an identity, or form of identification. National sovereignty is inseparable from the instantiation of juridical-political orders that shape, in profound ways, forms of identities, political spaces and experiences therein. It is always and immediately the bearer of the very insignia of partition, fortifying partition as the hallmark of being something that arrives to tear asunder and overturn the order of succession. Partition is said to free the new sovereign body from the restrictions of the old regimes in order to enrich itself with the material that is absolutely necessary for its proper functioning. By way of this strange upheaval, partition gives birth to itself as what is now finally separated, signing its own birth certificate in the process.

Again, we are brought to the thought of something like *catastrophe*. From the Greek word *katastrophē*, it means the conclusion, the final event, the dénouement—the end of a life. It also means a reversal, a sudden and tragic overturning of events that subverts an established order, bringing about its ruin and end. It refers at once to a surprise event that reverses a teleological course, accomplishing its conclusion, and to the truth of an event, the accomplishment of a life. And further still, a doubling contradiction in *strophe*. It means a turning toward that stays the course and a turning toward an unexpected destination, which derives from the Greek verb *strephein*. *Strephein* means to turn upon as in a type of change, as in repetition, as in *to repeat*. Especially in the contemporary Western philosophical tradition, catastrophe names the anticipation of threat as the indestructible horizon that opens toward every event. Partition: as if to say we hear a catastrophe or a philosophy articulated to a thought of the word which obliges.

This is what, from Heidegger to Derrida and onwards, via even the tenacious lineage of what is called the postcolonial critique of the subject, remains consummately problematic: catastrophe is a kind of transcendental destruction in which destruction is always already a structure, always already the repetition of a more originary trauma that constitutes a certain truth with regard to the subject's ancient history. Catastrophe appears as something like an ontological entity that is a positive principle of the function of separation without a subject, a cause of contemporary trauma. In this regard, partition becomes like a narrative of origin that takes on the task of investigating what *is* originary and of being a movement in the strong sense to produce historicity. It speaks about what is in reality and about what is enduring, not just as an experience of borders but as the schema of an explanation for the source that opposes, yet gives us the reasons why life is always at issue with itself in its actions.

Especially as it pertains to the diverse realities manifested in partition and its afterlives, the thought of the instance of rupture is decisive, for it presupposes a demonstration of the thought of catastrophe as innate to the old and new subject as well as to the character of their relation. No matter the discipline specific discourse and the particular accounting of partition(s) produced therein, the very heritage of the idea of partition as constituting the foundation of the structure of subject and the subjectivity of the structure borrows from the assumption of catastrophe as immanent to the question of the theory of being. It takes as its starting point an initiatory reversal that both subsists and consists in an inversion to the order of succession or in a specific disclosure of a world against a horizon of appearing, which comes to affect the very immutability of the horizon of meaning. Here we touch upon a critical aspect of Heidegger's thought, which is that from the beginning, ontology is always put in terms of a hermeneutic of factical life, which implies a heritage that stores possibilities. Dasein, the Being-there who is its *da*, its 'there', its 'place', is always in the mode of having-to-be. Consigned to itself in its ways of being, Dasein is a problem for itself and exchanged into the object of calculation.[7] The royal remainder is evermore the split subject caught within a circular system that formalizes the form of life as needing to identify itself in a relation to an external object that is felt in the form of lack so that it can comprehend itself and make attainable the possibility of breaking traditional determinations.

The very thought of partition is a serious issue for itself since it poses, in the very formulation of its structure, the problem of differentiating between life and its actual situations, between constituting power and the nature of its relation to the sovereign body. In this way, the issues of partition (for example, juridical-political, geographic, colonial, postcolonial), or else the question of partition and its afterlives find themselves easily (re)moved to first philosophy.

To help present these problems in a different way, let us continue in the vein of the historical example of the 1947 Partition of British India, which simultaneously generated the end of British colonial rule and the establishment of India and Pakistan as independent nations. Rather than describe the empirical facts and different registers that make up this complicated history, I will instead pay attention to the case of the making of the name 'Pakistan'.

There are diverging accounts of who first conceptualized the word 'Pakistan'. However, its initial spoken and written nominations are generally attributed to Sir Muhammad Iqbal and Rahmat Ali. In his presidential address to the twenty-fifth session of the All India Muslim League on 29 December 1930, Iqbal outlined a territorial vision for an independent Muslim nation by identifying the Muslim-majority provinces in the northwestern region of the subcontinent. Three years later and in response, Ali, a student at Cambridge University at the time, self-published a pamphlet titled 'Now or Never: Are We to Live or Perish Forever'. These are the opening lines:

> At this solemn hour in the history of India, when British and Indian delegates are laying the foundations of a Federal Constitution for that Sub-continent, we address this appeal to you, in the name of our common heritage, and on behalf of our thirty million Muslim brethern who live in PAKISTAN by which we mean the five Northern units of India viz: Punjab, North-West Frontier Province (Afghan Province), Kashmir, Sind, and Baluchistan. And we ask for your sympathy and support in our grim and fateful struggle against political crucifixion and national annihilation.[8]

The passionate appeal against the threat of death, from which the demand for the compassion to protect and support the life of a people emerges, is clear enough. The subject at stake and under the threat of being crossed out appears as the effect of the concatenation of signifying elements ('solemn hour', 'in the name of', 'common heritage', 'brethren', 'political crucifixion', 'national annihilation'). The entire text is a very moving declaration of love, on 'behalf' of the life and political existence of the subject and subjectivity of Pakistan. In the effort 'to help' the addressee 'realise the full magnitude of this impending catastrophe'—that of potentially creating, via the process of decolonizing British India, a unified Indian nation—Ali 'reminds' the reader of the principles of Muslim life that find their resonance in everything from customs to census data. As Ali proclaims, there is nothing to be 'gained' from making the 'stupendous sacrifice' of 'our nationhood in order to make India one nation'. Further still, he expresses that 'in this settlement', which, at the time of writing, has yet to be decided upon, 'our body and soul are at stake. Our very being and well-being depend upon it. Not only ours, but also those of every other people in India'.

Now, what is very interesting is that there is something missing in Ali's text—namely the letter *i*—and that this missing something is what supports the discourse ('discourse' understood here as link, not firstly as a succession of historical emergences or only as a particular discourse). Not completely without significance, depending on the source from which one retrieves the text of Ali's writing, the word 'Pakistan' is written in one of two ways, with capital letters: 'PAKSTAN' or 'PAKISTAN'. In either case, and since its status and functioning as missing is not limited to the actual writing of the word, the *i* is still missing. What is important is the reference to writing, a writing that supports a tangible idea of the real situation.

Certainly, then, what immediately stands out is the intermediary place of the *i* (whether actually there or not there). It introduces a gap between the other letters, which are themselves standing in/for the place(s) that signal territorial orders of the political, religious, economic and juridical principles that sustain the demand for the establishment of a sovereign nation-state separate from India. The main function of the letter is thus not its signification but the hole in language and meaning it both opens and comes from with respect to what comes before and after it in a series.[9] The letter here reveals itself as being in force without signification insofar as it posits its own essential undecidability in a series, in the endless exchangeability of the roles of the signified and signifier. 'Pak(i)stan' (which I write in this way to help establish a neighborhood of letters between the two versions of the name) thus turns upon itself as a linguistic syntagm that shows its own signification by rendering impossible any determinate meaning. It operates to mark its terms as an excess of its signifying function over the field of signifieds that marks itself as such. With respect to its role as something missing in a series, the *i* stands for any number of subjects ad infinitum. *I* for India; *i* for British India; *i* for Iqbal; *i* for the fifth northern province of India not included by Iqbal in his address; *i* for Indus Valley and River; *i* for Islam; *i* for inside, interior; *i* for identity; *i* for identical; *i* for idea(l). In its turns, the *i* at once appears and disappears as the signifier of partition (its multiple conceptions, the territorial boundaries, the ideals of Islam, the political demand and so forth) and as its signified.

In this series of substitutions, infinite negation allows us to grasp the very system of nomination in its excess, which implies the passage from one system of naming to another, or else the exchange of a system and the change into another. With a little undue play, we can say that the *i* is not quite working out and that, in a certain respect, it is causing the subject we are calling 'Pak(i)stan'. This can only be noted by *a* writing, or more accurately, by an *i* that is what does not stop being written. In the neighborhood between 'Pak' and 'stan', there is concentrated for us the letter functioning to indicate the place where there is suspended in the signifier the very question of its guarantee in the advent of truth of another era.

To establish things only from say, an original writing—from the reprieve of writing, the separation from writing by its own its graphic force—is only to make the alternative between the synchronic and the diachronic the presupposed joint of the text we've been reading. Like two faces of a single coin, a single reality, 'Pakstan'/'Pakistan' consist in the different same and the same different, or else, the same difference. It is the sense of this opposition that keeps its solidarity to anterior and posterior, between structure and what, for example, Derrida calls arche-writing, in order to guarantee that its structure precedes its elements in order to reproduce the founding structure itself. Whatever multiplicity of subjectivities may have been indicated from the outset are immediately and drastically contracted into the text of one body, of the politicization of the life of the body that institutes the political subject by partitioning itself into partial objects.

In this approach to Pakistan writing, the very life of India and Pakistan appear only as an empty structure, as a virtual form that economically connects up to a systematic negation whose productive values (historical, political, juridical, cultural, social and so forth) consist in giving every appearance of Pakistan's bodies and identities as issuing from the first and immediate referent to a life that needs to be partitioned and which has its paradigm in the figure that accomplishes itself by dividing itself from itself. Paradoxically, the immediate assumes partition to be in a presuppositional way, the structural symbolic. It is thanks to the economy of the double bind, which involves a real political double bind, that, as a juridical-political-geographic process, partition opens the space in which it is possible to mark the borders, and thus the differences and distances between inside and outside. In this way, it is a familiar crisis of space. Further still, it is thanks to the production of the value of this binding economy that partition designates the field of a set of rules assigned to determinate territories. As the founding event and structure of the postcolonial subcontinent, the Partition of British India engenders its situation as immediately valid and applicable to every body and its actual situations, to every form of life, precisely by maintaining itself as the law that produces its economic value in the political body. The condition of the subject—the subject qua supposable, the subject qua eventual subject capable of receiving messages—is ever more the meaning-effect of the law as partition that takes its power from the law as at once code and model.

In Ali's text, the *i* that is being inscribed there functions to help designate Pakistan as a proper name after the initial appearance of the linguistic conception of partition. Here the *i* is also the *I*, a self-consciousness, a singularity. The subject encounters its partitions before the actual Partition of 1947; in a way, it anticipates its own possibility to partition. Pak(i)stan comes before itself as the official heir of a new regime of independence and national sovereignty, before its division from its twinned, sibling nation, before the Muslim League's 1940 demand, before the juridical-political processes of decolonization, before the installation of new geographical borders, before the emergence of its territorial form for which there is no prior geographical referent. Before it happened in the empirical, parliamentary and geographic senses, partition is there before the beginning. From this, we can begin to see that the political becoming of Pakistan, or nation formation moves in at least two possible directions: the orders of anteriority and posterity.

First, it was an acronym in which each letter abbreviated and represented the names of the Muslim-majority provinces that comprised the territory of such a state. Second, Pak(i)stan is a sequence of grammatical elements, which are themselves cognates of a prefix [*pak*] and suffix [*stan*], whose combinatory derivative meaning is 'land of the pure'. Third, it was, as we can now see, incomplete. The *i* is/was not yet there, Pak(i)stan is still to come, still wanting itself to be realized. Already we can see that Pak(i)stan comes before its proper name, before the different political processes of decolonization and of establishing a new map of the subcontinent, and before the birth of the twinned nations at midnight between 14 and 15 August 1947. (Let us recall the motif of twinness, prominently figured by Saleem and Shiva, that runs ahead of *Midnight's Children* to the extent that the text builds itself afterwards.) It's as though both Pakistan and India have two ages and that these two ages develop in tandem and in only analogous ways. Paradoxically, midnight is the first partition, which is also the departure point insofar as everything issues from it. Everything is born of that first *i* which repeats itself out of m*i*dn*i*ght.

For as rich in difference becoming is, what is not working out here in the substance of this knowledge, which consists in returning us to exchange, to the insistence that the only thing that counts, is whether a piece has or has not exchange value even as it undoes the weave of its text. No matter how difficult it may be to pin down the time of generations, the concern for the timing of partition, which involves orders of direction and succession, moves only by the force of the negative schematic. The life of Pakistan and India and their subjectivities are instituted by a structure of partitioning that obliges its subject to follow along in the way of opposition and negation, to be the form of a *via negativa*.

From the view of the conceptual status of partition as operating with the disorienting, emptying play of the symbolic, the real causal power lies in the structure of separation as always already a structure of effacement that discovers and invents itself only in and with the force of the negative. We see this, for example, in the Derridean thought of the eternal return of the same, which is a principle of distinction between living beings and their spectres, and in the Deleuzian thought of the eternal return of the same, which, for its part, is a principle of singling out weakness in order to ensure the reproduction of difference.[10] In both, we see a particular economy and strategy of the exchangeability of difference that destroys the Hegelian dialectic and Hegelian model of the end of history as imaginary. However, it is important to recall that according to Hegel, repetition plays a very precise role in history. When something happens only once, it can be attributed to being a pure contingent accident. But when the same event repeats itself, then this is a sign of a deeper historical necessity that is illuminated by a self-reflective redoubling. So the Hegelian dialectic itself is not exactly another old ideological narrative but more precisely an innate capacity to dodge the progressive teleology in which prior epochs are understood as stages in the building of a civil state in the civilized, modern epoch.[11] Nevertheless, and as Frederic Jameson shows in his book *The Hegel Variations*, the materialist answer to the dialectical teleology has been to substitute the dialectical teleology with the retroactive process of positing presuppositions.[12] This is especially the case in the responses and strategies of postcolonial critique, which work to reveal how this grand teleological narrative ensures the survival of the myth of modernity and guarantees the destiny of the human as a political subject and the living being to be the necessary transition from nature to culture.

Until now postcolonial scholars, however effective their critique of the dialectic, of capital, of deconstruction or of poststructuralism (of everything that stands for the West), have maintained something of it in the end, calling it orientalism, the subaltern, the native informant or the hybrid, for example, because even if the death of the dialectic and deconstruction have been proclaimed, the *threat* of a return of the eternal same nevertheless circumscribes the minimal creed of a given critical theory in general. The minimal creed that exists is a set of structures, of both theoretical and practical experiences, that remain irreducible to each other, to purely formal, symbolic logic on the one hand and to material, empirical facts on the other. It is a set of concepts that demonstrate how the subject's historically given self-identity is something to be deconstructed, something always already deferred and therefore that it must, in some way, rely upon the processes of exchange that undermine its negations in order to produce itself as a subversive novelty that presents itself to itself and to the world.[13]

Why is this the case? Because no matter how radical the critiques of sovereignty, hegemony, and Western discourse, or how suspicious of the universal, there is no discourse on partition, whether geographic, historical, political, juridical, philosophical, literary or anthropological, that does not in some way borrow from the idea of the thought of the structure of man as fundamentally partitioned between the natural, biological aspect of living and the spiritual, intellectual or symbolic domain of life. This is indeed an old border inherited from Aristotle's description of man as an intermediary between God and animal. What is proper to the human is always identified as first a concept or meaning in its essential partition from any empirical content.

How then to address the study of partition from within the constraints of discourse? How to borrow from different discourses to think about the history of the subject and theoretical ideologies, that is, about cultural and political formations without falling back upon all language as determined by *logos*?

We touch here upon the thought that every 'theory' is a language insofar as it aims either to consume or introject all others while forming its own path(ology) within a territory of thinking. The particular structure of theory thus discloses itself to be a presupposition of language. Accordingly, a 'theory' necessarily carries a multiplicity of idioms that it can never master except as a certain stabilization of itself into its own accent, its own style of projection. Like that which is 'my' language, a given theory of partition must be perpetually invented so that it can enter into discourse in its own way while establishing the cartography of its style. In order for a 'theory' to speak, it cannot universalize discourse; yet it must describe something that everyone can hear. Any theory therefore shows its own signifying and, in this way, suspends its own meaning insofar as the particular structure of theory founds itself in the presuppositional structure of language.[14] A theory is always a text firmly installed in the nonderivatory logic of the order of succession as the paradigm of heritage and inheritance.[15]

What then remains for us in theory, of a given theory, except to say how a text is made and the ways its texture is elaborated according to the law of reversal of before and after, between what Derrida calls arche-writing and structure? Moreover, we are left to ask: what form of posterity, which would not simply distribute meaning differently but would provoke a transformation of the process of the exchange of terms through several different spaces, can this approach to the theory of partition and the conceptualization of its afterlives really produce? Does this mean that any thinking, any theory of partition made of concepts, is fated to mime, to repeat critically the problem of the inherited double concept of the border? Is every thought of partitioning doomed to fulfill the old problem of the essential border (nature/culture, immortal/mortal, infinite/finite), in critiquing the status of discourses (like modernity, postmodernity, idealism, materialism and so forth) whose successions borrow from the very sources of their heritage in order to overcome it? Does partition already say everything or at least offer the master key that unlocks every possible explanation about the subject in its different forms?

Let us here briefly consider Homi Bhabha's concept of the finitude of the modern nation, defined as the meeting point between the accumulative temporality of modernity and the lived temporality of the living localities of cultural difference.[16] Before anything else, the concept of 'difference' for Bhabha expresses an irreducibility to negation as what functions to produce a new subject. All presence—forms of the nation, of identity, of the subject and so forth—results from an originary *diapherein*.[17] Accordingly, difference is a mode of the being of the splitting and the multiple that is not, in itself, self-overcoming because its constancy is assured through mimicry. Mimicry is not a simple restoration to the identical, but it nonetheless cannot produce a new form of nation that overcomes the prior structures of powers it aims to subvert. In a manner reminiscent of Deleuze's 'phantom of affirmation', Bhabha presents us with an idea of posterity and of nation—of the advent of the birth of a new subject—that is produced by an automatic differentiation, or else, programmatically selected for reproduction.[18] For Bhabha, the form of the nation always founds itself on being the advent of writing anew. What chance, then, are we actually giving, in the sense of a *histogenetic* potentiality, to the inheritor, to the subject (on the level of the individual and at the level of the community) to whom legacies and territories have been bequeathed?

We arrive here at a very crucial point: that of the importance and stress put on the idea of the double inscription in (the) theory, the presumed status of which underwrites the treatment of the modern political subject in the problem of sovereignty, from philosophical discourse to what is called 'postcolonial critique'. Let us consider in passing Spivak's exercise of the classical figure of sovereignty in the production of capital forms of the West as the knowledge of the subject in 'Can the Subaltern Speak', Foucault's concepts of biopolitics and biopower in the inclusion of the simple facts of man's biological life in the mechanisms, technologies and calculations of State power and Agamben's category of bare life as it enters into the zone of irreducible indistinction between the body of *homo sacer* and the body of the sovereign.[19] Without entering into the details of their specific critiques, it will here suffice to say they share the treatment of the subject as both a spontaneity of synthesis capable of erasing all substantial content, which is irreducible to a prior cause, and as a power of differentiating and pluralization—as both an effect of partition and a power to partition. Through the experience of plurality, life, and thus modes of the living being, constantly endows and supplies itself with the very material that is absolutely necessary for its proper functioning, which, again, is to partition. To become an effect with a new meaning value, to become like a language, to be resisting bodies with their economies of pleasures: such is the way the subject, no matter what form of it finally arrives, is rooted in and remains faithful to the traditional, presuppositional primacy of the symbolic economy as designating what is uniquely sanctioned to resist and overcome old regimes of power.

How then to overcome the difficulty of the discourse of partition, whether it speaks of the conceptual elements or of the material aspects, or of their conjunctions, as limiting itself to acting only in the artefact? How to free partition from the fields of the linkages between symbolic and imaginary that fix the study of partition as designating an objective genitive in the epistemological drive, that is, in its have-to-know about the subject?

Here I cannot answer all of these questions. I can only offer a modifiable hypothesis, which does not go without its obscurity: partition is a potentiality of the structure containing all of its elements[20] that supports the different modalities of the nation.

What the configuration of Ali's text gives us to read and extract is the supposition of both Pakistan and India (either together or apart from each other) as a subject and a constituted subject (a nation, a community, a people, for example). This subject is a subject conscious of its own identity insofar as it is aiming to possess and accomplish the recognition of its identity so that it can constitute its own unity, so that it can reappropriate and reconfigure the homeland into an independent, sovereign nation-state to which its identity can return home. Yet in this rather strange radical abstraction in Ali's text, the *i* is the object that he designates and which he writes with the figure of 'PAK(I)STAN', and about which nothing pertaining to the nation of Pakistan as a sovereign nation is *thinkable*—except for the fact that everything that is subject is determined by it. The point is that between the unity of meaning and the *i* as the object causing the subject to appear there, there is no actual determinable relationship even though there is a passionate appeal to one's senses of space.

We can see this expressed in the juridico-political-geographic process of establishing a new map of the Indian subcontinent and the corresponding regions of the autonomous nation-states of India and Pakistan, which the particular work of the Boundary Commission helps uncover. The commission, chaired by Cyril Radcliffe and composed of eight High Court judges, each of whom was elected by the Indian National Congress and the Muslim League, was charged with the task of determining the precise location of the new borders according to criteria and concerns for existing administrative boundaries, census figures on population distribution, and infrastructure elements such as power lines and waterways. Crucially, the commission was also asked to divide and distribute territory as the answer to the onslaught of communal tensions and violence. In the end, and after multiple proposed maps and disputes, the final decision consisted of what Jinnah famously called a 'moth-eaten Pakistan', the geographical formation of a nation whose eastern and western regions did not at all geographically touch each other, but were instead fully partitioned from its sibling nation, India.[21] It was not until 17 August 1947, after the declaration of independence at midnight between 14 and 15 August, with the announcement of the Radcliffe Award that the precise locations of the actual geographical borders were publicly disseminated.

During the summer months of 1947, before the announcement of the Radcliffe Award, the subcontinent was embroiled in an unparalleled onslaught of communal violence and exchanges of populations. The traumas happening throughout the different regions, cities and villages came to affect ideas of where the borders between India and Pakistan would be and needed to be in order to quell the violence. Indeed, the violence (mass migration, communal violence, forms of gendered violence, the loss of home, scissions to communities and so forth) that created and guaranteed the specificity of the 1947 Partition of British India turned upon the confrontations between the different types of contingencies of the necessity of borders and the different types of necessities of the contingency of the borders. It is in this way, as Pandey puts it in *Remembering Partition* via an emphasis on the status of the double inscription and negation, 'violence happens—can only happen—at the boundaries of community. It marks those boundaries. It is the denial of any "violence" in our midst, the attribution of harmony *within* and the consignment of violence to the *outside*, that established "community". Violence and community constitute each other. [. . .] The category of "violence" is reserved in this genre of writing [disciplinary historiography] for "exceptional", disorderly actions, and not for events for which there is a ready political name'.[22]

Regardless of the method of the specific study of partition and the question of its afterlives, in partition, we find ourselves not only in a crisis of jurisdiction over space, but also in a crisis of space, one in which the capacity to make the distinction between inclusion and exclusion in the law is being blurred in the very process of rendering the difference between a lawful outside and inside. Important here is once again the reference to writing, insofar as the starting point for it is the reference to the body and its real and diverse situations. Namely, in this case study of partition, we see the endlessly mutual interchange between the law of violence passing over into community and the law of community passing over into violence. To establish from a genre of writing what can be imagined from the very fact of its writing and thus of writing it (that is, the exceptional), as Pandey does, partition as a decisive point of space finds itself in the model of the subject that consists in ordering the spaces of the communal bodies that mark the inscriptions of the immediate unity between the law of violence and violence as the law. What thereby allows there to be an accounting for the very questionings that are brought by experience to the real partition itself is denial, or else the functioning of negation to ensure the annulment of the subject that one is.

Yet, the trait which is written in Ali's writing of Pak(i)stan—and this is what makes his text so remarkable—is precisely an inkling, a dint of potentiality that *accepts* rather than denies or refuses privation in its existence. Pakistan's process of making for itself a name and body that practically functions with a lack (an *i*) in constituting the localization of a place, which included and involved a diversity of other processes, such as the drawing of new geographical borders where they had not actually before been. This way of functioning with lack and privation braided together the material and the symbolic dimensions of the concerns for Pakistan by removing the references to the question of origin as that which means it is from there something starts as new to a different space which had no jurisdiction over which territories belong to the potential of an independent nation called Pakistan. Pak(i)stan is a signifying density that shows how different regimes of partition, exchange and transformation that consist in the interplay among the geographic, the political, the linguistic, the psychic, the cultural, the social, the symbolic and so forth in order to be assembled and manifested in different ways at each of its historical occurrences. To be sure, all of this subsists from what is written. So this trait supports the idea of the real Pakistan, differentiated in itself, which is also a modality of the existence of, let us say, the nonbeing of a unified India.

What slides behind Ali's text is something of the way Pak(i)stan makes for itself a body marked by lack, yet practically functions with what is missing. Thus the letters do not designate the assemblages of Pakistan; they constitute assemblages and are taken as functioning like those assemblages. Pak(i)stan is like a potentiality of all the elements of signifying network augmented by certain discrete elements in relation to the zone that inscribes the lack in structure. This does not mean that it is simply an actuality that manifests forms of lack in its affective bodies of knowledge. Rather Pakistan and India, which do not go without the continuous solicitation of the privation of the other, are different modalities of the subject in the lack of the one from which enumeration begins.[23] In other words, Pakistan and India, which are spaces that imply the privation of the other space and consequently of the other nation, share the same structure called partition but use this bipartitioned structure in different ways.

We arrive at a question of the teaching of partition. On which principles to base the teaching and study of partition? On what do we base the formulation of something called a theory of partition? In the expressions of the different discourses about the 1947 Partition of India we see that writing makes a step in the theory. Yet, writing is not enough. A signifier is a mark, a writing, but it cannot be read alone. Indeed, what we catch a glimpse of here in the subjectivities of India and Pakistan that present themselves in Ali's writing is that which we call partition—what, as an assemblage of letters, is not a theory made by concepts. It is not a structure of representation that merely functions to put into place a new subject endowed with the capacity of nomination. It rather has to do with the presentation—not a representation—of the structure of spatiality as a space that continuously modifies and transforms in being used differently by the nation-spaces as subjective spaces. In this way, a theory of partition is not a matter of finding, in a particular case, the differentials of it, but rather consists in the continuous reformulation of the concept of partition on the basis of a subjective structure of spatiality. If there is a theory of partition to be made, and which, in act and in potential is realized, then perhaps it would consist in being what continues to develop through different hypotheses.

NOTES

1. With regard to philosophical discourse, for example, we can here consider Heidegger's notion of ontological difference, which is the difference between the horizon of an appearing of a world (the background of withdrawal) and appearing entities who appear within this historically given horizon-world of appearing. Or more simply, the difference between beings and their nonontic horizon of meaning, between appearing entities and the ontological horizon of their appearing. It is important to remember that Heidegger never confounds the ontological disclosure or withdrawal of entities with their ontic production, since there is a difference between worldly entities and the horizon of appearing, which is always grounded in human finitude. There needs to be this difference because it is impossible to demarcate a distinction between simple existence and the horizon of sense; historicity means that being is always already disclosed within a horizon of meaning. Ontological difference is this separation, this partitioning.

2. Homi Bhabha, *The Location of Culture* (New York: Routledge, 1994), 6.

3. Gyanendra Pandey, *Remembering Partition: Violence, Nationalism, and History in India* (Cambridge and New York: Cambridge University Press, 2001), 1.

4. Ibid., 3–4.

5. Ibid., 4.

6. To see this, let us think especially of Aristotle's definition of the *polis* as the distinction between the good life, or a politically qualified life, and pure, natural life, Hegel's structure of language as at once inside and outside itself, or Heidegger's later thinking on the history of Being accomplishing its end. In any case, the opposition between human history and natural history is a very old one. It continues to take human history as the other of natural history and meaning for the result of their difference.

7. Here we can again think of Heidegger and specifically of what he calls *Ereignis*—the 'appropriating Event', the hermeneutic horizon of meaning within which beings appear as they are, the very structure of finitude—which is the ultimate primordial gulf out of which Being reveals itself to us within a plurality of historically destined horizons. This is the fundamental historicity of Being, which reaches its formulation in the change from Being to being(s).

8. 'Now or Never: Are We to Live or Perish For Ever?', http://www.columbia.edu/itc/mealac/pritchett/00islamlinks/txt_rahmatali_1933.html (accessed 24 October 2018).

9. This is like what Levi-Strauss calls a 'floating signifier'. Characterized by its ability to represent an undetermined amount of signification while remaining capable of receiving an infinite plurality of meaning, the 'floating signifier' is utterly empty of meaning, yet nevertheless maintains the correlation between signifier and signified. Accordingly, it possesses a pure symbolic value, a 'value zero'. Claude Lévi-Strauss, *Introduction to the Work of Marcel Mauss*, trans. Felicity Baker (London: Routledge & Kegan Paul Ltd., 1987), 62.

10. See especially Jacques Derrida, *The Ear of the Other: Otobiography, Transference, Translation*, trans. Peggy Kamuf (Lincoln: University of Nebraska Press,

1988), and Gilles Deleuze, *Difference and Repetition*, trans. Paul Patton (New York: Columbia University Press, 1994).

11. We should here clarify that, while Hegel's thought of repetition involves sublation, in which something is idealized and then transformed from an immediate reality into an ideal universality, it is not precisely accurate to claim that he fails to think mechanical repetition. This bears noting because the minimal creed taken to be the mark of post-Hegelian materialism, such as the one we see in postcolonial theory, is that repetition gains autonomy with regard to sublation, creating an opposition between the two. It is this freedom of repetition, or the mechanism of repetition (we can here think of Freud's compulsion to repeat of Lacan's idea of the excess of repetition over organic processes) from the grip of sublation that is taken to be the mark of post-Hegel materialism. It is in his discussion of habit (§§ 409–12) in the section 'Anthropology' from the *Philosophy of Mind*, we see very clearly that Hegel in fact thinks of a mechanical, nonaccumulating repetition.

12. See Fredric Jameson, *The Hegel Variations: On the Phenomenology of Spirit* (London: Verso, 2010).

13. We impact here upon the immense question of the transcendental, which is the very question of the condition of possibility in general, and thus of the foundation of all experience and its circularity. Without entering into the details of the evolution of the critique of the transcendental, it will here suffice to say that it is in this way that whatever is finally called postcolonial critique circumscribes what since Kant has been a leading problem in continental philosophy: the nature of the correlation, or the necessity of the agreement between categories and objects of experience.

14. If we follow the Derridean thought of difference, this form of writing moves us back to the problem of catastrophe as that which immediately appropriates the diverse issues of partition. This is one of the immense legacies of deconstruction. For what Derrida brings to light is philosophy's dependence on an external, wholly other Other, while demonstrating the impossibility to locate a center outside philosophy. So, according to him, any antiphilosophical attempt to develop a different, critical theory and any anthropocentric discourse necessarily borrows from the economic and strategic resources of the very structure of knowledge (i.e. the finitude of the subject) they seek to exceed in the first place.

15. At the origin of (my) language, there is always an inscription of the beyond within the native, fertile soil of a language. I am therefore only capable of inhabiting my language from the position of alienation, which pertains to speech's estrangement from writing and the transcendental anteriority of writing to speech. Such is the thought and condition of the originary exile, which is a closed loop. But within this loop, there must and can be engendered the *event* of the stranger, or let us say the sudden emergence of otherness that cannot be separated from the name of the one who thinks it. Such is the original encounter. Therefore, there are two loops within the loop in which the Other is another subject with whom 'I' am always already together-with, sharing an intersubjective space of (mis)recognition. See Derrida, *Otobiographies*, 11.

16. Homi K. Bhabha, 'DissemiNation: Time, Narrative, and the Margins of the Modern Nation', in Homi K. Bhabha, ed., *Nation and Narration* (New York and London: Routledge, 1990): 291–322.

17. The English verb 'to differ' derives from the verb *diapherein*, which translates from the Greek 'as to differ'. It means to carry over or across, to put into motion or to carry from one to another. It also means to bear through to an end, to carry through with, to support, to carry different ways, to make difference and to tear asunder.

18. See Gilles Deleuze, *Nietzsche and Philosophy*, trans. Hugh Tomlinson (London: Athlone Press, 1983).

19. See Giorgio Agamben, *Homo Sacer: Sovereign Power and Bare Life*, trans. Daniel Heller-Roazen (Palo Alto, CA: Stanford University Press, 1998); Michel Foucault, *The History of Sexuality: An Introduction*, vol. 1 of *The History of Sexuality*, trans. Robert Hurley (New York: Vintage, 1978); and Gayatri Chakravorty Spivak, 'Can the Subaltern Speak?' in C. Nelson and L. Grossberg, eds., *Marxism and the Interpretations of Culture* (Urbana: University of Illinois Press, 1998): 271–313.

20. Here I mean the Aristotelian concept of potentiality. Though this emphasis may be quickly read as a contradiction to the argument regarding the classical roots of the thought of partition, it is important to understand that in the *Metaphysics*, Aristotle very precisely delineates the consistency of potentiality as the effective mode of potentiality's existence, and not simply as the logic of its possibility or probability. In other words, he attempts to establish the autonomous existence of potentiality that is not, in the first instance, captured by actuality as the accomplishment of potentiality.

21. For an excellent account of the Boundary Commission and their different maps, see Lucy P. Chester, *Borders and Conflict in South Asia: The Radcliffe Boundary Commission and the Partition of Punjab* (Manchester: Manchester University Press, 2009): 55.

22. Pandey, *Remembering Partition*, 188.

23. This subject, I will clarify, is not the accomplishment of the subject rendered through a demonstration of the Hegelian notion of reconciliation, which insofar as it posits the externalization of the internal opposition of the subject in the relation among other subjects, is a dynamic that does not immediately find itself in the internalization of external contradiction. This is also not an example of creation ex nihilo. Rather, what I am attempting to demonstrate, by way of tracking what shared ideas and presuppositions support in current, yet different discourses about partition, is that the very thought of partition demands a different approach to the familiar crisis of space, one that envisages space differently and the epistemology of space as not originarily related to the concept of force but rather to a cinematic of dimensions of space that constantly generates a signifying dynamic.

REFERENCES

Agamben, Giorgio. 1998. *Homo Sacer: Sovereign Power and Bare Life*. Translated by Daniel Heller Roazen. Palo Alto, CA: Stanford University Press.

Ali, Choudhary Rahmat. 1933. 'Now or Never: Are We to Live or Perish For Ever?'. http://www.columbia.edu/itc/mealac/pritchett/00islamlinks/txt_rahmatali_1933.html (accessed 24 October 2018).

Bhabha, Homi K., ed. 1990. *Nation and Narration*. New York: Routledge.

———. 1994. *The Location of Culture*. New York: Routledge.

Chester, Lucy P. 2009. *Borders and Conflict in South Asia: The Radcliffe Boundary Commission and the Partition of Punjab*. Manchester: Manchester University Press.

Deleuze, Gilles. 1994. *Difference and Repetition*. Translated by Paul Patton. New York: Columbia University Press.

Derrida, Jacques. 1988. *The Ear of the Other: Otobiography, Transference, Translation*. Translated by Peggy Kamuf. Lincoln: University of Nebraska Press.

Foucault, Michel. 1978. *The History of Sexuality: Volume I: An Introduction*. Translated by Robert Hurley. New York: Vintage.

Hegel, G. W. F. 1971. *Encyclopedia of the Philosophy of Mind [Spirit], Part Three of the Encyclopedia of the Philosophical Sciences (1830)*. Translated by A. V. Miller. Oxford: Clarendon Press.

Heidegger, Martin. 2010. *Being and Time*. Translated by Joan Stambaugh. Albany: SUNY Press.

Jameson, Frederic. 2010. *The Hegel Variations: On the Phenomenology of Spirit*. London: Verso.

Lévi-Strauss, Claude. 1987. *Introduction to the Work of Marcel Mauss*. Translated by Felicity Baker. London: Routledge & Kegan Paul Ltd.

Nelson, C., and L. Grossberg, eds. 1998. *Marxism and the Interpretations of Culture*. Urbana: University of Illinois Press.

Pandey, Gyanendra. 2001. *Remembering Partition: Violence, Nationalism, and History in India*. Cambridge: Cambridge University Press.

Spivak, Gayatri Chakravorty. 1998. 'Can the Subaltern Speak?'. In *Marxism and the Interpretations of Culture*, edited by C. Nelson and L. Grossberg, 271–313. Urbana: University of Illinois Press.

Index

Adams, Gerry, 173
Agamben, Giorgio, 237
Ahmed, Ishtiaq, 10
Ahuja, Ankur, 190
Airtel, 202–7, 212, 213, 216–17
Akali Dal, 5
Ali, Rahmat, 230–31, 233, 238–40
All India Congress Committee (AICC), 4
Ambedkar, B. R., 129, 145, 147, 148. *See also* Dalit activism
Aristotle, 235, 241, 243
AT&T, 202–3

Balfour Declaration (1917), 23–24, 32, 36
Balkans, the, 14, 83–84, 92, 96–98, 102,
Bangladesh, 3, 49, 181, 184–85, 187–88, 189, 197–99, 238; Liberation War (1971), 74, 181, 185, 187, 223
Barthes, Roland, 205–6, 213–14, 217
Bengal, 14, 51, 52, 70, 223; east Bengali. *See* Bangladesh
Ben-Kiki, Hayyim, 29
Benjamin, Walter, 208
Bhabha, Homi, xv, 226, 236–37
Bhasin, Kamla, 58, 70, 72, 182
Biermann, Wolf, 119, 125
body, 49–61, 63, 65, 164, 190, 226, 227, 231, 233, 237, 239, 240
borders ix–xii, xv, 2, 5, 6–9, 28, 39, 49, 50, 52, 53–54, 58, 74, 90, 94, 98, 109, 111, 112, 114, 115, 119, 122, 160–62, 172–74, 181, 183–85, 187, 191, 193–94, 197, 201–6, 208–14, 216–18, 225, 226–27, 229, 232–33, 235–36, 238–39; Berlin Wall, 109–11, 114, 122–23, 125, 202–3; Israel/Palestine Wall, 202, 215; Line of Control, 53–54; Wagah–Atari border, 53, 74, 204, 218; Western Wall, Jerusalem, 193–94
Brexit, xiv, 98, 157, 172–74; Referendum (2016), ix, 172–73
Brooke, Rupert, 50–51
Butalia, Urvashi, 13, 58–60, 72, 182, 190

Calcutta. *See* Kolkata
Campos, Michelle, 27–28
capitalism, x, 10, 33, 35, 37, 53, 85, 87, 99, 112, 123, 137–38, 146, 201, 216–18, 235, 237

caste, 10, 65, 70, 129, 131, 133–36, 138–41, 144–50; Dalit activism, 131, 134, 140, 144–48, 152; Bhima Koregaon, 144–47
Catalan independence, ix, 98
Cellcom, 202, 215–17
Chatterjee, Partha, 63, 67
Chattha, Ilyas, 12–13
China, 85
citizenship, ix, xii, 49, 50–51, 55–57, 59, 61, 64, 65, 66, 68, 71, 91, 94, 98, 112–113, 116–20, 122, 125, 134–40, 143, 157–58, 162–67, 172–73, 184, 187–88, 194
class, 10, 27, 41, 68, 70, 77, 131, 133, 135–39, 146, 147, 169, 188, 209, 214–15
Cleary, Joe, xi, 182
Coca-Cola, 202, 205–14, 216–18
Cohen, Hillel, 28–29, 31
Cold War, 109–11, 120
Communism, 70, 84–86, 88, 90–91, 96, 100, 110–11, 120, 129, 139
Congress, Indian National, 51, 129–30, 132–35, 138–39, 141, 143, 147–50, 194, 238
Crimean status referendum (2014), ix
cultural representation, x, xiv, 115–17, 132, 148, 159, 163, 201; advertising, xiv, 36, 112, 201–18; cinema, 168, 182, 183, 195, 243
Curran, Kevin, 168
Cypriot partition, ix, 94
Czechoslovakia, 86, 94

Das, Veena, 60–61, 68–69
Dayton Agreement (1995), 92–93, 101
decolonization, x, 50, 55, 56, 63, 85, 142, 161, 165, 181, 227, 229–31, 233–35
Deleuze, Gilles, 42, 234, 236
democracy, xi, xiii, 37, 56–57, 59, 61–63, 69, 84–85, 89–92, 95–96, 113, 121, 129–32, 134–40, 147–48, 173
Derrida, Jacques, 51, 58–60, 73, 75, 229, 232, 234, 236
Devji, Faisal Fathehali, 51
Doyle, Roddy, 166–67

east Bengal. *See* Bangladesh
empire, x, 1, 15, 23, 27, 37, 49, 56, 58, 60, 64, 68–69, 71, 72, 94, 142, 143, 144–47, 159, 165–68, 223, 227, 228, 230; British rule in India, 3, 9, 12, 14, 56, 58, 67–69, 94, 135, 145, 223, 231–32; British rule in Ireland, 157–60, 172; British rule in Palestine, 23–26, 32, 36–37, 94; Ottoman Empire, 27–28, 31, 38; settler colonialism, 26–27, 29–35, 38–41, 193
Enlightenment, 62–64, 77
ethnicity, x–xiv, 1, 2, 10, 27, 34, 36, 52, 84, 88–90, 92–93, 111, 135, 136, 140, 148, 157–74, 194; ethnic cleansing. *See* genocide
European Union, ix, xiv, 83, 86–99, 172–73

Fascism, 110–11, 120, 136
Fatah, Sonya, 188–99
Fateh Ali Khan, Nusrat, 203
Foucault, Michel, 26, 51, 56, 59–60, 71, 223, 237
France, 94, 95, 98, 143, 147, 191
Fraser, Nancy, 64, 76
Frawley, Oona, 163–64, 166–67
Freud, Sigmund, 51, 242

Gaelic Athletic Association (GAA), 158, 205
Gaelic revivalism, 159–60, 166, 172
Gandhi, Mohandas Karamchand, 68–70, 129, 130, 132–33, 135, 147–48, 154
gender, x, xiv, 2–3, 10–11, 50, 56, 61, 63, 66–72, 91, 131, 138, 169, 170, 188, 214, 215, 223, 225, 233, 238, 242

genocide, xi, 1, 7, 9–10, 24–25, 40, 50–54, 64, 71, 91, 95, 111
German Democratic Republic, xii, xiv, 109–24, 203, 216
Germany, Federal Republic of, 110–12, 114–17, 119, 121–23, 203, 216
Germany, xii, xiv, 51, 56, 89, 98, 109–11, 203, 217; Berlin Museum of German History 112; DDR Museum, Berlin 112–14; Museum of Everyday Life, Berlin 113
Ghosh, Vishwajyoti, 183–87, 189–91, 193–94, 196–98
globalization, 50, 66–67, 85–86, 89, 95, 130, 137–38, 140, 157, 163, 165, 201
Good Friday Agreement (1998), 161–63, 173–75, 202
Google, 202, 212–14, 217
Gupta, Malini, 191

Habermas, Jürgen, 62, 64
Hassan, Mashkur, 8
Hegel, G. W. F., 51, 234–35, 241, 242, 243
Heidegger, Martin, 229–30, 241
Helal, Wasim, 196
Hindutva, xiv, 129–49; Bharatiya Janata Party (BJP), 129–31, 138, 140–41, 147–48; Hindu Mahasabha, 132–33, 135, 144; Rashtriya Swayamsevak Sangh, 130, 148–49
Hitchens, Christopher, 197
Holocaust, xi, xii, 9, 56

identity, x, xii–xiii, 10, 27–28, 51–52, 55, 65, 68–69, 123, 129–32, 135–36, 138–39, 142, 144–48, 157–62, 164, 165, 170, 172, 173, 176, 188–89, 193, 218, 224, 226, 229, 232–33, 235–38
Iftikhar, Khawaja, 8
India, ix, xi, 1–15, 49–72, 94, 129–149, 158, 168–71, 181, 184, 188, 191, 194, 196–98, 202–4, 208–14, 216–18, 223, 227, 228, 230–34, 238–40; Amritsar, 4–6, 8–10, 13, 15; Bihar, 4, 187–188; Delhi, 3, 57, 140, 148, 188, 190, 212; Karnataka, 142–144, 148; Kolkata, 3, 4; Mumbai, 50; Patiala, 8, 10; Tripura, 129; West Bengal, 129
India/Pakistan partition, ix, xi, xiii, xiv, 1–15, 49–71, 130–48, 181–91, 194, 196–98, 202, 208–10, 212–14, 218, 223, 227–28, 230, 233, 239–40; Boundary Commission, 7, 14, 238. *See also* Radcliffe, Cyril
Iqbal, Muhammad, 230, 232
Irish partition, the 157–61, 163, 165, 172–74
Irish Republican Army, 172, 175
Irish Republican Brotherhood, 158
Irish Troubles, the, 161, 172, 174, 202, 214–15
Ireland, Republic, of, xi, xiv, 67, 96, 157–79, 217; Citizenship Referendum (2004), 158, 162–67
Islam, Khademul, 185
Israel, xi–xiv, 23–25, 30, 33, 35, 39, 41, 138, 181, 184, 187, 189, 192–95, 202, 211, 215–16; Israel Defense Forces, 33, 184, 193, 215
Istria, xiii
Italy, xiii, 94, 98

Jahn, Roland, 119–20
Jalal, Ayesha, 11, 130, 149
Jameson, Frederic, 235
Jawhariyyeh, Wasif, 28
Jinnah, Muhammad Ali, 4, 129–30, 132, 149, 151, 194, 238

Kant, Immanuel, 62, 77, 224, 242
Kalyvas, Stathis, 1, 13, 14
Kamasutra, 56
Kashmir, xii, 12, 53, 59, 196, 223, 231
Katrak, Ketu, 69

Khalidi, Walid, 26, 37
Khan, Yasmin, 52
Kumar, Ravish, 194

Lacan, Jacques, 242
League of Nations, 23, 25, 36
Lenin, Vladimir Ilych, 129; Leninism, 120
literature, xiii, xiv, 122, 145, 158, 166, 168, 182, 194; graphic novels, xiv, 182–98
Litwa, Maria M., 187–88

Malik, Salma, 196
Mallya, Prabha, 194
Manto, Saadat Hassan, 11, 194
Marx, Karl, 52, 74, 216; Marxism, 120, 129, 143
Master, Irfan, 194
McAleese, Mary, 157, 161
memory, ix, xi–xiii, 25, 53, 109, 114, 118–19, 123–24, 129–48, 159–60, 165, 184, 197, 226
Menon, Ritu, 58, 70, 72, 182
migration, x, xii, xiv, 1–2, 7, 14, 29–33, 35, 37, 39, 91, 97–98, 110, 137, 157–58, 161–73, 182, 187–88, 191, 223, 238
Mishra, Nita, 169–70
Mittal, Dyuti, 191
Mosse, George, 56
Mountbatten, Louis, 2
Murtuza, Mehreen, 198
Muslim League, 6, 8, 14, 51, 130, 132, 133, 144, 149–51, 194, 230, 233, 238

nation-state, the ix, xi–xiv, 15, 25, 29, 33–37, 41, 49, 51, 54, 56, 58, 61–63, 65, 68–72, 87, 89, 92–93, 96, 99, 111, 116, 118–19, 121, 122, 130–37, 139–40, 144, 148, 165, 168, 172, 181, 185, 187–90, 192, 194, 196, 207, 209, 218, 223, 226–34, 236–38, 240
nationalism, x–xiii, 1, 9, 26, 31, 52–53, 56, 63–64, 67, 69–70, 83–84, 86–87, 89–91, 94, 97, 99, 116, 129, 132–38, 141, 145–47, 158–61, 173, 218
Nazis, the, 56, 91, 111, 136, 140. *See also* Fascism
Nehru, Jawaharlal, 130, 134, 135, 139, 148, 152, 194
neoliberalism, 50, 66–67, 69, 98, 122, 130, 136–41, 146, 147, 209
Nirbhaya, 57, 71
Northern Ireland, 98, 157, 160–63, 172–75, 202, 204–7, 210, 214–16; Belfast, 161, 175, 215
nostalgia, xii, 50, 109, 114–16, 118, 123; ostalgie, xii, 113–16, 123

O'Toole, Fintan, 173
Oppenheimer, Franz, 34
oral history, x, xiv, 6, 54, 58, 109–10, 116–18, 122, 186
Oslo Accords, 24
Oz, Amos, 23, 25

Pakistan, ix, xi–xv, 4, 7–10, 49–51, 53, 55, 58–59, 132–33, 136, 140, 146, 181, 184–85, 187–90, 194, 196, 197, 202–4, 208–18, 223, 228, 230–34, 238–40; east Pakistan. *See* Bangladesh; Gujranwala, 12, 13; Lahore, 4–7, 9, 11–13, 197, 208, 212; Multan, 5, 145; Nizamabad, 12–13; Rawalpindi, 4–5, 10, 15; Sheikhupura, 5, 7–8, 11, 13; Sialkot, 12–13; Sindh, 3; Thoha Khalsa, 4, 5, 10, 54
Palestine, xii–xiv, 23–41, 181, 183–85, 189, 192–93, 195, 197, 202, 211, 215–17; Gaza Strip, 183–84, 193–95, 197; Nakba, ix, x; partition, xii, 23–41, 181, 183–85, 189, 191–92,

195, 198, 202, 217; West Bank, 183–84, 192–93, 195, 197
Palestine Liberation Organization, 24
Pandey, Gyanendra, 72, 182, 187, 227–28, 239
Parrey, Arif Ayaz, 196
Pepsi, 202–3, 212, 213
Plato, 51
postmodernism, xii, 49–50, 236
power, xiii–xiv, 3, 14, 24, 26–27, 30, 38, 55–56, 66, 71, 90, 94–95, 99, 122, 131–33, 137–38, 140–42, 148, 160, 163, 165, 208–9, 223, 226–28, 230, 233–34, 236–38
Punjab, xiii, 1–15, 51–53

Radcliffe, Cyril, 238
refugees, 1–3, 5, 7–10, 12–15, 49, 52, 54, 57–58, 69–70, 91, 111, 168–69, 184, 187–88, 191–92, 194–95, 198
religion, x, 1, 5, 10, 12, 15, 27–28, 49, 51–52, 54, 61, 73, 83, 91, 111, 131–32, 135–36, 138–44, 146, 148, 160, 166, 169–70, 174, 190, 194, 196, 199, 215–16, 232; Christian, 12, 27–28, 140, 142, 146, 169; Catholic, 91, 143, 159, 160, 165, 169–70, 204–5, 207–8, 214–16; Protestant, 159–60, 165, 204–5, 207–8, 214–16; Hindu, 4–13, 49, 51, 53, 57–59, 68, 129–48, 169, 181,188–89, 196; Jewish, 23–41, 56, 73, 111, 165, 181, 194; Ashkenazi, 27, 32–33, 36; Sephardi, 27, 29, 31–33; Muslim, xii, 4–15, 27–28, 34, 49, 51, 53, 54, 57–59, 68, 84, 129–33, 138, 140–48, 181, 187, 188–89, 194, 196, 199, 230–31, 233, 238; Sikh, 4–15, 51, 53–54, 57, 59, 68, 140, 149
Rifkin, Jeremy, 95
Robinson, Mary, 161–62
Rupnik, Jacques, 83
Rushdie, Salman, 234

Sabnani, Nina, 191
Sacco, Joe, 183–87, 189, 191–93, 195–98
Sahni, Bhisham, 4
Said, Edward, 74, 185
Sandhu, Ikroop 194
Sarma, Ursula Rani, 169–171
Sartre, Jean Paul, 186, 192
Scottish independence referendum (2014), ix
sexuality, x, xiv, 49–72
Singh, Tara, 4
Sinn Féin, 160, 161, 172, 173
Sen, Sarbajit, 185
Socialism, 29, 70, 84–86, 89–90, 95, 110–12, 116–20, 122–23, 130, 136
Socialist Unity Party (SED), 110, 112–14, 117, 120
south Asia, xii, xiv, 1, 49–53, 55–57, 64, 69, 72, 204, 209–10
Soviet Union, 84–86, 101, 110–13
Spivak, Gayatri Chakravorty, 60, 237
Sreenivasan, Archana, 188–89

Tipu Sultan, 134, 142–44, 147
Tiwana, Khizr Hayat, 4
trains, 1, 2, 4, 8, 10, 12, 13, 15
trauma, 71, 223, 229, 238

United Kingdom, ix, 25, 67, 68, 91, 94, 98, 160, 161, 168, 172, 173
United Nations, 24–26, 39
United States of America, 25, 64, 67, 85, 89, 92, 93, 94, 95, 126, 138, 160, 167, 168, 184, 194, 202

Vietnam War, 186
violence, x, xii–xiv, 1–15, 31–32, 49–53, 54, 64, 72, 83–84, 93–95, 97, 111, 112, 119, 130, 131, 133–35, 139–42, 144, 146, 148, 157, 161, 174, 181–98, 202, 204–5, 207–8, 214, 217, 228, 238–39;

gender–based, 14, 49, 52, 54–61, 65, 67, 69, 71, 111, 131, 188–91, 214, 223, 238
Viswanath, Gita 196

Weizmann, Chaim, 32
Williams, Raymond, 207, 211–13
World War One, 23, 27, 34, 94, 207
World War Two, xiii, 23–25, 91, 94, 181

Yugoslavia, xiv, 83–99

Zionism, xiii, 23–41, 138; Jewish National Fund, 32–34, 39
Zreik, Raef, 29

List of Contributors

Ronnen Ben-Arie is an Honorary Postdoctoral Research Associate at the School of Humanities and Social Inquiry at Wollongong University and teaches at the Faculty of Architecture and Town Planning at the Technion Institute. His research interests include spatialities of power and resistance; contested and shared urban spaces; and contemporary political theory and settler colonialism in Israel-Palestine. The title of his recent book, coauthored with Marcelo Svirsky, is *From Shared Life to Co-Resistance in Historic Palestine* (Rowman & Littlefield International, 2017).

Stefano Bianchini is Professor of East European politics and history at the University of Bologna and Rector's delegate for relations with Eastern Europe. Former director of the two-year Interdisciplinary Master of Arts in East European Studies (MIREES), a joint diploma of the Universities of Bologna, St. Petersburg, Vytautas Magnus at Kaunas and Corvinus of Budapest, he is currently a visiting professor of the State University of St. Petersburg and holds a HD in humanities of the Vytautas Magnus University, Kaunas. He is the author, among others, of *Liquid Nationalism and State Partitions in Europe* (2017); *Eastern Europe and the Challenges of Modernity 1800–2000* (2015); *Partitions: Reshaping States and Minds*, written with Sanjay Chaturvedi, Rada Ivekovic and Ranabir Samaddar (2005); *Sarajevo, Le Radici dell'odio. Identità e Destino dei Popoli Balcanici* (2003); *La Question Yougoslave* (1996) and coeditor of *Regional Cooperation, Peace Enforcement and the Role of the Treaties in the Balkans*, together with Joseph Marko, Craig Nation and Milica Uvalic (2007).

Vedita Cowaloosur teaches in the Mass Communication Programme at Curtin Mauritius. She completed her postdoctoral fellowship in the English Department at Stellenbosch University in South Africa and her PhD in English and comparative literary studies at the University of Warwick, United Kingdom. Her research interests include the politics of language in South Asian literary and popular culture, Indian literature in translation, and migrant literature. Her articles have been published in *Interventions*, the *Journal of Postcolonial Writing, Economic and Political Weekly* and the *MLA*. She also translates between English, French, Hindi and Bhojpuri.

Louise Harrington is Assistant Professor in postcolonial and South Asian literatures in the Department of English and Film Studies at the University of Alberta. She is working on a monograph on cultural representations of ethno-religious-national conflict. She has further research interests in critical border studies, spatial literary studies, and migration and intercultural studies. Her essays have appeared in the journals *TEXT: Writing and Illustrating Interdisciplinary Research, Postcolonial Text and South Asian Diaspora*, and in the edited collections *The Cosmic and the Corporeal: Interdisciplinary Explorations of Time, Space and Body* (2016) and *Tracing the New Indian Diaspora* (2014).

Radhika Mohanram is Professor of postcolonial studies in the School of English, Communication and Philosophy at Cardiff University and has published books and articles on imperialism, race and gender. She was PI of the AHRC-funded research network, 'Partitions: What Are They Good For?' (2013–2015) and is PI of the AHRC-funded 'Refugee Wales: The Afterlife of Violence' (2019–2022). She is a co-editor of the Rowman & Littlefield book series, *Critical Perspectives on Theory, Culture and Politics*. Currently, she is working on a monograph on the 1947 Indian partition.

Anindya Raychaudhuri is Lecturer in English at the University of St Andrews. His primary research interest is in the cultural representation and collective memory of war and conflict. He is also interested in postcolonial and diasporic identities and cultures. He is the author of *Homemaking: Postcolonial Nostalgia and the Construction of a South Asian Diaspora* (Rowman & Littlefield, 2018) and of the forthcoming *Narrating Partition: Agency, Memory, Representation* (2019). In 2016, he was named one of the BBC/AHRC New Generation Thinkers.

Samuel Sequeira is a Postdoctoral Researcher who did his doctorate in the area of critical and cultural theory at Cardiff University, United Kingdom.

He has published a monograph titled *Memory, History, Identity: Narratives of Partition, Migration and Settlement among South Asian Communities of South Wales*. Prior to becoming an academic, he worked as a journalist and newspaper editor in India. His areas of research are memory studies, partition studies, identity and cultural conflicts.

Marcelo Svirsky is Senior Lecturer at the School for Humanities and Social Inquiry, University of Wollongong. He researches settler-colonial societies particularly Israel–Palestine, and focuses on questions of social transformation and decolonization. He has published several articles in the journals *Cultural Politics*, *Interventions*, *Subjectivity*, *Intercultural Education*, *Deleuze Studies* and *Settler Colonial Studies* among others, and various books and edited collections: *Deleuze and Political Activism* (2010); *Arab-Jewish Activism in Israel-Palestine* (2012); *Agamben and Colonialism* with Simone Bignall (2012); *Collaborative Struggles in Australia and Israel-Palestine* (2014); *After Israel: Towards Cultural Transformation* (2014); and he has recently coauthored with Ronnen Ben-Arie *From Shared Life to Co-Resistance in Historic Palestine* (Rowman & Littlefield International, 2017).

Ian Talbot is Professor of modern British history at the University of Southampton. He has recently published *A History of Modern South Asia* (2016) and a coauthored study, *Colonial Lahore: A History of the City and Beyond* (2016). The latter work follows his long-term interest in the history of the Punjab and the partition of the region following the emergence of Pakistan. It builds on earlier publications such as *The Partition of India* (coauthored with Gurharpal Singh, 2009) and *Divided Cities: Partition and its Aftermath in Lahore and Amritsar, 1947–1957* (2006). This study was funded by a two-year Leverhulme Major Research Fellowship which was held in conjunction with a Visiting Fellowship in History at Balliol College, Oxford, during 2003–2004.

Chris Weedon is Professor Emerita of critical and cultural theory at Cardiff University. She is best known for her books and articles on feminist theory, women's writing, multi-ethnic Britain and cultural politics. Her recent research and publications are in two main areas: British black and Asian writing and the cultural politics of memory. She is currently working on a book of life stories from East Germany. She is co-editor of the book series *Critical Perspectives on Theory, Culture and Politics*, published by Rowman & Littlefield International. She is active in community projects outside the university.

Jennifer Yusin is Associate Professor in the Department of English and Philosophy at Drexel University. She is the author of *The Future Life of Trauma: Partitions, Borders, Repetition* (2017). Her essays have appeared in *Textual Practice*, the *Journal of Contemporary Literature* and *Culture, Theory and Critique*.

Lightning Source UK Ltd.
Milton Keynes UK
UKHW011936131119
353459UK00001B/32/P

9 781783 488391